Extreme Cuisine

To my wife Lamyai

Extreme Cuisine

JERRY HOPKINS

BLOOMSBURY

First published in Great Britain in 2005

Text © 2004 Haku 'Olelo

Photos © 2004 Michael Freeman

The moral right of the author has been asserted

Bloomsbury Publishing Plc, 38 Soho Square, London W1D 3HB

A CIP catalogue record for this book
is available from the British Library

ISBN 0 7475 7554 1

10 9 8 7 6 5 4 3 2 1

Printed in Great Britain by Clays Ltd, St Ives plc

All papers used by Bloomsbury Publishing are natural,
recyclable products made from wood grown in well-managed
forests. The manufacturing processes conform to the
environmental regulations of the country of origin.

contents

foreword by
Anthony Bourdain

I FIRST MET JERRY HOPKINS over a plate of crispy-fried frog skins in Bangkok. I was midway through another six week gastro-tour of Asia and I thought it was a good idea to meet the man whose book had for some time served as my virtual Fodors guide to the pleasures and terrors of extreme cuisine.

Before setting out on the road to film a television show of my adventures, I eagerly consulted his definitive collection of unusual eats, itemizing, country by country, what I absolutely had to try while in each place. Vietnam? Gotta have that *ho bit long* (half-term fetal duck egg). Singapore? Don't miss out on the scorpions! After a few years of this, when offered a spicy fry-up of crickets or worms, I'm likely to say, "Bugs? That is so last week!"

This book is the finest overview and users' guide to the wild and wonderful world of things people cheerfully put in their mouths in various places around the world. It's one thing to hear, third hand, that they drink snake wine in much of Asia—it's another to actually see the stuff—a nest of coiled serpents, a bird, still in plumage, trapped among them, in the bottom of a bottle. This book benefits from lush—even appetizing photography. It is quite another thing to actually try the stuff.

Which I actually recommend everyone do. The world is a big, scary, beautiful, dirty, multi-colored, multi-cultural, sometimes cruel, sometimes nauseating—but always marvelous place. People eat differently around the world. While a gourmet from Indiana might turn his nose up at bird's nest or bat, many Southeast Asians would be truly horrified by a Kraft single. Which, truly, is more strange and terrible to the greater part of humanity—the simple charms of a worm taco, or the terrifying heap we call a Grand Slam Breakfast?

Fortunately, Jerry Hopkins approaches his subject with a pure heart, free of prejudice—taking clear delight in his subject. If there is one sin in the world of gastronomy, it is lack of curiosity, and Jerry, in his book, and in person, makes readily apparent his interest and excitement in his subject.

I could not have written *A Cook's Tour* without this book. There is so much I would have missed. And experience has shown me that no matter how frightening a dish may look on the page, in front of you, on the table, with a proud host watching your first tasting—and the accompaniment of much local beverage, it's almost always worth the ride. For truly—how bad can it be? Compared to an olestra-greased faux potato chip, Cheez Whiz or pineapple pizza, a lot of this stuff is pretty damn good. One of the surprises of my trips has been the sadness, even pity with which poor citizens of faraway places receive sketchy accounts of what Americans put regularly in their mouths. This from nations whose peoples are traditionally insectivores. And there's a lot to be said for their argument. People enjoy, even celebrate with a lot of what you see in this book. And I'd eat most of it with a smile compared to the standard fare at most midwestern malls. While a lot of this stuff skirts the fine Asian line between food and medicine (shark fin, bear bile, snake blood), some of it is quite tasty. My frog skins with Jerry were delicious.

So dig in. Enjoy. Eat without fear or prejudice, secure in the knowledge that millions of people have been enjoying this fare for centuries without ill effect. Get away from your hotel dining room—and the tourist terrordomes and range wild and free. Eat. Eat adventurously. Miss nothing. It's all here in these pages.

If nothing else, when the money runs out and you find yourself cadging free drinks at your local saloon, you can always re-tell the anecdote of the time you ate the poisonous blowfish liver. That's usually good for at least one drink.

photographer's preface

MY SECRET TRAINING began as a child, at an English boarding school. I realise that few readers will truly appreciate the significance of this, but survival depended heavily on being able to eat, for weeks at a time, a food regime that was modelled loosely on that of Victorian prisons. A cartoonist called Ronald Searle once produced a book about these very English institutions, and to my mind no one has bettered his description of school dinner as "the piece of cod which passeth all understanding." There can be no finer education of the palate to accept the impossible than the one I and my fellow inmates received, and for that I am, as was intoned before each meal, "truly grateful."

As a photographer, I put my catholic tastes to work and began, many years ago, shooting the weird culinary habits that I came across. Much of this was in Asia, not because the region became something of a speciality of mine, but because the southern Chinese and their neighbors, particularly in Thailand, Laos and Vietnam, have a greater fascination with unusual foods than any other culture I know. So where more appropriate should I meet Jerry for the first time than in Bangkok, where we found that we shared many of the same tastes.

With very few exceptions, I ate what you see photographed here. Keeping or consuming the props, I should explain, is considered one of the perks of photography, and where a fashion photographer might get the clothes at the end of the shoot (or model if lucky), I would be left with the gooey parts. Yes, that includes the rats and the bats and the buffalo's penis—two-and-a-half feet, by the way, when flaccid. My only regret is that the publisher excised some of the best bits on the grounds of common decency. Surely you wouldn't have been offended by the breakfast of raw chopped dog, flavoured with its bile? On second thoughts, perhaps you would.

Michael Freeman

introduction

"He was a bold man who first swallowed an oyster."
— *Jonathan Swift*

ABOUT 150 YEARS AGO, an eccentric English gentleman named Francis Trevelyan Buckland invited a group of influential Earls and Viscounts and Marquis to dinner and in an attempt to expand their dietary horizons placed the freshly-killed haunch of an African beast on the table at London's famed Aldersgate Tavern. It was, he said, eland, a large antelope, and he thought they should be imported and bred on the green meadows of Great Britain, for the gustatory delight and nutritional benefit of all its citizens. The crusade that followed the dinner attracted considerable attention in the daily press, but no one seemed much interested in taking it any further, and the eland remained in Africa.

Buckland was not discouraged. He was raised by eccentric and imaginative parents and as a child he had eaten dog, crocodile, and garden snails, a habit he kept for life. To a fellow undergraduate at Oxford he confessed that earwigs were "horribly bitter," although the worst-tasting thing was the mole, until he ate a bluebottle fly. Later, guests at his London home were served panther, elephant trunk soup, and roast giraffe and it was reliably reported that whenever an animal died at the London Zoo, the curator called the Buckland home.

Buckland pressed on, forming, in 1860, the Acclimatisation Society of the United Kingdom, followed by sister societies in Scotland, the Channel Islands, France, Russia, the United States, the Hawaiian Islands, Australia, and New Zealand. His goal was the same: to introduce new food sources worldwide. In the end, his efforts failed. The world's dinner table did not welcome Tibetan yak, Eurasian beaver, parrots and parakeets, the Japanese sea slug, steamed kangaroo, seaweed jelly, silkworms, birds' nest soup, or sinews of the Axis deer, and Buckland died in 1880 in relative obscurity, where he remains today.

Since Buckland's failed effort, there have been several campaigns, both public and private, underwritten by the United Nations and individual countries as well as by ranchers, academics, and businessmen, to introduce "exotic" foods to the closed diet of what generally is called the "west," but in fact is epitomized by the gastronomical habits of Europe and North America. (And hereafter will be called Euro-America.) Nearly all have been unsuccessful and many were opposed vehemently. Yet, the debate continued.

"There are no more than one dozen species of domestic animals which are major food producers around the world," Russell Kyle argued logically in *A Feast in the Wild*, a book published in 1987. "If one adds the species with limited, local importance, such as the yak in the Himalayas, or the alpaca in the Andes, there are still fewer than twenty domestic species altogether with a major role as food producers. And yet the world as a whole contains over 200 species of herbivorous animals from the size of a hare upwards. Why have men apparently never considered making more deliberate use of so many wild animals for food production?"

Ten years later, in 1996, came "mad cow disease" and when British beef was banned by the European Union, the media published and broadcast stories about ostrich and kangaroo and other beef substitutes. As British Airways added ostrich medallions to its first class menu and other unusual protein sources appeared in European supermarkets, and more wild game became available in North America, a growing number started taking "strange foods" seriously. What was called "Extreme Cuisine" by the producers of a television series of that name for America's Food Channel suddenly became all the rage.

In Southeast Asia, Australia, and the United States, struggling alligator and crocodile farms found new markets, domestic and foreign. In Singapore, an established investment service began offering ostrich "futures": invest in a pair of breeders and reap the profits in the sale of their offspring, ranging from twenty to forty a year. From Sydney to Nairobi to Los Angeles, "jungle" restaurants, where game and other exotic dishes were served, became an overpriced trend. At the same time, a few naturalists made an interesting pitch to environmentalists, arguing that the way to save threatened species was to give them commercial value: guarantee their survival by eating them; once there was a market for these beasts as a food, they suggested, people would start breeding endangered species instead of killing them. A dubious argument, bearing in mind the value given to the tiger, the elephant, and many other threatened animals.

Through history and around the world, what is eaten has varied greatly from time to time and place to place, from one culture to another. Much of the dietary change has resulted from history's "natural" development—for example, the Portuguese introduced Brazilian chili peppers to Asian cuisine when they started trading there and Marco Polo packed spices and teas back to Europe following his first journeys to China. Similar change continues today as modern travelers return home with a newfound taste for foods experienced abroad, and as more migrants from one part of the world to another take their distinctive cuisines along with them; thus, most if not all Euro-American cities now have sushi bars and Thai restaurants (to name just two examples), unknown only a few years ago. Over the centuries, many other factors have influenced diet, from religious beliefs to hunger to flavor to status to medicinal (and, some insist, aphrodisiacal) properties and more.

What it all comes down to was stated simply and eloquently by M.F.K. Fisher, arguably the best writer about food in the 20th century, who wrote in a book aptly titled *How to Cook a Wolf* (published in 1942). "Why," she asked, "is it worse, in the end, to see an animal's head cooked and prepared for our pleasure than a thigh or a tail or a rib? If we are going to live on other inhabitants of this world we must not bind ourselves with illogical prejudices, but savor to the fullest the beasts we have killed.

"People who feel that a lamb's cheek is gross and vulgar when a chop is not are like the medieval philosophers who argued about such hair-splitting problems as how many angels could dance on the head of a pin. If you have these prejudices, ask yourself if they are not built on what you may have been taught when you were young and unthinking, and then if you can, teach yourself to enjoy some of the parts of an animal that are not commonly prepared."

Calf brains, sheep tongues, chicken feet, pig entrails, fish heads, the list goes on and on. Add "unusual" species such as ants and termites, beetles, bats, water buffalo, algae, cactus, rats and mice, flowers, elephants, whales, camel, bear, grubs, and earthworms, the start of another long list. And, yes, add all those protein sources that so many regard only as pets: cats and dogs, hamsters and gerbils, horses, exotic birds and fish. How many of us would push ourselves away from the table when such dishes were served, as the late Ms. Fisher said, because of what we learned when we were young?

All that said, much regional individuality remains in the world. In Taiwan, serpent blood is a tonic and many in the southwestern part of the United States swear by rattlesnake steak, just as kangaroo meat is a principal part of the diet for many Australian aborigines and appears on restaurant menus in dozens of Aussie restaurants. A small neighborhood in Hanoi and several in Seoul specialize in dog dishes (not to be confused with dishes from which dogs eat). Bulls' and sheep's testicles called Rocky Mountain Oysters are accepted in the American west, while in China, pigs' ears, fish eyes, and rooster wattle are chopsticked up with gusto. In Southeast Asia, fried locusts are regarded as tasty snacks, just as monkey stew is a staple in parts of Africa and the Amazon, guinea pig is an essential protein source in Peru, ants and termites are cherished in Africa and South America, yak milk is made into butter in Tibet and then added to tea, and horsemeat has an avid, centuries-old following in France, with another market expanding in Japan. These foods, accepted in one region, are rejected by diners in others.

I've followed Ms. Fisher's lead and tried to make this book a guide to how the other half dines and why. I'm no Frank Buckland, but over a period of twenty-five years I've augmented my meat-and-potatoes upbringing in the United States to try a wide variety of regional specialities, from steamed water beetles, fried grasshoppers and ants, to sparrow, bison and crocodile, the latter three served *en casserole*, grilled, and in a curry, respectively. I've eaten deep-fried bull's testicles in Mexico, live shrimp sushi in Hawaii, mice cooked over an open wood fire in Thailand, pig stomach soup in Singapore, minced water buffalo and yak butter tea in Nepal, stir-fried dog tongue and "five penis wine" in China, the boiled blood of a variety of animals in Vietnam, and paté made from my son's placenta when I lived (and he was born) in the UK. This list, too, goes on, and I share some of these experiences in the chapters following, along with many recipes. After all, no matter what humans eat, by choice or circumstance, the one thing all the dishes have in common is that they must be prepared properly.

Of course, there are some people who oppose such exploration. Conservationists are concerned, correctly, about the disappearance of endangered species. Others worry about animal rights, objecting to the manner in which even non-threatened species are penned or caged and slaughtered. A third group—called "bunny-huggers" in wildlife circles—cries out when people eat animals that they, the protestors, call pets, reminding me of Alice at the banquet in *Through the Looking Glass*, who turned away the mutton because it was impolite to eat food you'd been introduced to.

I will not engage animal rights people in debate. Their point of view is valid and, in fact, carries incalculable weight in a world where resources and environment are being threatened in a manner that is as alarming as it is unrelenting. Many argue that this alone will expand our gastronomical frontiers, whether we like it or not. As Mr. Kyle wrote, cattle are notoriously unkind to the earth and in time there won't be enough pasture to accommodate the world demand, forcing us to dine on alternate protein sources. The one mentioned most often? Insects.

An earlier version of this book was published in 1999 as *Strange Foods: Bush Meat, Bats, and Butterflies*. That material has been updated and expanded and nineteen new chapters have been added, along with a preface by noted chef Anthony Bourdain and an afterword that considers such recent food-related threats as SARS.

I don't insist that you add ostrich or dog or grasshopper to your menu, although I do suggest that you consider expanding your diet to include something outside the ordinary. However, as a frequent traveler, I do urge anyone who shares my passion for new places and peoples to heed that old but good advice about "when in Rome, do as the Romans do." Try some of the local food; I believe that it's a path to understanding the culture better than any other besides learning the language, marrying a native, or converting to the local religion.

Of course, species on the endangered list are not recommended, except under special circumstances. (There are chapters on elephants and whales.) There is no need. There are too many other tasty choices.

There also is the matter of curiosity and the pleasant surprise that frequently follows it. "I have always believed, perhaps too optimistically," Ms. Fisher wrote in a book called *An Alphabet for Gourmets* (1949), "that I would like to taste everything once, never from such hunger as made friends of mine in France in 1942 eat guinea-pig ragout, but from pure gourmandism."

Remember the person who first tasted the oyster. It's not just dinner, it's an adventure.

CHAPTER ONE
mammals

NO ONE IS SURE what the first humans ate, but surely other mammals were soon included in the diet if they weren't there from the beginning. In Neanderthal times, for example, the mammoth played a large role—courageously brought down with spears, then feeding, say, a dozen or more caves full of people for maybe a week or more. Many drawings found in such caves in Europe, North America and elsewhere show men hunting great, hairy beasts and archeological digs have uncovered the well chewed bones of dozens of animals to show that meat-eating has a long history.

Since then, of course, the number of mammals added to the diet multiplied as quickly as the number of species, while, in time, hunting, transport, and marketing advances were made enabling all types of meat to reach a larger audience, in smaller, more manageable portions. In other words, it is not necessary nowadays to deal with a dead mammoth outside the cave when there are steaks in the freezer and quarter-pounders at the corner fast food outlet.

That said, despite the advances and a current trendiness in the consumption of some exotic foods—mostly game meat—it can be argued that the number of protein sources for a growing number of people is shrinking rather than expanding, at least proportionately. Through history, humans have eaten virtually everything that walked, including each other. However, if it is true that in recent times the number and variety of mammals consumed in many parts of the world have increased, the consumption of the four herbivorous mammals that provide eighty per cent of the world's protein—cattle, pigs, sheep, and goats—has become more prevalent. Thus, as the number of species being added to the menu goes up, the proportions, worldwide, are running the other way.

That many mammals have disappeared from the menu can be explained in part by the unfortunate number of species added to the endangered lists, and their removal from the approved diet may be applauded. At the same time, the Gang of Four—beef, pork, lamb, and goat—has gained ground because of fashion and the outside influence that accompanies the press of history. In Japan, for example, meat was virtually untouched before the country opened up to the West in the mid-19th century, and in China, where bean curd was first produced some 2,000 years ago and meat-free diets were common-place, McDonald's outlets now outnumber vegetarian restaurants in Beijing.

Notions of class and caste exerted other forces. Some animal foods, such as possum in the United States, became associated with the poor, the "lower class," and thus were not accepted at "better" tables, just as what is called "bush meat" in Africa and "bush tucker" in Australia traditionally was consumed by ethnic minorities, thus was shunned by those who fancied themselves fancier. At the same time, a number of specific mammal parts—blood, brains, certain innards, and sexual organs, for example—were disdained because they were not consid-ered a "proper" food for the proper lady and gentleman.

Certain religions also played and continue to play a role. Hindus do not eat beef, Muslims and Orthodox Jews do not eat pork, and not so long ago many Catholics ate only fish on Fridays. Some of these guidelines and taboos have their origins in practicality. Pork has been banned for thousands of years in the Middle East and remains on the taboo list for many hundreds of millions today because it spoils quick-ly; modern refrigeration has eliminated most of the threat, but the belief remains in force. It may also be argued that beef in modern India is an inefficient food source because grazing cattle would take away land required by more productive crops such as rice and vegetables; before 800 B.C., however, when India was lightly populated, beef was welcome at mealtimes.

In the chapters that follow, I talk about mammals ranging in size from the mouse and the bat to the elephant and the whale, including animals both domesticated and wild. I've also selected foods from all corners of the earth, from horse tartar in France to monkey stew in West Africa to dog soup in Korea to yak butter tea in Tibet to grilled lamb's testicles in the United States.

Some of the chapters may offend Euro-Americans because the animals are regarded by many as pets or partners. Perhaps with no other food is the gastronomical gap made clearer than when what is called "man's best friend," the dog, finds a welcome place on a plate in Asia and only on a lap in Euro-America. Second to the dog is the horse as man's closest companion and helper through history. Yet, they are regarded highly at mealtime in many countries, as are cats, hamsters, gerbils, and guinea pigs.

I also include chapters about animals on the world's endangered lists. I am not irresponsible. First, all have a long history as food that continues to the present time, so they cannot be denied from any survey that has any pretensions to historical comprehension. More important, they give me a chance to argue that some of these animals are not always threatened, depending on location and circumstance.

I have not deliberately tried to offend. Southeast Asians adore grilled field mouse and rat, the Chinese put a lot of faith in beverages and soups made from animal penises, a recent Indian prime minister began each day with a glass of his own urine, and on a program produced by the BBC in London in 1997, human placenta was blended into a delicious paté. (As did I twenty-five years earlier.) What is strange in one place, in another is merely lunch.

Where's the beef?

The figures speak for themselves, says World Bank economist Nicholas Stern, who has been crunching numbers to determine how much the developed world pours down the toilet in farm subsidies.

The average cow in Europe, he concluded, was subsidized to the tune of US$2.50 a day, while the figure for Japan's prized herds was $7 per animal.

While the world's rain forests are denuded to create pasture or produce grain for the same quarter-pounders.

In time, he thinks, the protein choices must change.

Dogs & Cats

In most Euro-American countries (except in some immigrant communities), dog is man's best friend, or so they say. Which explains why so many westerners get so upset when this animal is eaten so matter-of-factly in many Asian and Latin American countries, and why a one time movie sex goddess in France, Brigitte Bardot and so many animals rights groups campaign so vigorously to get the eating of Fido banned.

Ms. Bardot gained prominence in her crusade when the animal rights foundation bearing her name urged soccer fans not to attend the soccer World Cup in Seoul if eating dogs was not outlawed and all the restaurants in the city offering dog on the menu weren't closed. While hers was a valid point of view shared by many in the so-called West, in other parts of the world, especially in numerous Asian countries, it was regarded as incomprehensible. Not only in Korea, but in most of southern China (including Hong Kong) and much of Southeast Asia, as well as in parts of Latin America, dog was just an available and affordable protein source.

There were precedents for Ms. Bardot's proposed ban, however. In 1988, the South Korean government ruled that restaurants serving dog soup, or *poshintang* (literally, "body-preservation stew"), closed to present a better image for foreigners attending the Olympic Games. Ten years later, in 1998, Philippine President Fidel Ramos signed into law a statute banning the killing of dogs for food, although its extreme popularity in the north made success of enforcement questionable.

Similar action has been taken elsewhere. In 1989, two Cambodian refugees living in southern California were charged with animal cruelty for eating a German Shepherd puppy. The charges eventually were dropped when a judge ruled that the dog was killed by the acceptable practices of slaughtering agricultural livestock. That did not satisfy animal activists who later the same year convinced the California legislature into passing a law making it a misdemeanor to eat a dog or a cat, punishable by up to six months in jail and a fine of US$1,000. Later still, the law was amended to include any animal traditionally kept as a pet or companion. Presumably, those charged with enforcing this law were expected to look the other way when 4-H Club members led their prize cattle and pigs to slaughter, animals they had raised from birth and for whom they frequently developed great affection. Furthermore, rabbits could still be killed and eaten and so could tropical fish, because they were legally categorized as livestock and fish, not pets.

There is no mystery why so many Euro-Americans oppose the eating of dog. There have been too many dog heroes in literature, TV and film—in stories by Jack London and dozens more, in movies like *Rin Tin Tin*, *Lassie*, *Benji* and Disney's enduring *101 Dalmatians*, in virtually everything writ large in popular culture, from the heroic K-9 Corps in the US military to the St. Bernard who carries a flask of life-saving grog to humans lost in the Alps. In addition, the dog—believed to be a domestication of a Neolithic Asiatic wolf—through the years has proven his usefulness to man because of its speed, hearing, sense of smell, hunting instinct, and herding abilities.

All that said, dog has been a welcome dish across much of the world's history and geography. The recorded eating of dog goes back to Confucius's time in China, circa 500 B.C., when the *Li Ji*, a handbook of ancient ritual translated in 1885, offered recipes for delicacies prepared on ceremonial occasions. One of the dishes was canine, fried rice with crispy chunks cut from a wolf's breast, served with dog liver basted in its own fat, roasted and seared over charcoal. During the same period, an emperor who wanted more warriors, encouraged childbirth by awarding what was described in the literature of the time as a succulent puppy to any woman bearing a boy.

The Chinese (and other Asians) regarded dog meat as more than a culinary treat. It was considered to be very good for the yang, the male, hot, extroverted part of human nature, as opposed to the female, cool, introverted yin. It was believed to "warm" the blood and thus was consumed in greatest frequency during the winter months. As early as the 4th century B.C., a Chinese philosopher named Mencius praised dog meat for its pharmaceutical properties, recommending it for liver ailments, malaria and jaundice. Along with many other foods, it also was believed to enhance virility. The Chinese also served a sort of dog wine, believed to be a remedy for weariness.

Later, the Manchu Dynasty that ruled China from the 17th century banned dog meat, declaring its consumption barbarian. However, southern Chinese continued to eat it and Sun Yat-sen's opposition Kuomintang followers began their meetings by cooking dog, believing the act symbolized their anti-Manchu revolution. The code name was "Three-Six Meat," a play on the Chinese word for the number nine, which rhymed with the word for dog. Even today in Hong Kong, where since 1950 it has been illegal to catch or kill dogs or to possess their meat, butchers and customers use the expression "Three-Six Meat" when selling and buying it. Because Hong Kong Chinese are from southern China, where dog is still regarded as a staple, enforcement of the law has been negligible, punishment (up to six months in prison and a fine of US$125) has been lax, and the law is widely ignored, especially during the winter months when demand is greatest.

It is well known that the American Indian originated in what is now Mongolia, and it's believed that they brought the dog with them when they crossed the Bering Sea and eventually settled the wilderness that became North America. When European explorers and settlers arrived in the New World, they counted seventeen dog varieties, many of them raised specifically as food, although it was noted that not all tribes indulged. Those that did included the Iroquois and several Algonquian tribes of the central and eastern woodlands and the Utes of Utah, who cooked and ate dog meat before performing sacred ceremonial dances. While the very name of the Arapahoe means "dog-eater." David Comfort writes in *The First Pet History of the World* that puppies were generally preferred because of their tenderness: "They were fattened with a special mixture of pemmican and dried fruit. After harvest with a tomahawk, the puppy was suspended upside down from a lodge pole, and the carcass hand-marinated with buffalo fat. Then it was skewered."

Many of the early European arrivals contentedly, or at least circumstantially, joined in. Cabeza de Vaca, the Spanish explorer, was shipwrecked in the Gulf of Mexico and wandered for eight years on foot throughout the American Southwest, eating canine regularly. In Christopher Columbus's time, Mexico's only domesticated livestock were the turkey and the dog and according to a history written in the 16th century, the two meats were served in a single dish. Meriwether Lewis, leader of the Lewis and Clark Expedition that opened the American Northwest, wrote in his journal in 1804, "Having been so long accustomed to live on the flesh of dogs, the greater part of us have acquired a fondness for it, and our original aversion for it overcome by reflecting that while we subsisted on that food we were fatter, stronger, and in general enjoyed better health than at any period since leaving buffalo country." As recently as 1928, the Norwegian explorer Roald Amundsen ate his sled dogs in the Arctic in his attempt to reach the North Pole, although that was, admittedly, for reasons of survival and not by choice.

Nor was canine cuisine limited to Asia and North America. For at least a thousand years, Polynesians cherished the *poi* dog, so called because the animal's diet was vegetarian, consisting largely of *poi*, or cooked taro root. This was one of the food animals taken to what is now Hawaii on primitive sailing ships from Tahiti and the Marquesas (along with the pig). At large feasts in Hawaii in the early 1800s, hosted by local royalty and attended by sailors from England and the United States, as many as 200–400 dogs were served at a single sitting.

In 1870, a cookbook was published in France with recipes for dozens of dishes based on the meat of dogs. Across the English Channel, however, the British typically rejected anything enjoyed by the French and in the 1890s Punch, the humor magazine, published several cartoons demonstrating their disapproval. The same magazine also satirically described an anonymous Englishman's encounter with a canine meal:

...he brightened up
And thought himself in luck
When close before him what he saw
Looked something like a duck!

Still cautious grown, but, to be sure,
His brain he set to rack;
At length he turned to one behind,
And, pointing, cried, "Quack, quack?"

The Chinese gravely shook his head,
Next made a reverend bow;
And then expressed what dish it was,
By uttering, "Bow-wow-wow!"

Today, dog remains popular in southern China, Hong Kong, parts of Japan, Korea, much of Southeast Asia, and to a lesser degree in Mexico, Central and South America, but not without controversy. For years, organizers of the world's most famous dog show, in England, welcomed sponsorship from the Korean electronics giant Samsung, until the International Fund for Animal Welfare protested in 1995, claiming that up to two million dogs were processed for the Korean food industry annually.

Men in the dog business must be selective. If the dogs haven't eaten well, the meat may be stringy and possibly unhealthy. In some Asian countries today the movement is not only to regulate the slaughter and promote cleanliness, but also to identify establishments where dog meat is served, because sometimes it is substituted for something else. For example, I was served "wild boar" in Saigon that I'm sure wasn't boar—this, the day after seeing a flat-bed truck loaded with caged dogs on the highway leading into the city. A coincidence? Perhaps.

I have also eaten dog in China and Vietnam. As a photographer friend took pictures of a skinned dog just delivered to a restaurant in China's Yunnan province, a woman beckoned to us to come in. On the stove, she had some bite-sized, stir-fried haunch in a wok, left over from lunch, with a taste like cooked beef, slightly greasy, as dog, I've learned, often is. Two weeks later, in the mountainous region of north-western Vietnam, near the China border, I was served thin slices of dog tongue stir-fried with garlic and vegetables and while visiting a week-end marketplace in the same province I saw more than a dozen well-fed dogs of various breeds for sale (for about US$10 apiece), and later I observed members of the hilltribe prominent in that area leading din-ner home on a leash. The same year, 1998, the Ministry of Agriculture and Rural Development said there were at least fourteen million dogs in Vietnam, their numbers swelling as more and more farmers turned to raising dogs instead of pigs.

In Thailand, I found dog in the open markets as well, butchered and ready to go, but also cooked into a rich stew that sold for about eighty US cents a portion, and deep-fried into a sort of jerky. This was in Sakon Nakhon, a province in Thailand's northeast, where on the average day, I was told, approximately a thousand dogs were killed for markets in the region. This area was known for a kind of Oriental dog tartar, where raw dog meat was chopped almost to a mince, mixed with a few spices and finely chopped vegetables and served with the dog's blood and bile. Unlike Vietnam, where most of the dogs that are cooked are tender puppies, the adults wind up on the plate in Thailand, so tough that minced is the easiest to chew and most digestible.

In Korea in 2003, an estimated 4,000–6,000 restaurants served rich soups (costing about US$10 for a medium-sized bowl), casseroles (US$16 per serving), and steamed meat served with rice (US$25). It was, as in other places, technically illegal to sell cooked dog meat, and restaurateurs did so under threat of having their licenses revoked. However, an appeals court in Seoul in 1997 acquitted a dog meat wholesaler, ruling that dogs were socially accepted as food.

So, too, in Hanoi, where the Nhat Tan neighborhood by the Red River on the capital's northern outskirts is made up almost entirely of dog restaurants, while the village of Cao Ha, forty kilometers to the south, makes a living keeping them in meat. Here, at least ten or a dozen dishes will be on the menu, including steamed dog, minced and seasoned dog wrapped in leaves, fried intestines, spare ribs, and fried thighs. A kind of sour dog curry is also made with fermented wine and served with noodles. The most expensive dish on offer is a bamboo shoot dog soup. This normally is only eaten in the second half of the lunar month when it is regarded as auspicious. It is believed to help general health and fitness as well as male virility and wipe away bad luck.

As a protein source for human consumption, cats have a briefer history. At least, there are fewer historical references and while felines continue to find their way to the supper table, from South America to Asia, consumption level is comparatively quite low. This may be explained by the fact that through the ages, human regard for the cat has swung so widely—from worship to blasphemy and back—and at neither extreme did the small creature with the heart-warming purr and sharp claws ever seem as right for a stew or grill as their larger relatives, the cougar, the panther, the leopard, the lion, and the tiger.

There are, of course, numerous cases of the small, domestic cat being eaten for survival, just as Mr. Amundsen ate his sled dogs in the last century. In 1975, for example, the British correspondent Jon Swain was held captive in the French embassy in Phnom Penh following the invasion of the Cambodian capital by the Khmer Rouge. "With no end to our internment in sight, the shortage of food was becoming serious," he wrote in *River of Time* (1996). "Reluctantly, Jean Menta, a Corsican adventurer, and Borella, the mercenary who had been keeping a low profile in case he was recognized, strangled and skinned the embassy cat. The poor creature put up a spirited fight and both men were badly scratched. A few of us ate it, curried. The meat was tender like chicken."

So, too, in 1996, cats were skinned and grilled in Argentina under the media's harsh glare, causing an uproar in homes throughout the country and in the legislature. The press and politicians asked, were people so poor they had to eat pets? The answer, of course, was yes.

The same year, in Australia, Richard Evans, a member of Parliament, recommended the country do everything possible to eradicate the country's eighteen million feral and domestic cats by 2020 to prevent them killing an estimated three million birds and animals every year. John Wamsley, the managing director of Earth Sanctuaries, went a step further, urging people to catch and eat feral cats, recommending what he called "pussy-tail stew." Another uproar shook the media.

It isn't always need that puts the cat in the pot. At Guang's Dog and Cat restaurant in Jiangmen, a city in southern China, the owner, Wu Lianguang, told reporters in 1996, "Business couldn't be better. The wealthier the Chinese become, the more concerned they are about their health and there's nothing better for you than cat meat."

In northern Vietnam in the 1990s, cat joined its canine cousin on many restaurant menus in the belief that asthma could be cured by eating cat meat and that a man's sexual prowess could be aroused or enhanced with the help of four raw cat galls pickled in rice wine. As a food, it was enjoyed raw, marinated, grilled over charcoal, or cut into bite-sized chunks and dunked into a Mongolian hotpot with vegetables. According to a report from Agence France Presse, a dozen restaurants specializing in cat meat opened in just one district of Hanoi and about 1,800 cats were butchered every year in each of them, with the cost to the consumer rising from US$3.50 to US$11 in just two years.

Cat meat—generally not so greasy as dog—was a favorite of Hanoi gourmets until 1997, when the government forbade all further slaughter. Why? Official figures showed that as the country's cat population dropped, the number of rats multiplied at an alarming rate, ravaging up to thirty per cent of grain produced in some districts around the capital city. The restaurants were held to blame.

The same year on the other side of the world, in Lima, Peru, a last-minute appeal from Peruvian animal-lovers persuaded authorities to halt a festival of cat cookery intended to celebrate a local saint's day. Organizers of the event announced with regret that the annual festival honoring St. Efigenica, scheduled in the southern coastal town of Canete, had been cancelled at the insistence of animal rights activists. However, cat continues to be considered a delicacy and it remains on local menus, without any public display.

A Swiss chef who worked in a five-star hotel in Asia smiled when I mentioned cat cuisine. He said he ate cat in northern Italy and enjoyed it, and if anyone wanted to do the same and lacked a recipe, it tasted so much like squirrel or rabbit, all they had to do was find a recipe for one of those and substitute.

How Much Is That Doggie in the Paddy?

"The Lao [residents of Laos and northeastern Thailand] say eel is the best water meat and that dog is the best land meat," Chavalit Phorak, a man in the dog slaughtering business in Thailand told *The Nation*, a Bangkok newspaper, in 1997. "It's much tastier than beef and not as tough. In the past, families used to kill a dog to eat each week. People liked the meat, but they had to be careful not to exhaust their supply. After all, there's not much meat on a big dog, let alone a pup, and a dog takes time to grow, so farming them is still impractical."

In most countries where dog is eaten, farming is not necessary, as strays and other unwanted canines are plentiful. For this reason, there are men like Mr. Chavalit, who travels the back roads and barters for village dogs, then sells the meat, entrails, and skins. "My truck has a loud speaker," he said. "Everywhere I go I tell people that I will give them pails for their naughty or lazy dogs."

A healthy dog, in 1997, was worth two buckets. It took Mr. Chavalit three or four days to collect 100 dogs, the number at which he broke even and possibly earned a small profit, as each trip cost as much as US$400 for petrol and pails. He then returned to the slaughterhouse, where butchers were paid twelve cents for every dog they kill, with a blow to the head with a hammer so as not to damage the skin.

Another twelve cents was paid for skinning the dogs, plus sixteen cents for butchering the meat. The meat was then sold for up to US$2 a kilo, with each dog contributing about three kilos, and the skins were sold for between US$1 and US$2 to factories in Thailand, Taiwan, and Japan, where they were turned into golfing gloves. (Think about that next time you step up to the tee.) The genitals were also sold, for about forty cents, and used in soup and wine, mainly in China, Korea, Vietnam, and Japan.

Stir-Fried Dog with Coconut Milk

1 lb dog haunch,
    cut into bite-sized pieces
1 medium onion, thinly sliced
2 small green chilies, seeded and sliced
4–6 mushrooms, sliced
1 cup coconut milk
5 tablespoons peanut oil

2 tablespoons soy sauce
2 tablespoons fresh ginger,
    chopped
1 teaspoon ground cumin seed
1 teaspoon cornflour (mixed
    with water to form paste)
Salt and pepper to taste
Fresh mint leaves

Heat oil in wok or frying pan, then add meat, stir-frying until lightly browned. Add coconut milk and soy sauce and stir for 1–2 minutes. Add onion, chilies, mushrooms, and seasoning and continue to stir. When the mixture begins to bubble, stir in cornflour paste. Garnish with mint leaves and serve with rice.

Sweet & Sour Dog

1 lb dog, cut into thin 2-inch strips
1 yellow or red pepper,
    seeded and chopped into pieces
1/2 onion, chopped into pieces
1 tablespoon catsup

2 teaspoons vinegar
3 tablespoons red wine
1 tablespoon cornflour
3 tablespoons vegetable oil
Salt and pepper

4 tablespoons sugar
1 tablespoon soy sauce

1/2 cup water
Oil for deep-frying

Batter:
2 egg yolks, beaten
2 tablespoons flour
2 tablespoons water

Sprinkle meat with half of the red wine and a pinch of salt and pepper. Add catsup, sugar, soy sauce, vinegar, remaining red wine, cornflour, and 1 teaspoon salt. Set whatever is left aside for later use.

Make a batter from the eggs, flour and water. Heat cooking oil in wok or frying pan to 350°F and dip meat into batter, then fry until crisp. Keep warm on the side.

Clean wok or pan and heat vegetable oil, adding pepper and onion and stir-fry for 1–2 minutes, then add soy sauce/sugar/catsup blend and stir until it thickens, then mix in meat, serving hot, with rice.
—*Based on interviews with Chinese cooks,*
Bangkok and Guangzhou, 1998

Cat Ragout

2 lbs cat meat, sliced on bias
1 1/2 lbs potatoes,
    boiled and cubed
2 large onions, sliced
2 large carrots, cut into 1/2-inch slices
2 leeks, sliced
2 stalks celery, sliced
2 cloves garlic, chopped finely

1 1/2 cups red wine
Flour
Butter
Pinch each rosemary,
    oregano and paprika
Salt and pepper to taste
Parsley or coriander,
    chopped finely

Skin cat, remove ribs, using only the trunk, cutting away the fat from the fillets, then slice into thin pieces. Dip into flour and cook in a pan until lightly browned. Boil potatoes. Cook other vegetables in butter, removing while still firm.

Put cat in casserole pot and add wine, cooking for 1 hour, until brown gravy forms. Add vegetables for final 8–10 minutes. Serve with polenta. (This is the traditional corn porridge of northern Italy; may substitute creamed corn.)

Horse

My friend Richard Lair, an elephant expert living in Thailand, where he says he has eaten just about everything except elephant, was attending San Francisco State University in the early 1960s when he was introduced to horse meat. A pal of his was a chef who often shopped for his dinner at a pet store, the only place where horse meat could be purchased (in America) easily—this, because it was regarded (in America) as food fit only for dogs.

This gentleman knew the various cuts of horse, my friend told me, and he knew freshly slaughtered meat when he saw it, so when the "pet food" met his approval, he purchased some of the rump and took it home and prepared the horse meat in the same way he prepared beef bourguignon, coating the cubes of lean meat with flour and frying them in a heavy saucepan with onions and shallots, and perhaps a tot of brandy, set aflame just before serving with potatoes and vegetables.

Horse meat? Most Euro-Americans would giddyup and go at the thought. This was, after all, the mammal most closely identified with human activity. From approximately 2,500 B.C., the animal has been an indispensable part of society, primarily as a beast of burden and a means of transportation. As early as 900 B.C., the Assyrian horse was drafted into the forerunner of what became called the "cavalry." At the same time, in Greece, horse racing was included in the earliest Olympic games. They also pulled chariots into battle and plows across fields.

The horse was introduced to the "New World" by Spanish conquistadors in the 17th century, where it proliferated on the vast, grassy plains, and became a cowboy's (and in Argentina, a gaucho's) best friend and essential partner. Before trains traversed the United States, mail was delivered by Pony Express, people in stagecoaches were drawn cross-country by teams of four and six. Later, horses pulled trolley cars and fire engines. Teamsters and tradesmen transported their goods in horse-drawn wagons, much as the Budweiser Clydesdales pull beer carts for TV commercials today. In time, of course, the horse was replaced: by the train (initially called the Iron Horse), the tractor, the car, and truck.

The horse performs both essential and romantic tasks. Today, there are horses that pull carriages through New York's Central Park, others that perform tricks in circuses. There are horses that still help cowboys herd cattle and horses that race around tracks and horses that jump over fences. Polo is an international sport, dating back to ancient

India, when a goat's head was frequently used as a ball. There are police horses and horses on dude ranches and there are ponies for little girls to ride on their birthdays. There also are horses on merry-go-rounds and, over the past century, dozens of horses that were stars in movies and in the international racing circuit. Clubs and competitions and shows are everywhere.

With this background, it is no surprise that there are organizations, mainly in the United States, determined to halt the killing of wild horses in the American West and Canada for export to Europe as food. A 1996 equine survey counted seven million horses in America, about twenty per cent more than a decade earlier. Of those sold at auction, most were "going to Paris," the local euphemism for the European horse meat market.

We know that prehistoric man hunted the horse as a source of meat from cave paintings dating back to the Ice Age showing hunters and their equine prey. In fact, some historians believe the horse was domesticated as a source of food before it was used as a beast of burden. Although the flesh was forbidden by Mosaic law, Joseph raised horses for food during a famine and the Greek historian Herodotus told how horse was boiled and then cooked with ox.

Calvin Schwabe wrote in *Unmentionable Cuisine* (1979) that in pre-Christian times "horsemeat eating in northern Europe figured prominently in Teutonic religious ceremonies, particularly those associated with the worship of Odin. So much so, in fact, that in A.D. 732 Pope Gregory III began a concerted effort to stop this pagan practice, and it has been said that the Icelandic people specifically were reluctant to embrace Christianity for some time largely over the issue of their giving up horsemeat."

Marco Polo told of the Mongols draining small but regular quantities of the blood from their mounts as they moved across central Asia, taking milk to make foods of the curd or yogurt type, and drinking mare's milk as well for sustenance. (See the chapter on Blood.) "First they bring the milk [almost] to the boil," the early trader and explorer wrote. "At the appropriate moment they skim off the cream that floats on the surface and put it in another vessel to be made into butter, because so long as it remains the milk can not be dried. Then they stand the milk in the sun and leave it to dry. When they are going on an expedition they take about ten pounds of this milk; and every morning they take out about half a pound of it and put it in a small leather flask, shaped like a gourd, with as much water as they please. Then while they ride, the milk in the flask dissolves into a fluid, which they drink. And this is their breakfast."

Another early traveler in the east was William de Rubruquis, who published a record of his *Remarkable Travels into Tartary and China*, 1253, in which he told how the Mongols made kumiss, a fermented liquor. Just as the standing horse milk was about to ferment, it was poured into a large bladder and beaten with "a piece of wood made for that purpose, having a knot at the lower end like a man's head, which is hollow within; and so soon as they beat it, it begins to boil [froth] like new wine, and to be sour and of a sharp taste; and they beat it in that manner till butter comes. After a man hath taken a draught it leaves a taste behind it like that of almond milk, going down very pleasantly, and intoxicating weak brains, for it is very heady and powerful." The consumption of horse milk and its by-products is not so common today, although a weak version of kumiss is drunk in parts of China. (Where the alcoholic strength is at a low two percent, no match even for the feeblest beers.)

The French, especially Parisians, have eaten horse meat common-ly and openly since 1811, when it was decreed legal following a long ban. Today in France, especially in the Camargue in the south where herds of wild horses dashing through water is a photographic cliche, some breeds are raised for meat and as is true of most meat sources, the young—the colts—are preferred for their tenderness. Easily digested, horse meat has fewer calories than beef—ninety-four per hundred milligrams, compared with one-hundred and fifty-six for lean beef.

To satisfy the market that now includes Japan, thousands of wild horses, donkeys, burros, and mules are killed and butchered in the American west each year, despite efforts by animal activists who want to see the Old West left alone. Running free across parts of ten western states, the estimated 50,000 wild equines are far too many for the range to sustain, according to the US government. The Bureau of Land Management wants nearly half removed by 2005.

Oddly, it is an expensive government program that has created, or at least abetted, this industry. The program, managed by the Bureau of Land Management, is intended to protect wild horses on public lands, where they compete for water and forage with grazing cattle. What this means is that "excess horses" are rounded up and offered to the public for adoption. The government spends over US$1,000 to collect, vaccinate, brand, and administer the paperwork for each horse and adopters pay US$125 for a healthy horse, as little as US$25 for one that is old or lame. The new "parent" agrees to keep the animals for at least one year. Some do, many don't, most selling them for slaughter eventually, usually receiving US$700 apiece. More than 165,000 animals have been rounded up since the program was started in 1982, costing the government over US$250 million. A tenth of that sum is considered a good year in the sale of the meat by export to Europe and Japan.

So it is not a big business, but it is a medium-sized one that likely will not go away. Some conservationists say it is a billion-dollar-industry, a figure that makes people at U.S. slaughterhouses laugh and say, "I wish."

"Killed on Friday, processed on Monday, Thursday we load the truck and then it's flown to Europe," said Pascal Derde, proprietor of the Cavel West, a packing house in Redmond, Oregon. "Tuesday eaten."

However popular that horse may be today, it is unlikely there ever will be an event to top one held during the mid-19th century, not long after Napoleon's pharmacist, Cadet de Gassicourt, and others publicly testified that horse meat had sustained a number of lives during the general's military campaigns. On February 6, 1856, a number of butchers and chefs organized a banquet at one of Paris's grand hotels that offered horse-broth vermicelli, horse sausage, boiled horse, horse stew, fillet of horse with mushrooms, potatoes sautéed in horse fat, salad in horse oil, and a rum pastry with horse bone marrow. Guests at the feast included the novelists Alexandre Dumas, who not only wrote *The Three Musketeers*, but also the 1,152-page *Grand Dictionaire de Cuisine*, and Gustave Flaubert, author of *Madame Bovary*.

The flesh of the horse (*Equus caballus*) may be substituted for beef in many recipes—the animals are related, after all—as can donkey (*Equus asinus*) and the mule, a hybrid of the two, both often sold under this title. However, as animals which do not have cloven hooves or chew cud, they are prohibited for both Muslims and Jews.

Especially in France, Belgium, Sweden, and Japan, it is particularly enjoyed in raw dishes, the lean flank sliced thinly and presented with a hot sauce (horse radish is not inappropriate) or as "horse tartar," mixed with chopped onions and herbs and spices and served with Worcestorshire sauce. In Japan, *umasashi*, horsemeat sashimi, is widely prized; in the south of France, the local sausage is based on ground horse meat, and is grilled, baked or fried; in Italy it is included in a recipe for spaghetti sauce Bolognese; in Switzerland it is deep-fried; in North and South America it is made into jerky.

Other members of the horse family also are eaten, notably the zebra in Africa, where their extraordinary number have made them an inexpensive and readily available protein source for centuries. Laurens van der Post, a South African writer whose book *First Catch*

Your Eland (1977) recalled his gastronomic adventures as a child and maturing adult, said zebra fillets and steaks provided "the tenderest and tastiest meat of all."

From the Plains to the Plate

BIG HORN, Wyoming – Last year, 85,000 horses met their end in the four horse meat packing plants left in America. In 1996, these businesses shipped US$64-million worth of horsemeat to Belgium, France, Switzerland, and Mexico. The prime candidate for slaughter, say buyers, is a ten- to twelve-year-old well-muscled quarter horse. The hind quarters are chilled and flown to Europe; the front quarters are cooked and minced and sent by boat.

"This is an all-but-invisible trade. Even the United States Department of Agriculture, the government agency responsible for inspecting horse-meat, is stingy with information. Studies and analysis of the industry are practically non-existent. Packing plants are about as open as a frozen oyster. The Central-Nebraska Packing Company of North Platte politely but firmly rejected this reporter's request to visit it. 'With people burning down plants, we don't make a habit of giving tours,' said the manager. He was referring to an incident in July 1997, when arsonists did $1 million of damage to the Cavel West packing house in Redmond, Oregon, which specialized in horsemeat. A torch-happy group, the Animal Liberation Front, claimed responsibility."

—The Economist, 1998

Horse Tartar

5–8 oz lean horse flank or rump (per person)	1 teaspoon capers
1 egg	Worcestershire sauce or tabasco to taste
1 tablespoon red onion, chopped	Salt and pepper to taste
1 garlic clove, minced	Catsup, olive oil, soy sauce
1 tablespoon parsley, chopped	

Grind meat and form into a ball, working in egg yolk, garlic, Worcestershire sauce or tabasco, salt and pepper. Flatten one side so the ball will hold its position on a plate or use a mold. Place the onion, parsley, and capers on the plate around the meat; these are then added to the fork while eating. Serve with catsup, olive oil, more Worcestershire sauce, and soy sauce as desired for additional flavoring.

Veterinary Students Meatloaf

Mix together ground horse meat and ground pork (3:1) with bread soaked in milk (2 slice per lb of meat), some finely chopped onions and chopped celery, beaten egg (1 per 2 lbs of meat), salt, pepper, dry mustard, crushed garlic, and a little Worcestershire sauce. Form into a loaf and bake at 350°F. After the first half hour, pour off the fat and ladle over the load a mixture of canned tomato sauce and water (2:1) and some crushed garlic. Sprinkle with grated Parmesan cheese and bake until done.

—*Calvin Schwabe's original, from his days as a veterinary student*

Bison, Water Buffalo & Yak

Roasted American buffalo, more accurately called bison, was the main dish served to me at a Boy Scout ranch in New Mexico in the 1950s after a month spent hiking and riding horses across the rough, dry mountains and plains. At the time, one of the coins in any American pocket had a picture of an Indian chief on one side, a bison on the other; thus, it was called a "buffalo nickle," and as a Boy Scout, Indian lore was something I knew well. At home, my mother hated to cook and my father's bland dietary demands made dinner time quite mundane, so eating the same food that nourished countless American Indians was quite exotic, permitting me to ignore the fact that it tasted like a slightly pungent version of my mother's undercooked roast beef. (Sorry, mom.)

The bison was once so numerous, its shaggy, humped-back herds roamed the Western plains like zebra and gazelle still inhabit parts of the African veldt. Before the white man arrived, an estimated forty- to sixty-million bison ranged from central Canada south into Mexico, where it was a primary source of food for the nomadic Indian tribes, including the Cheyenne, Cree, Kiowa, Sioux, Osage, Blackfoot, and many more. Native hunters frequently approached the herds on their hands and knees, with wolf skins hiding their human forms, their bodies smeared with buffalo fat to hide their human odor, bows and arrows at the ready. (Like other grazing animals, bison relied more on a keen sense of smell than sight and hearing to detect approaching harm.) The hunters also constructed high walls of brush along either side of known buffalo migration routes, forming a sort of funnel leading to a rough corral, where they easily killed the targets of their choice. When the geography permitted, they stampeded the buffalo over cliffs. After acquiring horses and rifles from early western hunters and explorers, the tribal hunt became more efficient.

One kill, averaging between 1,000 and 1,500 pounds, could provide for a tribe for days. Usually the first parts consumed were the offal, although the favorite parts—generally either roasted or dried for future use—were the tongue and meat from the hump, which was considered the tenderest and sweetest. Eaten soon after slaughter, the meat was roasted on a spit or boiled in a skin bag with water and stones heated in an open fire, a process that produced a nutritious stew or soup.

The Indians wasted nothing, using every part of the shaggy, horned, black-bearded beast. Clothing and moccasins were made from the tanned hide, along with river rafts and boats; the cured hide also covered the Indians' tall, conical tents, or tipi. With the hair left on, the hides became blankets for the bitter winter cold. Tanning agents were produced from the brains, fat, and liver, soap from the leftover fat, glue from the rendered hooves. War shields were crafted from the tough neck hide, arrowheads and knives from the bones, powder flasks, spoons, and drinking cups from the horns. Sinew was used as thread. Hoes were fashioned from the shoulder blade, and stomachs were sewn into water bags. The long hair was plaited into halters. Even the dried dung was used, as it is today when no wood is available, for campfires, producing little smoke.

The Indians killed an estimated 300,000 bison a year, well below the natural replacement rate. That changed tragically in the early 19th century, when a vogue for big game hunting swept much of the world and white settlers with rifles began populating the American plains, followed by entrepreneurs and adventurers. The bison were killed by white hunters first for their meat at a rate of about two million a year, but frequently only the tongues were taken for the menus of fashionable restaurants in Chicago and New York and the huge carcasses were left to rot. The slaughter accelerated to about three million a year in the 1870s, when bison hides were first made into commercial leather.

William F. Cody, an early plainsman, acquired his nickname "Buffalo Bill" for shooting bison as food for railroad construction crews and is reported to have killed 4,280 animals within one seventeen-month period. Once the railroads were in place, the white man shot millions more each year, blasting away from trains passing through the diminishing herds. Some contend that this was a plot to beat back the native Americans; slaughter the primary source of their survival and you wipe out the Indians, too. More likely, the hunters got some sort of thrill from banging away at the beasts.

Whatever the motivation, now the entire animal was left to waste and with the introduction of fences erected by sheep herders and other homesteaders, the surviving animals' freedom to range was restricted, their natural lifestyle inhibited. By the end of the century, the American bison was driven to the point of extinction; unbelievably, from tens of millions, only about a thousand still grazed the plains.

Happily, the tide has turned. Small wild herds survived in parts of the U.S. (notably in what became Yellowstone Park) and Canada and in the 20th century, efforts were introduced to protect the animal and reconstitute the once-great herds. Today, the buffalo's future seems secure and more than 300,000 animals range parklands and private ranches from New York to California, from Canada to Oklahoma. Some of the herds, including the largest in existence—numbering 25,000—are on ranches owned by American media mogul Ted Turner.

Many of today's herds, including Turner's, are being managed at least partly for the production of food, so today it is becoming more common to see charbroiled bison steak and stew on menus in the U.S. and Canada. Because of its resemblance to beef, in appearance as well as in taste, it has found ready acceptance wherever it is available; limited quantity and distribution has kept the meat unknown in most places, however. The bison also is being cross-bred with cattle, producing what is called "beefalo," and sometimes "cattelo." (However, the male of the mixed breed so far is infertile.) The North American Bison Cooperative, backed by scientific studies, boasts that the meat is lower in cholesterol and saturated fat than beef, non-allergenic, and free of chemicals.

Bud Flocchini of Gillette, Wyoming, president of the American Bison Asociation, says membership has doubled to 2,300 since 1993. "We've never seen such interest," he says. "These animals are much tougher to work with than beef cattle. To produce income, you need between fifty to one hundred head and around fifty acres of good pasture, with supplementary feed in the off season." Farmers also say they are naturally disease resistant and are easier on the land, although they remain a wild animal; an irritated bull, weighing up to a ton, can outrun a horse in a short burst, meaning even the most experienced rancher will not turn his back on one of his animals.

Much of the bison consumed by the Indian nations was in the form of jerky, or pemmican, a word that comes from the Cree, meaning "journey meat." To make pemmican, or jerky, the Cree dried strips of buffalo meat in the sun, a process that took a few days. They then pounded it into a pulp, mixing it with the fat from a bear or goose, or the bison itself, and, if available, pulverized dry fruit. More colorful was the description by C. Levi-Strauss in *The Origin of Table Manners*: "They placed thin slices of hard meat carefully on a bed of charcoal, first on one side then on the other. They beat them to break them into small pieces which they mixed with melted bison fat and marrow. Then they pressed it into leather bags, taking care that no air was left inside. When the bags were sewn up, the women flattened them by jumping on them to blend the ingredients. They put them to dry in the sun."

The rising numbers are not an altogether good thing, at least not for ranchers who have seen the price of the animals and the meat sink. In 1999, one was selling his calves for US$2,500 apiece and in 2001 they went under the hammer for US$300. Encouraged by Sen. Kent Conrad of North Dakota, the U.S. Department of Agriculture bought one million kilograms of bison burgers over a three-year period to be sold for school lunches and poverty-reduction programs. While on some ranches, hunters pay to shoot a bull, which gives them an impressive wall mount, a robe or tanned hide, and a freezer full of steaks.

The bison has numerous "cousins" around the world, many of them also cherished as a renewable, non-threatened protein source. These include the Cape Buffalo in Africa, and in Asia, the water buffalo and yak. Of these, surely the water buffalo is the most commonly consumed. With an estimated 130 million in existence, this largely domesticated, cud-chewing, plant-eating animal is now spread over much of the world, but it is in Indonesia, Thailand, Malaysia, the Philippines, Myanmar, China, Laos, Cambodia, and Vietnam where the majority live. Here, they labor as the developing world's tractor, while serving as family friend, object of competitive sport (battling head-to-head during festivals or in long, bouncy dashes in a race against the clock, riders clinging precariously to their asphalt hides), and household symbol of status, wealth, and tranquility. Sacrifice a buffalo at a funeral or in a religious rite or offer one as part of a dowry for a bride and your local status goes up, or put them to work in the paddy fields and, between shifts in front of primitive plows, let them and children mind each other in muddy peace. Surely no other Asian beast of burden is so revered.

Given this status in Asian society, it may seem surprising that the water buffalo so easily becomes dinner. In fact, until most Southeast Asian countries first imported real beef from Australia and elsewhere about twenty years ago, most of the "beef" consumed in Asia was water buffalo—sadly much of it rather chewy, due to the animals' advanced age; after all, there was no advantage in butchering a key member of the family work force.

Related distantly to domestic cattle, the water buffalo—so called because they like to wallow in mud and water—labored in fields in Iraq and the Indus Valley as long as 4,000 years ago, and domesticated populations existed in southern China a thousand years later. Wide hooves, flexible joints, and tremendous strength allow them to pull a plow knee-deep in mud. They also have a docile nature and thrive on low-quality forage, surviving happily on wild grass and the stubble left behind following a rice harvest. Despite such a humble diet, adults often reach nine feet in length, can be nearly six feet high at the shoulders, and weigh more than a ton, as much as a small automobile.

Today, water buffalo are a major source of milk, contributing about half of the milk consumed in India. This liquid, which has much more fat, more nonfat solids, and less water than cow's milk, is also important in China and the Philippines. In India, the milk is also used for making a kind of liquid butter and herds created for commercial purposes as far apart as Italy and Australia provide the milk that is turned into soft cheeses, the most notable being mozzarella. Similarly, the Cape buffalo contributes much milk to the diet in Africa. Still, mainly the beast is valued for its flesh.

Water buffalo may be consumed raw (usually ground, as in steak tartar), dried, or cooked as beef would be prepared. Some of the earliest written recipes survive from the 19th century, when, in Laos, the king's chef included instructions for making "hot boiled water buffalo sauce" to be served with slices of raw eggplant or cucumber, "slow-cooked water buffalo tripe," and the meat in a kind of stew seasoned with lemon grass and chili peppers. Even today in Laos, there is a restaurant in the capital, Vientiane, known for its buffalo specialties, including placenta, fetus, udder, and brains. As is true for other animals, the older the beast, the tougher the meat, so tenderizers may be warranted.

Sliced Water Buffalo Meat Stew

2 pieces water buffalo meat,
   each the size of a hand,
   with the tendons removed
   —wash them, rub salt into them
   and toast them over the fire
   until the outside is golden
5 slices galangal
1 large onion, sliced vertically

2 (small) heads of garlic—
   place them in the embers of a
   charcoal fire until they are
   partly cooked but not well
   done, then remove them,
   take off the charred outer
   skin, and chop them
   vertically

4 straight-bulbed spring onions
—chop the bulbs and adjacent
green parts only (not the leaves)
2 fresh red chili peppers,
chopped crossways

chopped coriander leaves
salt, fish sauce and ground black
pepper
2 limes
2 Kaffir lime leaves,
finely chopped

Put into a pot the meat, galangal, onion, a sprinkling of salt and enough water to cover the meat. Put the pot on the fire. When the water boils, sprinkle in some fish sauce and keep boiling until the water is reduced and the meat tender.

Take out the meat and slice it thinly. Spoon out and throw away the galangal. Return the sliced meat to the pot. The amount of water should be just sufficient to keep the meat moist. Taste, and check the saltiness. Stir in the chopped ingredients and the juice of the two limes.

Put the soup in a large bowl, garnish it with ground black pepper and the chopped coriander leaves, and serve it with young cucumbers.

Today, the water buffalo population is shrinking, worldwide. The average population growth rate in Asia has, over the past three decades, declined by more than half. As farmers replaced these four-legged tractors with three-wheeled ones (the earliest were called "iron buffalo"), interest in breeding dropped. At the same time, more and more farmers sought work in the cities, leaving much of the rice farming to large conglomerates. In the past, 400 families in one village might have owned as many as a thousand buffaloes. Nowadays, the same number may have only twenty-five.

In the high plateaus and mountains of Central Asia, in eastern Kashmir, Nepal, and Tibet, ranging from the lower valleys to 20,000 foot levels, where the climate is cold and dry, is another cousin of the bison and buffalo, the yak. Known for an unusually luxuriant coat almost reaching to the ground and its long, curving horns, it looks like a large brown or reddish shag rug that's been thrown over a long-horned steer with a hump. Despite their relative immensity—they, too, weigh as much as a small car—they are agile, nimble climbers and sure swimmers, roaming icy mountainsides and valleys, grazing on native grass.

Like other members of the same family, they are favored for the variety of their uses and services. They are valuable as pack animals. The hair is spun into rope and woven into cloth. The hide is used for leather, shoes, coats, bags for storing grain, and the construction of simple boats, as well as for tent-like, temporary housing. (More permanent homes may include some of the bones for structural support.) Its horns serve as a bugle, emitting a distinct sound when properly shaped and blown, used by monks or yak herders to signal the time of day, to call for help, signal danger, or simply to communicate. And, as is true for its American relative, the dried dung is used for fuel.

Yet, it is its use as a food that gives the yak its reputation. The milk yields excellent butter and curd, and the flesh is of high quality, eaten roasted or dried, fried, boiled, baked, broiled, or made into a stew or soup, with or without noodles. Its meat is available everywhere in Lhasa, Tibet's capital, where it is found on most restaurant menus, stuffed into dumplings, sliced into steaks, air-dried, and minced into "yak burgers." When China invaded the country and the Dalai Lama and some 80,000 Tibetans fled to neighboring Nepal and India, they took this cuisine with them. In Nepal's capital, Kathmandu, a center for Tibetan refuges, there are several Tibetan restaurants offering a full range of yak dishes.

Because the yak, like other animals, tends to get tough and stringy with age, some of the meat will have been ground to ease the chewing process. Yak is as lean as venison or bison (about five per cent fat, compared to three times that for beef) and if the animal is young, to many diners it tastes juicier, sweeter, and more delicate. Originally brought to the Western Hemisphere for zoos a century ago, yaks have been bred commercially in the U.S. for about fifteen years. There are now more than thirty yak ranches in North America, principally in the mountainous west.

However popular the flesh, it is the milk and its by-products, including cheese but mainly butter, that likely will give this mammal its culinary immortality. Read any book about Nepal or Tibet, or check the staggering number of web sites on the Internet about these countries—hundreds and perhaps thousands of them posted by foreigners who recall their visit as if in a state of religious transcendence—and it is inevitable that the subject of yak butter is mentioned.

Yak milk is rich, valued for its seven per cent fat content, compared to half that for cattle, but it spoils in two hours and local herders had no way to keep it fresh. "When the Swiss faced the same situation," says Ethan Goldings of Trace Foundation, a New York-based NGO that started bringing medicine and food to Tibetan farmers, "they invented cheese technology." A cheese maker was hired to teach others and in a mountain nunnery encircled by snow-capped peaks, by 2001, they were producing a thousand kilograms of cheese per year.

The butter is better known and is used as a thickener for soups and mixed with ground barley in a tea called *tsampa*, a drink consumed in vast quantity at all hours of the day and night. The whitish yellow fat may also be burned in lamps to illuminate tents, homes, and temples, and is applied as a body lotion or hair pomade. In Buddhist monasteries, monks boil up huge cauldrons of the stuff to offer visitors in tea. The natives' clothing is redolent, committing to the air a sort of greasy, smoky smell. The odor is strong—some insist rancid—yet it is so pervasive that because you cannot avoid it, after a while you stop noticing it. It becomes a part of you.

And you hold out your cup for more.

Herb- and Dijon-Crusted Yak Tenderloin

1 yak tenderloin, trimmed (about 20 ounces)
1/4 cup vegetable oil
3/4 cup dried bread crumbs
2 tablespoons Dijon mustard
Salt and freshly ground black pepper
2 tablespoons chopped mixed fresh herbs (including thyme, basil and rosemary)

Heat oven to 375°F. Brush tenderloin with 1 tablespoon oil, sprinkle with 1 tablespoon herbs and season with salt and pepper.

Heat a large sauté pan over high heat, and sear tenderloin on all sides until golden brown, about 10 minutes. Transfer to a large roasting pan, and roast to desired doneness (10–12 minutes for medium rare). Remove from oven, and let rest 3 minutes.

In a bowl, combine remaining herbs with bread crumbs, and season with a little salt and pepper. Spread mustard over top of tenderloin, and press seasoned bread crumbs onto mustard to form a crust.

Heat remaining oil in a sauté pan over high heat. Place tenderloin crust side down in pan, and cook until crust is golden brown. Transfer to a board, and let rest until ready to carve.
    —*Adapted from De la Tierra at the Sunday House in Delray Beach, Florida*

Rats & Mice

The first time I heard about the rodent as a comestible was when I was told about a restaurant in London where a French couple reportedly served a savory rat stew. The way the story went, the couple immigrated to England following the Second World War, bringing with them a recipe developed during the German occupation of Paris, a time of severe shortages. Meat was particularly scarce and of necessity, the couple caught rats in traps in the alleys and cooked them with whatever vegetables and herbs they could find, creating a distinctive and delicious dish.

"Unfortunately," my friend told me, "the rats were as stringy and tough as the Parisians, so it was pretty chewy. Not to worry about that today, my lovely. The day of the alley rat is done. Today, they raise their own rats, feed them grain until they're plump and juicy."

My friend said the dish was listed on the menu in French for "rat stew," and next to it were the words "When available." That permitted the waiter to make sure it was understood just what kind of meat the customer was ordering. The only surprise the owners wanted to offer their patrons was how good it tasted. They did not want to hear anyone cry, "I ate WHAT!?!"

Sadly, the elderly owners of the restaurant had died and the establishment had closed, so it was many years before I actually got to eat a rodent. It finally happened the first time I stayed with some rice farmers in northeastern Thailand, where field mice are not only savored as a gastronomical treat, but also are considered a superb way of disposing of agricultural pests, hated for their damage to the rice crop. My friend, Samniang Changsena, the daughter of those farmers, told me that the rats and mice lived in burrows in the mud dikes between the paddy ponds and generally were regarded as healthy, unlike the rats of Bangkok. Because they lived mainly on a diet of rice, they were fattest at harvest time, from November to January, which was when I was planning my trip.

My friend said she and her sister poured water into a hole and when the small, furry residents ran out, they hit them on the head with a stick, and if they didn't come out, they dug for them. They then took them home and placed them directly on the coals of the outdoor wood fire that served as the family stove, turning them over with a stick until crisp. She said the babies were the tenderest, popped into the mouth and eaten bones and all, with or without a spicy dipping sauce.

And so it was when I visited my friend's family. On one of her visits home, she had brought an electric wok, but they still cooked nearly everything they ate over a wood fire outside their home. It was there that I watched several mice turned over coals until they were crispy, then ate them, bones and all, with a chili and fish sauce dip.

When I returned to Hawaii and told my friends, they said, "You ate WHAT!?!"

Rodents, after all, have an unfortunate name worldwide. For all the good Mickey and Minnie Mouse and other cartoon characters may have offered the rodent population's reputation, the rat and mouse are still creepy creatures that not many seem to love and few might welcome to the dinner table.

In fact, in recent years the rat has been a detestible epithet, usually applied to someone who betrayed ("ratted on") his or her friends. Who can forget James Cagney calling some movie enemy, "You dirty rat!" (Or was it Edward G. Robinson?) When you joined the nine-to-five work routine, you were in the "rat race," from which escape was deemed desirable. With their twitchy pointed noses and whiskers, ominous yellow buck teeth, and hairless tails, rats weren't considered pretty to look at either.

Worse, rats bit children in their cribs and spread a host of awful diseases, and newspaper stories appeared all the time about how health departments in modern cities, from Bombay to Berlin to Beverly Hills, struggled to stay a step ahead of rat infestation. A report in 1997 said one in twenty homes in Britain were infested, that there were about sixty million rats in that country, compared to a human population of fifty-eight million.

Having said this, rats, mice, and other members of the rodent family have a long, palatable history, based in part on their vast numbers and variety. This is an order, after all, whose members constitute nearly forty percent of all mammals on earth, all of which are edible, among them the rabbit, squirrel, marmot, beaver, chinchilla, guinea pig, porcupine, gerbil, hamster, and in Latin America the agouti, coypu, and capybara, large, tail-less creatures that are cooked in the same way as a suckling pig. In some areas, some of these rodents are considered common dinnertime fare. Between one and a half and two-million squirrels are killed by hunters each year in the American state of Illinois alone. But most are eaten less frequently. And some are anathema to the prevailing Euro-American taste, most remarkably the mouse and rat.

The common black rat, sometimes brown in color, most likely

came from Asia, reaching Europe on trading ships by the 13th Century. Not long after, the fleas it carried were blamed for spreading bubonic plague, killing twenty-five million people, a quarter of the population. Around the world today, rats and their parasites spread at least twenty kinds of disease, from typhus to thrichinosis to Lassa fever. It is no surprise that the *Guinness Book of Records* calls this species "the most dangerous rodent in the world."

Yet, there are rats and mice that are easy to catch and not only safe to eat, but commonly eaten, both in times of hardship and as a staple or delicacy. And so it has been for millennia. In ancient Rome, caged dormice were stuffed with nuts until they were plump enough for an emperor's demanding appetite. These animals, which reached a length of twenty centimeters (eight inches, not counting the tail), were so popular, they also were farmed in large pens and exported to satisfy the appetites of Roman soldiers then occupying Britain.

In imperial China, the rat was called a "household deer" and considered a special treat, and Marco Polo wrote that the Tartars ate rat in the summer months, when they were plentiful. In Columbus's time, when a ship's food store ran low due to unanticipated delays in oceanic crossing, the ship's rat catcher became a man whose low station was elevated and highly paid, as rodents usually thought to be pests now became a valued protein source. In 19th century France, many in Bordeaux traditionally feasted on grilled or broiled rat with shallots and Thomas Genin, a noted cook and organizer of that country's first culinary competitions in the 1880s, considered rat meat to be of excellent quality. When Paris was besieged by Prussian forces in the Franco-Prussian war (1870–1), brown rats and roof rats went onto the menu.

Henry David Thoreau is reported to have said he enjoyed fried rats, served with relish, although some insist he was talking about muskrats, which probably lived beside Walden Pond. During Vietnam's war with America, the Viet Cong considered rats an important food group. More recently, G. Gordon Liddy, one of the engineers of U.S. President Richard Nixon's Watergate scandal, boasted that he ate rat in the all-American way, fried, although it's generally believed that he did so to prove his courage.

In much of Latin America, Asia, and in parts of Africa and Oceania, it remains a common hors d'oeuvre or entrée today. In parts of China, rat still is prepared in over a dozen ways in popular restaurants. In the Philippines, the farmers go after the field mice and rats with machetes and flame throwers. In Taiwan, they hunt with traps and nets and dogs. From Peru to Ghana, they constitute a significant protein source.

Even in America, there are commercial sources for rats and mice. One outfit, called the Gourmet Rodent, will deliver the critters dressed and frozen by UPS, Express Mail, or alive by Delta Air Freight, collect. (In 1998, mice cost between forty-seven to sixty-seven US cents apiece, rats from sixty-two cents to $2.17 for the 300–400-gram "jumbos." Discounts were offered on orders over five-hundred units.) It should be noted that such companies advertised in magazines for people who kept snakes and that, according to the editors, it was known that some of the buyers were recent immigrants to the United States who did not keep snakes.

The Rat Catchers of India

The greatest consumption of rats may be in India, where every year, swarms of mole rats, rice rats and field mice steal enough grain to feed the country's close to a billion people for three months. Many are killed by chemicals that also poison the water and earth, at the same time rendering the animals hazardous to eat. Meet the nomadic Irula tribe, India's master rat catchers.

Not so long ago, the 28,000 Irulas, from the Chingleput District, earned a reputation and living as snake catchers, selling the serpents to the snake-skin industry. In the mid-1970s, when the government banned the trade, they offered their services as rat catchers and in the late 1980s, they proved their worth when a study conducted by the international aid organization Oxfam Trust showed that in fifty audited hunts, the Irula captured several thousand rats at a cost of about five cents (US) per pest, where in parallel trials, the per-rat price using pesticides cost ten times as much.

The hunt is so simple it mocks modern eradication techniques. The men go into the fields and when they find a burrow they build fires in clay pots using grass and leaves to create a lot of smoke. The pots are then placed over all the exits of the underground tunnels and the smoke is blown into the burrows. After a while, the Irula dig into the earth to harvest the rats and mice, asphyxiated by the smoke. Some of the catch is sold to crocodile farms in Madras. The rest is taken to the market for human consumption, or taken home, where the small animals are prepared in a curry or grilled.

Gold and Rats

In China, rat soup is considered equal to ox-tail soup, and a dozen fine rats will realize two dollars, or eight or nine shillings. Besides the attractions of the gold-fields for the Chinese, California is so abundantly supplied with rats, that they can live like Celestial emperors, and pay very little for their board. The rats of California exceed the rats of the older American States, just as nature on that side of the continent exceeds in bountifulness of mineral wealth. The California rats are incredibly large, highly flavored, and very abundant. The most refined Chinese in California have no hesitation in publicly expressing their opinion of 'them rat's. Their professed cooks, we are told, serve up rats' brains in a much superior style to the Roman dish of nightingales' and peacocks' tongue. The sauce used is garlic, aromatic seeds and camphor.

—*Peter Lund Simmonds, The Curiosities of Food (1859)*

Deep Fried Field Rat

4 mature rats or 8 small rats
2 tablespoons salt
1/2 teaspoons pepper
10–15 garlic cloves, crushed

Gut and skin the rats, removing the head and toes. Mix garlic, salt, and pepper into a paste, spread on the meat, then place in direct sunlight for 6–8 hours, until dry. Fry in deep vegetable oil for about 6–7 minutes, until crispy and yellow in color. Serve with sticky rice, sweet-sour sauce, fish sauce, or a hot chili paste, and raw vegetables.

—*Traditional Isan recipe, courtesy Samniang Changsena*

Curried Rat With Noodles

6 mature rats (the larger, the better)
1 lb rice noodles
1 pt canned coconut milk
2 large onions, peeled
6 cloves garlic, peeled
4 green chilies, seeded
3 teaspoons turmeric, ground
6 fl oz oil
4 tablespoons yellow chickpea flour
2 tablespoons fish sauce
Salt and pepper, to taste

Skin, gut, and clean meat, then place in a large pan, cover with water and bring to a boil. Cover and cook for about an hour, until the meat is tender. Cool. Remove meat from the bones by hand and cut into pieces. Keep at least 2 pints of the stock.

Chop onion, chilies, and garlic and mix with tumeric until it becomes a thick paste.

Heat 4 oz of the oil in a wok or a large pan and fry 2 oz of the noodles, until they are crispy; this will take only a few seconds. Dry on absorbent paper and put aside.

Fry the onion/garlic/chili/tumeric mixture in the remaining oil. Stir in the stock and coconut milk and simmer for 10–12 minutes, then put aside.

Blend the flour with a small amount of water to produce a thin cream, adding a few spoonfuls of the onion/garlic/chili/tumeric mixture, then stir it all back into the pan containing the rest of the onion/garlic/chili/tumeric mix. Simmer for a few minutes before adding the rat and fish sauce. Cover and keep warm on stove top.

Bring a large pan of salted water to a boil, adding the rest of the noodles. Return to a boil and put the noodles aside to cool when done, then drain and rinse in a colander or strainer and remove all excess liquid.

Serve noodles in bowls, topping with the curried rat mix. Garnish with the crispy noodles.

—Traditional Burmese recipe

Hamsters, Gerbils & Guinea Pigs

"I'm not as adventurous as you are, dad..."

It was my daughter's first time in Asia, and we'd just walked past a street vendor selling a variety of deep-fried and steamed insects, a popular snack in Thailand. I asked her if she wanted to try some of the grasshoppers. "They're pretty good," I said, reassuringly.

She shook her head no and said, "I'm willing to try new stuff, but I won't eat anything that's cute or disgusting."

She was referring to what the foods looked like when they were alive. Insects were in the disgusting category, she said, and a lot of small mammals were cute, such as cats, dogs, rabbits, and three small rodents raised in parts of the west as pets—hamsters, gerbils, and guinea pigs. Cuddly pets they may be in the US and many other places, yet they, too, have a long, appetizing history and they remain an accepted and important source of protein in Peru—the rodent's birthplace—and in Ecuador and parts of Venezuela, Bolivia, and Colombia.

Russell Kyle, in his survey of edible herbivores, *A Feast in the Wild*, called the guinea pig's present status in the Andes in South America "the most ancient case of rodent farming in the world," dating back to 2,500 B.C., pointing to an excavation site in Peru that had guinea pig runs (exercise yards) built into the foundations of every house. So important was the animal to the local diet, Mr. Kyle said, that when the Spaniards arrived in the 16th century and began converting citizens to Catholicism, in a cathedral at Cuszo there was painted a localized version of the Last Supper showing Jesus Christ and his disciples at a table laden with local fruits and vegetables, the main dish, on a plate before them, roasted guinea pig. Even today, the species (*Cavia porcellas*) is so commonplace in Peruvian villages that it "can be seen scuttling around the floor, feeding on scraps of vegetable waste and anything else they can scavenge, in the same way that chickens used to be part of poor, peasant households in Europe, and like the chickens, guinea pigs finally end up in the cooking pot."

There are an estimated twenty million domestic guinea pigs in Peru today and, according to Mr. Kyle, they produce a crop of edible carcasses over three times that figure at sixty-four million a year, thanks to a rapid reproduction cycle. Females customarily produce a litter of three or four following a gestation period of only seventy days, and tend to have three or four litters in succession, taking a few weeks off before starting again. With breeding as recommended by experienced farmers, one pair could produce about 260 new pairs in two years. Young guinea pigs reach sexual maturity at two months and are ready for slaughter at three, when the new "super-pigs" may weigh as much as a kilogram (2.2 pounds). Most weigh about half that and are bred for the table in West Africa and the Philippines.

The animal does not gnaw, cannot climb, does not bite, but is timid and can scratch when afraid. Its senses of smell and hearing are very sharp. And, they are noisy, squealing when hungry or when attacked, murmuring as they eat. Their cry of "cooee" is the source of a common name in the Andes Mountains, *cui* or *curi*. It takes its English name from Guiana, where Europeans arriving in South America first found it.

The cleaned animal can be mounted on a spit and cooked in rotisserie fashion or cut into pieces. At the time of the Spanish occupation, they were roasted with heated stones placed in their abdominal cavity in much the same way pigs are cooked in Polynesia. Because of the animal's small size and the desirability of making maximum use, generally the meat is cut into several large pieces and boiled until soft. The flesh then can be shredded and the small bones removed. The meat is then included in soups, stews, and fricassees, which are seasoned conventionally. The small intestines (tripe) are often cut up, washed and boiled, usually appearing in soups and stews, while the heart, kidneys, and liver are cooked separately and served as a special treat. Roadside vendors sell frequently the animals deep-fried.

The taste is dark, similar to rabbit and, like mice and rats, sometimes the small bones are eaten along with the meat, depending on how the animal is cooked. The skin is crisp and chewy when the guinea pigs are young, becoming somewhat rubbery with fat as they age. (Although normally the animal is low in fat and the fat is bland and odorless.) The guinea pig generally is identified with the poorest people of Peru, but the meat can also do justice to the most discriminating dinner party and today has joined the list of many foods worldwide to leap social taboos and barriers. That they are high in B vitamins and seem resistant to disease and the negative effects of in-breeding adds more to their desirability as a food source.

After eating guinea pigs, the custom in Peru is to remove the tiny bone from the animal's middle ear, called the anvil, and drop it in a wine glass. The wine must then be drunk in a single gulp without swallowing the anvil, and if this can be achieved, reportedly it brings good luck.

While the smaller hamsters and gerbils are not so widely eaten, or farmed for the dinner table, they, too, have a long gastronomical chronology. Marco Polo wrote that the Tartars ate gerbils in the summer, when they were most numerous. Archeologists who have studied ancient campfires and garbage piles tell us that hamsters have been eaten for thousands of years as well. Of the twenty-four species, the largest, weighing a pound and a half, is the common hamster (*Cricetus cricetus*) of central Europe and Russia.

Gerbils and hamsters are versatile animals, valued as pets for the same reasons other animals are welcomed into the family home, mainly because they are friendly and cute. (As my daughter will firmly attest.) They also are easy and inexpensive to house and maintain and young boys, along with their sisters, may find a reason to justify the animals' presence in their bedrooms by including the small mammals in a school science project. Because they are so easily tamed, handled, and trained, they also have found a place along with mice as research animals for behavioral and medical research, while the gerbil's keen sense of smell once prompted the U.S. Federal Aviation Agency to invest in a program aimed at training them to sniff out bombs at airports. However, a London tailor who made clothes for Queen Elizabeth II and Prince Charles—Gieves and Hawkes, a 200-year-old firm best known for its staid pinstripe suits—dropped plans to make a US$4,800 hamster-fur jacket after an outcry from animal welfare groups.

Bats

The Tri Ky Restaurant doesn't exist in Saigon any more, replaced by a highrise office building not long after the city was renamed for the country's founder, Ho Chi Minh. A pity, too, because it had one of Southeast Asia's pre-eminent "strange food" menus, offering dog, bat, turtle and a variety of wild game, as well as a selection of blood cocktails for the end of the difficult work day. The restaurant was in a fair-sized ground floor room in a building near the Saigon River. I discovered it in 1993, during its last days, when such drinks were supposed to gird your loins—so to speak—for what came later in the evening, probably in Cholon, the city's notorious Chinatown.

I entered, taking a seat by the large windows in the front near the door, looking out at a cluster of men in peaked caps napping in the seats of their three-wheeled cyclos, waiting for customers. I read the menu casually, as if I were used to encountering such dishes regularly. I recalled when I had decided not to drink snake blood in Taipei a few years before and figured this was the time to correct what I now hoped was a show of culinary cowardice.

"I'll have one of these," I said, pointing to a line in the menu. "The, uh, cobra."

"Bat bery good, sir," the waiter said, pointing at the menu.

Obviously, I hadn't read far enough down the drinks list. "Bat blood?" I said. I tried to play it cool.

"What sort of bat?" I asked, as if it really mattered and I would know what he was talking about, whatever he said.

"The fruit bat, sir. Also hab bat stew. Bery good."

I told the gentleman (actually about a third my age) that I'd try it. With a glass of 333, the local beer. A chaser.

What happened next surprised me. After the cold beer was delivered, the bat was brought to my table still alive, its legs and wings gripped in the waiter's hand as he cut the creature's throat with a small, sharp knife. The blood fell into a small glass.

"*Chuc suc khoe!*" the waiter said. The standard Vietnamese toast meaning good luck.

I raised the small glass and drank the warm liquid, tried to roll it around my tongue as if it were vintage wine, but then chased it rather quickly with a swallow of 333. The waiter smiled, still holding the limp bat in one hand, cupping the head with the other in a small bowl to prevent any blood falling onto the floor.

"One more, sir?" he asked.

"Maybe after the meal." Still trying to be cool. As for the bat stew, think about Dinty Moore with very stringy meat.

"How many foreigners order bat?" I asked as I paid the bill.

"You are the first this year," the waiter said.

Tom Cruise's presence in a 1994 film about vampires and a number of actors playing Batman may have done something to soften the poor reputation held for so long by bats, but the fear of these creatures prevails in much of the world. The author Bram Stoker, who wrote the original *Dracula*, must take some of the blame for this sorry state of affairs, but the American writer Anne Rice must share it for her series of best-selling vampire novels. It was her first one, *Interview with the Vampire*," that starred Mr. Cruise.

With a hundred years of such inglorious history—Mr. Stoker's book was published in 1897—and images of neck-biting men who sleep during the day in coffins, who are killed by having stakes driven through their hearts or shot with silver bullets, is it any wonder that people turn away from the notion of deep-fried bat for dinner, or a glass of warm bat wine?

Nor is this all. Bats are grimly prominent in much folklore. The Bible calls it an unclean bird—although it is a mammal—and from India to Ireland to the United States it is regarded as a symbol of death. In many folk tales, the devil takes the form of a bat and there is a belief in much of the western world that bats will become so entangled in a woman's hair that nothing but scissors or a knife can get them free.

Bats may command such a prominent role because they've been around so long—fifty million years, according to fossil evidence—and because they're so widely distributed and numerous; it's estimated that one out of every four mammals on earth is a bat. There are more than 900 species, ranging in size from the bumblebee bat of Thailand that weighs less than an American penny, right up to some flying "foxes" in South America and the Pacific, with bodies the size of small dogs and a wingspan of nearly six feet.

They're not very attractive, either. The furry bodies that look like those of rats or mice, the leatherlike wings stretched on a framework similar to an opening umbrella, the outsized, translucent ears ribbed with cartilage and laced with blood vessels, and pig-like snouts spoked with whiskery projections, sleeping while hanging upside down, clinging to a cave's ceiling with their feet...well,the picture is not appealing.

That said, bats are one of the most interesting of nature's creations, mainly because of their echo-location, or sonar, talents. Similar to radar, which uses radio waves to detect location of another object, bats use sound waves to accomplish the identical task: the sound goes out and bounces back, giving them the precise location of obstacles—they don't want to be flying into buldings and trees, after all—and prey that may be moving at speed.

Most of the sounds humans perceive may be counted in hundreds of vibrations per second and we can, with difficulty, hear sounds with a frequency of, maybe, 20,000 vibrations per second. Bats hear sounds between 50,000 and 200,000 vibrations per second, and send out a series of clicks at the rate of thirty or so per second. This keen sense of hearing is unequalled in the natural and technical worlds. Scientists say fishing bats have echo-location so sophisticted that they can detect movement of a minnow's fin as fine as a human hair, protruding only two millimeters above a pond's surface, while African heart-nosed bats can hear the footsteps of a beetle walking on sand from a distance of more than six feet. It also keeps them from banging into things. Most (but not all) bats are, as the old saying goes, quite blind and able to react to a "sonar" bounce with unerring and astounding speed.

So, how in the hell does anyone catch one? Easy. It doesn't take much effort to position several men with a fishing net outside one of the caves from which the bats emerge by the thousands at dusk to feed. A man with a shotgun at such times also can bring down twenty to thirty with a single blast, although when the cook prepares the meal, care must be taken to remove the pellets.

The easy catch is part of the bat's appeal, but there's more. Images of the devil and Count Dracula aside, there are millions in the world who believe that eating bats increases male sexual potency and one's chances for long life and happiness, and if there are any other, more important reasons for my indulging in Saigon, may the reader please write me care of my publisher. To the Chinese, a symbol of five bats indicates the five blessings: wealth, health, love of virtue, old age, and a natural death. Eating bats also is believed to improve eyesight and in India, their oil—made from melted fat mixed with blood, coconut oil and camphor—is sold as a cure for rheumatism and arthritis. In Cambodia, it is prescribed for a child's cough. And, it's low in fat.

The bat is regarded as food today mainly in Asia and the Pacific. One species of flying fox in Guam has been hunted to extinction, but elsewhere they're numerous and the bat is isn't considered threatened. Probably the most cherished is the fruit bat, found in much of the western South Pacific, from the Philippines to Indonesia and most of

Micronesia, and westward into India. "They are clean animals living exclusively on fruit," noted *The Oxford Companion to Food* (1999), "and have a taste which has been compared (like so much other exotic animal fare) to that of chicken." But imagine a baby chicken.

The preparation of bat is simple. Bat has not yet breached the barrier that might one day make it more acceptable to a wider audience, much as ostrich and kangaroo have done in Australia and various wild game meats have in Africa, where "native" foods are now fashionable and chefs are dreaming up fancy recipes. Some day, there may be recipes for Bat Lasagna and Bat en Casserole, but for now, it's mostly soup and curry, or maybe a stir-fry with a little ginger and soy sauce or coconut cream. In the wonderful *Unmentionable Cuisine,* by Calvin Schwabe (1979), a Samoan recipe is given: "Flame fruit bat to remove hair, or skin them. Eviscerate and cut the bats into small pieces. Bake them in the ground oven, or *umu*, over hot rocks or fry them with salt, pepper, and onions."

Eating bat may also be difficult for those put off by their appearance on the plate. Rabbits don't look like rabbits when they are served, after the flesh has been hygienically distanced from any resemblance to the Easter Bunny, but bats often do still look like bats when they arrive on your plate. Because most of those available are small, and generally grilled or deep-fried, the entire creature may be cooked and consumed, including the wings and head and brittle bones, bringing a crunchy sound to the table, along with the undeniable reminder of what you are eating. Alternatively, the bat may be skinned, the head and wings removed and the body cut into cubes for soup or stew, but they contain little meat and if this is done, it'll take many bats to make a stew.

A word of caution: most species exude a somewhat pungent odor as they cook. This can be alleviated by the addition of chili peppers, onion, or garlic, or any combination. (An American friend living in Indonesia says that the cook's consumption of several bottles of the local beer also helps.)

There's a bat that lives on my street in Bangkok. I don't know where he or she hangs out during the day, but I see the solitary creature, swooping unevenly in the purpling dusk—sucking up mosquitoes, I guess. I don't know why I see only one.

I do know that every time I see this small animal I remember cocktail time in Saigon.

More Reasons to Love a Bat

The larger species additionally are hunted for their skins and bat guano, the droppings deposited inside caves, valued for more than a century as an excellent fertilizer. In the wild, important agricultural plants, from bananas, breadfruit, and mangos to cashews, dates, and figs rely on bats for pollination and seed dispersal. A single brown bat can catch 600 moquitoes in one hour and the twenty million Mexican free-tails that live in a large cave near Austin, Texas—the largest urban colony in the world, and now a tourist attraction—eat 250 tons of insects nightly.

Grilled or Barbecued Bat

6–8 bats
4 garlic cloves, finely chopped
4 chili peppers, seeded and finely chopped
Salt & pepper to taste

Remove hair by singeing over fire. Remove head and wings if desired. Grind salt, pepper, and garlic together and work it into the butchered meat, leaving it for at least an hour. Grill on medium heat , or over an open fire or barbecue until crispy Sprinkle peppers on the meat and leave for about ten minutes, until the strong odor dissipates.

Serve with rice.

Stir-Fried Bat

6–8 bats
2 medium onions, sliced
2 turnips or similar vegetable, cut into small pieces
Salt & pepper to taste

1 red chili, seeded and finely chopped
2 garlic cloves, finely chopped
Cooking oil

Remove wings and heads and cut meat into bite-sized chunks. Fry meat in a wok with minimum amount of oil over a medium heat until tender. Vegetables and other ingredients are added only for the final 2 or 3 minutes.

—Collected personally in Thailand and Indonesia, 1997

Elephant

1 elephant
Brown gravy
Salt and pepper to taste
2 rabbits (optional)

First, find your elephant. Cut elephant into bite-sized pieces. Be sure to allow adequate time. In a large pot, cover pieces with brown gravy and simmer. Cook over an open fire for four weeks at 465 degrees. This will serve about 3,800 people. If more guests are expected, 2 rabbits may be added, but do this only if necessary as most people dislike finding a hare in their stew.

Elephant conservationists may not think this is funny, because both surviving species of elephant—the Asian and the African—are listed by every environmental group worldwide as endangered species. Where once large numbers of elephants roamed Africa from the shores of the Mediterranean to the Cape of Good Hope and occupied Asian forests nearly everywhere, now the numbers are small nearly everywhere and the prospects are grim. Poachers continue to kill them for their ivory, a trade that is blamed for the slaughter of 700,000 elephants in the decade before it was banned in 1989. Deforestation has removed much of their natural habitat, especially in Asia. Except for small numbers required in the tourism trade, few are needed now for transportation. At the same time, logging restrictions in many countries have taken away other traditional work.

That said, the African elephant is still being killed for food. Legally. And it is possible, if you visit one of the countries where elephant finds it way to a restaurant menu, to enjoy elephant stew—without hare—as well as elephant trunk steak, which is believed to be the tastiest cut. You may even be able to find elephant meat in a tin to take home as a souvenir, to impress, or offend, your friends. (In Thailand, and perhaps elsewhere, the "finger" at the tip of the trunk is seen as an aphrodisiac.)

Elephant meat has been eaten for tens of thousands of years, going back to when primitive man hunted the modern pachyderm's ancestors, the mammoths and mastodons, with spears, as shown in drawings on the walls of prehistoric caves in Europe and elsewhere. (They also killed them by driving them off cliffs with fire.) Even in recent times, many African peoples included the animal in their diet. The pygmies of the Congo were known for their prowess in bringing down the giants with poisoned spears.

Such activity did not affect the population; those killed numbered fewer than those born. The harvest was sustainable.

Today in most African and all Asian countries, the elephant population is severely threatened. Most. But not all. In Zimbabwe, protection efforts were so successful that the government initiated a program to cull the elephant population. In 1995, George Pangeti, deputy director of the Department of National Parks and Wildlife, said there were between 70,000 and 80,000 elephants in an environment that could support only half that number. An adult elephant ate at least 450 pounds of vegetation a day, he said, and large areas of the national parks were being ravaged by overpopulation, upsetting the ecological balance needed to sustain other wildlife.

The same argument was voiced in South Africa, where in Kruger National Park, a game reserve the size of Israel, the elephant population grew to 8,000 from the few hundred the ivory hunters left in the early 1990s. With park officials warning that the reserve could sustain only 7,000 and that larger numbers would endanger other species, pushing them to the brink of extinction, or at least to hunger, the government proposed a culling program that included selling the hides (for expensive luggage and so on) and the meat, which in turn would bring up to US$500,000 a year, to be assigned to conservation programs.

An alternative is reminiscent of the days when Ernest Hemingway banged away at big game in Africa. In 1999, Mozambique lifted a ban on elephant-hunting safaris imposed during the country's sixteen-year-long civil war.

Unsurprisingly, safaris and culling are controversial, as the idea of killing any elephant upsets not just human sensibilities but also the strong social bonds of the animals themselves, and has led to bad behavior—including killing rhinoceroses—in young bulls whose mothers were killed. In addition, animal welfare groups in Europe and the U.S. argued that the culling would weaken the ivory trade ban as well as encourage more poaching by creating new markets for the meat and skins. Why not send the unwanted beasts elsewhere? South Africa did that, relocating hundreds to smaller reserves, as did Kenya, moving elephants from crowded areas to parks where the herds had been decimated. As might be imagined, such programs are logistically complex and expensive, and governments usually find something else to spend their stretched budgets on. Meanwhile, the overpopulation problem remains in some areas.

With politicians nervous about endorsing any law that sanctioned the killing of elephants, the beasts were put up for sale and "adoption." There were few takers and finally the herds were thinned by government hunters in helicopters using drugged darts, at last sending the meat and hides to the marketplace.

Such government programs were not cheap, either. Skinning an elephant required a team of people several hours and 500 pounds of salt to treat a single skin, while hauling a thousand or more pounds of meat a long distance was no easy matter. In fact, the scale of the economics brought one effort at culling to its knees in 1965. This was funded by the United Nations, creating an abattoir in Zambia that was designed to cut five per cent of the local populations of elephant, hippo, and buffalo. By 1970, the program was scrapped, due, largely to the cost of transporting carcasses over long distances and poor marketing. Because of the tropical heat, it also was required that such transport be made in refrigerated trucks. Today in South Africa, most elephant meat feeds the poor, who live in densely populated areas near the game reserves.

Historically, most elephant meat usually has been consumed on the spot, or smoked and dried for later use. According to *The Oxford Companion to Food*, "There were elephants in ancient Egypt, where their meat was regarded as a delicacy and King Ptolemy Philadelphus (308–245 B.C.) forbade killing them, but they did not survive." During the siege of Paris in 1870, when all food was scarce, elephants from the zoo started showing up in butcher shops and restaurants, along with other wild animals. One restaurant offered braised elephant's feet with ham, garlic, spices, and Madeira and at least one butcher sold elephant blood pudding. About the same time, a British explorer, Sir Samuel Baker, described how to dig an oven in the ground and cook a foot. He said that after thirty-plus hours, the food was dug up and the hard sole was removed like a shoe, exposing a delicate white meat beneath—best served hot; add oil and vinegar when cold.

Most of the elephant consumed in Asia today occurs when an elephant dies a healthy death. (Its life span is approximately that of a human.) Usually this occurs from old age, but in modern Asia, many pachyderms have their lives cut short by trucks, trains, and land mines, or when a rogue elephant is shot after tearing up crops and homes and killing villagers, as occurs most frequently in India. (As a rule, an animal felled by disease will not be eaten.)

In northern Thailand from 2000 to 2002, there also were numerous reports of their being deliberately killed for their meat, a strange fate for the animal that is the country's symbol and something many elephant experts contest, never having heard of any such incidents, adding that whoever did it would be ostracized. But, said Prasong Chumchoey, speaking for the Phrae province's government, "Elephant meat is a good seller. Believe it or not, when elephant meat is available, beef, pork and buffalo meat are ignored." Because domesticated elephants in Thailand were in the same official category as cattle, there were no laws forbidding its consumption, opening the door for its trade.

The trunks and feet are considered the choicest cuts and elephant fat has been rendered into cooking oil. Even after twelve or more hours of cooking (or long aging in the open air), the meat is regarded as somewhat chewy. The flesh, which is muscular and gelatinous, compares with beef tongue, which it also resembles in taste, only gamier.

If you wish to try this delicacy in Africa, book a flight early. In Johannesburg, the government already has introduced birth control.

Foot Baked by Hottentots

In *Travels from the Cape of Good Hope into the Interior Parts of Africa* (1790), Francois LeVaillant gave this account of a breakfast of elephant foot baked by the Hottentots:

"It exhaled such a savory odor, that I soon tasted and found it to be delicious. I had often heard the feet of bears commended, but could not conceive that so gross and heavy an animal as the Elephant would afford such a delicate food. 'Never,' said I, 'can our modern epicures have such a dainty at their tables; let forced fruits and the contributions of various countries contribute to their luxury, yet cannot they procure so excellent a dish as I have now before me.'"

Primates & Other Bush meat

Karl Amman discovered his burning "cause" in 1988 while traveling on the Zaire River in west Africa. Here, in what was the inspiration for Joseph Conrad's novel *Heart of Darkness*, in an open marketplace he counted 2,000 smoked primate carcasses and about a thousand fresh ones. Monkey. Chimpanzee. Gorilla. To Mr. Amman, it looked like a miniature human morgue.

Since then, Mr. Amman, a Swiss photographer, has spent most of his life investigating the bush meat trade in Africa, where the gorilla is endangered (and an estimated 800 are killed and eaten each year) and in Indonesia, where the orangutan is on the same long list of animals either at the edge of extinction or approaching it. Mr. Amman is a fanatic. He says there are tribes like the Fang in Gabon who practiced cannibalism until a few decades ago, a practice that was eradicated by missionaries and colonial powers. He then points out that chimpanzees share 98.6 per cent of the human genetic code, and asks whether shooting them is not 98.6 per cent murder and eating them 98.6 per cent cannibalism.

Not everyone is so emotional, but the conservationist has a point. Yet it's an inarguable fact that monkeys and other jungle animals have been the primary source of protein for tens, perhaps hundreds of thousands of years for the peoples of many parts of Central and South America, Asia, Africa, and Oceania. Even today, in west and central Africa, what is commonly called bush meat represents over half the animal protein consumed by millions of people and it is, in some areas, the only source of protein available. (Keeping livestock in the tropics is often impossible due to the lack of pasture, the tsetse fly which prey on cattle, and a variety of inhospitable epidemics.) The World Wildlife Fund (WWF) says:

- Bush meat comprises fifty per cent of the protein consumed in parts of Equatorial Africa, seventy-five per cent in Liberia.
- The half-million residents of the state of Amazonas in Brazil hunt and consume three million mammals every year (also half a million birds and several hundred thousand reptiles).
- Of the 214 species found in one forest in West Bengal, India, 155 are used by the local population for food fuel, fiber, fodder, medicine, and religious rites.

Mr. Amman's question is: how long can this go on? The Biosynergy Institute, an American conservation outfit that runs The Bush meat Project and is one of Mr. Amman's allies, is no less vehement, saying a "ragged army of 1,500 bush meat hunters" this year (1998) will shoot and butcher more than 2,000 gorillas and 4,000 chimpanzees in the forest region of west and central Africa, consuming more great apes each year than are kept in zoos and laboratories in North America.

That isn't all. It isn't just a centuries-old eating habit that's causing what CNN called "the biggest conservation issue facing Africa since the ivory crisis." Logging companies owned by Germans, British,

Japanese, French, and Americans operating deep in the rain forest have caused a dramatic increase in the demand to serve the needs of their workers. Hunters in remote villages once killed only enough game to feed their families—a sustainable number of animals, thus no species were jeopardized—and now they were setting up camps in logging townships and hunting on a commercial basis. The construction of the new roads through the forests also eased transport of bush meat to the region's large cities, in Doula and Yaounde in Cameroon, in Brazzaville and Pointe Noire in the Congo, and in Kinshasa in Zaire, where it is not unusual to see a truck pull into the marketplace with dozens of animals tied to its sides. Bush meat also is commonly sold smoked or by the part (arm, leg, etc.) or cut to steak and stew meat size.

Nor is the sale of such meat inhibited by any bans that exist. "Bush meat from a wide variety of species was available for sale in all the major markets, irrespective of it being closed or open hunting season," Mr. Amman wrote 1998 in one of his regular broadsides, published in various newsletters and on the Internet. "While the meat of protected species was disguised in some markets, it was openly on display in others. On our first evening in Ouesso, the gateway to the renowned Nouabale Ndoki National Park, we filmed a lorry carrying tons of bush meat, including the carcass of a silverback gorilla."

Mr. Amman said the bush meat trade had "been commercialized to the point where it has become an integral part of the economy, the problem well beyond the scope of conservation organizations. Even the loggers had to throw in the towel, he said: one executive of a major French firm told CNN that they were now afraid of the poachers, who had automatic weapons; some German loggers weary of the bad publicity in 1997 asked the transporters of their timber to tell their drivers to stop carrying bush meat. The drivers went on strike, and the loggers and transporters gave in.

Mr. Amman did some shopping to compare the price difference between bush meat and that of domesticated species, such as pork and beef. "We went to the Yaounde bush meat market and bought two gorilla arms," he wrote. "We then acquired the equivalent amount of beef. Next, we bought the frozen head of a chimpanzee and matched it with a much bigger pig's head. We took all this back to the hotel and stuck on price tags to illustrate that beef and pork were less than half the price of gorilla and chimp."

For nations outside Africa and other undeveloped areas, mainly in Europe and the United States, eating primates is not within the range of acceptable behavior.

"Understandably, many of us who study and conserve primates are uncomfortable seeing them on the menu," Dr. Anthony Rose of the Biosynergy Institute wrote in in 1998 in *Pan Africa News*. "This discomfort may be ego-centric, born of our own personal eating taboos or our concern that animals at our field sites may be killed before we've finished our research. It may be anthropocentric—a manifestation of our reluctance to eat anything so human-like as a gorilla or baboon. Or it may come from a bio-centric concern for individuals and species that are on the verge of extinction, high on the food chain, or demonstrably sentient and subject to suffering."

Whatever the reasoning, there is now an alliance of more than thirty international organizations trying to change a diet that has existed for millennia, not only in Africa, but also in South America and in South and Southeast Asia. Together, they argue urgency, because hunting methods have changed. Not so long ago, the animals were hunted with bows and arrows, spears, and nets, the only goal being to put food on the family table, with occasional surplus carcasses being sold in the village market or shared without charge with other villagers. Today, automatic rifles and shotguns are used and the same trucks that took the hunters into the forest also take the fresh meat out. Even some of the traditional river boats now have freezers.

Thus, more bush meat is reaching the marketplace faster and more efficiently, as the market itself continues to expand. A study conducted in 1997 in Ouesso, a small town in Congo (pop. 11,000), reported more than six tons of bush meat was sold each week in a market that offered eight different kinds of monkey and gorillas. Bush meat trading was banned in Cameroon, yet up to ninety tons of flesh arrived at Yaounde's four bush meat markets every month in 2002.

Nor is the market limited to African dinner tables. The World Wildlife Fund for Nature reported in 1998 that chimpanzee and gorilla were on menus as far away as Paris and London, where the meat was served dried, smoked, cut into steaks and cooked in a rich, gamey stew. Monkey is also a popular dish in rural areas of southern China and Southeast Asia.

However threatening all this may sound, many if not most of the jungle animals found on Equatorial restaurant menus or in diets in tropical countries around the world are not on any endangered list. While it can be said safely that so many primates are on such lists—the gorilla, the chimp, the orangutang, one species of babboon and more than a dozen species of monkey—probably they should not be eaten, even when their populations are sizeable. However, there are other kinds of bush meat that might be considered "acceptable" according to the numbers.

Three countries in Africa—Namibia, Zimbabwe, and South Africa—are exporting game meat to Europe and a number of private game ranches now invite hunters to go on an old-fashioned safari reminiscent of the time when Ernest Hemingway championed big game hunting fifty years ago. Here, today, if the hunter can pay the price, he can shoot eland, impala, kudu, duuiker, springbok, bush pig, zebra, and hartebeest.

It's easy to guess what Mr. Hemingway would think of the number of "jungle restaurants" that opened in many cities worldwide. These included two African restaurants, one in his beloved Kenya, the other in South Africa, called Carnivore, the first opened in 1980 just outside Nairobi, and now one of Kenya's most popular tourist attractions. Here, two different game meats are offered each day depending on what's available, cooked over a massive charcoal pit that dominates the entrance, then is carved right onto the diners' sizzling cast iron plates with a traditional Masai machete, or *panga*. During the peak winter season, more than 10,000 customers are served each month, seventy per cent of them tourists. The restaurant's standard dinner included crocodile raised on a farm near the coast, along with zebra, eland, Cape buffalo, hartebeest, gazelle, giraffe, impala, camel, oryx, wildebeest, and ostrich. They call it "gnu-velle cuisine." (Their joke, not mine.)

Similar restaurants exist around the globe. In Australia, there are dozens of places where what is called bush tucker is served, "tucker" being slang for food, the menu offering what once was considered fit only for the aboriginal population. Today, kangaroo fillets and ostrich steaks and crocodile satay are not only acceptable, but desirable. Here and elsewhere, the "exotic" or "jungle" restaurants resemble the Hard Rock Cafe and Planet Hollywood, where the theme seems as important than the food. For example, African Heartbeat in Singapore runs Discovery Channel documentaries on its closed circuit television system as it dishes up Ostrich *Potjiekos* (stew) with Polenta and Fresh Vegetables, African Caesar Salad with Venison Biltong Shavings, and Pan Fried Crocodile with Papadums and Spring Onion Relish. While the Carnivore in Nairobi seated 350 and an adjacent hall held 2,500 for concerts, there were six bars, a children's playground, an Internet café, a water park, and a go-kart track. Prices at such places are in the luxury class. It is as if the proprietors decided that the best way to make food that once was considered fit only for the "natives" attractive to others was to ask an exorbitant price for it.

Most game meats tend to be drier and less tender than meats of domestic animals, and more pungent in smell and taste. Because wild birds and mammals forage for food, their muscles may develop more connective tissue than the muscles of domestic animals, thus exercise can be given as a reason for less tender meat, although the younger the animal, the less tough, of course—just as veal is preferred by some over meat from an older animal. In addition, it is generally agreed that strong flavors associated with game animals are more pronounced in the fat of the species, so trimming fat from a carcass can be important.

To assure tenderness, the chefs at the Carnivore also marinate the meat for eight to twenty-four hours in a mixture of oil, water, soy sauce, lemon, tarragon, red wine, salt, white pepper, and cardamom seeds, and during cooking, baste it with a barbecue sauce made of honey, lime juice, oil, soy sauce, and cornstarch.

Almost all game animals lend themselves agreeably to stews and stroganoffs, or may be cooked on a grill, roasted in an oven, or baked. In South Africa, bush pig and a several members of the gazelle family are routinely turned into biltong, or jerky, an age-old way of preserving meat for another day.

In Trouble Again

Redmond O'Hanlon is an anthropologist-cum-travel writer of massive talent and eccentricity. His books, chronicling off-the-track treks into the jungles of Borneo, South America, and Africa have won bestseller and cult status. In the second of these, *In Trouble Again: A Journey Between the Orinoco and the Amazon* (1988), in search of a hidden tribe, he eats what the locals eat, as described when he tells a story about shooting a howler monkey "about the size of a cocker spaniel."

"Chimo and Pablo spread palm fronds on the ground and began to prepare the Howler monkey, scalding it with boiling water and scraping off the fur. Its skin turned white, like a baby's.

"That night, when Pablo had jointed the body and Galvis boiled it, Chimo handed me a suspiciously full mess tin. As I spooned out the soup the monkey's skull came into view, thinly covered with its red meat, the eyes still in their sockets.

"'We gave it to you specially,' said Chimo with great seriousness, sitting on a log beside me, taking another fistful of manioc from the tin and adding it to his own bowl. 'It's an honor in our country. If you eat the eyes, we will have good luck.'

"The skull bared its broken teeth at me. I picked it up, put my lips to the rim of each socket in turn, and sucked. The eyes came away from their soft stalks and slid down my throat.

"Chimo put his bowl down, folded his hands on his paunch, and roared with laughter.

"'You savage!' he shouted. 'You horrible naked savage! Don't you think it looks like a man? Eh? How could you do a disgusting thing like that?'"

How to Make Real South African Biltong

Game meat
Rock salt
Black pepper, coarsely ground

Dried coriander, ground
Vinegar, preferably apple-cider
  vinegar

Get some half-inch thick strips of meat. Make sure it's cut with the grain. The pieces should be about 6 inches long. Liberally sprinkle rock salt on each side of the pieces of meat and let them stand for an hour. The longer you let it stand, the saltier it will become.

After the hour, scrape off all the excess salt with a knife (don't soak it in water!). Then put some vinegar—preferably apple-cider—in a bowl and dip the strips of meat in the vinegar for a second or so—just so that the meat is covered with the vinegar. Hold the biltong up so that the excess vinegar drains off. Then sprinkle ground pepper and ground coriander over the meat on all sides.

Once you have done this, the meat is ready to dry. There are several methods of drying. One is to hang it up on a line in a cool place and have a fan blow on it. This method is a bit difficult because if the air is humid the meat can spoil. The method I use is a homemade 'Biltong Box.' This is basically a sealed wooden box (you can use cardboard if you like) with holes in it and a 60w light bulb inside. Just hang the meat at the top of the box, and leave the light bulb on at the bottom. The heat from the light bulb helps dry the meat (even in humid weather) in about 3–4 days. Remember, the box must be closed on all six sides except for a few holes. The whole theory behind this method is that hot dry air rises, thus drying the biltong. The holes are quite important as they promote good air circulation in the box.

Kangaroo

The way it'd been done for centuries, perhaps millennia, was that the original inhabitants of what later came to be called Australia, the Aborigines killed kangaroos with spears and after dressing them and filling the cleaned body cavities with heated rocks, wrapped the corpses with bark and buried them in the ground over hot ashes. Building a fire on top, thus forming a sort of oven, the bounding marsupial was baked. When ready to eat, the animal was cut into parts and divided amongst the villagers. Thus the Aborigines enjoyed their favorite protein source.

In 19th century Australia, after the boatloads of English arrived, the animal was hunted for sport as well as food and early recipe books had more for kangaroo than for other game. Compared to hare or venison in taste, the meat was cooked in a "steamer," minced or finely diced, with fatty bacon, salt, and pepper added. The tails were made into a soup and steaks were grilled over an open fire.

These dishes appeared in hotels until about 1900, when interest in "bush foods" declined following the introduction of mutton and beef, and in the years after that, as ranches took over much of the country's arable land and cattle and sheep became Australia's leading herbivorous money-earner, the kangaroo—or "roo," as it was commonly known—fell into gastronomical disfavor.

According to Barbara Santich, writing in *Looking for Flavour* (1996) and later in *The Oxford Companion to Food* (1999), "There were no absolute prohibitions on its sale or consumption in the 20th century, but food regulations made it difficult or impractical for retailers and restaurants to offer kangaroo and it virtually disappeared from Australian tables until the late 1970s." During that period, kangaroo meat, the byproduct of annual culls to keep the population in check because they were considered pestiferous—competing for grazing land with cattle and sheep—was canned and fed to dogs and cats.

Everything changed again, as it does so often in culinary history, and when regulations discouraging human consumption of the meat were lifted and some Aussie entrepreneurs began talking about roo as meat that might find not only a domestic human market but also a commodity that might drive up the country's exports, the ranchers panicked. I must hand it to them, the cowboys put up a hell of a fight.

The ranchers' appeal was to Australia's heart. The kangaroo was regarded as a national symbol, a part of the national coat of arms and as a design on the tails the national airline's planes (Qantas). In addition, the Aussie football team called themselves the Wallabies, named for the roo's smaller cousins.

Besides, kangaroos carried their young in a pouch, presenting a rough sort of Madonna and child image. The young "joey," as the newborn was called, immediately crawled up following birth, unaided, to settle in the pouch and attached itself to one of the mother's teats, where it remained for about eight months while finishing gestation. The picture of a tiny, but fast-growing, baby roo peering out of its mother's "pocket" was an image that argued sympathetically against the kangaroo's value as a meal.

In addition, the kangaroo was—and is—an admirable beast. Born the size of a large lima bean (as the *National Geographic* once put it), many grew taller than a human. Of 250 existing marsupial species, more than half—including wombats, bandicoots, and kangaroos— lived only in Australia and its immediate surroundings, ranging in size from a mouse-like creature weighing only fifty grams when mature, up to the red kangaroo, standing on its highly developed hind legs and heavy tail to a height of seven feet and weighing as much as 200 pounds. (All the rest, except the American opossum found in the United States and Canada, lived in Latin America.) The elongated tail, strong legs, and large feet, gave it the ability to "hop" or "bound" a distance of forty or more feet (easily clearing a six-foot fence), propelling these ungainly animals at twenty-five miles an hour, up to thirty-five miles an hour in short bursts. The kangaroo also was known for its fighting prowess. A full-grown male, known as a "boomer," standing on the wide tip of its tail, was able to destroy a foe with the sharp claws of both hind feet, a feature softened by Hollywood animators when they put a happy-go-lucky roo in boxing gloves and shorts.

The cowboys didn't leave it at that. Even if there were more damned kangaroos in the country than there were people—twenty-five million roos vs. twenty million humans—and two million animals had to be culled every year to keep the population from getting out of control, they argued, had the people forgotten that the meat was used for pet food! The campaign got racial, as well, when it was pointed out—quietly, mind you, nothing was overt—that black Aborigines had eaten kangaroo for centuries. Did the people who wanted to market the animal in markets and restaurants really think white people would eat food fit for "Abos" and dogs?

A "Save the Roo" campaign was launched. In addition to street marches, people reserved large tables at restaurants serving kangaroo, then failed to show up, as a means of economic protest. They publicly charged those who ate kangaroo with being unpatriotic, and bombarded the newspapers with indignant letters to the editor.

The reason for the campaign was clear. Annual beef consumption in Australia was eighty-four kilograms (185 pounds) of beef per person, nearly double the forty-six in the United States, and more than four times England's twenty. Thus, by far, beef had a grip on the protein market that cattlemen didn't want challenged by a cheaper, more abundant meat whose slaughter was being paid for by the government.

Despite the opposition, the taste for roo caught on and by 1998, ten years after the "bans" were lifted, kangaroo meat was being sold in butcher shops nationwide and served in some 900 restaurants, from pizza parlors to steak houses to the dining rooms of five-star hotels. "Bush tucker," as the indigenous food of Australia came to be called and marketed with great success—not just kangaroo, but also ostrich, emu, crocodile and a number of other local creatures, including a species of grub—was suddenly all the rage, flavoring menus from Melbourne to Sydney to Perth. In Cairns, for instance, in 1998 in a place called Dundee's, named for the popular movie character Crocodile Dundee, a bowl of kangaroo soup cost about US$3, a serving of roo satay $8, a "Kangaroo Mignon" $12, a skewer shared with the meat of water buffalo, emu, barramundi, and crocodile (with a choice of sauces) $18.

As a rule, only the large hind quarters were used, butchered into fillets of rump, saddle (porterhouse), tenderloin, and braising or gravy steak. The flesh was dark and had a slightly gamy but inoffensive taste. Of the dishes served, the most popular seemed to be in the form of steaks, but in 1994 a small press in South Australia published a book called *Kangaroo Cookin'*, a collection of "88 Simple Roo Recipes" that included soups, pastas, one-pot dishes, pies and pastries, meals that were stir-fried and char-grilled, and a selection of recipes for children, from tacos to burgers to sandwiches. Where once there was dog food, now there was Kangaroo Lasagne, Kangaroo Escalopes with Green Olives and White Wine Sauce, and Hot and Sour Kangaroo Soup. It was also cured and smoked and served in salads. When grilled or roasted, it was thought to be best served rare.

Advocates said that the animal was able to survive on less and poorer forage than domestic livestock, while producing more protein pound for pound than Australia's sheep and cattle. Nutritionists said the meat was rich in iron, low in fat, and free of contaminants, a healthy alternative to other red meats. Roo was also reportedly lower in cholesterol, was as rich in color and taste as beef, and it cost less than lamb or pork. Southern Game Meat, a large kangaroo slaughterhouse and distributor, advertised its product as "Australia's health meat." Even the local National Heart Foundation gave the roo its stamp of approval.

Advocates of kangaroo ranching differed on the specifics, but, as was reported in the New York Times in 2002, they agreed that it had a place among a variety of long-term actions needed to halt chronic soil degradation and diversify the sources of farm incomes. They urged turning the prolific kangaroo into an export product and saw such a strategy as a way to jump-start economic and conservation reforms in Australia's arid range-lands. Animal welfare activists in Australia and the US and elsewhere still opposed the shooting of kangaroos and argued that mass harvesting could lead to the extinction of major species.

In the end, the success of the kangaroo as a protein source likely will come down to economics. By 2002, kangaroo populations exploded after strong vegetation growth, and the official cull rate went to seven-million, the highest ever. What was to be done with all that meat? The dog and cat market was limited. Will the McDonald's and KFC step into the fray?

Hey, Captain James Cook liked it when he stepped ashore in 1770. He called it "very good eating."

Kangaroo Escalopes with Green Olives and White Wine Sauce

4 thin kangaroo steaks
2 tablespoons olive oil
60 ml dry white wine
200 ml water
1 garlic clove, crushed
8 whole green olives

4 medium mushrooms, sliced
2 teaspoons fresh oregano
Crushed rock salt to taste
Crushed black pepper to taste
1 teaspoon corn flour mixed to
    a thin paste with cold water

Heat oil in heavy pan, then fry meat until browned on both sides. Add mushrooms, garlic and olives, and fry for 2 minutes. Add wine and water, simmer gently for 2 minutes, then add oregano, salt and pepper. Add corn flour mix and stir over heat until thickened. Serve with vermicelli and green salad.

—*Kangaroo Cookin'*

Bear

"Bear stew special order. No bear in Indonesia now. Get from China. Take one week, two week."

I was sitting opposite the chef of a lavish private club in Jakarta, who said he prepared bear paw soup for many of his Chinese customers—ethnic Chinese who lived in the Indonesian capital, others from Taiwan and Hong Kong, all very rich businessmen who came to gamble and sing in private karaoke rooms.

"Not easy cook bear paw," the chef grumbled. "Pull hairs from back with tweezers. Many hair. Many, many hair."

I confess that I did not order it, using the excuse that I wasn't going to be in Jakarta long enough for a shipment of bear parts to arrive. In fact, this was true, but there were other reasons I think that at bear I would draw the line when it came to trying new foods.

Soon after I moved to Asia in 1993 I met a woman in Bangkok who operated a refuge for abandoned and captured wild animals. Around her spacious garden were cages containing gibbons who had been displayed in bars where customers fed them salted nuts and cigarettes until at about age six the animals turned mean and the bar owners no longer wanted them. There were monkeys and pangolin and an assortment of colorful wild birds. The tragic centerpiece was a bear, called "Stumpy" because he'd had one of his paws cut off. Eventually, the woman found a home for him in an upcountry zoo, but last I heard, he still withdrew to the rear of his cage when any humans approached.

I also started keeping a file marked "Bear." One report included this description of a "typical evening in a bear restaurant":

"A live bear would have its feet chopped off and either barbecued or made into bear paw soup. The hapless animal would then be placed in a string net basket and lowered, still alive [muzzled to stifle it's cries], into a cauldron of boiling water where it is slowly cooked to death before being chopped up and served to the diners. Sometimes, as a variation, the bears are placed in a small cage with their feet ticking out, and are lowered onto hot coals so that the paws are cooked first. This sadistic ritual serves as a spot of pre-dinner entertainment. The people who indulge in this practice believe that the bears must be cooked alive because the pain and terror they experience somehow tenderizes the meat. They also believe that bear gall bladders are a cure for liver diseases and cancer, and that bear meat is a good all-round health tonic. None of these notions can be scientifically verified."

It gets worse. Bear gall bladders are even more prized than the flesh as it is believed to enhance sexual potency. These are reportedly sold in tens of thousands of traditional apothecaries and herbalist shops not just in Asia, but wherever there are expatriate Chinese and Korean communities. An undercover agent found thirteen out of twenty such Chinatown shops in Vancouver, Canada, were selling dried galls, with one of them offering a volume discount for orders of fifty or more. While back in Asia—the largest market for galls—there were numerous "farms" where bears were kept in rows of cages, drains attached to their bladders to collect the bile.

By 2000, virtually all the bear populations in China, Southeast Asia, and Russia were approaching extinction. Of the world's eight species of bear, only the giant pandas has not been targeted for its galls. Galls from every other species have been found in trade. Bladders from Russian bears have been smuggled into Vancouver, while Koreans export Canadian galls back to Seoul. In North America, some enforcement officers estimate that in addition to the 40,000 bears killed legally each year, another 40,000 are poached.

Illegal trafficking in endangered species—of which the bear is just a part—is estimated to be valued at US$6 billion annually, with profit margins second only to those of the illegal drug trade. Historically, demand for bear originated in China thousands of years ago, when it was regarded as a delicacy for the elite. So, too, today, where only the rich can afford it. A full-sized bear sold in a restaurant to a tour group from Hong Kong, Taiwan, South Korea, China, or Japan may cost between US$1,000 (in Vietnam) to ten times that amount (in Thailand). Tiny quantities of bile from an Asiatic black bear was worth up to eighteen times the price of gold. No wonder laws banning trafficking of bear parts have been ineffective.

The bears indigenous to North America, including the Brown, the Black, and the Grizzly, were killed matter-of-factly during early settlement; Davy Crockett's heroic status tells the story of his killing a "bar" with a knife. Bear grease, or fat, was valued by French pioneers in the Mississippi Valley and reportedly was preferred over butter or hog's lard in New Orleans during the 19th century.

Commonly, bear today is boiled and braised. After braising the paw in soda water for ten minutes, then stewing it in fresh water for about four hours, the hair, crust, nails, and bones are removed and the meat is wrapped in cloth and further braised in water again with chicken breast and/or ham and duck, changing the water several times to remove the odor. The meat is then sliced and everything is sautéed with a choice of seasoning (chives, ginger, garlic, water chestnut powder, etc.) and a generous splash of Chinese rice wine. This is stewed for a further three minutes and served. Bear is roasted in the same way that pork is, until the meat is tender and leaving no trace of pink.

Not everywhere is this trade illegal. In parts of Asia and Russia and in Canada and the United States (Alaska), the Native American Inuit, formerly called Eskimos, are permitted to hunt bear in the traditional manner, along with seal and caribou for food and skins; a limited number of whales also may be killed. When the Inuit go after what is the world's largest land carnivore—weighing up to 675 kg, or about 1,500 pounds—they wear the fur-lined parkas and pants and gloves of wolf or beaver, appearing little changed from their ancestors. However, where once all hunted from dog-drawn sleds, now many use snowmobiles, and the harpoon has been replaced with a powerful rifle.

After the kill, the knives are drawn and the animal is skinned and butchered, at home or in a cabin in the wild. Within two hours, the meat is bubbling over a fire, filling the room with its rich, gamy scent. The paw, regarded most tender, may be marinated in bacon fat if available and if not, in its own fat, then grilled. Usually the manner of preparation is simple. The Inuit hunt bear for sustenance, not for fun.

That said, they also serve as guides to foreign sport hunters, who pay as much as US$20,000 for the privilege. Until recently, polar bear trophies could not be imported into the United States, but the regulatory act was amended to allow hunters to return home with huge, stuffed, white bears so long as they had been killed in approved locations, which seem to change fairly regularly, and always are limited in number, according to the fluctuating local count. In the 2002–2003 season, foreigners shot sixty-nine.

Barbecued Bear

1/3 lb bear roast	1/4 teaspoon chili powder
Salt and pepper	1/8 teaspoon cayenne pepper
1 clove garlic, crushed	1 tablespoon paprika
2 teaspoons brown sugar	1/4 cup catsup
2 tablespoons Worcestershire sauce	1/4 vinegar
1 teaspoon dry mustard	1 cup tomato juice

Clean bear immediately and cure for several days. When ready to cook, remove all fat. Do not lard. Broil or roast according to specific recipe directions. Do not undercook bear; treat it like pork, leaving no traces of pink in the meat.

Place roast in small roaster. Season to taste with salt and pepper; rub with garlic. Bake at 350°F for 1 hour or until well done. Cut into thin slices. Combine 1 teaspoon salt, brown sugar, seasonings, vinegar, tomato juice, catsup, and 1/2 cup water in heavy skillet. Simmer for 15 minutes. Add meat; simmer for 1 hour or until roast is tender.

Whale

All hell broke loose in 1998 when the school district of the seaside city of Shimonoseki in Japan announced an addition to the upcoming year's school lunch menu: whale meat.

Greenpeace and thousands of save-the-whale crusaders world-wide, along with fans of the *Free Willy* movie, were angry. When the Japanese defended their move, saying it was designed to teach some 25,000 elementary and primary school students pride in their town's historical role as a major port for their country's whaling fleet, that only made people madder.

No food in the present time is more controversial than that sur-rounding the killing of whales. Not the tiger, the panda, the elephant, not the dolphin, monk seal, or manatee, not the bald eagle, the gorilla, the orangutan, the gibbon, or the chimpanzee, nor any other endan-gered or threatened species. People who killed whales were crazy, they argue: "Didn't you read Moby Dick?" Of course, it's not that simple.

Surveys show that most people believe Japan is the only country defending this age-old harvest and that only the Japanese continue to regard the meat, blubber and other by-products as a part of daily life. While it's true that Japan leads all other countries in its whaling activi-ty—sending the meat into markets and onto dinner plates, as well as including it in school lunches—Japan is not alone. There are other countries that approve whaling, Iceland, Denmark and Norway among them, and Canada, Russia and a handful of South Pacific nations, have refused to agree to international bans as well. In addi-tion, aboriginal subsistence whaling is permitted by native peoples in Alaska, the far-eastern part of Russia, in Greenland, and in Saint Vincent and the Grenadines. What's more, there is a strengthening international voice to cancel the commercial whaling ban altogether.

In fact, as long ago as 1972 and 1973 the Scientific Committee of the International Whaling Commission (IWC), the committee responsible for counting the world's whales, by consensus at its meetings said that "there is no scientific justification or need for a whaling moratorium." This opinion did not match that of the anti-whaling member nations who controlled the IWC, however, and the judgment was ignored. This same opinion was put forth by the committee once more in 1993, but again brought no change.

Then, in 1997 at the bi-annual meeting of the highly esteemed Convention on International Trade in Endangered Species (CITES), the organization generally regarded as having the last word on the subject of any creature thought to be in jeopardy, member nations stunned environmental advocates everywhere by supporting the sustainable use of abundant whale stocks, voting to allow trade in whale products, fifty-seven to fifty-one. Thus, the majority endorsed the notion that whales could be killed and eaten, but a two-thirds majority was needed, so the prohibition remained in place.

The operative phrase in the frustrated proposal was "abundant whale stocks." What, after all, is "abundant"? There are nearly two-million sperm whales; is that "abundant"? Certainly that number would make the defenders of many other endangered species ecstatically happy. Yet, the sperm whale, found in all the earth's oceans, is still one of the eight whale species on the CITES list. (The others are the blue, the bowhead, the finback, the gray, the humpback, the right, and the sei, whose populations are far smaller, many in the tens of thousands and one, the right, estimated to be down to the last 3,000.)

It is important to note that Japan reportedly claims to hunt the minke whale almost exclusively, a species whose estimated numbers, while smaller than those of the sperm whale, are regarded as sufficiently large to justify limited hunting and are, therefore, not on anyone's endangered lists. (Smaller numbers of the Pacific Brydes whale are also taken; another whale not on any threatened list.) According to the Scientific Committee of the IWC, charged with maintaining population figures, there are approximately 760,000 minke whales in the Antarctic, another 118,000 in the North Atlantic, a further 25,000 in the Okhotsk Sea and Western Pacific.

Moby Who?

To understand how whale meat found their way into school lunches in Japan and onto grills in faraway Iceland, Norway, Denmark and elsewhere—and why it is not eaten in most places today—suggests a fast look at whaling history.

Many whales are threatened with extinction today because unregulated whaling activity once led by the United States, England, and Norway, annihilated the oceanic population in much the same way many other large mammals were hunted to near extinction in the North American and African continents. Whaling by these countries was conducted to collect whale oil, the market for which died with the discovery of petroleum. (Whale bone, used in the construction of corsets and other female foundation garments, also became obsolete.) It wasn't concern for the survival of the great beasts that ended whaling. It was commerce.

With the market for the oil gone and no apparent interest in the meat, commercial whaling became unprofitable and the United States quit whaling in 1940, the United Kingdom in 1963. A resolution calling for a ten-year moratorium on commercial whaling was adopted at the United Nations Conference on Human Environment in 1972 and the IWC followed with an open-ended moratorium effective from 1986. Iceland withdrew from the IWC six years later and Norway resumed whaling in 1993.

Initially, Japan objected noisily to any controls, but then it discovered it could continue limited whaling with IWC approval under the cloak of "scientific research"—where it was believed that safe management of marine resources was not then possible because knowledge of the number of whales, age composition, sex ratio, and natural mortality rate was unknown or ambiguous. The research catch by Japan was thus introduced, with the IWC limiting the capture to two thousand whales a year, to answer such questions and eliminate uncertainties.

Now, population figures can be estimated by simple counting, with research limited to spending lots of time at sea with binoculars, every now and then saying, "Over there!" and making a tick on a note pad. Such non-lethal enquiry was acceptable even to Greenpeace and other environmental organizations that had assumed a very visible role by 1987 when Japan was given its Special Permit in the Antarctic.

However, non-lethal research, by itself, did not work for determining age, pregnancy rates, and the effects of marine pollution. A whale's age could be determined, for example, only by removing a part of the inner ear and a study of the whale's fertility involved a look at the ovaries. Environmentalists objected strongly, insisting that killing something in the name of saving it didn't make any sense. Nonetheless, in the spirit of cooperation, perhaps, the IWC went along.

While it is true that the Japanese are completing their task, contributing to the world's knowledge of the Antarctic and its cetacean population—Greenpeace vigorously disputes that—it may be noted that they also get to keep the whales. After scientific examination and removal of necessary tissue and organ samples, the remains of the whales are frozen and marketed in compliance with further provisions of the IWC, which forbid any part of the carcass to be wasted. Voila! Whale blubber and steak.

Environmentalists contend that Japan is hiding behind "research" to keep their whaling fleets intact, and whether or not this is true, there is ample evidence that eating whale meat in that country has a long history. Discoveries at archeological digs in Japan show that whale meat has been eaten at least to the 2nd century B.C. (Whaling began in Norway, France and Spain in the 9th century.) Furthermore, after the acceptance of Buddhism in Japan, which in its early years prohibited the consumption of flesh from four-legged animals, whale meat became an important source of protein. It has been found recorded on menus from a thousand years ago and by the Muromachi Perod (1333-1568) it had come to be regarded as so important as to merit inclusion on a menu contained in official literature on Japanese food culture.

Japan's whale meat consumption was about 10,000 tons in the early 1920s, jumping to 40,000 tons by 1939. Its popularity accelerated again following World War Two, when other protein sources were severely limited, reaching a high of 200,000 tons in 1962. Since then, the market has fallen, to just under 15,000 tons in 1985. Today, it appears to be less than that, although figures are not revealed because of the controversy.

The Japanese people know that the whale is a mammal, but it is commonly treated as a "fish." (As is the dolphin or porpoise.) For instance, a quarterly journal published by the Japan Whaling Association is called Isana, a word from the ancient Japanese language composed of two Chinese characters, for "brave" and "fish," denoting a whale. The whale to the Japanese in earlier times was, therefore, a kind of courageous fish, thus it was served at joyous occasions such as weddings and other communal celebrations.

Japan has long been, and still is, a nation of fish-eaters and the whale was regarded as just another part of the harvest from the sea, just as it has been judged by indigenous peoples from the northwestern United States, where the Maah Indian tribe won the right from the IWC to resume a 1,500-year-old whaling tradition, pointing to a treaty with the US government that dated back to 1855. On the southern tip of South America, where the Yahgen people used smoke signals to summon neighbors whenever a whale was caught or found beached, families would come for miles around and camp out and feast for as long as a month.

For a tribe of native North Americans, the Kwakuitl, such a find was highly ritualized. Preparing food was women's work and the honors, in this case, went to the daughter of the hunter who found the whale. The choicest piece, the dorsal fin, was given to the village chief and others received a share, according to their status, starting with the neck and working from the top down and from head to tail.

The harvest was then loaded into the canoes and taken home, where the blubber was cut into half-inch strips and boiled in water. When the oil separated, it was ladled into watertight storage containers and the remaining strings of blubber were threaded onto long thin pieces of cedar bark and hung to dry in the rafters of the house for at least a month. It could then be taken down and boiled again as needed.

It was back in 1931 when the International Convention for Regulation of Whaling (ICRW), one of the earliest monitoring groups, set rigid standards for "aboriginal/subsistence whaling." The concept was to aid local, aboriginal, indigenous or native communities in meeting their nutritional, subsistence and cultural requirements, but the regulations soon proved unworkable. Aborigines, who themselves were never very clearly defined, were to use only canoes or other exclusively native craft propelled by oars or sails and were forbidden to carry firearms. In effect, IRCW was saying that if an exception was going to be made for the hungry natives, they would have to stick to ancient means of pursuit and capture, an inefficient hindrance that resulted in much wasted time, effort and meat. Over time, the rules were relaxed and today, modern whaling boats usually assist in providing the limited catch.

Some of these ships are from the former Soviet Union, one of several countries—Japan is another—accused of illegal whaling. According to figures released in a report commissioned by the Australian government, one of the loudest anti-whaling voices, Soviet fleets between 1947 and 1972 killed 48,000 humpback whales, one of the most endangered species, yet reported a catch of fewer than 3,000. The Russians also were charged with killing 8,000 pygmy blue whales, while admitting to a catch of only ten. Anti-whaling critics also said, as recently as 1998, that in Japan, DNA testing of whale meat on sale in local fish markets showed some of the meat was not from Japan's "scientific" catch, but from protected species caught thousands of miles away from the authorized hunt areas.

Whatever its legal—or ethical—status, there is no doubt about the healthy nature of whale meat. Though richer in protein, whale meat has fewer calories than beef or pork, and it is substantially lower in cholesterol. To many peoples, salted whale meat has long been an indispensable part of the diet during the winter months, as it keeps longer than salted fish and tastes good as well.

Whales are classified into two groups, baleen whales and toothed whales. Unlike toothed whales, which actively hunt their food, baleen whales "graze" on zooplankton called krill, comprised of extremely small shrimps and fish. It's believed that this is what makes the meat so tender and juicy. The Japanese consume nearly all the whale, including the internal organs, the blubber, even the tail and flukes. The tastiest part is thought to be the *onomi*, the marbled flesh found at the base of the tail.

Surely, the controversy over killing whales will continue. Many whale species are now increasing in numbers and the climate is changing. When CITES voted fifty-seven to fifty-one, supporting the trade of whale products in 1997, Ginette Hemley of the World Wild Life Fund told the Associated Press, "This indicates a significant decrease in opposition to whaling. The whole tone of the whaling debate has changed."

Peter Bridgewater, chairman of the ICW, added, "The numbers [favoring an end to the ban] were much stronger than they have ever been. The interpretation being put on this by a number of countries is that the way is open for trading and people are interested."

In 2003, the IWC was polarized. The forces for loosening or even eliminating the ban gained strength, as Japan was accused of increasing foreign aid to small voter nations in exchange for their support. Also in 2003, Iceland's government issued permits for "scientific whaling" and three vessels set sail a few days later with explosive harpoons to resume the hunt for the large sea mammals for the first time in fourteen years.

At the same time, anti-whaling countries introduced an initiative to transform the commission into a body dedicated to safeguarding the whale rather than regulating the whaling industry for which it was originally created. Japan responded by threatening to quit the organization.

While Greenpeace and other conservationists continued to say: no way! Feed the people something else!

Whale Steak with Vegetables

2 kg whale meat	2 dessert spoons black currant
4 dl red wine	cordial
2 dl water	Cream
15 juniper berries	Cornflour

Brown the meat on all sides in a stew pan, add the red wine, water and mashed juniper berries. Simmer under lid for about 30 minutes. Remove the meat and wrap it in aluminum foil while finishing making the gravy.

Gravy: add the black currant cordial to the juices in the pan. Add cream to taste and thicken with corn flour. Cut the meat into thin slices and serve with potatoes, green peas, sprouts and mountain cranberries.

—*High North Alliance, 1994*

Camel

Think of a camel and, putting aside all thoughts of a cigarette and so-called "adventure wear," most of us think of Bedouin nomads loping across the desert sands, strange, humped beasts with ridiculous lips and dreamy eyes that are known to have a nasty temperament and for going long distances between drinks. Think of a camel and up pops Lawrence of Arabia, or three wise men at Christmas, but certainly not a meal. So it was no surprise when many young American and British soldiers sent to fight Saddam Hussein in 1991 and again in 2003 were shocked when they arrived in the Middle East and learned that pork products were forbidden and that many people ate camel meat instead. Enjoyably.

To those who own them, the camel is an amazing beast. They may have bad breath and like to kick and spit, but camel hair is admired worldwide for high-quality coats and artists' brushes, as well as for making traditional Bedouin rugs and tents. Camel racing is such a big business, children are kidnapped to serve as jockeys, and a good breeding female can be worth up to US$1 million at auction. Camels also still pull ploughs, turn waterwheels, and transport people and goods to market along desert routes unfit for wheeled vehicles, and where wheeled vehicles do exist, frequently the animals are fitted with red bicycle tail lights as a warning to motorists. In many parts of the Arab world, with or without warning lights, camels have the right of way and colliding with one of the lumbering ships of the desert can be lethal and expensive; half a ton of dromedary can write off both you and your car and if you injure or kill the animal, then the responsibility is yours.

No surprise that the Bedouin name for the dromedary is *Ata Allah*, God's gift.

Camels additionally command respect for their adaptation to the relentlessly harsh environment. They do not pant and rarely sweat, accepting the awful desert heat with passivity; they are not victims of their unkind place but a product of it, like cactus and desert rats. Because their body temperatures are lower than the air temperature, a group of resting camels will avoid excessive heat by pressing against each other, what other mammals might do to find warmth. Camels can go five to seven days with little or no food and water and may lose a quarter of their body weight without its affecting their performance. When a camel does find water, it may drink as much as twenty gallons in ten minutes, a feat that would kill any other animal, but the camel's metabolism enables it to store the water in its bloodstream. A double row of long, curling eyelashes helps keep out sand and dust, thick bushy eyebrows shield the doe-like eyes from the sun, and large, muscular nostrils can be opened and closed at will to cool the incoming air and condense moisture from its outgoing breath. As in most mammals, food and liquid is stored in the form of fat, but this is not distributed around the body where it might prevent natural cooling, it is concentrated in one place, in the humps on their back. Dehydrated, a camel's hump will hang like an old woman's teat.

The camel originated in North America approximately forty-million years ago and today ranges mainly from Morocco to Mongolia. The U.S. Army imported some camels in the mid-19th century for use in the American southwest, primarily for mail service, but in the end they were turned loose. The same thing was done in Australia, where today camel safaris play a role in the tourism business and otherwise the animal is regarded as a pest, roaming the central districts in large numbers. (In the U.S., they no longer exist in the wild.) The Arabian camel, *Camelus dromedarius*, has one hump and the Bactrian camel in Asia, *Camelus bactrianus*, two, and it is the latter that is most popular for personal transport, as the two humps form a natural sort of saddle.

Camels are all domesticated in the Middle East and North Africa, and the last wild herds of any size in the world are in Australia. Camels were used instead of horses in Australia's arid and desolate interior, where temperatures may rise above fifty degrees Celsius during the day and fall to freezing at night. They helped explorers search for gold, settlers carry building materials and supplies, and policemen patrol remote areas. By the 1920s, they were overtaken by the internal combustion engine traveling on new highways and an estimated 12,000 were shot or turned loose. Those that survived flourished and they now live compatibly alongside kangaroos, emus, and dingoes (the wild Australian dogs). The population is now estimated to be around 200,000 and there are breeding programs in place.

Much that can be said in gastronomic praise of the horse can be echoed when talking about the camel. "They are genetically clean and disease-free," said Peter Seidel, chairman of the Central Australian Camel Industry Association, one of the individuals who think a range of products can prove to be profitable export items. In recent years, the market in Australia for ostrich and kangaroo meat has expanded rapidly, but so far, the local market for camel meat remains small, so Seidel has his eyes on China and Southeast Asia, where an unusual protein source usually is not considered unusual. This is a market only to think about now. About ten ranchers in his association are primarily cattle ranchers, supplementing their herds with camels to provide the 300 or so camels needed to satisfy the domestic market annually.

In Biblical times, Moses banned the consumption of the camel, but the milk was used and is prized even today and usually is consumed fresh and the warm. However, the frothy liquid, heavy and sweet, is an acquired taste for Western palates. Tiny fat globules also make it difficult to churn butter, but it can be used for yoghurt. The Institute of Food Science in Zurich, Switzerland, reports that of the eighteen million camels in the world, fourteen million live in Africa and the Middle East, the rest in Asia, where in many arid areas camels play a central role as a milk supplier. Said Seidel, "The comparative advantage of the camel as a dairy animal over the other species in the same environment is shown by the continuity of supply even during long droughts when other animals cease to produce."

Like so many other foods, camel milk in some areas is given credit as an aphrodisiac. In the Arab world, there is a saying: "One liter [quart] a day, five times a night." Bull camels are notorious for their sexual appetite, which lasts two or three months each year, when one bull can service twenty females—giving rise, perhaps, to theories about the milk's special powers for flagging libidos. Camel's milk also is rich in Vitamin C and believed to have liver-healing properties.

Camel is unlikely to find much of a market in developed countries, if not for an aversion to eating such an animal, because of stringent trade barriers. To illustrate the point that rich countries were helping keep poor nations poor, in 2002 the World Bank's chief economist, Nicholas Stern, told a story about camel cheese. The exotic delicacy, made by nomads in Mauritania, one of Africa's most destitute countries, had become popular among a group of European dairy connoisseurs, but import to the cheese gourmands was halted by the European Union's high tariff levels. Stern also cited hygiene rules in Europe that stipulated the camels had to be milked mechanically, an economic impossibility.

Nomadic cuisine has it roots in tent cookery. Nomadic tribes could only use easily transportable foods such as rice and dates, or ambulatory stock like sheep and camels in their recipes, which tended to be rough sketches rather than strict formulae. Even so, camel meat is rated highly by international adventurers, who say it tastes much like veal, although it may be, even in the younger beasts, somewhat on the chewy side. Praised by Aristophanes and regarded as a gourmet treat in ancient Rome, and a staple to the present day, the whole camel can be consumed, from the thick tongue to the rope-like tail, as it was at ancient Persian banquets.

The meat from the hump is considered the prime cut, and usually is roasted. The thigh may be minced and formed into meatballs or patties, or baked whole in a marinade. The wide, soft feet—designed for walking in the sand—have been eaten from the days of the Roman empire, most often grilled. The stomach, heart, and offal are savored in stews. And in Mongolia, the fat from the hump is used to make butter.

The small herds in China are endangered now, numbering under a thousand, down from two or three times that in 1980. Here, unlike in Australia, the hunters of China's Muslim Uighur and Kazakh minorities have long stalked the wild beasts for its cherished hump and other delicacies. It is Mr. Seidel's aim to replace the meat of the two-humped Chinese Bactrian with meat from its cousin, the single-humped Australian dromedary.

Camel Hoof Paste

250 gr camel hoof	Chives
40 gr dried scallops	Ginger
40 gr dried mushrooms	Gourmet powder
30 gr done ham slices	Rice wine
Green soybeans	Vinegar
Coriander	Soy sauce
Salt and pepper	Soup

Clean the hoof and pull its hair out, braise it for 30 minutes, remove the bone and put it in a bowl, then steam it together with knotted chives and sliced ginger for about 1 hour, knife it into slices, then stew them with more knotted chives and sliced ginger for 45–60 minutes to make them into a thick paste.

Steam the dried scallops with chives, ginger, wine to be done, put them with the dried mushroom slices, ham slices, green soybeans in the camel hoof paste, then add salt, pepper, gourmet powder, rice wine, vinegar, soy, braise them for 20 minutes, place them in a bowl, add coriander.

Guts

"Guts" is an interesting word.

Literally, it is a reference to the alimentary canal, a tubular passage functioning in the digestion of food and extending from the mouth to the anus, a path that includes a lot of anatomy...and provides a great deal of food itself.

It's also now thought of—colloquially, at least in English—as a synonym for courage. So, a robust and daring individual may be described as being "gutsy" or "having guts," and to be without such character is to be "gutless." Sometimes, this attribute is called "intestinal fortitude." The famous World War Two army general George Patton was known as "Blood and Guts."

In addition, many people talking about their instincts say, "I feel it in my gut."

This is one of those rare instances when positive endorsement—using the word to mean courage and intuition—don't do anything to make the word's origin appealing, gastronomically. However many people in the world today savor the deliciously prepared parts of the alimentary canal, many more would never even consider putting "guts" on their dinner plate. And it is interesting how many of those who will eat guts often give the meat an innocent-sounding euphemism, as if that might distance the food from its anatomical derivation. Just as feet are called "trotters," the pancreas and thymus glands are called "sweetbreads," lungs are called "lights," the spleen is called "melt" (or "milt") and testicles have a variety of more socially acceptable names, the stomach of ruminants, especially the ox, calf, or sheep, is called "tripe," as, sometimes, are the intestines, while the intestines of young pigs are called "chitterlings" and udder is called "elder." Such foods, along with other internal organs, are called offal, meaning, literally, the "off-fall" or off-cuts from the carcass; many call these items "variety meats." Similarly, offal from birds usually is referred to as "giblets." Even in Chinese households, you will never hear anyone say, "Pass the stomach" or "Could I have some more intestine, please?"

Eating entrails has a history as long and twisting as the gut itself—proving that no matter what something may have once contained, with the proper preparation, a tasty meal can be made of it. Many European countries are known for their sausages; Germany alone boasts nearly 1,500 varieties. What is used to hold all that beef, pork, mutton, chicken, game meat, fat, egg, cream, beer, wine, blood, bread-crumbs, oatmeal, potato and soybean flour, dried milk solids, onion, garlic, herbs and spices, salt and pepper and assorted additives and preservatives together? Although some of the casings are now made from digestible plastic—the horror, the horror!—the tube-like sleeve tied off at the ends more usually is a length of pig's intestine. For large sausages, the large intestine is used, and for the smaller ones and chit-terlings, meat packagers employ the small intestine or the caecum, the latter being an abdominal appendage that is also used, from sheep, to make condoms that are sometimes called "skins." (Falling into disfavor nowadays because they are porous and while it will keep back spermatozoa, the HIV virus may slip through.)

The intestines themselves also may be minced and added to the sausage's other ingredients. Chitterlings, for instance are not only encased in short sleeves of pig intestine, the insides are pork intestine, too. Their use dates back to 16th century England when they were a primary ingredient in a sort of "white pudding." Today, they are enjoyed in France, as well as in the US, and usually are fried or grilled. While calf's mesentery, part of the peritoneum, the membrane lining the abdominal cavity, is a sausage ingredient that may also be fried or prepared in the same way as tripe, about which more in a minute.

Ox intestines also are a common ingredient in blood sausage (black pudding), a dish most often associated with the north of England, but found in many other European countries as well. In Asia, the carefully cleaned bowels of pigs are chopped and simmered along with other innards, such as the stomach, in anise-flavored broth and poured over noodles...and the large intestine, also thinly sliced, is simmered and deep-fried, then served as a snack that goes down well with beer. In Singapore, I've eaten entrails cut into quarter-inch wide rings and cooked in a rich soup with blood used as a thickening. A disadvantage: improperly cooked, such foods have the chewyness of thick rubber bands.

Sweetbreads is the butchers' word for both the pancreas, the organ that sends digestive enzymes into the intestine and insulin into the bloodstream, and the thymus gland, located in the throat and so named for its resemblance to the bud of the herb thyme. Like much organ meat, it deteriorates rapidly and should be consumed quickly. They may be added to stews or sliced into cutlets that can be egged, breadcrumbed, and fried. In France, they are cooked in butter and served with sorrel purée. It's a fairly bland meat and benefits from spices and seasonings.

Spleen, or melt, is less commonly encountered. This is the vascular organ near the stomach that restores worn-out blood cells and stores blood, a word that for reasons I don't know also means, according to my dictionary, "ill humor, peevish temper, or spite." Most often, it is but one of several offal ingredients that go into faggots, sausages, and patés, although a popular sandwich sold on the street in Sicily contains beef spleen with warmed ricotta and caciovallo, a hard cheese made from cow's milk.

Even rarer is the use of mammalian lungs, or lights. Although they contain more protein than T-bone steak and only six per cent as much fat, their vitamin content is low and in 1971 the U.S. Wholesale Meat Act was amended to declare the meat unfit for human consumption, another example of dumb American law out of sync with much of the world's needs and taste. The flesh is especially popular in Europe, where it is poached, then fried with onions, tomatoes and wine sauce (France); boiled and sautéed with paprika and other vegetables (Hungary); cooked with kidney beans (Italy); or stewed (France, Austria, Germany). Most are calf, sheep, and pork and it's one of the cheapest meats.

Rarer still is cow's udder, described by Calvin Schwabe in *Unmentionable Cuisine* (1979) as "one of the foods which is doing a slow disappearing act, at least in western countries." Sometimes this is counted as a form of "tripe," and in England it's called "elder," a word apparently imported from Holland in the 17th century. Sam Pepys recorded it in his famous diary in 1660, but since then it's been downhill. Nowadays, it's found almost exclusively in industrial West Yorkshire in the UK, parts of Belgium, and, more widely, in Asia, where, as it is well known, the people will eat just about anything. Long simmering is required and the taste and texture are reminiscent of tongue.

The somewhat snooty *Larousse Gastronomique* calls offal, "particularly intestines and tripe," inferior, saying that only kidneys, liver, calves' sweetbreads, lambs' brains, and *animelles* (testicles) have any "real gastronomic importance." Having said that, *Larousse* then devotes two pages to stomach—tripe if you and *Larousse* insist—to outright praise and delicious recipes.

Tripe is the catch-all word for the stomach of ruminants (even-toed, hoofed animals with three- and four-chambered stomachs such as the cow, ox, sheep, and deer) and most often comes from the first and second stomachs of oxen, the former called the rumen, providing "plain" tripe, and the latter looking much like a honeycomb, and regarded as the tastiest. As is true for intestines, preparation of tripe is lengthy, requiring ninety minutes of simmering before becoming tender; tripe sold commercially usually is white, the result of lengthy and tedious soaking in lime, then in brine, and boiling.

The good news is that most tripe is sold in stores cleaned and prepared for cooking, so the repeated lengthy washings and soakings at home are unnecessary, although it still must be simmered before eating. Tripe also is available ready-cooked or pickled. Tripes a la mode de Caen, the most famous of French tripe dishes—cooked with calves' feet, garlic, thyme, bay leaf, beef fat, cider, and Calvados—is available tinned. Pickled tripe is usually sold thoroughly cooked, but should be parboiled before using. Canned tripe is ready to heat and serve.

Tripe is eaten throughout most of Europe. In France, tripe may be cooked with pig's trotters, goose fat, or white wine, and the pig's caul, the lace-like, fatty membrane around the paunch, is the binding used for crepinettes, small forcemeat sausages made from lamb or pork. The French also use it to wrap pates. (Occasionally found fresh, usually caul is sold frozen; thaw it until you can peel off as much as needed, then refreeze.) Another French sausage, the *andouillette*, is made almost entirely of tripe and mesentery. The Spanish garnish tripe with chorizo, chili peppers, garlic, and thin strips of sweet red pepper. In Bulgaria, there is a popular tripe soup. In Arabian countries, it is boiled with cumin, pepper, and the rind of citrus (oranges and lemons most commonly). In Mexico, it is a part of menudo. It also may be cut into one-inch squares and batter-fried or dipped into egg and breaded and fried until crisp, another beer snack. Almost everywhere, the classic dish is a white stew with onions.

In China, honeycomb tripe is simmered for an hour and a half with soy sauce and star anise, then sliced and eaten. Bruce Cost in his book *Asian Ingredients* suggests simmering in water or a light stock with wine and ginger, then sliced and stir-fried or tossed in a Beijing-style salad with a mustard-sesame sauce. Asian cooks also use caul fat to wrap pork liver. In Sri Lanka, it is cut into one-inch cubes and cooked in a rich curry. It may also be marinated, then fried or grilled; stewed with tomatoes and other vegetables; and cooked in broth, wine, or cider.

Americans may be surprised to learn that it is often one of the ingredients in hot dogs.

Pass the mustard.

Sausage for the Duke of Este

"Take pigs' throats and cut out the fat, but keep the clean, smooth glands. Slice the loins finely; also the ears (well scoured), and the snouts; peel the tongues and wash them thoroughly in hot water; bone, scrub and singe the trotters; clean the testicles. Lay the ears, snouts and trotters on the bottom of a good clean pot and cover with coarse salt. On top put the tongues, then the throats, loins and testicles sprinkled with fine salt. Let the pot stand for 3 days, then swill out with red wine. Soak the lot with red wine for another day. Drain, rinse several times to get rid of the salt, and dry with clean white cloths. Pack the ingredients tight into a sausage skin. Use at once or store."

—Cristoforo di Messisgbugo,
chef to the Duke of Este in Parma, 16th century

Ears, Eyes, Noses, Lungs, Tongues, Lips, Gums, Glands & Feet

I was fourteen or fifteen, a Boy Scout going cross-country by train from the US East Coast, where I lived, to New Mexico, where I would spend a month on a Boy Scout ranch (and eat my first bison meat). On the way, we stopped in Chicago, where one of our stops was the Hormel slaughterhouse. Our guide led us past hundreds of cattle, sheep, and pigs, crammed together in rough plank pens between the rail lines and the slaughterhouse and then into a huge building where the butchering of pigs was done. As we entered, a large hog was released into a space about the size of my small bedroom back home, except this one was wall-to-wall cement and there was no furniture, only a large handcuff-like device hanging from the ceiling at the end of a chain.

A man in a blood-splattered butcher's jacket that went to his knees grabbed the disoriented pig by one of its hind legs and attached the handcuff. Instantly the hog was lifted up so that it was suspended at a height that made it easy for the man to open its throat with a knife. Gravity quickly emptied the beast of its blood supply, which fell to the cement floor and disappeared down a drain. The hog was then transported along an overhead rail, still hung by its hind foot, to the next station in the slaughterhouse, to be steam-cleaned and have its bristly hair removed.

We were told that we would follow that hog through the building, to watch it being butchered and packaged for sale nationwide, and that it would provide the nourishment that kept our nation great, building fine young bodies like ours. Maybe when we got home, we were told, we'd have some of the bacon from that pig for breakfast. Our guide then said something that I remember to this day: "Every part of the pig is used, everything except the oink."

And so it is with many animals. Little or nothing is wasted. Other sections of this book consider blood, guts, and genitalia. In this one, I consider the other bits: the feet, the ears, the bones and marrow, the tails and snouts and tongues, the heads, some of the glands, the eyes, the gums, the lips, even the noses.

A friend of mine tells a story about why he won't eat sausage. He says he once took the time to read the list of contents on the package and while he found it (barely) acceptable to consider consuming most of the ingredients that went into the pulpy mix, when he got to the ingredient identified only as "parts," he blanched. No way, he said, would he eat "parts." Which is too bad. Because probably most of those parts are not only edible, but tasty and nourishing.

The head of the animal offers such nutritious variety, I wonder why it is discarded or ignored by so many when the eyes, ears, the tongue, the brain, and the flesh on the skull itself, especially the fleshy cheeks, give up such valuable protein, minerals and vitamins, as well as a succulent taste. Many cultures, now and in the past, have savored the head of the ox, pig, and calf as a delicacy, most notably nowadays in Asia and Asian groceries, where you will find heads of animals staring at you, usually between the pigs' feet and the gigantic slabs of tongue.

Many nice things can be done with the heads—which have a surprising amount of meat attached to all that bone—although usually they are roasted whole in much the same way any other large piece of meat or poultry is cooked, for three to four hours on a rack in a baking pan, basted every thirty minutes or so, served when the skin is crisp, or as the centerpiece for a hearty stew. They may also be boiled until the meat falls off the bones, this becoming either a soup (in warm climates) or jellied (in colder regions). Calf's head also provides much of the protein for Mock Turtle Soup.

The heads of pigs and calves, and sometimes sheep, are the most common in Oriental and specialty meat markets, usually bought whole and skinned, although it is sometimes sold split in half with the tongue intact and the eyes removed. The flesh is tender and gelatinous, perfect when corned for making head-cheese (called brawn) and other jellied meat dishes. In Britain, smoked pig's cheeks, called "bath chaps," are usually boiled and eaten cold like ham, while the meat of the calf's head is eaten cold as a luncheon dish with a light vinaigrette sauce. Sheep's Head Broth is a popular Scottish dish, in several countries in the Middle East a dish of broth and meat of slowly simmered sheep's head and trotters is made, and in South Africa the head of an ox is baked.

Some internal organs may comprise some of the "parts" that my friend is worried about. For example, the pancreas and thymus glands, called sweetbreads; the spleen, called melt; and the lungs, called lights. The spleen is a fine sausage ingredient and with the heart and lungs may be used in stews, while the pancreas and thymus glands from the neck and heart of young animals can be braised, fried, or sautéed. In some areas, however, lung is a major taboo; in the US and Japan and several other developed countries, the import of haggis, a Scottish dish, has been banned because sheep's lung is an integral ingredient.

Holding the head and all those body parts upright are the feet, or trotters, of slaughtered animals. Although they consist principally of skin, bone, and cartilage, they also contain some meat and, when boiled, provide gelatin, at one time an essential step in making jelly. The hooves of pigs, sheep, and calves and a number of other animals are eaten today in Asia matter-of-factly, and are sold with other offal in groceries wherever Asian populations have taken up residence.

Lambs' and pigs' trotters generally are sold already blanched, but must be boned, singed (to remove the little hairs between the hooves) and generally are cooked in a bouillon, then braised, broiled, grilled, or fried and eaten hot with or without a sauce, added to stews for extra richness, or jellied for eating cold. The poor in England traditionally have brined then boiled pig's trotters for several hours, serving cold with vinegar, and in Poland served with in saurkraut soup.

Shoppers for pigs' feet might keep in mind that the front ones are meatier than the hind ones, and may also wish to ask the butcher to cut them into eight pieces each. (They are hellaciously difficult to chop into sections with a cleaver at home, unless you have a huge chopping block and a wicked overhand swing with the cleaver, or perhaps will use a chainsaw.) The Chinese use the feet to make a somewhat bony but delicious stew, with sweetened black vinegar and fresh ginger. While in Sri Lanka it is more common to boil the trotters, adding cinnamon, coconut milk, and curry leaves, serving the meat with boiled potato or cucumber. In Italy, a pork sausage that is stuffed into a hollowed-out pig's trotter instead of a casing is called *zampone*.

Bones and marrow play a larger role in what we eat than most of us realize. How many times did I watch my mother put leftover chicken or turkey bones into a pot of boiling water to produce a healthy soup stock? Experiments carried out as long ago as the 17th century and as recently as 1988, show that bones cooked under pressure sufficiently long enough disintegrate, yielding both marrowfat and a pulp which may be used for thickening sauces.

Some bones may also be crushed and browned in an oven then cooked with vegetables and herbs to make stock for sauces. Lamb chops, chicken legs and wings, turkey drumsticks, and most other bones are also fun to gnaw on, and nourishing, although it is considered by some to be coarse or impolite. (Except in yuppie bars where Buffalo Wings—which have nothing to do with buffalo—are dipped into catsup by hand between cell phone calls.)

Marrow, the soft, fatty goop in the centers of long bones (shoulder bones, fore and hind legs), is one of the richest protein sources available. Just breaking the bones and sucking the marrow is a wonderful experience, even when it's the little dollop of glop found in the middle of a slice of baked ham. Marrow is used in sauces, soups, stews, and in the Italian rice dish (cooked in fat and stock) called rissoto. Elisabeth Luard in her book *European Peasant Cookery* (1988) recommends marrow bone as "a treat for high tea or a savory after the meal instead of a pudding."

Now, imagine a tongue that is more than a foot long and weighs two kilograms (four to five pounds). That is about average for an adult ox and even the smaller tongues of calves, young pigs, and lambs have impressive heft and size. The most commonly served tongues, those of the larger mammals—including wild game and horse—may be prepared in a variety of ways: in stews or ragouts, boiled or grilled, pickled and smoked, au gratin, and often cold, sliced thinly and delivered to the table with a vinaigrette sauce or in sandwiches. Pork tongue may be marinated and roasted, simmered, and fried. Tongue sliced thinly and served with mustard and fresh, sliced onions makes a delicious sandwich. And dog tongue—I tried it once near the China border in Vietnam—sliced and stir-fried in oil with Chinese cabbage makes for a tasty, if somewhat chewy dish. In fact, the tongue has been cherished all the way back to Roman times, when flamingo tongue was on more than one emperor's dinner plate.

Tongue often is sold ready to serve, but it is more usual to buy it fresh, smoked, corned or seasoned in brine, for cooking and eating hot or cold, with or without a sauce. Beef and veal tongues are the commonest, lamb tongues thought to be the most tender, although all tongue is tough and requires long, slow cooking. (Stop for a minute and pinch your own tongue between your thumb and first finger; that is not a piece of meat that is quickly tenderized.) If purchased fresh, it is necessary to soak the tongue for up to twelve hours in water that is changed several times. Fat is then removed and the tongue is placed in boiling water and skinned. (After making an incision at the root and along the top, pulling the rough outer layer toward the lip.) Sprinkle with salt and let sit in the refrigerator for about twenty-four hours. Now you're ready to go.

Pigs' and calves' ears offer another protein treat that may be boiled, fried, sautéed, braised, grilled, stuffed, made into a gratin, or added to a stew or soup. In parts of China, they are cooked for up to two hours until the cartilage is crunchy, then cut into narrow strips and mixed with sprouts and garlic, and served with soy sauce and chili oil. They may also be cooked until tender and combined with thinly sliced carrots, cucumbers and onions and tossed lightly with plum sauce, then served on lettuce, chilled. (This is a salad that could also incorporate sliced duck web or jellyfish.) Brushed with crushed garlic and deep-fried until crispy, they also make a delicious alternative to potato crisps. Before cooking, they must be cleaned thoroughly, blanched, scraped, and dried.

Now we get to the funny bits, the "parts" that some may consider the most difficult to eat: the eyes, the snouts, the gums, the lips. Even *Larousse Gastronomique*, known for its patrician but generally open mind, doesn't mention eyes, lips, or gums, although calves' and pigs' ears get a full page of mouth-watering recipes. *The Oxford Companion to Food* is marginally more complete, giving brief attention to eyes, while ignoring lips and gums.

Eyes may be plucked from virtually anything cooked—from chicken to cow to fish—and chewed or chased with a shot of liquor. In many cultures, they are considered a delicacy, although making a meal of them is logistically challenging. In the Middle East, sheep's eyeballs are considered a great delicacy, as well as a great challenge to any western visitor who might be offered one, especially if it is removed with the point of a dagger and presented straight from the skull.

Lips and gums comprise an even rarer treat. I've seen them on a menu only once, at a Laotian restaurant in Bangkok where *nguak wua thot* (fried beef gums) is one of the dishes that pulls the crowds who ooh and ahh over the choice, but usually order something else. (The same restaurant also served a piquant salad with ant eggs, but that isn't one of the favorites, either.)

Perhaps my friend, who rejected sausage that contained "parts" might welcome them if they were identified and served as good parts should be served, rather than hidden in mystery.

Moose Nose Jelly

Among the Eskimos, the head of the moose—or at least a prominent part of it—is turned into Moose Nose Jelly. In recipes from both Canada's Ministry of Indian Affairs and the Cooperative Extension Service of the University of Alaska, the upper jaw bone of the moose is cut just below the eyes and boiled, then chilled and after the hairs have been removed, washed and boiled again, this time with garlic, spices and vinegar. The large, fleshy nose is next simmered until the meat is tender. When cool, the meat is removed and the bones and cartilage are discarded. The meat—white from the bulb of the nose, dark from along the bones and jowls—is sliced thinly, the original broth is brought to another boil and poured over the meat in a loaf pan. It is then cooled until the jelly sets, sliced and serve cold.

Mannish Water (Sheep's Head Stew)

4 qts water (or enough to cover head)	2 dasheens, peeled and cubed
2 lbs sheep head, feet, or both	2 lbs potatoes, peeled and cubed
2 lbs lamb stew meat	1/4 pumpkin (Big Mama squash),
2 small onions, chopped	peeled and cubed
2 garlic cloves, minced	6 green bananas, peeled
10 pimento (all-spice) berries	5 scallions, finely chopped
10 whole black peppercorns	3 whole Scotch bonnet peppers
3 bay leaves	2 cups Jamaican Overproof
1/2 cup vegetable oil	white rum
4 carrots, diced	Salt to taste

In a large, heavy pot, combine the water, head, meat, onions, garlic, pimento, peppercorns, bay leaves, and salt. Bring the mixture to a rolling boil, and skim off any scum. Cover the pot, and over medium heat, cook for 30 minutes, or until the meat falls off the bone.

Sauté the carrots, dasheen, potatoes, pumpkin, green bananas, scallions, and peppers in the oil for 3–5 minutes, then add to the stew. Cook the stew at least an hour, 2–3 hours is better, and then add the rum. Cook 1 hour more before serving. This should serve 10–12. Adding finely chopped banana peel makes the soup extra mannish.

—Courtesy, Maple Leaf Farms

Marrow Bones

2 thigh or femur bones of beef cattle   Bread for toasting
Flour and water paste

Have the bones sawn into 3-inch lengths and seal the cut ends with a stiff paste of flour and water. Wrap the bones tightly in a floured cloth and put them to simmer in plenty of salted water for an hour. Or bake them at 300°F in the oven for an hour. Serve the bones as they are, with a knife or a long thin spoon to scoop out the delicious marrow onto fresh, hot toast.

—Elisabeth Luard European Peasant Cooking

Pickled Lamb Tongues

6–8 lamb tongues   2 bay leaves
3 peppercorns   2 tablespoons salt
6 whole cloves   1/2 cup vinegar (5% acid)

Place tongues in saucepan and cover with hot water. Simmer for 1 hour.

Add peppercorns, cloves, bay leaves, salt, and vinegar. Cover simmer until fork tender. Cool in broth. Peel and clean.

Put peeled tongues in sterile canning jars. Skim fat off broth and bring to a boil again. Pur broth through a strainer over the tongues. Seal and refrigerate or freeze.

Serving suggestions: slice and use in sandwiches; dice, brown in butter, add claret wine and simmer 45 minutes, then addraisins and/or mushrooms, and serve hot on biscuits, toast, or rice; dice or thinly slice, marinate 1 hour and add apple, celery, or olives, and serve on lettuce.

—Maine Whole Lamb Cookbook by Sarah Miller,
courtesy Maple Lawn Farms

Brains

To many movie-goers, one of the most upsetting scenes in recent cinema history was one in *Indiana Jones and the Temple of Doom* , the 1984 film in which Harrison Ford, playing Jones, an adventurous anthropologist, is served a meal of unusual foods, including monkey brains. The way the scene played out, live monkeys were strapped into position beneath the dining table, into which there were cut circular holes. The monkey's furry skulls were then fitted into the holes from beneath, the cap of the skull was neatly removed, and Mr. Jones was given a spoon.

I bet I've heard someone tell me that story a dozen times, always in horror or disgust. "You wouldn't really eat monkey brains, would you?" they ask. I don't know what upset them most, the fact that it was a monkey—a small primate distantly related to humans and bearing a sort of resemblance—or the fact that the little creature was being consumed alive. Either way, I don't think I've ever met anyone who thinks eating monkey brains might be acceptable, let alone tasty.

Or the brains of any other animal, for that matter. Let's face it, brains have earned an esteemed place in gourmet cooking, but most Westerners withdraw in abhorrence, and possibly hostility, at the very idea of eating something that once housed even the most primitive thought. In a list of 143 foods presented to a sample of Americans, brains, together with tripe and kidneys, were overwhelmingly rejected.

However unappetizing the scene in the movie may have been to many cinema fans, eating monkey brains with a spoon was not the invention of a screen writer looking for shock. Digging into a just-opened primate cranium is far from common, but it is reportedly practiced in some restaurants in China today, as well as in some "underground" restaurants elsewhere in Asia where customers pay a premium for the exotic experience. (The price a Hong Kong journalist quoted me was US$300 for a small monkey.)

There are, however, some that say that the tradition of eating live monkey brains is an urban myth or, at best (or worst), something that the demand created, rather than the other way around. Not so, the eating of brains of other animals.

Technically, the brain is the part of the central nervous system enclosed in the skull of vertebrates, serving to control mental and physical actions. In the culinary world, brain is considered white offal, offal being a term used to describe "variety meats," those internal organs and extremities of an animal which usually are removed (in this case, along with the rest of the head) before the carcass is cut up into chops and steaks. The editors of *Larousse Gastronomique* insist that lamb's brain and sheep's brain are the best—sheep being the older and larger of the two—although the brains of calves and oxen are also commonly sold. Pig's brain is eaten less frequently and generally is harder to find, even in Chinese butcher shops, but some say it's tastier than calf brain.

In Europe in the 18th century, the brains of large animals were served to the most honored guest, the skull being pre-sawn so that it could be lifted off at the end of the meal, then eaten with a spoon; it was considered poor form to put a knife into so esteemed a body part. The brains of many game animals were also eaten matter-of-factly in Asia, Africa, and South America and Richard Burton, the 19th century Middle Eastern scholar and explorer, not the actor, wrote that gorilla brains were believed to be an aphrodisiac.

Sometimes the preparation has been simple, little more complicated than that which was done for Mr. Jones. In *New System of Domestic Cookery*, a book published in 1806 in London, Maria Elizabeth Rundell urged chefs serving hare to "cut off the head; put your knife between the upper and lower jaw, and divide them, which will allow you to lay the upper flat on your plate; then put the point of your knife into the center, and cut the head in two. The ears and brains may be helped then to those who like them." While in Norway in more recent times, there was a delicacy called *smala hove*. This was a sheep's head, cut in half and grilled on an open fire, using the skull halves as the cooking receptacles. The brains were then consumed with a spoon when done. They can also be made into fritters. In Evansville, Indiana, there is supposed to be a restaurant called the Dogtown Tavern where pig brains are breaded, deep-fried, garnished with sautéed onions and served on a bun. No doubt with catsup.

Care should be taken in buying and preparing brains. Because they are highly perishable, they should be fresh—bright pinkish-white in color, plump and firm when purchased—and used the same day. Preparation before cooking requires washing the organ with your hands. First, there is a thorough wash in cold water. (Some suggest the water be acidulated, with a small amount of vinegar or lime juice added.) Then the membranes and blood vessels are removed and again the brain is soaked in cold water for at least an hour. A final washing follows that—by which time the cook should be getting used to handling this specialty meat, or will have ordered a pizza by phone—and then the brain is blanched in salt water and, finally, cooked.

In the 1700s in France, brains were marinated in lemon and fried in a terrene or cooked in a pastry shell or loaf of bread (*en croutes*). One contemporary recipe suggests slicing an ox brain thinly, marinating in vinegar, salt, pepper, and lime, frying in deep fat after dusting with beaten egg, flour, or bread crumbs. In India and Sri Lanka, there are recipes for brain curry. The editors of *Larousse Gastronomique* are so enamored of the pale, lobed flesh they offer eight recipes under "brains"—more than the average number for most of the encyclope-dia's entries—and a dozen cross-references to other sections of the book, suggesting they be cooked in *court-bouillon* (a spiced, aromatic liquor or stock), fried in butter, battered and cooked in scorching-hot oil, served with glazed onions and mushroom caps after cooking in red wine...and once you start checking the cross-references, rubbed through a sieve to create forcemeat or stuffing, pureed in a blender or food processor, baked in a soufflé, or braised whole and left to cool, then cut in half and arranged on a bed of lettuce sprinkled with vinaigrette.

France may be at the forefront of brain gastronomy, but recipes in *Unmentionable Cuisine* (1979) include instructions from England (Brain Cakes), Russia (Brains in Lemon Sauce), Norway (Brain Dumplings), Germany (Brain Soup), Colombia (Calf's Brain with Tomatoes), and Indonesia (Brains in Coconut Cream).

Bruce Cost in his book *Asian Ingredients* (1988) prefers pork brains, saying they "are wonderful as a part of a Chinese custard that is steamed and cooled, then lightly fried in cubes." Still another source suggests baking, broiling, poaching, or frying, and serving with *buerre noir*, " black butter," butter that has been cooked over low heat until dark brown (but not black), usually flavored with vinegar or lemon juice, capers and parsley. While the *Woman's Day Encyclopedia of Cooking* provides recipes for Brain Batter Cakes (finely chopped brains and onion with sugar, Worcestershire sauce, curry powder, folded into batter and dropped by tablespoonfuls into hot fat) and Brains and Scrambled Eggs. Probably without catsup.

Two warnings are imperative. Mad Cow Disease is a fatal brain disorder that has led to the slaughter of more than 160,000 British cat-tle and, in the late 1980s and early 1990s was blamed for killing humans who ate the infected beef. In 1989, Britain banned the feeding of cow remains back to cows and in the years following ranchers were required to slaughter their herds to regain lost credibility in the marketplace. In 1997, two American doctors reported a possible link between eating squirrel brains, a backwoods delicacy in the southern United States, and the same disease. Dr. Eric Weisman, a behavioral neurologist who practices in rural Kentucky, reported in the distinguished British medical journal *The Lancet* that he had treated eleven people for Creutzfeldt-Jakob (the official name of the malady) in four years, and all had eaten squirrel brains at some time.

The second warning is more benign. Diners should be aware that while the brain of any animal is rich in phosphorous, proteins, and vitamins, and the fat content is only about one-fourth that found in a T-bone steak, the fat is extremely rich in cholesterol.

Scrambled Eggs with Brains

1 lb beef brains	6 eggs
Salt	1/8 teaspoon white pepper
Water	2 tablespoons butter
1 tablespoon cider vinegar	Chopped parsley
or lemon juice	Paprika

Soak brains in salted cold water for 15 minutes; drain and carefully remove membrane with tip of paring knife. Cover with boiling water; add 1 teaspoon salt and vinegar; simmer for 15 minutes. Drain, plunge into cold water, and drain again. Chop coarsely. Beat eggs slightly; add 1/2 teaspoon salt, pepper, and brains. Melt butter in frying pan; add egg mixture. Cook over low heat, stirring often, until set. Sprinkle with chopped parsley and paprika. Serves 4.

—Woman's Day Encyclopedia of Cooking

Genitalia

It is not difficult to understand why most modern diners might turn their noses up and roll their eyes in despair at the idea of eating an animal's genitals. Offer a soup made from deer or cow penis, or sheep testicles that have been deep-fried, and he or she likely will flee.

There is, however, one compelling reason that has made the genitals of four-legged creatures attractive to two-legged diners. In a word, it's called "testosterone," the sex hormone secreted by the testes. A feminist friend of mine calls the whole macho syndrome, of which slurping penis soup and masticating sheep testicles is a small part, "testosterone poisoning," defined as man's desire to be manly, and more manly, and even more manly than that. I confess I may be one of the men she's talking about.

It first happened in Mexico City, when in 1969 I found myself traveling with an American rock and roll band, the Doors, a group not known for its sissyness, whose lead singer wore leather trousers made from cowhide and unborn horse and who called himself the Lizard King. So when we all were taken to one of the Mexican capital's finest restaurants and one of the dishes served was a platter of deep-fried bull's testicles, most of us nervously tucked in. Some joked about how they'd always wondered what happened to the bull's balls following its humiliation in the corrida. Some pushed the gristly meat around the plate, as they had done with so many other uninvited dishes as small children, hoping it would appear that they were eating, when in truth they were trying to hide the evidence under a taco shell or beneath a pile of refried beans.

Still, most of us did consume at least a portion. Why? Because we were men, that's why. And that is why in parts of the world today there is something on many menus that has been euphemized for more than a century. They were called "lamb stones" in 19th century England, and today they are called "lamb fries." *Larouse Gastronomique*, the French encyclopedia of cookery that has a fancy French word for everything, calls them *animelles*, the latter being the culinary term for testicles (and sometimes *rognons blancs*, literally, "white kidneys"), and in the US they are called mountain or prairie oysters. Sometimes, they're found under the vague linguistic umbrella called "variety meat."

This macho attitude—testosterone poisoning, if my friend is correct, and I suspect she is—may have its variety meat cloaked in euphemism to suit contemporary conservatism, but it has historical roots that sink deep. Animal genitalia have been devoured to improve one's bedtime prowess and cure a number of ills as well as one's status among male friends for thousands of years in many parts of the world. What is termed "organotherapy" dates back at least to Roman times, when it was believed that eating a healthy animal's organ might correct some nagging ailment in the corresponding human organ, a belief and practice that continues to the present day.

In a Pharmacologia published in 1696, deer testicles, were hailed as an aphrodisiac and in 1739 and 1750, in medical texts sold in Sweden, the deer's penis was also prescribed against poisoning, bladder stones, and blood in the urine. Another, better known text, the notorious *Kama Sutra*, the Hindu guidebook whose origins dated back to the 4th century B.C. and was first translated into English in 1883, recommended ram's testicles boiled in milk and sugar.

The same 19th century Victorian explorer and amateur anthropologist who translated that text was named Richard Burton (not to be confused with the actor, although he probably suffered from testosterone poisoning, too) also translated a 15th century middle-eastern treatise entitled *The Perfumed Garden for the Soul's Delectation*, a book now regarded as an erotic classic. (Burton is better known for his translation of a book of *Near Eastern tales, Thousand and One Nights*, placed in what is now Iraq, which may explain you-know-who's testosterone level.) The author of the *The Perfumed Garden*, originally written in Arabic, was Shaykh Nefzawi, who claimed, "Pleasure is only given and felt by those who are well developed. He then who, having a little penis, wishes to improve and strengthen it for its task, should bathe it in warm water until it becomes red and swollen by the blood which will be drawn to it; let him now anoint it with honey mixed with ginger, and he will then be fully primed for his part. So great a pleasure will he now bestow upon the woman that she will be loathe to let him go. Another method is to make use of a donkey's pizzle. The organ is boiled with onions and wheat, and the resulting mess is fed to fowls with care afterwards killed and eaten. Or the pizzle may be soaked in oil and the oil then drunk..." What kind of oil was not specified, although likely it didn't matter.

Such genital imagination runs rampant in cookery even today, especially in Asia, where the belief that tiger penis soup will improve one's sex life has been blamed for helping drive the tiger to the doorway of extinction. The Wildlife Conservation Society in 1996 used this notion as the basis of an international advertising campaign, showing a bowl of soup with the headline, "SOME MEN BELIEVE THAT TIGER PENIS SOUP IS A POWERFUL APHRODISIAC. ACTUALLY, IT'S A LOAD OF OLD BULL." The advertisement went on to say that a single bowl of "tiger" soup cost as much as US$300, warning buyers that they should expect to be disappointed: "Firstly, because tiger penis soup usually is a load of old bull. Or ox. Or deer. Or any number of more commonplace substitutes. The counterfeiting of tiger penises (and tiger bones or other potions) is something of an art in Hong Kong and China. (At US$300 a bowl, it's something of a temptation.) And for those drinking the real thing? More depressing news. Testosterone simply cannot, we repeat, cannot be ingested through eating animal genitalia. Cooking steroids only inactivates them."

What the conservation society didn't mention, and might consider in any future campaigns, is that it isn't such a wondrous thing to gain the sexual prowess of a tiger, a beast that normally makes love for only fifteen seconds and then goes into the jungle to take a nap. Just like you know who. (And me.)

The society also failed to warn that what is sold as a tiger's penis may not even be a penis. "Many people, including staff at non-governmental organizations and members of the media, slam the trade in wildlife and their body parts, which seems to continue in Thailand," said Dr. Schwann Tunhikorn, head of the wildlife research of that country's Royal Forestry Department, in an interview in the *Bangkok Post* in 1998. "What they don't realize is that most of the merchandise is fake. I have never seen a real tiger's sexual organ in the market." The doctor went on to say that the phony penises usually were carved from cattle tendons. I have seen several for sale in northern Thailand. Even if I never saw a real tiger's penis to compare them to, the ridiculously low price of US$20 to $30 should have made it clear; the price for what is claimed to be the real thing is ten to twenty times that amount.

The illegal slaughter of tigers and sale of the great cat's genitals goes on, of course. Despite widespread efforts to control poachers, another conservationist group, the Wildlife Protection Society of India, estimates there are still 100 million potential users of tiger-based potions in the world. Most of these consumers are in Asia and with the increasing cost and illegality attached to eating an endangered species, other genitals are being used widely as substitutes. In 1994, for example, a Canadian company delivered 50,000 seal carcasses to China. And while the pelt, meat and oil of one seal sold for US$20, the genitals each went for more than $100.

All that said, it is not difficult to include genitalia in your diet without endangering any threatened animals. As mentioned, many restaurants in the United States serve Rocky Mountain Oysters, which generally are made from lamb's or sheep's testicles, and in Mexico, deep-fried bull's testicles are still a savored delicacy, thirty years after I passed a plate of them to Jim Morrison. They're also popular in Spain, Italy, the Middle East, and throughout much of Asia where there is a large Chinese population.

In Singapore there's a pricey place called the Imperial Herbal Restaurant, only a few steps from the famous Raffles Hotel. It may be the only restaurant with a resident Chinese herbalist, Dr Li Lian Xing, who emigrated from Tianjin, China, and now diagnoses customer ills or imbalances, recommending certain dishes or drinks on the menu as being helpful. On entering the restaurant, the first thing you see are large glass display cases containing deer antler and dried penises from assorted unthreatened species, and behind that a full-scale herbal pharmacy where, if one's luck holds, Dr. Li will suggest one of the house specialties—Bull Pizzles with Chinese Yam, perhaps. Prices start at about US$20 and go up, depending on the number of pizzles, to $40. The restaurant also offers a choice of wines where the ingredients include deer penis, starting at $12 a glass, with a two-liter bottle costing as much as $450!

At smaller sidewalk establishments in Singapore, penis soup is less expensive, but not always available. When I visited one, shortly after the Chinese New Year, the sign on the wall advertised cow penis soup for about $6 a bowl, and turtle penis soup was double that, but I was told that the restaurant's compete supply of penises had been consumed. (In Asia, those prices are much higher than those for, say, a bowl of noodle soup with pork or chicken, selling for under a dollar.) The taste? Nothing special, sad to say, as it's rather like any red meat broth. It's the anticipation of pleasures to come and the story westerners may tell once they get home that gives the dish its kick.

No less interesting is the Five Penis Wine available at the Snake King Completely & Restaurant in Guangzhou in China. Although this is a place that focuses on the reptile in its odd name, this wine reportedly is a drink that blends the snake penis with the genitals of ox, sheep, deer, and dog. When I tried it during a visit in 1997, it went down quite smoothly, although the dark sediment floating in it was a bit worrying. I was the only foreigner in the restaurant that night and was asked to join several tables for after-dinner drinks of it.

"*Ganbei!*" my new friends cried again and again. "Empty glass!" And perhaps empty of subsequent performance, too.

Like other organ meats, testicles may be cooked in a variety of ways—deep-fried whole as I experienced in Mexico; cut into broad, thin slices and marinated in oil, lemon juice, chopped parsley, salt and pepper, then fried in batter; and sliced and cooked in butter and a cream sauce with blanched and sautéed sliced mushrooms.

Like the heart, kidney, and some other organ meat, genitalia tend to be a bit chewy.

Will Viagra Save the Tiger?

The scientists who invented Viagra were awarded a Nobel Prize in 1998 for giving millions of men a pharmaceutical solution to impotence. Because the prescription drug also found widespread acceptance as a sex-enhancer, even when erectile dysfunction was a minor factor or didn't even exist, those scientists may soon be given an award by organizations struggling to protect endangered species.

According to a report from Tokyo by Agence France Presse in early 1999, "ancient cures, most based on Chinese medicine, are being swept aside" by Viagra sales. "Viagra, already a hot black-market item in Japan before its official release, is threatening sales in Tokyo of tiger and seal testicles..." the news agency said.

Add the outbreak of SARS in 2003, which was blamed on a virus that jumped from numerous exotic animals eaten in China for similar purposes, and it's reasonable to think Viagra, and alternative pharmaceutical boosts, may, in fact, save several endangered species.

Bull's Ball Pie

Boil 4 bulls' testicles together with salt. Cut into slices and sprinkle with salt, pepper, nutmeg, and cinnamon. Then, in a pie crust, place layers of sliced testicles alternated with mince of lamb kidneys, ham, marjoram, cloves, and thyme.

—*Bartomolo Scappi, chef to Pope Pius V, 16th Century*

Rocky Mountain Oysters

40 lamb testicles	1 cup white wine
1 or 2 cloves garlic, chopped	Salt & pepper to taste
1/2 onion, chopped	A little Tabasco to taste
2 tablespoons corn starch	1 cup water

Wash and clean oysters thoroughly. Boil until tender, about 30–45 minutes. Drain thoroughly. Fry oysters, onion and garlic until brown. Dissolve corn starch in water; add the oysters. Add wine and let simmer until sauce thickens. Add wine and let simmer until sauce thickens. Add seasonings and serve steaming hot. Serves 4.

Lamb Fries

1 qt lamb testicles
1 onion, chopped
1 to 3 cloves garlic, chopped
3 tablespoons parsley
1 7 oz can Ortega salsa

4 green peppers, chopped,
    or 1 small can Ortega chilies
1/4 cup white wine
Salt & pepper to taste

Cook fries in salted water for about 20 minutes or until done. Skim foam from water as it appears. When done, drain and rinse in cold water. Fry onion and peppers in small amount of oil. When onion and peppers are limp, add garlic and parsley. Add fries and fry to a few minutes. Add salsa, salt, pepper, and white wine and simmer, covered, for about 15–20 minutes.

—*Courtesy, Maple Leaf Farm, 1997*

Double-Boiled Penis Soup

4 oz penis (deer, beef, etc.)
1 cup rice wine
10–12 cups water

Herbs & spices a packaged
    at Chinese pharmacy

Soak meat in rice wine for a few minutes to remove the strong smell. Scrub with salt, rinse with hot water, and boil for 1–2 minutes. Take out and scrub again, then chop into small pieces.

Put meat and herbs together in the double-boiler with water and cook over a high heat for 1 1/2–2 hours. Usually there are several herb packages available, the mixtures created according to the customer's needs. Some are for the blood (circulation), others for stamina, etc. When purchasing, merely tell the pharmacist what you are doing and ask his advice.

When ready to serve, remove the meat and drink only the broth.

Urine

Some years ago, when my then-wife and I were unsuccessful in our efforts to have a child together, we sought means by which we might better our odds and fertility. One of our friends at the time was Dave Guard, a musician and singer who was one of the founding members of the Kingston Trio, American recording artists popular during the early Sixties folk music boom. Twenty years later, he was spending much of his time in Tibet and when we told him about our predicament, he said that when Tibetans wanted to get pregnant, the husband and wife drank each other's urine. We were aghast. We told him that we'd think about it.

As it turns out—and neither my wife nor I knew this at the time—there were many besides Dave Guard and the childless Tibetans who believed in "urine therapy," a field of study that says human urine—usually your own, not someone else's—may be a cure for a number of illnesses, good for the skin tone, and a way to cleanse the physical body of impurities as well as promote spiritual growth, while offering something nutritious. So widespread was this belief that in 1996 some 600 delegates from seventeen nations traveled to India, meeting in Goa in what may be one of the most unusual "scientific" gatherings in modern times, the first World Conference on Auto-Urine Therapy.

The three-day meeting was organized by the Indian chapter of the Water of Life Foundation, bringing together leading proponents of what was declared to be a 5,000-year-old therapy that fell into disuse in this century and was considered taboo in most of the world. Conference delegates didn't care, thumbing their nose at the world's majority by hanging posters that showed a young boy urinating into a glass.

They also paid loud and approving tribute to Morarji Desai, who, shortly after succeeding Indira Gandhi as India's prime minister in 1977, shocked the international community by announcing that his excellent state of health could be explained by his longtime practice of drinking his own urine, a glass each morning, taken in much the same way others have a cup of coffee or tea. At the time he was in his eighties and to this day—he died aged ninety-seven—in India, urine has been called *Morarji Cola*.

This isn't just one of those quirky habits that seem to be so numerous in India. Books on the subject, advocating the daily intake principally for medicinal purpose, have been written not only by Indians, but also by Germans, Englishmen, Dutch, Japanese, Chinese, and Thais. Quoting another speaker at that conference, an estimated five million Germans drank their own urine and in 2001, the official Xinhua news agency in China said three million Chinese did the same thing.

There were celebrity adherents, too. Delegates at that convention in Goa also acknowledged Sarah Miles, the English actress who starred in *The Servant, Ryan's Daughter*, and many other films, who said it improved their health. And J.D. Salinger's daughter Margaret wrote in her memoir *Dream Catcher* (2000) that her author-father did the same thing.

Are these people quacks, or what? Drinking urine certainly seems radical. As it turns out, consuming the yellowish liquid excreted by the kidneys has a long history, much of it in India, where it has been associated with the yoga and tantra tradition for perhaps as long as five millennia. A document said to be that old, called *Shivambu Kalpa Vidhi* ("the method of drinking urine in order to rejuvenate") calls urine "a divine nectar...capable of abolishing old age and various types of diseases and ailments. The follower should first ingest his urine and then start his meditation." *Shivambu* literally means "the water of Shiva," the highest god in the Indian pantheon, whose name means "auspiciousness." In India, at least among urine enthusiasts, one often hears the phrase "drinking *Shivambu*," which simply means drinking the water of auspiciousness. Urine also is described as harmless in the Buddhist text *Phra Traipidok* (or *Triptaka*).

Definite rules for ingesting urine were established early. Only "midstream" liquid was recommended, meaning that the first and last ten milliliters were to be discarded, because the first flow was too pungent and the last was lacking in strength. Before drinking, the mouth was to be cleansed, and the liquid was to be sipped like tea and drunk one to four times a day, usually upon awakening and following meals. The rule-makers also suggested a urine fast, where it was consumed only with water and no other food or liquid. It's clear that believers take this urine drinking seriously.

In 1747, German author Johann Heinrich Zedler wrote, "One can best heal injuries to eyes with honey dissolved in the lightly-boiled urine from a young man." He also said that mixing it with sulfur and potato helped prevent hair loss and "in the beginning stages of dropsy, one should drink one's own morning urine on an empty stomach for a prolonged period of time." In the same century, French and German physicians used it to treat jaundice, rheumatic disorder, gout, sciatica, and asthma. In more modern times, Dr. John W. Armstrong, a British convert to urine therapy and author of a book called *The Water of Life*, claimed to have treated over 40,000 patients starting in 1925 for ailments ranging from cancer to tuberculosis. In the 1940s, many German doctors routinely gave urine enemas to children exposed to measles or smallpox and today it is credited by various "experts" as helping alleviate the symptoms of or cure everything from cancer to sinusitis, from mad cow disease to the flu.

Mainstream physicians scoff. There is general agreement that small amounts probably won't hurt anyone—although the *U.S. Army Survival Manual* warns readers not to drink it, saying it contains "harmful body wastes"—and it is difficult to find anyone in the Western medical establishment willing to endorse it. They say there hasn't been sufficient study and insist that the literature of urine therapy is not scientifically based, that it is based on anecdotal evidence, i.e., the unsubstantiated testimonials of enthusiasts. There also is a substantial body of medical opinion that insists becoming exposed to any body fluids—from blood to saliva to urine—is to risk becoming HIV+.

Supporting literature is substantial, nonetheless. Numerous books on the subject have been published, and remain in print, although sometimes they're difficult to find. These include *A Miracle of Auto-Urine Therapy, The Fountain of Health and Beauty* by Dr Ryoichi Nakao, chairman of the Miracle Cup of Liquid Institute in Japan (which has been translated into Thai) and, what is regarded as the definitive book, *The Golden Fountain: The Complete Guide to Urine Therapy*, a text written by Coen van der Kroon of the Netherlands, who said, "I splash it on my face as an aftershave." In addition, *A Very Special Juice*, written by a German radio journalist, Carmen Thomas, reportedly sold 750,000 copies.

Adherents contend that it is not a toxic waste. They agree that urea, making up 2.5 per cent of urine, can be poisonous when present in large amounts in the blood, yet it also is urea that is used worldwide as a key ingredient in many skin products. They also warn that urine therapy is based on the principle of "natural cycles." So long as we do not interfere chemically with the body's natural cycle, they say, the body produces urine that is suitable for re-cycling. However, if you ingest chemical substances—and processed foods contain chemicals—some of them will end up in the urine, in which case the composition of the urine changes.

The literature suggests a variety of ways of ingesting this pungent yellow liquid: drinking it, of course (morning urine is claimed to be the best, starting with a few drops, building up to a glass a day), and using it as a gargle (good for toothaches, colds, and sore throats), as an enema, ear- and eye-drops, or vaginal douche (for yeast problems). For those for whom the idea of drinking urine is a problem, the Water of Life people suggest mixing a few ounces with the morning juice. Many modern adherents also suggest including it as an ingredient in traditional Indian dishes.

Urine has other uses. When you step on a sea urchin or get a bee sting, and you don't have any meat tenderizer handy (this being the most widely accepted first aid), urinating on the wound is the next best thing to do. I've done that. But, drink it?

Who knows? In *Waterworld*, one of the most expensive Hollywood movies ever made up to that time (1995), in the opening scene, a web-toed Kevin Costner urinates into a cup and drinks its contents. It could start a small trend. Even if it doesn't, the movie is certain to find an audience in India.

By the way, my wife and I did not drink each other's urine, as the singer Dave Guard suggested. And we did not get pregnant.

Mango Urine Lassi

1 cup unflavored yogurt
2 tablespoons sugar
1/2 cup urine

1/2 cup mango pulp
Ice cubes

Put all the above into a blender. Blend well and serve immediately. Other fruit may be used when mangos are out of season.

—*Vanda Balbir, owner-chef,*
Mrs. Balbir's, traditional Indian restaurant, Bangkok

Human Flesh

When I tell people that I took the placenta home following the birth of my son and the next day served it as a paté, they generally (1) don't believe me, or (2) recoil in horror, calling me a cannibal. My dictionary defines the word as "a person who eats human flesh" or "an animal that eats its own kind." I guess that makes me, technically, a cannibal, but I feel a long distance from all the images of cannibalism in history, where a missionary or white hunter is being cooked in a large iron pot by natives with bones in their noses.

This is how it happened. I was married, I had a daughter about two years old, and I was living in London, where my wife gave birth to our son in a private nursing home near our flat. I think it was right after he emerged that I told the doctor that I wanted to take the placenta home with me.

The placenta is the organ attached to the lining of the uterus that provides for the nourishment of the fetus. It is expelled by the woman's body following the child's delivery and as a rule is discarded, at least in developed nations. In some other places—including our London flat—it was considered food, and trashing it along with bloody bandages and used rubber gloves and other medical debris seemed to us a waste. After all, this was the organ that had nourished our unborn child and although the baby no longer had a need of it, it remained rich in protein, vitamins and minerals.

My wife was to return home the day following and my plan was to cook the placenta and make it into a paté to serve visitors who had been invited to meet the baby. When I asked, the doctor agreed in wonderment and said there was no danger so long as it was kept refrigerated and eaten promptly. He told us that it would taste much like liver.

There then arose the question about how to get it home. Unlike restaurants, medical clinics don't have Styrofoam take-away containers. We settled on a large, plastic bag of the sort used for garbage. As I was walking home, at four in the morning, the bag slung over my shoulder, I wondered what I'd say if a British bobby stopped me and asked what I had in the bag.

Fortunately, I encountered no policemen and the next day I sautéed the placenta in butter and garlic, then chopped it into small pieces, and turned it into a dark brown paste in the blender. Oops. I had forgotten to de-vein the organ, so there were small bits of gristle throughout. This was a major *faux pas* in cooking, I guess, but I served it anyway, chilled, with whole wheat crackers and slices of raw onion for garnish. Much to my amazement, a couple of our guests actually tried it.

Our serving placenta paté may seem a deliberate oddity, designed to shock our friends, or may be written off by some as something only hippies would do. (My wife and I then would have admitted we belonged to that group, happily.) The truth is, from a historical perspective, what we were doing was not unusual. The consumption of human flesh had a long and sometimes approving history. From the days when Neanderthals walked the earth, from southwestern Colorado to southeastern France, grilled human leg was okay.

The evidence is in. In 1981, archeologist Tim White of the University of California Berkeley in 1981 found a 60,000-year-old skull from an early human ancestor in Ethiopia, noticing that the skull had a series of fine, deep cut marks on the cheekbone and eye socket where the flesh appeared to have been stripped away with a knife. The marks were judged to show the "signature of cannibalism," which differed from damage done by war, normal injury, burial practices, and scavenging animals. Dr. White compared that skull to the bones of twenty-nine individuals from the Anasazi pueblos in Colorado in the United States, the spectacular, apartment-like cliff dwellings that are now a major tourist attraction. Carbon dating the bones, tools and pottery found back to the 12th century, and using an electronic microscope to examine 2,106 bone fragments to identify cut marks, burn traces, and so on, he proposed a new category of bone damage called "pot polish." These were the shiny abrasions left on bone tips that came from being stirred in pots. He concluded that the Anasazi people processed their colleagues by skinning them, cutting the muscle tissue into chunks and roasting it, baking their long bones, crushing their skinny bones, putting all of the pieces into pots over open fires, stirring vigorously.

White's investigation was taken further in 2000 by Richard Marlar, a pathologist at the University of Colorado, who reported in Nature magazine the discovery of butchery tools stained with human blood and the scattered, battered bones of even people bearing the marks of those tools. In addition, human myoglobin was found present in a cooking pot, as well as in a human coprolite, a piece of ancient, desiccated fecal material.

The consumption of human flesh continued for centuries. Beginning in the Tang and especially during the Ming and Ch'ing dynasties in China (7th through 18th centuries), for example, it was common when all normal medical resources failed to cure a dying parent, the daughter or daughter-in-law (or, less often, a son) would cut a piece of flesh from her or his thigh and cook it in a broth to offer it to the patient to drink. Evidence to the contrary, it was believed that miraculous recovery would be made.

The consumption of human flesh as medicine, called *ko ku*, or *gegu* in Chinese literature, may be rooted in a story about Princess Miao Shan, the human incarnation of Kuan Yin, the goddess of mercy, who offered her eyes and hands to save her dying father. This theme is also prominent in the stories of the previous lives of Buddha, representing the Buddhist tenet of compassion.

Most of the incidence of modern cannibalism has been reported by explorers, missionaries, and others from the west who discovered it in primitive societies and always cited it as evidence of native savagery. In literature, this attitude goes back to the Greek myths of Saturn devouring his children and the Cyclops eating Odysseus's sailors. Homovores also are a staple ingredient, so to speak, of early tales as diverse as the *Thousand and One Nights*, in which Sinbad the Sailor was shipwrecked and rescued by a king who then fed him human flesh, and Marco Polo's highly imaginative narrative in which he said the soldiers of Kublah Khan ate the flesh of men who died on the battle-field. "I assure you," Mr. Polo wrote, "that they go about every day killing men and drink the blood and then devour the whole body."

The 18th century satirist Jonathan Swift, best known for writing *Gulliver's Travels*, used the same subject when he penned an essay in 1729, *A Modest Proposal*, suggesting that the solution to the food short-ages in England and Ireland might be to eat some of the children. Even novelist Robert Louis Stevenson, who lived his final years in the 19th century in the Marquesas in the South Pacific, reported seeing "the last eater of long-pig in Nuka-Hiva" striding along a beach with a dead man's arm across his shoulder. "So does Kooamua to his enemies!" Stevenson said the man roared to passers-by, taking a bite from the raw flesh.

Missionaries returning from Latin America told similar stories and one writer described a tribe of man-eaters in Africa as having pointed teeth that fit together like those of a fox; that he had never been to Africa, nor had any hard evidence to support his claim was unim-portant. The invading Spanish in the Caribbean similarly said that the Caribs salted and dried their victims' flesh at a time when salting was unknown to them. While some of the tales appeared to ring true—the Aztecs are thought to have eaten thousands of prisoners of war—much of what was reported at the time is now known to be poppycock, although it does seem to be true that they made cakes with grain and human blood shaped into the forms of their gods. What emerged from the overwhelming attack was, however, as one contemporary writer put it, "greater evidence of a prurient curiosity within developed cul-tures about cannibalism than of its widespread practice outside them."

In fact, many cannibalistic practices had strong cultural roots, in the belief that existed in many parts of the world that eating one's ancestors would incorporate their benevolent spirits, or that making a meal of one's enemies would give the diner the deceased's strengths; eat the brains and you gain his wisdom, eat his heart and you ingest his courage, and so on. When Captain James Cook was killed by Hawaiian natives in 1779, his body was returned the following day to his surviving officers reduced to a heap of bones wrapped in native cloth, the flesh having been cooked and eaten so that the natives might absorb the great explorer's numerous powers.

Even the tyrant who ruled Uganda in the early 1970s, Idi Amin, was known to boast at mealtime that he had consumed human flesh, justifying his act by saying, "In warfare, if you do not have food, and your fellow soldier is wounded, you may as well kill him and eat him to survive. It can give you his strength inside. His flesh can make you better, it can make you full in the battlefield." Perhaps it was for a similar reason that at about the same time Michael Rockefeller, the young, adventurous son of American millionaire Nelson Rockefeller, disappeared into the jungles of Papua New Guinea and was presumed eaten by some of the last remaining cannibals on earth.

Not far away, in Fiji, cannibalism was practiced as early as 700 A.D., when Fijians sacrificed captured enemies to appease the warrior-gods. Afterwards, the flesh was consumed by the victors because to eat your enemy was the ultimate disgrace to the victim, having a lasting effect on the victim's family. Thus, religious ritual and revenge justified the practice. So common was this—lasting into the early 20th century—that most Fijian households included among their belongings what came to be called "cannibal forks," carved from wood and varying in size much as modern forks are, depending on what is to be eaten with them (an eye, perhaps, or a chunk of rump). "Tender as a dead man" is an old Fijian phrase occasionally heard today to compliment a modern dish.

It was Christianity and not the emergence of a "civilized" society that changed the west's view of such behavior. Spanish missionaries in Latin America, for example, set about to change the diet as well as the religion they found, both of which were declared barbaric. If they recognized the irony in espousing a faith where the blood and body of Christ are fed to believers during communion as wafers and wine, as a replacement for the real thing, it was never recorded. For the Christians, in the phrase of one scholar, Gian-Paolo Biasin, "cannibalism is [thus] metaphorized," as it was in the *Bible* itself, when Jesus said (John 6:51-57): "I am the living bread which came down from heaven. If anyone eats of this bread, he will live forever; and the bread that I shall give is My flesh, which I shall give for the life of the world. Most assuredly, I say to you, unless you eat the flesh of the Son of Man and drink His blood, you have no life in you. Whoever eats My flesh and drinks My blood has eternal life, and I will raise him up at the last day. For My flesh is food indeed, and My blood is drink indeed. He who eats My flesh and drinks My blood is in Me, and I in him."

Of course, much human flesh has been consumed in modern times not for eternal life, but for immediate survival. The story of American settlers snowbound in a blizzard while crossing the Donner Pass into California in 1846, eating their friends as they died, is well known. In an almost identical situation, British explorers on a doomed 19th century Arctic expedition to find the imagined

Northwest Passsage between the Atlantic and the Pacific Oceans in Canada's frozen wastes, resorted to cannibalism in what turned out to be a vain attempt to survive—a story substantiated by the recent discovery of their remains, which showed knife marks on over ninety bones. There is also the somewhat humorous account of a man named Alfred Packer, who, while prospecting for gold in Colorado in 1873, became trapped in a shack during a blizzard, surviving by eating his fellow prospectors. "You are a low-down, depraved son-of-a-bitch," the judge said when sentencing Mr. Packer to thirty years. "There were only seven Democrats in Hinsdale County, and you ate five of them."

In a more contemporary tragedy, the members of an Uruguayan rugby team whose plane crashed in 1972 in the Andes Mountains in South America, survived by eating their dead teammates, their story later told in a best-selling book and movie, *Alive*. Some Vietnamese boat people reportedly avoided death the same way. In a story not acknowledged until recently, in Guangxi, China, during the Proletarian Cultural Revolution of 1966–76, there was widespread cannibalism practised against "class enemies"; a book published in 1996, *Scarlet Memorial: Tales of Cannibalism in Modern China*, by Zheng Yi, quoted an official saying that some 10,000–20,000 people from that county alone ate their fellow citizens. More recent reports have come from North Korea, where widespread famine in 1997 and 1998 drove the hungry to eat family members and neighbors who had already starved to death.

Other contemporary reports about cannibalism are focused on the grisly aspects of cannibalism. This, in fact, seems to be all the media care about. In England some years ago, there was a well-credited story of the infamous Kray brothers, who controlled much of London's organized crime, cutting out the liver of an enemy and frying it on a sizzling shovel held over an open fire. Similarly, the American serial killer Jeffrey Dahmer, called the "Milwaukee Cannibal" by the press, slaughtered and ate his victims. Except for the contents of his freezer—which included lungs, intestines, a kidney, and a liver—police found no food in his apartment, only condiments. Dahmer asked prison physicians after his arrest in 1994 if there was anyone else in the world like him, or was he the only one? He was not, of course.

So it is difficult to imagine when, or how, attitudes about the consumption of human flesh might ever change, even if what I served my guests as a paté in 1972 became a sort of yuppie fad in England in 1998. At that time, *Esquire* magazine interviewed several people who had eaten it, as well as a number of professional chefs. One cook suggested braising it slowly and serving it with herb dumplings. Another advised cooking with olive oil, onion, vin santo capers, and anchovies, blending in a food processor, spreading it on a toasted crostini—"the perfect canapé for a Christening party," he said.

In 2002, an American television program, *Robert Ripley's Believe It or Not*, said they'd send a camera crew to Thailand if I'd recreate the dish on camera. I replied, saying, the original placenta party occurred long before AIDS and it was my wife's placenta. How would it look in Bangkok—of all places!—to start calling hospitals to ask for a placenta. I told them it would be a first, though—the first time that a recipe included a HIV test. I never heard from them again.

The Horror, the Horror...

Wanna know why cannibalism has a realllllly bad image? Bad press.

I have hundreds of stories from 1994–2003 in my files telling, for example, how eight people in Brazil unwittingly ate the liver of a murder victim served up fried with onions and garlic in a bar in Rio de Janeiro; how a seventy-six-year-old woman in Moscow was arrested for killing her husband, then eating and canning his remains; how two men in northeastern India murdered a neighbor they thought was trying to kill them with black magic, cutting his heart in half and eating it raw; and how a Portuguese historian studying World War Two atrocities uncovered documents showing that a hotel in Macau bought babies, who were fattened, then cooked and served to the hotel customers.

From a small village in Russia's Ural Mountains in 1995, came a story that police had arrested four men who were selling human flesh, telling restaurants it was veal. Another the same year tells of two Cambodian men who were helping a friend bury a stillborn child and, with the father's permission, made a soup instead. In Hong Kong in 1997, a police officer's head was chopped off by a doctor who said his wife was having an affair with the man; when police, tipped off by the policeman's wife, arrested the physician, they found the head in a pressure cooker.

Year after year, the stories appeared. In 1998, in Thailand a man drowned his six-year-old niece, believing that eating her brain would restore his mental health, and in Egypt three brothers were condemned to death for killing a man and drinking his blood. A year later, a London man was given a life sentence for killing and eating part of his victim's thigh and a Ukrainian was given the same for strangling his young lover, boiling her brains, eating her tongue, and keeping her skull on his television set.

In 2000 in Sri Lanka, a man who killed and ate his wife ten years earlier was arrested on charges of doing the same thing to his father, the body of a Hong Kong woman who went missing after a visit to northern China was found marinated in a jar of salt, and in Kathmandu, a twenty-two-year-old was arrested for devouring his older brother's ear, claiming he was driven by a drunken urge for meat. Cannibalism went onto the front pages and CNN in 2001 when Dyaks slaughtered and then ate their Madurese enemies in Borneo, cooking and shredding their flesh, then offering it to the public, and in Kathmandu, two brahmins ate the brains of the just assassinated king and his murderer, then ritually rode over the valley wall, taking the "bad luck" with them.

The next year, a German man confessed to murdering and eating a fellow homosexual who volunteered to be killed and two men accused in Cambodia of eating human body parts, washed down with a bottle of wine, were freed by provincial court because there was no law against cannibalism. And in 2003 in Los Angeles, an aspiring rap star was charged with murdering his roommate and eating part of her lung so—he claimed—he could cultivate a "gangsta" image and thus become a star.

Selling Cannibalism

There may be no social taboo greater today than cannibalism. Yet its pull is exceptionally strong, taking us to market, no surprise.

The most visible commercialization is Hollywood's. At one end of the spectrum were exploitation films such as *Cannibal Attack* (1954), *Blood Feast* (1963), *The Undertaker and His Pals* (1967), *Night of the Living Dead* (1968, followed by two sequels and one remake), *The Folks at Red Wolf Inn* (retitled *Terror on the Menu*, 1972), *Cannibal Girls* (1973), and *Return of the Living Dead* (1985, with two sequels), to name, believe it or not, just a few.

At the other end were productions made with larger budgets and by more talented film makers. In the novel from which the satirical movie *Soylent Green* was crafted (1973), the title referred to was a food made of soybeans and lentils, but when Hollywood got through with it, detective Charlton Heston discovered that it was made from human flesh. In Jean Luc-Godard's satirical *Weekend* (1968), terrorist wannabes who claimed "the horror of the state can only be answered by horror" demonstrated their return to a "natural," anti-industrial way of life by dining on captured bourgeois picnickers. Similarly, in *The Cook, the Thief, His Wife and Her Lover* (1989), an iconoclastic assault on sacred cows set in a smart restaurant, the meal served in the final scene is a whole, naked, roasted human. While Thomas Harris's character Hannibal (rhymes with cannibal) Lecter in *The Silence of the Lambs* (1991) and its lesser-known predecessor *Manhunter* (1986) and sequel, *Hannibal* (1999), is a human ghoul jailed for, among other things, his taste for human liver washed down with "a nice Chianti.".

In Fiji, replicas of traditional forks are still sold as souvenir items, made from a local wood, buried in black mud for several weeks and then polished, or merely painted. They come in a variety of sizes, small forks for eating the eyes and brains, larger ones for consuming the fleshy parts. It is also possible to buy "cannibal chutney," based on a real recipe for a vegetable relish which accompanied human meat in cannibal feasts.

And then there were the restaurants. In Ecuador in 2002, restaurateurs admitted using human thigh bones in stock to give a boost to soups and stews. Femurs, stolen from cemeteries, were the bones of choice as they imparted a "special taste." A year later, in China, women's skeletons were being excavated from graves in Shejiang province to make "ghost soup" and in another province, Hunan, a restaurant offered two dishes cooked with human breast milk, abalone and perch; the milk came from rural peasants. When the media learned of it, Beijing shut them down.

Placenta Paté

1 placenta
6 strips bacon
6 oz red wine
1 egg
Salt and pepper to taste

3 garlic cloves, minced
2 shallots, chopped finely
Green onion
Paté pastry

Use a thin, pointed knife to remove all the veins, opening the larger end where the main vein can be spotted easily. It should come out with a tug. Remove other, smaller veins. Cut meat into thin strips, sprinkle with salt and pepper, and marinate in wine for at least 6 hours. Mince about half of the meat, garlic, and shallots.

Line a mold with paté pastry, covering the bottom and sides with the bacon, then add the minced forcemeat and remaining slivers of meat mixed together. Cover the top with pastry and glaze with egg. Bake in a preheated oven at 375°F for about one hour. Let cool.

Serve with unsalted crackers and garnish with green onion.

CHAPTER TWO
reptiles & water creatures

AFTER HOLLYWOOD DISCOVERED THE DINOSAURS, many people probably thought reptiles ate us, even if most, in fact, were then and are now vegetarians. Whatever the reason, in today's world, there are many who consider eating reptiles unattractive. However, there are others who think a lizard on a spit quite ordinary, really nothing to talk about, except enthusiastically.

In Colombia, natives open the abdomens of pregnant female iguana and remove the eggs, then smear wood ash into the wound and release them into the wild, where the wound quickly heals, while in Mexico they grill the iguana, males as well as females. Crocodiles and alligators are on the menu wherever they are not on an endangered list and sometimes where they are. Armadillo is a treat in Texas, geckos are eaten matter-of-factly in parts of Asia, and snakes are consumed almost everywhere that they're found.

Yet, these descendants of ancient reptilian majesty are scorned and loathed at most Euro-American dinner tables. Probably only insects are more repellent. Perhaps it is the bony skeletons and the covering of dry scales and horny plates that are so off-putting. The word "reptilian" itself is an epithet when used as an adjective to describe someone regarded as cold-blooded and sneaky. In science fiction's long history, both in literature and film, many of the most terrifying villains were reptiles or had reptilian features, as epitomized by the *Godzilla*, *Jurassic Park*, and *Alien* movies.

I've always liked reptiles. When I was young, I had turtles as pets and while I don't think I ever thought of them as food, I don't believe I would have rebelled if someone suggested it. Nor do I find lizards and their limbless, scaly, elongate cousins, the snakes, very threatening today, however many movies I've seen that employed the image to scare. (Remember when Harrison Ford found himself in a pit with 6,000 snakes in *Indiana Jones and the Temple of Doom*? Did you see *Anaconda*?)

Such widespread prejudice is now beginning to fall in the developed world, where "jungle" restaurants and gourmet dining are coming together in a way that may make such creatures acceptable as food, even if the notion is wrapped in a sense of adventure and fashion. Never mind. However a reptile finds its way to the dinner plate, it can only enhance one's protein choice.

Some of the other creatures in this section come from the sea or freshwater lakes and rivers, among the greatest sources for nourishment since the first humans started grabbing fish from the tide pools with their hands. However much a staple most fish are today, there are several that are widely dismissed. Shark, for instance—like reptiles, rejected because of what it represents alive rather than cooked. And *fugu*, the highly publicized poisonous fish that continues to be regarded as a delicacy in Japan despite the lock put on wallets when the economy collapsed in the late 1990s.

This is an amorphous section of the book, with chapters on an assortment of unrelated creatures, including not only foods from both the land and sea, but also both vertebrate and invertebrate, the latter category represented by the fish eggs, jellyfish, and worms, none of which are related to each other, as well as the frog and toad, and the delicious snail and slug.

Snake

When I was in secondary school in the United States a long, long time ago, a classmate of mine told me and his other pals a story he thought was hilarious. Over the weekend, his father, a respected local physician, had hosted a barbecue at his home, serving what appeared to be small fish steaks, with potato salad, and plenty of beer. Everyone assumed the meat was fish, although it tasted a bit like chicken and was a little on the chewy side. The consensus was that it was delicious. Many went back for more.

After the meal, my friend's father announced that what he had served, and everyone had consumed, was rattlesnake. My friend, practically falling on the floor as he told the story, said that several of the guests promptly rushed to a toilet and vomited.

Happily, the dietary tolerance of many Americans has changed, with rattlesnake appearing rather matter-of-factly in restaurants and on home barbecues in the American southwest, where rattlesnake round-ups are now an established tourist attraction. However, snake still has not slithered very far onto the Euro-American plate, not as it has in Asia, anyway. In Asia, snake is king. And in much of Africa and Latin America, at least prince.

This was made clear when I visited one of the top destinations of culinary adventurers, Guangzhou, an easy commute from Hong Kong, where I went to one of the city's most famous eating places, the oddly named Snake King Completely and Restaurant, a nice tablecloth joint that offered—and I swear this is true, I copied the entire menu; there was only one in English, well worn by years of use, and they wouldn't let me take it with me—seventy-five different snake dishes! The live serpents were stored in cages on the ground floor and on order were brought to the second level where the kitchen was, to be sliced, diced, minced, flaked, shredded, stuffed, cut into fillets, and rolled into balls, then baked, salted, steamed, boiled, double-boiled, stir-fried, pan-fried, deep-fried, stewed, braised, baked in a casserole, cooked in paper, served raw (cut like sashimi), and presented with rice, vermicelli, a staggering selection of vegetables, herbs and spices and sauces, as well as with other protein, including quail, abalone, silk worm, and cat.

The cat was not in stock, I was told—I noted that a live one wandered confidently around the restaurant, mouthing dropped morsels—but I was assured that they did have the seventeen different snake wines listed on the menu, along with steamed fish lips with sour bamboo shoots, baked fish intestines, pig's blood and marrow with Chinese chives, and something called "cattle oil and flower rolls." Overwhelmed by the choice, I forgot to ask what that was. I ordered a baked snake plate "with special sauce" that tasted like sweet soy, a stir-fried snake with vegetables, and a glass of the five-snake wine. The snake tasted like—what else?—chicken and the wine looked like and burned like tequila going down; I also quickly learned to be careful of the tiny snake ribs, about the size of fish bones.

I was the only *gwailo* (foreign devil) in the restaurant and so I was as much an attraction to the local residents as the menu was to me. Several of the diners asked me to join them for a drink. In this way, I got to experience Five Testes & Penises Wine, a dark liquid with a worrying sediment that was said to be made from the genitals of deer, ox, sheep, dog, and snake, but had less of a kick than that made from snake alone.

"*Gan bei!*" my new friends cried. Mandarin for "empty cup," or bottoms up. And then they refilled my glass.

Snake eating has long been a valued part of the diet in southern China, especially in Guangdong province (Guangzhou is the capital), where it was praised by Liu An, a sage during the Han Dynasty (206 BC-25 A.D.), who said, "Whatever good southerners can do with a snake, it is useless in the rest of China." Snake meat later became a delicacy in the north as well, and figured as one of the dishes in a famous banquet of Qing Dynasty emperors (1644-1911), an indulgent, 196-course culinary marathon that reportedly went on for three days.

Usually snake is consumed in the cooler months, from late September, say, to March. The Chinese believe that during this period, when the snakes are entering winter dormancy, their flesh is more delicious. Snake also is categorized as a yang food, representing the positive, bright and masculine half of the Chinese yin/yang philosophy, yin being negative, dark and feminine. Eaten in winter, it is believed that its consumption (along with that of many other exotic fare) will warm the blood. However, good quality snakes are available throughout the year and if there is a real snake-eating "season," it is determined by customer demand.

Such interest is year-round at the Snake King Completely and also in a village called Le Mat, five kilometers north of Hanoi, in Vietnam. For generations, people have come here to eat snake. Other exotic dishes are sold in the restaurants lined up along a rough street—including porcupine, lizard and raccoon—but it is the signs for *thit ran* (snake meat) that line the street where customers come seeking the serpent's medicinal properties.

Once entering one of the establishments, the snake of choice—cobra is preferred by connoisseurs—is brought to the table still alive and washed in a tub of water. The snake is then held by two men as one of them cuts a hole in the abdomen, allowing the heart to pop out, falling onto a dish where it continues to beat. The blood is drained into a glass and mixed with snake wine made from rice whisky and the fermenting corpses of several snakes. The heart is added last and the glass is offered to the customer before his or her order is taken. There is one dish on the menu called, in the poetic Chinese fashion, "South of the Five Ridges with Fresh Snake Balls." Who could say no?

Many do, of course. Snakes have been denigrated for as long as history has been written. Was it not a snake that was the evil symbol in the Garden of Eden? An asp that killed dear Cleopatra? How many movies have used snakes as threatening props? There is also the inarguable evidence that of the some 2,400 species, 200 are poisonous to man, and who the hell knows which one is which?

Practically all snakes, dangerous or not, are edible: the cobras of Asia, the boas of South America, the pythons of Africa, the garden snakes of Europe, the rattlesnakes of North America. Snake venom is in the head area only, and the flesh may be safely consumed. And all parts of the snake are used—the blood and bile for rejuvenating drinks, the flesh as a nourishing protein source, the skin for crispy snacks (deep-fried), as well as for shoes, purses, and belts.

It is as a food that the snake is most cherished. "People can now afford it," says Yip Kwok-leung, owner of one of several snake restaurants in Hong Kong. "They don't see it so much as exclusively a tonic any more, but take it like ordinary food, like porridge." At Yip's, a bowl of soup costs under US$2 and at the Snake King Completely, the only dishes over $10 called for the addition of tortoise or cat. The price of snake wine varies widely. In 1998 I spent US$40 on a pint-sized bottle of cobra wine at the airport in Hanoi and three years later saw bottles double the size in both Hanoi and Saigon going for a quarter of that price. The meat itself almost everywhere is reasonably priced. In Jakarta, after completing a meal of cobra prepared three ways (satay, baked, and stir-fried with vegetables), I took home several packages of dried and crumbled cobra meat about the size of the palm of my hand, to be used as seasoning, for just $1 apiece. And the bill for the meal for two, including snake wine with blood and beating hearts, came to under $10.

In Europe, the eating of snake has a long history, too, although its consumption has declined in the past hundred or so years. "Until the 18th century, adder diets were very fashionable in France for their beneficial effects on health and beauty," according to *Larousse Gastronomique*. "Mme de Sévigné, who obtained her address from Poitou, advised her daughter to go on a month's adder diet once a year. Recipes of the period full of suggestions: the adders should be skinned and gutted, cooked with herbs, used to stuff a capon, cooked in stock, jellied, made into oils, etc. Louis XIV controlled the adder trade by restricting their sale to doctors and apothecaries." Recipes of the time suggested baking the snake with herbs, using it to stuff a capon, simmering it in a soup stock, and making it into a cooking oil.

It is not only weekend adventurers (like me) and middle-income diners who relish snake. In the 1990s, restaurants in Hong Kong alone imported nearly 50,000 snakes a year to satisfy the local demand, in the American west there were at least fifty restaurants serving rattlesnake chili and steak, and in some Asian cities with large Chinese populations there were an equal number.

It is another story in the jungles of equatorial Africa, Central and South America, and rural Southeast Asia, where snake may be considered quite ordinary, consumed not as a special treat but as a regular part of the diet along with monkey, rodents, grubs and insects, whenever it is available. While in parts of Latin America, "rattlesnake salt" is sprinkled on other dishes at least once a day; to make it, a rattlesnake (rattles and all) is chopped up and salted, and after six months the dried meat is discarded and what is left is ready for use.

If the snake isn't roasted or grilled over an open fire—the most common preparation—the basic dish found in Asia, as well as in parts of Africa and the Americas, generally is a soup or stew, many of them hard to tell apart; the ingredients may be identical, only the amount of liquid varies. Some soups and stews in these regions—usually tropical—are thickened with arrowroot, rice, tapioca and other local starches, while in other areas the snake meat is merely cooked with vegetables and seasonings.

Last I heard, my high school friend, who went on to become a thoracic surgeon, was living in a section of southern California where snakes probably outnumber humans. I wonder how he would react to a snake dish today. Would he still fall down laughing, or tuck in?

Rattlesnake Round-Up!

In the United States, several rattlesnake "round-ups" are held each year—a scheme originally dreamed up by farmers and ranchers to cut back the swarming rattler population, and now a tourist attraction in a number of cities and country towns, from Kansas to Texas and through much of the American southwest.

The largest and oldest of these is administered as a charitable event by the Junior Chamber of Commerce in Sweetwater, Texas, drawing tens of thousands of visitors the second weekend in March. The round-up's promotional brochure—boasting that over 100 tons of Western Diamondback rattlers have been captured and consumed since the event's introduction in 1958—says it all in the section called "Things to See & Do," offering a calendar that begins with a Rattlesnake Review Parade, includes a Miss Snake Charmer Queen contest and Friday and Saturday night "Rattlesnake Dances" (with country and western bands), snake-handling and milking shows, brisket and chili cook-offs, a rattlesnake meat-eating contest, guided snake hunts and bus tours (for those who want to either capture snakes or merely photograph the critters in the wild—an experienced guide is provided, and the awarding of prizes and trophies to individuals and groups who turn in the most pounds of rattlesnake and the largest one. An "OFFICIAL RATTLESNAKE ROUND-UP SOUVENIERS SALES BOOTH" offers tee-shirts, caps, pins, jackets, and key-chains with a rattle attached.

Breaded Rattler Snacks

An "official" Jaycee rattlesnake recipe from the Sweetwater round-up may be unimaginative, but it's easy: "Kill it; remove head, suspend by tail for 1 hour. Skin; gut. Chop into chunks. Marinate in sweet milk for 2 hours. Dredge in corn meal or bread crumbs, or a combination of both. Deep-fat fry until brown. Serve with Louisiana Hot Sauce, Texas Pepper Sauce, or Tartar Sauce."

Marinated Snake Cooked with Rice

The snake is skinned, gutted, and cut into pieces of a size manageable with chopsticks. These are marinated in mixture of soy sauce, garlic, ginger, and bourbon whiskey. The Snake meat is placed over partially cooked rice and the cooking continued until the meat and rice are done.

—*Calvin Schwabe, Unmentionable Cuisine (1979)*

Cobra a la Pol Pot

"The cook of Pailin flashed a toothy smile, banged her ladle against the bubbling pot and said, 'I cooked cobra for Pol Pot.' She carried on stirring and dictated the recipe as if from page one of the Khmer Rouge Cookbook: 'First, kill the cobra. Then cut off its head and hang it on a tree for the poison to dry in the sun, away from the children. Collect the snake blood in a cup and serve it with white wine. Chop the cobra into little pieces and mash it into a pulp with a handful of peanuts. Add boiling water, bitter leaf of the vine, the herb of the lemon grass, and yellow ground ginger. Simmer for 1 hour. Serves 1."

—*John Sweeney, The Observer, April 2000*

Lizards

In a Hollywood movie called *The Freshman* (1990), Marlon Brando, portraying a mafia don named Carmine Sabbatini, hired Matthew Broderick, who played a college student in desperate need of cash, to pick up a "package" at the airport in Newark, New Jersey. The "package" turned out to be a live Komodo dragon on a leash—the Komodo being named for the remote Indonesian island where only a few thousand remain. Once upon a time, this largest of the world's lizards, growing to eleven feet and weighing up to 400 pounds, was hunted for meat, but today it's an endangered species, protected by the Indonesian government.

Much of what followed in the movie detailed the silly adventures involved in transporting the lizard, when it got loose at a petrol station, ran wild inside a shopping mall, and so on. Finally, came the flimsy plot. Each year, Brando invited members of a private gourmet club to a banquet comprised entirely of endangered species. Cost per serving started at US$200,000 and went to US$1 million, depending on the animals' rarity. In the film, there were supposedly only eight Komodos left in the world—the actual figure is between 2,000 and 6,000—so the price tag for the meal was $350,000. Per person.

The movie, so far seeming politically incorrect, to say the least, became socially acceptable in the final scenes when it was revealed that no matter what endangered species Mr. Sabbatini promised the club members—after marching the poor beast on-stage during cocktail time, to prove the animal was real—year after year they always got smoked turkey; after all, didn't every unusual food taste more or less like chicken? And afterward, the animals were donated to the Carmine Sabbatini Wing of the Bronx Zoo.

The point that must be made is that every unusual food doesn't taste like chicken, and certainly that's true of lizard, whose flavor is more like, well, smoked turkey, but varies from species to species, the reptiles' diet and locale.

Lizards live on all seven continents, from the southern tips of South America and South Africa all the way to the snowy arctic, but most of the 7,300 or so species make their homes in more temperate climes, and many of the largest and most unusual—and most popular at mealtime—are in the tropics. Especially in Asia and Latin America, the lizard is considered ordinary or a delicacy.

One of the most popular is the iguana, standard mealtime fare in

Mexico, Central America, South America, and parts of the Caribbean, at least since the days of Christopher Columbus, whose sailors reported it "white, soft, and tasty." (As recorded in *The Life of the Admiral Christopher Columbus*, written by his son.) Today, it is sold in markets, restaurants, and such places as Iguana Park, a tourist attraction whose name surely was inspired by *Jurassic Park*, a book and brace of movies that have done nothing to improve the image of ancient lizards. In the park's first five years in Costa Rica, owners say more than 80,000 iguanas were released into the wild, claiming that the population is now of such size that the park managers have a permit to sell iguana meat and make other commercial use of the animals. (The skin may be turned into leather belts, purses, and shoes.)

In size, the iguana is no match for a Komodo, but males can reach six feet in length, over half of which is tail, and females usually grow to four feet. They also have a distinct, prehistoric appearance, characterized by large round scales beneath their ears that look sort of like hi-fi speakers, prominent spines along the neck, back and tail, and a large dewlap hanging beneath their chins, which they display to defend their territory and attract mates. And, they are bright green. The effect is that of a miniature dinosaur crafted from pistachio ice cream.

Sold in native markets, the iguana is far cheaper than when sold in a store as a pet, and usually they're sold live, although some of the smaller ones are grilled on skewers and in small cafes sold in a stew or soup with local vegetables, and seasoned with garlic, cumin, cloves, and nutmeg.

Iguana eggs are valued highly, too, so in Colombia when the mama lizard is thought to be ready to lay her eggs, hunters capture the slow-moving creature, slit open the abdomen with a sharp knife, gently remove the eggs, rub wood ash into the wound, sew her back up, and away she goes, waddling into the underbrush to resume life and, presumably, seek another mate, while the Colombians go off to cook the eggs or sell them in the marketplace. Of course, the eggs may be dug out of the ground once laid, but many aficionados and hunters know that it is easier to spot a pregnant iguana than follow one until she lays her eggs.

Iguanas are not difficult to catch, although they can sprint for short distances at considerable speed and are skilled at climbing trees. Usually, hunters creep up on them as they lounge on low tree limbs, snoozing in the sun.

Opinion differs about lizard as food. Some say most species are hard to catch and don't have enough meat on them to justify the energy spent capturing and butchering them. However, most of the beast is meat, as opposed to, say, small birds, that seem to be all bones and feathers. Lizard is also regarded as an exotic delicacy and restaurant diners must expect to pay a premium, just as exotic leather goods cost more than those made from cattle, pig, or other domestic species.

That said, at Easter in Nicaragua, superstition, religion and tradition are the cultural ingredients that go into Nicaragua's Easter iguana soup, cherished for its nutritive and hoped-for aphrodisiac powers. As the holiday approaches, the lizards are sold for US$1.50 to $10 apiece, depending mainly on size. Iguanas are a protected species in many countries, but Nicaragua's ban on hunting and eating them goes largely ignored. Usually they are cooked in a rice and vegetable soup called *sopa de garrobo*, or made into *pinol*, a paste that's consumed with bread.

Another popular, large lizard is the chuckwalla, found in the mountains and deserts from Utah in the United States across the border into Mexico. Here, it is happiest in barren, rocky ground where there are small caves and crevasses in which to hide while pursued by hungry Indians. Once inside such a hole, it hyperventilates, filling its lungs to maximum capacity, causing its body to increase up to sixty per cent in size. To get the chuckwalla out, hunters pierce its lungs with a sharp stick to deflate them.

This grisly routine is deemed worthwhile. (And, after all, is sending a pack of dogs after a wild boar, then gutting it in the wild, a pleasanter exercise? Or slaughtering a hog in an abattoir?) A large chuckwalla may be a foot to a foot and a half long and can measure about three and a half inches wide, its thick tail as long as the head and body and containing nearly 100 per cent meat. Usually it is roasted, grilled, broiled, or cooked on a spit over an open fire and consumed with vegetables, tequila and lime. Sometimes, as with other lizard species, the chuckwalla is cooked in its rough, leathery skin. After gutting it and removing the head, it is placed directly on hot coals and turned continually. When the skin splits apart, the meat can be removed.

A number of monitor lizards, looking like small versions of the Komodo, also are hunted from the Nile to Southeast Asia to Australia, where the aborigines coat the animals with mud before roasting them on hot coals, realizing the same "baked" effect accomplished when fish or poultry are cooked in clay or *en papillote*. These and other smaller lizards are usually clubbed when caught basking in the sun, or snared by a noose at the end of a stick.

By comparison, even the largest geckos of Southeast Asia are smaller and it always takes more than one to make an entré, especially if you're using the smallest (up to three inches long) variety found zigzagging along the walls and ceilings in a house. This is the variety I watched in my home when I lived in Hawaii and now watch chase mosquitoes and other insects in Thailand, where the small creature is called a *jing cho* for the clicking sound it makes. There is really only one practical way to cook geckos and that's by deep-frying them in hot oil, although the larger species, maybe six inches in length and found in the jungle and infrequently in the home, may be gutted and grilled as any other lizard.

In Vietnam, Hong Kong, and China, the gecko also is made into a strong alcoholic drink, by adding the reptiles to a bottle of strong rice wine or whisky, then left alone for about a year. In restaurants—usually where snake is sold—the wine sells for about US$1 a shot-sized glass, and is drawn from five- to ten-liter jars. Smaller bottles, most containing one large gecko, can be purchased for under $2 in Oriental groceries and some airport souvenir shops in Asia. Dried geckos are also sold in street markets in China and in herbal shops in most of the world's Chinatowns, to be ground up and mixed with hot water and drunk to cure a variety of ills.

Live lizards are available in many pet stores, as well as through the mail, but the cost almost gives Mr. Sabbatini competition. Some common species are priced as high as US$100 and more, while many of the larger monitors cost up to $500 apiece. The sources also sell them as pets.

Lizard Therapy

A landscaper who recently took a ninth wife says he has no need for Viagra because eating two or three live geckos a day keeps him virile.

Veera Raungsri, from Bangkok, said his gecko diet had made him more virile than his first eight wives could handle. Mr. Veera, forty-two, said he started eating geckos twenty years ago on the advice of a Cambodian he had consulted after doctors told him he had an incurable liver condition.

—*Associated Press, June 18, 1999*

Iguana Soup

1 iguana	1 onion, studded with 3 cloves
1 1/2 qts iguana broth	1 green pepper, quartered
(or chicken broth)	1/4 small cabbage
2 chicken bouillon cubes	1 teaspoon cumin
1 clove of garlic	1 dash nutmet
1 leek	Salt and pepper
1 tomato, coarsely chopped	2 oz vermicelli

Kill, clean, skin, and cut the iguana into serving pieces.

Prepare chicken broth in heavy kettle, add garlic, leek, tomato, green pepper, and cabbage. Bring to a boil, reduce heat and simmer for 30 minutes. Add the iguana and simmer an additional half-hour, or until the meat is tender. Remove from the fire. Strain broth, discarding vegetables. Bone the iguana and set the meat aside.

Return the broth to the fire and add cumin, nutmeg, vermicelli, and salt and pepper. Simmer for about 5 minutes until the vermicelli is tender. Add the iguana and heat thoroughly. Serve piping hot with corn meal mush. Serves 6.

—Collected by Bert Christensen

Alligator & Crocodile

"See you later, alligator,
After a while, crocodile."
—Popular song by Bill Haley & the Comets (1955)

When this refrain topped the pop music charts around the world in the 1950s, the alligator and the crocodile had a cheery, unthreatening image. An American television show of the time, *Kukla, Fran & Ollie*, featured a friendly, gregarious character named Oliver Dragon, a gator or croc, take your choice, who engaged in happy repartee with the other hand puppets and the program's hostess, an ageless ingenue named Fran Allison. In the popular comic strip *Pogo*, one of the regular characters was Albert Alligator, a cartoon figure that stood on its two hind feet and was always non-threatening and frequently funny. More recently, the world flocked to see Australia's Paul Hogan in somewhat screwy films about an adventurer named Crocodile Dundee.

On the other side were films depicting this large, scaly creature as some sort of junior-varsity Godzilla, where alligators and crocodiles became a cliché in cinema fright. For decades there has been a persistent "urban myth" that baby alligators that had been kept as pets were flushed down toilets when the owners tired of them, thriving thereafter in the city's sewers. When floods hit Thailand in 1996, several crocs escaped from commercial farms, leading the government to send armed teams in boats with orders to shoot to kill.

At the same time, alligator "wrestling" has been a staple roadside attraction in the American south for generations, just as crocodile shows are a tourist draw in Australia and Southeast Asia; how many hundreds of thousands (millions?) have gasped when one of the trainers opened the reptile's mouth—full of teeth the size of a man's thumb—and stuck his or her head inside?

Of course, people actually do get killed by gators and crocs in the wild occasionally, just as they're killed by sharks every now and then, and surely there is some hazard in sticking one's head inside a toothy mouth. The thing is, the media always report such things with more than appropriate drama. It makes for a good story, but the truth is, the crocodile and alligator are, like snakes and most other "dangerous" carnivores, totally uninterested in humans, unless they themselves feel jeopardized.

Such clichéd reporting and the attitude attached to it by both the reporters and the audience, clearly affects how we now feel about alligators and crocodiles. Most people in the developed parts of the world think of them as animals that are not only threatened (some species are, anyway), but also personally threatening. It's too bad, because, the unthreatened species offer a tasty, healthy meat that is now finding a growing market on several continents.

In Singapore, stir-fried crocodile is a staple on many restaurant menus, while in some parts of India the preferred dish is a crocodile curry, and in Australia, crocodile pie is a part of that country's traditional cum trendy "bush tucker." In Japan, crocodile dishes are served as a delicacy at pricey Tokyo restaurants. In the U.S., alligator gumbo is a recognized southern dish, a part of Creole cuisine, and alligator ribs are barbecued in the same region, while in black ghettos in the north, they're served with collard greens and black-eyed peas. The meat is also eaten matter-of-factly in parts of Latin America and Africa, usually grilled on an open fire or as part of rough stews and soups.

Crocodile and alligator lend themselves to wide culinary artistry and choice. They mix well with many herbs, spices, and vegetables. They are well suited for numerous dishes, including not only soups and stews, but also casseroles, stir fries, omelets, pies, pasta, and pastries. The meat beneath that armor-like skin is easily butchered and cut into chops and steaks, to be char-grilled like a chicken thigh or breast, whose flavor it resembles. (The preferred, or most tender, meat is from the legs and tail of the young.) More exotic recipes abound, from crocodile tripe, a delicacy in Ethiopia, to omelets made from the eggs and "Dragon's Palm," the roasted crocodile foot, offered in some restaurants in Southeast Asia. In Thailand, the meat is tinned with Chinese herbs and black mushrooms and sold in supermarkets and a hotel dining room at Victoria Falls in Africa regularly offers crocodile thermidor.

Alligators and crocodiles are found in tropical swamps around the world—the two related species visibly differentiated by the fact that gators have narrower snouts and generally are somewhat smaller—from the Nile River to Southeast Asia and Australia to the southern United States, from Texas as far north as the Carolinas. All are surprisingly agile and fast, both in and out of the water, and have powerful jaws designed for gripping and swallowing rather than chewing. There are both freshwater and saltwater animals—some are at home in both—and all are carnivores.

Several species are endangered, but others are described as "controlled," meaning that the populations are closely monitored and carefully culled for commercial use only when the numbers warrant it. The American alligator went onto the endangered species list in 1967 when its number dropped to about 100,000, for example, and today the gator is thriving both in the wild and in captivity There are an estimated million in the wild in Florida alone, another hundred thousand on commercial ranches. No longer on the endangered list, this species today provides hides for a variety of products and meat for the table through much of the American south, especially in Florida, Louisiana and Texas, the primary alligator farming states.

Similarly in Australia, where the menacing saltwater croc once stood on the verge of extinction, after years of protection the population of "salties" living along the northern coast has rebounded to the point where they are now on the verge of being a dangerous nuisance. In the tropical Northern Territory, the population grew from an estimated 5,000 in 1971, when hunting was banned, to approximately 70,000 in 1998. The prohibition remained in force, keeping the meat from the Aboriginal diet, where it had been for thousands of years. This was a touchy issue, as the Aborigines argued for revival of traditional ways. During a state visit by German Chancellor Helmut Kohl in 1997, however, croc stew was served along with kangaroo satay. Why? The meat came from a licensed farm. Since then, the pale flesh has joined the shrimp on Australia's "barbie."

If you want crocadillia on your plate nowadays anywhere, it must (legally) come from one of the commercial ranches and farms that stretch from Cuba to Cambodia, where even governments are in the business. Although some facilities are still small, as is one in the

Philippines, also government-run, large commercial operations exist in many parts of the world, many in the southern United States, where alligators are now hunted in the wild and trucked to slaughterhouses and factories that process them into steaks and shoes. Not surprisingly, the U.S. dominates the world market and is the biggest exporter. The big buyers include France, Italy, Germany, and Japan, mainly for the leather. In Australia and Southeast Asia, where the beasts are raised in captivity, China and other Asian countries are the big markets, for the meat.

Oil derived from crocodile flesh also is in demand, widely used as a stabilizing agent in cosmetics and perfumes. In Brazil, Bolivia, and Madagascar, crocodile oil is praised as a cure for everything from asthma to baldness. While the reptile's teeth, head and bones are sold as souvenirs. And, because the commercial use of the beasts is almost everywhere rigidly regulated, limiting the numbers allowed to reach the market, the cost of anything made from alligator or crocodile is high.

In Southeast Asia, the most famous commercial operation is located only a half-hour's drive from Bangkok in Samut Prakarn. Called simply the Crocodile Farm, it is the source of the croc meat sold at many other restaurants in Asia. By its own boast, it is also the largest reptile ranch in the world, claiming a population of some 40,000 crocs of nine varieties. Whatever the census may be, it's clear that there is no shortage. When I visited in 1997, I saw thousands on open display in cement enclosures behind metal mesh fencing or in shallow ponds, ranging in size from almost newborn (six to eight inches in length) to old enough to be gathering real moss and large enough to qualify for the scariest movie you've ever seen. The farm insists that it—and not the sanctuary in India—has the world's longest in captivity, more than six meters in length, a claim I wouldn't even think about challenging.

The crocodile is virtually extinct in the wild in Thailand, but once past the turnstiles of the Crocodile Farm (admission: US$6 for foreigners, a twelfth that for Thais), it is threatened only by the farm's owners, who have a habit of turning the reptiles into profit-making leather and soup. One store near the entrance is full of luggage, briefcases, purses, shoes, belts, key chains, and other items made from the polished, brown skin. In another shop, stewed crocodile meat is sold in cans whose labels boast: "Product of our crocodile farm. It is selected by the first class breeding crocodile and prepared under the Chinese medicine with the modern stew processing. Stewed croc-meat strengthens the libido. It is a nutritious and a tonic food for good health. It provides a pleasant taste. Stewed croc-meat stimulates the appetite, good for

Clockwise from top: **Figure 1.** In April 1871, *Le Monde Illustré* depicted scenes of the Franco-Prussian War and the Siege of Paris, when market stalls selling cat and dog meat drew lines of people. **Figure 2.** A mobile horsemeat butcher's shop does brisk business in a French Provincial town, selling freshly slaughtered steaks and mince. **Figure 3.** *Saucisson d'ane* – donkey meat dried sausage – is one of the specialties of the town of Arles in the south of France, seen on sale at the Saturday market and served with olive bread and a glass of *Côte du Rhone*.

This page, from top: **Figure 4.** Two handfuls of rats that will either be eaten, or sold for one-and-a-half rupees each under a program set up by the Oxfam Trust and India's Department of Science and Technology. **Figure 5.** Grilled whole baby mice, served with a Vietnamese dipping sauce of finely chopped ginger, garlic, chilis, and coriander in fish sauce and rice vinegar.

Facing page: **Figure 6.** Grilled bat is a local specialty of the foothills of the mountain range separating Burma and Thailand. Limestone provides abundant caves for the bats, and several small restaurants near Ratchaburi (about an hour and a half's drive west of Bangkok) serve them whole, grilled or fried.

This page, clockwise from top: **Figure 7.** A waiter at the Carnivore restaurant in Nairobi serves up the bush meat *du jour*, carved right at the diners' table. **Figure 8.** The northern Thai town of Phayao is known for its culinary use of all possible parts of cattle and buffalo, including the cloudy green liquid called *phia*, from the second ruminant sac. Locals call it *khi phia*, the prefix being the word for excrement, and use it to flavour dishes such as spicy salads. **Figure 9.** Gorilla meat is easily smoked and passed off as buffalo, which makes it easier to sell openly in some areas. The nine-ball Chevrotine cartridge designed to bring down a gorilla is sold over the counter.

Facing page: **Figure 10.** Monkeys are smoked over open wood fires in the wild, then packaged for shipping to the city or put aside for later consumption. In the Congo Republic in 1997, the prime minister officially announced that all school children should spend their holidays hunting and fishing, an announcement made during the closed season.

This page, from top: **Figure 11.** Roasted bone marrow is a starter dish on its own at the fashionable London restaurant St. John. Chef Fergus Henderson has a passion for more unusual parts of animals, and the restaurant's motto is "nose to tail eating." **Figure 12.** Dr. Li, herbalist at the Imperial Herbal Restaurant in Singapore, displays one of his prize deer penises infusing a jar of wine. The wine is sold by the glass, but dried penises are also sold.

Facing page: **Figure 13.** So-called "whale bacon" is a popular snack in Japan—thin slices that include the blubber, for sale in a Kyushu fish market.

This page, from top: **Figure 14.** This archival print depicts cannibalism in what is now Brazil. **Figure 15.** A vendor offers fresh snake blood to passers-by in Taipei's Hwa-Hsi Street, known popularly as Snake Alley. The blood and bile are believed to strengthen eyesight and the lower backbone, to invigorate and to promote virility.

Facing Page: **Figure 16.** A cobra, artfully arranged so that its hood is spread, infuses a bottle of Chinese snake wine. The small red lozenges are wolfberries.

Figure 17. Iguana eggs, with their rich and tasty spherical yolks, are a favorite snack to accompany the local white rum on the Caribbean coast of Colombia.

This page, from top: **Figure 18.** To harvest iguana eggs, the gravid female is not killed, but felled from a tree with a slingshot. An incision is them made with the blade of a machete, and the string of eggs pulled out. The iguana's ability to recuperate is remarkable—once the wound has been protected with a coating of old ashes, the animal runs off back into the forest. **Figure 19.** The lizards are grilled both sides over an open stove, together with their eggs.

Facing page: **Figure 20.** The preparation of a giant frog in Northeast Thailand for a spicy soup known as *om kob* begins with cutting the ventral side from throat to tail and pulling the skin off in one piece, after which the frog is lightly grilled over an open fire. The meat and accompanying spices and vegetables, including chilies, bay leaves, ginger, lemongrass, and fish sauce, are then ready to place in the pot with water.

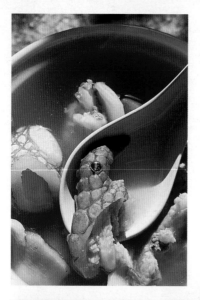

This page, clockwise from top: **Figure 21.** A bowl of crocodile soup served at the Crocodile Farm near Bangkok. **Figure 22.** A giant reproduction of a puffer-fish lantern hangs over a Tokyo street to advertise a *fugu* restaurant. The real lanterns are made from the dried skin of the inflated fish. **Figure 23.** Even after the lengthy process in preparing the shark's fin for use, it takes a long time and many stages to prepare sharks' fin soup. First soaked for at least three days with several changes of water, the fin is then simmered for up to five hours. The sandy skin is removed, as is the decayed bone hidden in the meat at the tip. The fin is then cooked for a further ten hours in stocks that are regularly discarded to remove any smell from the curative process.

Facing page: **Figure 24.** Creamed slugs on toast make use of a mushroom cream sauce, garnished with sesame seeds. Lacking the protective shell of a snail, slugs protect themselves with a tougher skin on the upper body and a coating of slime. In order to remove the slime completely, the animals must be simmered with several changes of water, before being arranged on the slice of toast.

Figure 25. One hundred tiny slices of raw *fugu*, shaved paper thin, are arranged in the traditional design of a chrysanthemum flower, with a tassel of fin and skin. The transparency of the flesh makes the plate itself an important part of the meal, and *fugu* restaurants have special and valuable designs on which to display this costly dish. Depending on the market price and the status of the restaurant, each slice on the plate like this will cost the diner the equivalent of between one and two U.S. dollars.

old people and growing children. It is an appreciated gift." The same shop also sells "essense of crocodile" in small bottles, reputed to be a healthy drink that can be served hot or cold, as well as a "crocodile oil," which is sold as a massage oil.

Near the two shops is a small, open-air restaurant, where those who have seen the crocodile show and exhausted the rest of the farm's low-key amusement park-like entertainment before getting back into Bangkok traffic, may relax over a bottle of beer or soda and a zesty bowl of soup. Only the most tender (young) crocs are used, so visitors should be prepared to see—as I did—little crocodile feet taking a final swim in the broth. Those little feet were on the bony side, but the taste was quite sweet. And a bargain at US$1.50.

Crocodile, 39 Ways

Crocodile Steak
Hot Spicy Spare Rib Crocodile Soup
Fried Spare Rib Crocodile with Peppers & Garlic
Fried Crocodile with Chili Paste
Fried Crocodile with Crispy Basil Leaves
Sweet & Sour Crocodile
Fried Crocodile with Ginger and Chili
Fried Crocodile with Cashew Nuts
Fried Crocodile with Pepper & Garlic
Fried Salted Crocodile
Crocodile Spicy Salad
Crocodile Tail Soup
Crocodile Satay
Crocodile with Chinese Bread
Baked Crocodile Egg
Dried Crocodile Meat
Crocodile Roll
Fried Crocodile with Vegetables
Crocodile Curry
Deep Fried Crocodile Meat
Crocodile French Bread
Fried Crocodile with *Matsu-take* Mushrooms
Fried Crocodile with Tiger Palm Mushrooms
Fried Crocodile with Beef Liver Mushrooms
Fried Crocodile with Chinese *Kong-chai* Vegetables
Fried Crocodile with Asparagus
Fried Crocodile Liver
Baked Crocodile Egg
Fried Crocodile Egg with Ham
Crocodile Gastro

Dragon Palm (the foot)
Crocodile Palm in Red Sauces
Fried Crocodile Tongue with Garlic & Pepper
Dragon Soup with Ginseng
Tian-chi Crocodile Soup
Crocodile Liver Soup
Tian-ma Crocodile Soup
Bamboo Tissue Crocodile Soup
Steamed Crocodile Egg
—*Menu, Sri Racha Tiger Farm Restaurant, Thailand, 1998, where tigers are just for show, not to eat*

World's Biggest Croc!

Fossil crocodiles appear in the rocks at about the same time as dinosaurs, varying little in size and appearance from the beasts today, preying on small antelope-sized dinosaurs when they came to the rivers and streams to drink. Through recorded history, they have played a widely varied role. An ancient Egyptian god, Souchos, was a crocodile himself and at one period the creatures were believed to be oracles and were embalmed after death. The custom of "ordeal by crocodiles" was popular for a while in Arabia, where the accused's guilt was determined by whether the crocodile ate or rejected him. In the Philippines, Borneo, and parts of West Africa, crocodiles were regularly fed prized livestock and other animals for religious reasons, although it isn't difficult to see that a well-fed croc is a better neighbor than a hungry one. Numerous popular tales from the South Pacific tell of women who had crocodiles for lovers.

Many people use the words alligator and crocodile interchangeably. Technically, both may be called "crocodilians," but they are two distinctly different, if related, species, the shapes of their heads providing the most obvious variance. The snout and jaws of the crocodile are broad, from the eyes to the tip forming a sort of rounded, lumpy rectangle, while the alligator's head tapers so that it appears almost triangular in shape. The alligator is also known to be far less aggressive than the croc when it comes to interaction with humans. I once watched a photographer get into a soupy Florida swamp almost nose-to-nose with a gator to take his picture; the gator looked totally bored.

Like most cold-blooded animals, they spend much of their time basking on sandbanks, maintaining an even body temperature. They also open their massive jaws and gape, so that air plays over the soft skin inside the mouth. This being a natural posture for the animals may make it easier for those who work in alligator and crocodile tourist attractions to put their heads between those rows of awesome teeth—although, of course, there are never any guarantees, so most of the head-in-mouth shows take place after the animals have been fed.

Records show that the estuarine or salt water croc, now extinct in many areas, is the largest reptile on earth, ranging from India, Sri Lanka, southern China, and the Malay Archipelago to northern Australia, Papua New Guinea, and the Solomon Islands. One, killed in Bengal, India, about a hundred years ago, was thirty-three feet long; a twenty-nine-footer was killed about the same time in the Philippines. The largest alive today, according to the *Guinness Book of Records*, is believed to be nineteen feet, eight inches from snout to tail, and is in a wildlife sanctuary in India. Most mature males average about fourteen to sixteen feet in length and weigh from 900 to 1,150 pounds, although old individuals may be half again as heavy.

Frog & Toad

On one of my early visits to the farm in northeastern Thailand that I now call home, the woman who is now my wife served lunch, the first course being something that looked like miniature game hens without legs.

"*Gop*," said Lamyai, sending me to my Thai-English dictionary without success. Lamyai's mother then brought a metal pot full of live frogs and Lamyai said they'd been caught in the flooded rice fields that morning.

"Oh," I said, "that *gop*."

Lamyai explained that their insides had been removed and finely chopped along with the legs and head, then mixed with basil and egg and stuffed back into the frogs, which then were sewn closed and grilled. The skin was crunchy and the insides tasted like a meaty sort of sawdust gone slightly sour.

How many cartoons have we all seen about frogs' legs? Remember the one showing a leg-less frog sitting on one of those wheeled platforms, begging with a tin cup? Or the ones with frogs on crutches? How funny has it ever been to call a citizen of France a "frog?" And how about all those gags (pun intended) a few years ago about putting a frog in a blender. It's all pretty sick, if you ask me.

I don't know why so-called humorists pick on frogs. Do they tell jokes about cattle being turned into hamburgers? Or fish showing up in a soup? I don't think so. I guess that in the quirky world that determines what is funny and what is not, frogs get more laughs than cattle or fish.

In modern gastronomy, the legs of this web-footed amphibian are not so uncommon at some of the finer tables, especially in Europe, where they are an expensive delicacy. Although many of the frogs consumed in Europe are raised in Yugoslavia (to name one primary source) and elsewhere, more are imported frozen from Cuba and the United States, where the meat has not yet found a great audience, except in the southern states, where midnight frog hunts produce a key ingredient for stew. Nor are they popular in England, where when the esteemed Auguste Escoffier was chef of the Carlton Hotel in London, he craftily sneaked them onto the plate of the Prince of Wales only by calling them *cuisses de nymphes l'aurore*, legs of the dawn nymphs.

Why the rejection? Who knows. Maybe it's because frogs are funny looking and the subject of all those jokes. With their moist, hairless, featherless, scaleless skin and large blinking eyes, wide mouth, an ability to live happily in both water and on dry land (where they hop rather than walk), and their deep, croaking voice, perhaps they are just a little too odd to consider. (Although when it comes to looks, I think chickens are funnier.) Perhaps, too, because they are so small, like song birds they are overlooked because it takes so many to make a meal. Kermit the Frog from *Sesame Street* probably doesn't help much, either. In any case, they are not easy to find in supermarkets, although they may be found in specialty shops in tins that are, like the legs on a menu, wildly overpriced.

"Prejudices against eating frogs or salamanders as food center upon their cold and slippery feel, their unappealing swampy or algae-grown habitats, and the expectation that they will smell and taste fishy," said Calvin Schwabe in his excellent survey of unusual foods, *Unmentionable Cuisine* (1979). "In my experience, these expectations are never realized, and the individual who puts squeamishness aside sufficiently for just one bit of frog meat or is tricked into eating frog meat even once finds that it is, in fact, like a more delicately flavored and textured chicken than he has ever eaten."

Another mystery lies in the belief—endorsed, wrongly, by *Larousse Gastronomique*, the French encyclopedia of cookery—that only the legs are edible. While it is true that this is where most of the meat is, in many parts of the world the entire frog is eaten happily and healthily, as Lamyai and her family do in Thailand every year during the monsoon season and the frogs emerge from hibernation in their hidey-holes in the rice paddy dikes.

The French encyclopedia also would have us believe that preparation of the legs is somewhat complex. First, the frog is skinned then cut at the hips so that the legs remain in pairs. After the feet are removed (to disguise the meat's origin and make them look like small chicken legs?), they are soaked in cold water for twelve hours, with a change of water every three or four. This causes the flesh to whiten and swell as it absorbs the water.

They are then cooked in a variety of ways, marinated and grilled on skewers, dipped in flour and fried, sautéed in butter and chopped onion, or form the basis of a soup seasoned with shallots and a sweet white wine. In fine restaurants in Thailand, where they are sometimes euphemistically called "paddy chicken" because they came from the rice farms in the north, the legs are cooked in a wok with peppercorns, red chilis, palm sugar, basil, and galangal. They may also be served in a curry, tomato sauce, or boned and included in egg fritata. Small frogs frequently are battered, then deep-fried, and eaten whole, with or without a sprinkle of salt and a spritz of vinegar.

In much of Asia, Africa, and Latin America—there are 3,500 species found virtually everywhere in the world, except in arctic regions—the preparation is simpler and less wasteful. Here, frogs are not farmed as they are in Europe and North America, but caught in the watery woods, swamps. and rice fields where they range freely, by villagers who stalk the creatures at night, following the sound of their throaty voices, "blinding" them with a light so that they freeze in place. They catch them with sharpened sticks, nets, or their hands and carry them home in buckets and sacks, where they are kept alive until the next day, when they are gutted and washed, then skewered on bamboo sticks and grilled for a hearty meal with rice and perhaps a spicy dip. They also are seen in open markets, hopping like mad by the dozens (hundreds?) in large pans with a wire mesh cover, strung like garlic or peppers on a long string, or grilled on bamboo skewers and sold ready to eat. Deep-fried, they look like men in suits—bloated plutocrats?—and disappear almost magically in the mouth, like cotton candy. Never are the legs removed, the rest wastefully thrown away. Here, they are consumed, bones and all. In one of my favorite restaurants in Bangkok, the skin is deep-fried to produce crispy, paper-thin snacks.

Toads are another matter. If the frog makes some wrinkle their noses, its fellow amphibian, the toad, probably makes them go googly-eyed and consider removing your card from their Rollodex if you dare to offer it to them. Again, I think it has to do with appearance. Where the frog is smooth and moist, most toads are dry and covered with warty bumps. Also, in recent years, one species of toad, found in the Sonoran Desert in the southwestern United States, acquired a nasty reputation for secreting a liquid that was dangerously hallucinogenic when dried and inhaled. ("It tasted like model glue," said one woman who went "toading." "I took a few really deep breaths and got it into my lungs. You feel it immediately creeping down your spine. Within a minute, I was on the ground, thrashing around. I had no control of my coordination and a total loss of muscle control. I couldn't speak or anything. It was great.") Toads also have shorter legs, thus less meat.

All that said, many species are edible and if it is necessary to put five or six pairs of legs on the plate, instead of the recommended three or four for frogs, so be it. Preparation is basically the same.

Finally, a word about toad wine. Just about anything from the worlds of insects and reptiles—and let's not forget genitalia—has been used to flavor whisky and wine, usually in the belief that the combination of the two—gecko plus rice wine, snake plus corn whisky, etc.—will generate some medicinal benefit, usually connected to longevity and sexual potency. Thus there was in 1995 a fad that swept across Cambodia that nearly wiped out that small country's toad population.

So great was the demand for the wine, a stout-like liquid that was cheaper than beer or whisky, Dr. Mok Mareth, Cambodia's Environment Minister, appealed to toad hunters to halt their killing as they were upsetting the balance in the ecosystem. Chay Seang Y, a traditional healer in Phnom Penh, said that unlike gecko wine, which is believed to have originated in China and Vietnam, toad wine was entirely Khmer. In the recipe he recommended, the toads were dried, fried, crushed and stirred into white wine along with some herbs, including black sugar cane, producing a drink almost thick enough to require the use of a spoon.

What was the attraction? A belief, unproved, that consumption of toad wine would cure syphilis and a number of other kinds of sexually transmitted diseases, as well as promote appetite and good sleep. A tough combination to beat

Under Secretary of State for Environment Pou Savath was unimpressed. "I'd sooner see toads catching harmful insects that destroy crops in the field," he said.

Spoil sport.

Mssr. Escoffier on Frogs

"For various reasons, I thought it best in the past to substitute the mythological name 'nymphs" for the more vulgar term "frogs" on menus, and the former has been universally adopted, more particularly in reference to the following *Chaud-froid a L'Aurore*:

"Poach the frogs' legs in an excellent white wine *court-bouillon*. When cooled, trim them properly, dry them thoroughly in a piece of fine line, and steep them, one after the other, in a *chaud-froid* sauce of fish with paprika, the tint of which should be golden. This done, arrange the treated legs on a layer of champagne jelly, which should have set beforehand on the bottom of a square, silver dish or crystal bowl. Now lay some chervil bunches and tarragon leaves between the legs in imitation of water-grasses, and cover the whole with champagne jelly to counterfeit the effect of water.

"Send the dish to the table, set in a block of ice, fashioned as fancy may suggest."

—*The World of Escoffier, Timothy Shaw (1994)*

Deep-Fried Froglets

100 tadpoles
5 large eggs (chicken)
1 gallon pond water in a bucket

3 cups bread crumbs
Dash of cayenne pepper
4 cups oil heated to 500°F

Put tadpoles into water and wait until they develop legs and lose their tails. While waiting, combine bread crumbs, add cayenne pepper, write a mystery novel, raise kids, take a round-the world cruise. Once frogs have developed, put in egg, then coat with bread crumb-cayenne pepper mixture. Fry frogs until golden brown. Serve alone, or in a fresh frog fajita.

Shark

People who keep track of such things—called actuaries in the insurance industry—say that the chance of being hit by lightning is one in two million, of dying from a hornet sting one in five million, of being struck by a falling piece of an aircraft one in ten million, and of being killed by a shark one in 300 million! And more people die each year by choking on toothpicks than have been killed by sharks in the last decade in North America.

Thus, the shark has an undeserved reputation when it comes to gastronomy. Most people think it dines on you, when the opposite is immensely more common. So common, in fact, that of the 350 species of shark, over eighty per cent are threatened with extinction due to humankind's desire for its flesh and fins.

Yes, it is true that sharks are nasty creatures when crossed. During the 450 million years sharks have patrolled the world's oceans, they have evolved into skilled predators who are at the top of the food chain among marine life. A shark can pick up sound waves over five kilometers and home in on the source to within a square meter, even in zero visibility. It can smell blood in the water at two kilometers, detect increased electrical current in the bodies of wounded fish or panicking humans, even hear their heartbeats. It can move at forty miles an hour, plus. It has no dental problems; if a tooth breaks off, the next automatically takes its place.

Is it any wonder that author Peter Benchley and director Steven Spielberg made names for themselves when they spawned a series of movies called *Jaws*? Can anyone forget the blonde teenybopper who left the beach party, slipped out of her clothes and swam off into the moonlight in that classic 1975 film? The music built to a crescendo and suddenly the water around the teenager foamed, we heard the sound of a human body being ripped apart and the screams of the girl before she disappeared amid gurgling noises into the depths.

Such scenes occur, but rarely. Paddling surfers resemble favorite shark meals, the seal and turtle. A woman who is menstruating may also be at risk if a hungry shark is nearby. Injured victims of maritime accidents are recovered infrequently. Yet, today, more often it is man who is the predator, as the hunter has become the hunted. Nowadays, shark meat may be eaten more widely in South America, Europe, Africa, and Asia than in the United States and Canada, but even those reluctant markets are expanding rapidly because of a trend toward eating more broiled and grilled fish, as the supply of tuna and swordfish shrinks. Shark meat also is praised for its high protein content and it contains almost no fat or cholesterol. One-third pound of raw shark meat yields about four ounces of lean, cooked fish, with more than an ounce of high-quality protein and only about one hundred calories.

In a pamphlet published by the University of Hawaii Sea Grant Marine Advisory Program as early as 1977, the shark was called not a swimmer's nightmare but "a chef's dream" whose "bland flavor allows it to conform readily to many tastes, with the use of sauces, herbs and spices, and flavorings. The boneless, all-meat fillets turn perfectly white when cooked, and this fish cooks easily and quickly." The flesh of the mako, which grows to twenty feet, was compared favorably to swordfish; in fact, even today, although restaurateurs may not admit it, some serve shark and call it swordfish, while others offer it under the names "whitefish" or "greyfish." Because the taste is indistinguishable from some other firm, pale fish, it is infrequent when anyone notices.

Usually, they are caught on "long lines" with baited hooks—300 hooks on a heavy nylon line that may be up to nine miles long. (Nets are destroyed by the sharks and because they don't swim in schools, they prove economically inefficient using nets, anyway.) And once in the boat, sharks must be cleaned immediately. If the blood is not drained from the system right away, the urea deteriorates into ammonia and gives the meat an unpleasant odor and taste.

The University of Delaware Sea Grant Marine Advisory Service suggests putting the shark on ice (after gutting and bleeding it), then at the dock cutting the shark's head all the way around, further making a cut from the head to the tail on both the top and bottom sides. Using a pair of pliers in one hand and holding the head or tail in the other, skin the shark. Then cut the head and tail off, remove the underlying layer of dark meat, and cut the shark into fillets. Wash thoroughly and package the shark for freezing or cooking as you would any other fish.

Once ready to cook, the options are as numerous as for any other fish. A quick check on the Internet shows there are many shark connoisseurs offering recipes for Shark *Hors d'Oeuvres* (deep-fried and served with Creole mustard), Shark Kebobs, Broiled Shark with Anchovy and Caper Sauce, Cape Shark in Essence of Fennel, Shark Tacos, Shark Amandine, Oven-Fried Shark, Shark *Marseillaise*, Shark Curry—Bengal Style, Crispy Shark with Sweet-Sour Sauce, Shark Teriyaki, and Poached Shark Remoulade. To insure good flavor, a quarter teaspoon of vinegar or lemon juice per pound of shark meat may be added to any recipe during cooking to eliminate any residual ammonia.

The University of Delaware offers more tips for preserving shark. Double-wrap the meat before freezing, wrapping only enough in one package for a single serving. Smoking does not preserve shark—it only enhances the flavor. The salt for salting and curing shark should always be non-iodized salt such as kosher salt. Iodized salt will turn the flesh black or it will spoil. To salt shark in a crock, glaze the inside of the crock or the salt will leach the crock and cause the shark to spoil. Plastic containers work well for salting shark. Before salting shark in a plastic container or crock, soak the shark in a brine solution overnight to remove all blood. Then wash the meat with clear water, lay flat, and let drain. After one to two hours, place the shark in a container and layer with salt, covering the final layer with about one inch of salt.

In a category all its own, of course, is shark's fin soup, and this is where, since the start of the new millennium, conservationists have made the biggest waves, declaring as their enemies the millions who think the soup increases social status and virility (nearly all of them Chinese males). It is this dish, one of the most expensive on any menu that includes it, that is blamed for so many shark populations going into steep decline. According to Julia Baum and colleagues from Dalhousie University in Halifax, Canada, writing in the journal *Science*, most affected is the hammerhead, whose numbers in 2003 reportedly were down eighty-nine per cent from 1986. While thresher sharks fell eighty per cent, tiger sharks by sixty-five per cent, blue sharks by sixty per cent, and the white shark, also known as the Great White, star of *Jaws*, by seventy-nine per cent.

Those most alarmed by this say that in some countries, India and Brazil among them, the whole carcass is kept for the protein offered, but claim that the majority of shark fishing is done purely for the fins, as the fins are worth so much more than the relatively inexpensive meat. Thus, to save space on the boats for more valuable fish and shark fins, and to stop the contamination of the taste of other fish from the ammonia that a shark carcass releases, the fins may be cut off the still live shark, then it is thrown back into the sea, where it either drowns slowly or is eaten by other sharks. So vivid is this image, even Peter Benchley has joined the anti-fin brigade, saying that he could not "in good conscience" have written *Jaws* today.

Several countries have already declared a shark-finning ban in their waters, Brazil, the United States, Costa Rica, and Australia among them. Only a few years ago, Singapore Airlines and Thai Airways International both removed the soup from their menus due to public pressure. Hotels worldwide are doing the same. Yet the number of restaurants abound, especially in cities where there is a large ethnically Chinese population; there are more than eighty in Bangkok's Chinatown alone.

This soup is made from the noodle-like, amber-colored gelatinous strands extracted from the dorsal "comb fin" or the two ventral fins of any of a variety of sharks. Some historians say it has been consumed in China since the Han Dynasty that began 2,000 years ago. Others contend it didn't come into vogue until the Song Dynasty, beginning in 960 A.D. Either way, it has a long, savory history, closely linked to the mandarins.

According to a 16th Century *materia medica*, shark fin "opens the stomach," meaning it is an appetite stimulator. Thus, said one food writer, "it may start a meal, or served at the peak of a banquet, it readies you for the onslaught of dishes to follow."

This is a specialty that costs more than most if not all other soups (save, perhaps, those made with birds' nests) because, well, because it's made from shark, of course, but also because it is not prepared quickly or easily. In fact, on reading the instructions in Bruce Cost's *Asian Ingredients* (1988), a book hailed by Craig Claiborne as "by far the most comprehensive guide to the essential ingredients for Asian cooking ever published," I'm compelled to ask why anybody bothers. Only the status attached to its consumption, along with the hope that it will bring sexual stamina, could create such a market.

To prepare shark's fin, Mr. Cost says, it was necessary to soak the fin for twenty-four hours, changing the water several times, then after a vigorous scrubbing, the fin was to be boiled, drained, and then soaked again. A stock with wine was then poured over the fin. Steaming for three hours followed. Then the liquid was discarded and after more rinsing in several changes of water, it was—finally!—ready for use in most recipes.

It is no surprise that shark's fin soup rarely is prepared from scratch at home, but rather is purchased frozen, dried, or in tins or, most often, enjoyed at exorbitant prices in Chinese restaurants. There also are "instant" soups vacuum-packed in plastic trays that may be stored at room temperature for what the manufacturer calls "a long period of time." What would the mandarins think?

The really odd thing about shark's fin soup is that after all the soaking and boiling and rinsing, the fin is rendered nearly tasteless, contributing only a gooey thickening to the dish. By itself, it is remarkable only for its blandness. It's chewy and it has a pleasing texture, but it is the crab meat, roe, shrimps, sweet-smelling mushrooms and other vegetables, ginger, bamboo, thinly sliced ham, shredded chicken, ginseng, and other ingredients that give the soup its flavor.

Steven Spielberg probably never goes near the stuff.

Sharkbait Fritters

1 1/2–2 cups chopped or
    grated shark meat
1/2 cup flour
2 eggs, beaten till foamy
1 small carrot, finely chopped
1/2 small onion, finely chopped

Salt and pepper to taste,
    depending on whether or
    not a sauce is used and the
    type of sauce
Dash of monosodium glutamate
    (MSG)

2–3 teaspoons green onion,
    finely chopped

1–2 drops of yellow food
    coloring, if desired

Optional: 1/4 cup any combination of the following: sliced Chinese peas or string beans, slivered gobo (burdock), chopped water chestnuts, chopped Chinese parsley

Combine all ingredients. Batter should be stiff, but should drop easily from teaspoon. If not, add more flour or moisten with water as needed. Deep fry at 350°F till evenly browned. Drain on paper towel. Serve with tartar, tempura, or soy sauce.

—University of Hawaii Sea Grant College, 1977

Fugu

When I was young, spending my summers on an island off the New Jersey coast in America, my brother and I greeted the fishing boats in the morning as they were rolled up onto the beach on logs. The fishermen then sorted their catch, throwing the ones they didn't want over the side to the dozen or so of us who gathered there most days. For the fishermen, and the shops to which they sold their catch, the discarded fish were trash. For us, it was lunch or dinner.

One of the unwanted species was the blowfish, so called because it was able to inflate its abdomen like a balloon, a defensive talent used to frighten away predators who might be intimidated by the sudden increase in size. Some of our friends told us the fish was inedible, even poisonous, but my brother and I believed it was thrown away because it offered so little meat, only two small finger-sized strips along both sides near the tail. To get a meal, you had to catch and clean quite a few.

It wasn't until many years later, when I was living in Hawaii and exposed to Japanese nationals on holiday, that I heard about another species of blowfish, a deadly toxic variety generally known as *fugu*. I was told that the Japanese regarded it as a delicacy and that there were in Japan hundreds of restaurants specializing in the dish. For those who could afford the price, and were willing to take the risk, *fugu* was an essential treat, a sort of ultimate edible.

How risky is it? Estimates range widely, but some say as many as twenty diners die each year, mostly from fish improperly cleaned at home. Whatever the figures may be, care must be taken and *fugu* chefs are meticulously trained and must serve a long apprenticeship before being licensed and permitted to work under strict government supervision. So rigid are the tests, in fact, that fewer than a third of the applicants pass.

Actually, the word *fugu* is a general name for what my brother and I called blowfish and others know as the puffer, globe, or swell fish. When inflated and dried, it may be sold as a souvenir and seen in seaside restaurants in many parts of the world, hanging from the ceiling with a light bulb inside. There are nearly 100 kinds worldwide, thirty-eight of them found in the waters surrounding Japan and the rivers emptying into them. Most are quite safe to eat. However, those containing tetrodotoxin (TTX) are riskier. A pinch of the poison, the amount found in a six-pound tiger *fugu*, is enough to kill an entire wedding party of thirty. The lethal dose for an adult, one to two milligrams, could be put on the head of a pin. Scientists say its molecular structure is unlike anything else in organic chemistry, making it 1,250 times deadlier than a comparable dose of cyanide. And like curare, a poison with which it is closely compared, there is no known antidote.

Over the years, many well-known names have either described or been exposed to the fish, going back to 1774 when Captain James Cook ate a bit after catching a fish in New Caledonia. J. Reinhold Forster and his son, George Forster, the naturalists for the expedition, sketched it before it was prepared for dinner. "Luckily for us," Captain Cook wrote in his journal, "that only the liver and roe was dressed of which the two Mr. Forsters and myself did but just taste. About three or four o'clock in the morning we were seized with an extraordinary weakness in all our limbs attended with a numbness or sensation liken to that caused by exposing one's hands or feet to a fire after having been pinched much by frost. I had almost lost the sense of feeling nor could I distinguish between light and heavy bodies, a quart pot full of water and a feather was the same in my hand. We each of us took a vomit and after that a sweat which gave great relief. In the morning one of the pigs which had eaten the entrails was found dead."

Years later, in Baja California, the writer John Steinbeck reported he and a friend tried to buy a puffer from a boy they met on the beach, but the boy refused, "saying that a man had commissioned him to get this fish and he was to receive ten centavos for it because the man wanted to poison a cat." It wasn't a cat but a spy who was poisoned, no less a figure than James Bond when Ian Fleming's novel *From Russia With Love* ended with Agent 007 being kicked in the leg with a boot containing a poisoned dart.

"Numbness was creeping up Bond's body...Breathing became difficult...Bond pivoted slowly on his heel and crashed headlong to the wine-red floor." Mr. Bond survived, of course, and in the next novel, *Doctor No*, it was revealed that he had been poisoned with *fugu*. "It comes from the sex organs of the Japanese globefish," a neurologist told Mr. Bond's chief. "It's terrible stuff and very quick."

The toxin works by blocking the nerve impulses, quickly shutting down the entire nervous system. The onset of poisoning ranges from twenty minutes to two hours following consumption, thus often strikes while the diner is still at the table. The first hints that there may be trouble are numbness of the lips and tip of the tongue, spreading to the extremities, followed by headache, stomach pain, a tightness in the throat, facial flushing, dizziness, and nausea.

The violent vomiting that is characteristic in some cases may permit the victim to expel enough of the poison to survive, as happened with Cook and his naturalists, but for those who do not regurgitate, the prognosis is grim. Convulsions hit, followed by fatigue, feelings of doom, and a wish to lie down. It becomes difficult to speak. Breathing is labored. Blood pressure and pulse accelerate, then fall as paralysis sets in and the skin takes on a bluish tint. Death follows within two to six hours.

Why, one wonders, would anyone want to take such a gamble and pay such a high price for taking it? *Fugu* is one of the most expensive foods in Japan and in Japanese restaurants elsewhere, from Hong Kong to New York. A single kilogram can bring as much as $130 wholesale and when served in a restaurant in a variety of ways, as much as $400 for a four- or five-course meal.

Millions seems content to take the chance, betting their lives each year; it is, they say, no more dangerous than flying—a tragedy when a plane goes down, but don't most passengers arrive at their destinations safely? More important is the status attached to paying the high price and experiencing what is, after all, both hazardous and avoidable. For males in a macho society, it is a way of proving one's mettle far more admirably than singing in a karaoke bar. Even some foreigners are willing to put their lives on the line. And for a rapidly expanding tourist population in search of thrills, it requires far less effort than mountain climbing or whitewater rafting.

In the Haedomari Market in Shimonoseki, where most of the country's catch is sold, the fish are auctioned in a peculiar manner. As the auctioneer describes the catch, buyers approach him and slip a hand into a long black sleeve that covers the seller's hand, grasping the auctioneer's fingers in a code that reveals what they wish to pay.

The auctioneer, whose sales pitch continues to fill the air, may keep track of as many as ten secret handshakes before he announces the winning bid. In this fashion, more than two tons of *fugu* may be sold in under an hour.

As is true in many Asian restaurants serving seafood, the fish is kept alive until it is prepared. The customer selects his meal, the chef slaps it onto a nylon carving block, holding it firmly in place with one hand, then with a sharp, triangular knife, removes the toothy mouth, the pectoral and dorsal fins, and tail. Mouth, fins and tail are placed on a black tray for additional preparation. Next he slices the fish from gills to tail on both sides, removing the skin and adding it to the same tray. Now his demeanor becomes that of a surgeon, as he cuts away the gills, placing them on a red tray, where all the dangerous bits go. He then slits the belly to remove the ovaries and roe if it's a female, the gonads if a male, the heart, and then the liver, kidneys, gall bladder and intestines. All join the gills on the red tray, as do the eyes and a thin membrane from the abdominal cavity. Finally, the *fugu* is thoroughly rinsed in cold water, patted dry, and cut into two fillets. There are thirty steps required by law, taking up to twenty minutes for a practiced chef, compared to less than a minute for other species.

It is served only between October and March and thought to be best from December to February. Many diners happily settle for an order of *fugu* sushi (or sashimi), cut into almost transparent slices which are beautifully arranged (typically in the shape of a chrysanthemum or flying crane), and served on a large round plate or tray with a slightly sour sauce for dipping (usually soy), chopped chives and grated radish.

Some diners will order a full meal, with *fugu* prepared in a number of ways. *Hirezake* is strongly flavored, toasted *fugu* fins soaked in hot sake, more a drink than a dish and consumed while eating any of the following. *Fugu chiri*, or *chiri nabe*, is a one-pot dish with pieces of *fugu*, bones, head, thin noodles, and assorted vegetables, boiled together; this may be cooked at the table, with the diners adding the ingredients as desired. *Fuguzosui* adds rice and egg to the liquid remaining in the *fugu chiri* pot. The fish may also arrive at the table whole, deep-fried in a light batter. And for those who wish an "aphrodisiac," the pulverized genitals may be mixed with hot sake—although, as noted, the organs may only be served illegally, something that rarely is done except, perhaps, for a customer of long standing, a friend of the chef or restaurant proprietor, or an insistent and persuasive celebrity. (See Sidebar.)

The *fugu's* bland taste—aficionados prefer the word "subtle"—

and dense, chewy texture may be explained by the fact that the meat is
without fat. When the poisonous organs are removed, they may leave
a slight tingle behind, spreading delicately throughout the skin and
the meat. This may cause a slight buzzing sensation in the lips and
tongue, adding to the thrill of the meal, inasmuch as these are among
the first symptoms of *fugu* poisoning.

When Japan's economy slid toward recession in the early 1990s,
many *fugu* restaurants closed, as white collar workers no longer could
afford the luxury. Still, *fugu* remained big business, with fishermen
catching the fish during the spring spawning season and raising the
hatchlings in huge cages in the sea. Some of the cages hold as many as
30,000 fish. The Japanese also have learned how to reproduce them
through artificial insemination. In 1996, 10,000 tons were consumed in
Japan. A cooperative agreement between the US Food and Drug
Administration and the Japanese Ministry of Health and Welfare
ensures *fugu* is properly processed and certified safe for consumption
before export, the rules changing slightly from state to state.

In New York, restaurants that serve *fugu* must import fish that
have been detoxified in Japan by having the poisonous parts removed
and shipped deep frozen. In 2002, there were about ten restaurants in
New York that served *fugu*, and perhaps fewer than twenty across the
United States. Most were frequented by expatriate or visiting Japanese.

The fish called *fugu* are not without their own risks in life and many
die as violent a death as the feckless or reckless seafood fancier. The
puffer is a tough and aggressive fish known for biting the tails of other
fugu, rendering them helpless. In addition, the *fugu* is raised on a fresh
seafood diet of mostly sardines and, ironically, because the fish lacks a
proper stomach, one of the primary causes of death is indigestion.

Some people call that justice.

Death of a National Treasure

The story of one death is told frequently in Kyoto, where restaurants specializing in *fugu* may be identified by the picture of an inflated fish, or a
lantern made from one, displayed over the entrance. In 1975, Mitsugora
Bando VIII, a kabuki actor of such stature in Japan that he was described
as a "national treasure," visited a *fugu* restaurant with a group of his fellow actors and insisted upon eating the liver. It is in the liver, intestines,
gonads, ovaries, and other internal organs that the toxins are concentrated and it is illegal to serve these organs. The actor was told no, deferential-
ly. He asked again, and then again.

After a time, the chef relented and served each actor one small serving. Those who ate one piece survived. However, three of the men declined and Bando ate their portions as well as his own. In less than an hour he collapsed in convulsions. His final words were, "I have eaten the death number." In Japan, the number four is considered cursed.

Jellyfish

In their natural state, as they go bobbing merrily (or malevolently) along, carried by the wind and ocean tides, jellyfish offer an unlikely source of food. Like so many other food sources in this book, in addition to an unseemly appearance, many species have a nasty reputation for painfully intruding on human lives, in this case, stinging bathers enjoying the sea.

It's no surprise that many people think jellyfish are a strange thing to eat. The beast itself floats to a different drummer. They have been on the earth for over 650 million years, going back to pre-dinosaur and shark times (and, some might say, rudely, given all that time, they still haven't developed much talent or personality). It gets its name from its "jelly bag," a sort of skin filled with a gelatinous secretion that makes it more than ninety-five per cent water—human beings, one of the other wettest creatures on earth, measure a little more than seventy per cent—and it has no heart, brain, or bones, being held together by muscle fibers. Its stomach is connected directly to its mouth, the only opening in its body. This means that food enters here and the waste passes out there, too. Jellyfish also use their mouths to swim, taking in water to fill their stomachs, then pumping it out to propel themselves forward. Their favorite foods? Small, drifting animals called zooplankton, which include other jellyfish, juvenile fish, baby seahorses, and larval crustaceans. There are 200 different species ranging in size from the tiny, spherical thimble jellyfish of the Caribbean to the Arctic "lion's mane," with a bell nearly nine feet across and tentacles that stretch half the length of a football field.

Those tentacles, used to paralyze and move food to the mouth, can be something to worry about. The umbrella-like form of some adult jellies are called a "medusa," so named because of its resemblance to the Medusa of Greek mythology with a head topped with a nest of writhing snakes. The small Portuguese Man of War, with its colorful pink sack that floats on the ocean's surface, to catch the wind and its luminescent blue trailing tentacles, has pestered bathers and beach walkers with nasty stings probably for millennia. While Australia's box jelly's toxin is more potent than cobra venom and can kill in minutes, statistics show that more people are killed by jellyfish than by great white sharks.

Is it any wonder that many don't think of this as food?

Nonetheless, once you get away from Euro-American menus and go to Asia, jellyfish is as commonly seen as it is on the beach following a storm at sea. It appears on restaurant menus from Tokyo to San Francisco to Lima, Peru, usually but not exclusively in Japanese (and to a lesser degree Chinese) restaurants. According to industry figures, nearly 360 tons of edible jellyfish were sold in 1997 by Tokyo wholesalers alone. I've even been served jellyfish salad by several Asian airlines.

The really weird thing about jellyfish—putting aside their peculiar looks and dubious renown—is that the edible ones have no taste. None. If it isn't served with a light soy or sesame oil dressing, for example, or as part of a salad that also offers chicken or fish and vegetables, the question arises: why is this considered food? Some people go so far as to complain that it's like eating rubber bands.

That's part of it. Its crunchy, chewy texture gives it much of its appeal, just as the tactile nature of many foods contribute to their attractiveness. Jellies also offer a fat-free protein related to albumen, the egg white protein, providing vitamins A and B. Like so many other exotic foods favored in the Orient—from snake to bird's nest soup—it's also believed to bring long life, cure a number of common ills, and, in fact, it is now being tested in responsible clinics and labs in some kinds of cancer research.

The creatures also are appreciated across much of the Pacific. In Samoa they're pickled and in the Gilbert Islands, even highly venomous jellyfish called "sea wasps" are considered a delicacy, their ovaries dried and deep-fried (and said to taste like tripe).

It is in its natural form that it is offputting, but so are many other delicious foods. Once harvested—besides Japan, Malaysia and the Philippines are prime sources—and the tentacles are removed, and the large, flat tops are dried, it looks no more threatening than a large, dried mushroom. The most popular species reaches fifteen to twenty inches in diameter and when dried is sold in one-pound bags. Preparation requires soaking them for about eight hours, changing the water two or three times. The blubbery flesh is then parboiled quickly and rinsed under cold water, and sliced thinly.

"It's a nuisance to some people, but a delicacy to others," Charles Blume, executive director of the Apalachee Regional Planning Council in Blountstown, Florida, said when announcing a plan to establish the state's first, authorized jellyfish harvest in 1997. The Asian market for the delicacy was growing, he said, and the fishing industry in Florida, as elsewhere, was in need of a new cash crop.

So, too, elsewhere. In Georgia, the next state to Florida, with shrimp catches falling precipitously, jellyfish were discovered, in 2003, to be a lifesaver, if reluctantly. To George Marra, director of the Georgia Shrimp Association, catching jellyfish was a sign of desperation. "If the shrimp prices were still at a level where we could make a living, ther's no way we would do jellyballs," he said, a reference to the "cannonball" jellyfish, rubbery blobs that once were discarded as trash.

The jellyfish-as-junk mentality made Yao-Wen Huang, a professor of food science at the University of Georgia, the butt of jokes. But he knew from a childhood in Taiwan that jellyfish were a healthy food because of their collagen-rich tissues, believed to help alleviate arthritis, gout, and high blood pressure. The trick was to accelerate the usual forty-five-day salting and drying process to make production worthwhile. Huang got it down to a week, fast enough to make harvesting profitable.

One fisherman shook his head and said, "That's quite a thing. It don't look like it'd be edible. But I guess you can just about eat anything nowadays."

Jellyfish Salad

1/2 lb salted jellyfish
1 large cucumber, julienne
1 tablespoon creamy peanut butter
1 tablespoon soy sauce

1 tablespoon vinegar
1 tablespoon sugar
1 teaspoon sesame oil
Dash of hot chili oil

Wash jellyfish. Rinse under running water for 20 minutes or until it is no longer salty; cut into strips. Put in boiling water for 5 seconds and rinse in cold water; drain. Arrange cucumber on serving plate. Place jellyfish on cucumber. In a bowl, combine remaining ingredients; mix until smooth. Serve with salad.

—*"The Electric Kitchen," Hawaiian Electric Co., Honolulu*

Snails & Slugs

"I have eaten several strange things since I was twelve, and I shall be glad to taste broiled locusts and swallow a live fish. But unless I change very much, I shall never be able to eat a slug. My stomach jumps alarmingly at the thought of it."

Thus begins an essay by Mary Francis Kennedy Fisher, better known by her initials M.F.K., arguably the best writer about food in English in the 20th Century.

"I have tried to be callous about slugs," she continued. "I have tried to picture the beauty of their primeval movements before a fast camera, and I have forced myself to read in the *Encyclopedia Britannica* the harmless ingredients of their oozy bodies. Nothing helps. I have a horror, deep in my marrow, of everything about them. Slugs are awful, slugs are things from the edges of insanity, and I am afraid of slugs and all their attributes.

"But I like snails. Most people like snails."

In this essay, first published in 1937, called "Fifty Million Snails," Ms. Fisher said that once, when she was living in Dijon, France, she ate so many she was dizzy for two days when the gastropods "changed into old rubber boiled in garlic." No matter. She still loved them, as did most other residents of France, who consumed, she said, fifty million snails each year, a figure that has increased to such a degree over the years that consumption is now counted in tons—some 35,000 tons a year; Parisians alone eat twenty tons during the December holidays.

I like snails, too, although I'm not sure why. (The truth is, I think I'd eat anything dipped in hot butter, even pieces of the rubber sandals I wear in Bangkok, my home.) Nor am I sure why history reports that snails were among the first animals to be eaten by man, a claim more or less verified by evidence in the piles of shells found in prehistoric caves. Perhaps it was because they were so easy to catch.

The Romans are believed to be the first to cultivate snails as a food, fattening them on wine and grain, and Pliny the Elder, wrote in the 1st century in his thirty-seven-volume *Natural History* of grilled snails eaten with wine as an appetizer before supper or as a snack between the feasts and orgies for which its countrymen were notoriously famed. While the Gauls in what is now France served them as a dessert, in the Middle Ages the Church permitted consumption of snails on days of abstinence. Usually they were fried with oil or onion, cooked on skewers, or boiled.

One of early acclamations to this culinary tidbit appeared in 1394 in a French newspaper, *Le Managier de Paris*: "Snails, which are called escargots, should be caught in the morning. Take the young small snails, those that have black shells, from the vines or elder trees; then wash them in so much water that they throw up no more scum; then wash them once in salt and vinegar, and set them to stew in water. Then you must tick these snails out of the shell at the point of a needle or a pin; and then you must take off their tail, which is black, for that is their turd; and then wash them and put them to stew and boil them in water; and then take them out and put them in a dish to be eaten with bread. And also some say that they are better fried in oil and onion or some other liquid, after they have been cooked as above said; and they are eaten with spice and for rich people."

By the 17th Century, the consumption of snails declined and in much of Europe for centuries afterward, they were regarded not as a delicious food, but as a garden pest. Which indeed they were, wickedly reproducing in great numbers and eating virtually anything that was green. In France, they made a fashionable comeback when Talleyrand had some prepared for a dinner he hosted for the Czar of Russia. Since that time, France has been the snail's gastronomical champion.

In England, they were still detested for the agricultural damage done and shunned as a food. In a curious little book called *Why Not Eat Insects*, published in London in 1885, the author Vincent M. Holt devoted twelve pages to this edible mollusc (including it because he believed it was, like most insects, another example of diet prejudice that failed to recognize an abundant and available protein source). In the small book, he argued that "Something could be done by force of example. Masters might prepare savory snail dishes, according to the recipes used in all parts of the Continent and in course of time the servants would follow suit." One stumbling block, he said, was that many thought only one species was edible, when the only superiority of this particular snail over its fellows was its superior size. To the contrary, Mr. Holt insisted, all species were edible.

Mr. Holt further reported that in Italy and elsewhere in Europe, many households raised snails in a sort of "snail-preserve, or escarcogotieres, consisting of odd corners of gardens enclosed with boards and netted over the top. In these enclosures hundreds of snails are kept and fed upon wholesome vegetables and such herbs as to impart to their consumers an agreeable flavor. I should like to see a simply constructed snail-preserve in every cottage garden in England."

Snails Cooked in the French Way

" 1. To dress snails. —Snails that feed on vines are considered the best. Put some water into a saucepan, and when it begins to boil throw in the snails and let them boil a quarter of an hour; then take them out of their shells, wash them several times, taking great pains to cleanse them thoroughly, place them in clean water, and boil them again for a quarter of an hour. Then take them out, rinse them and dry them, and place them with a little butter in a frying pan, and fry them gently for a few minutes sufficient to brown them; then serve with some piquante sauce.

" 2. Snails cooked in the French way. — Crack the shells and throw them into boiling water, with a little salt and herbs, sufficient to make the whole savory. In a quarter of an hour take them out, pick the snails from the shells, and boil them again; then put them in a saucepan, with butter, parsley, pepper, thyme, a bay-leaf and a little flour. When sufficiently done, add the yolk of an egg well beaten, and the juice of a lemon or some vinegar.

"Now, don't you think those recipes sound nice?"
—*Vincent M. Holt, Why Not Eat Insects, 1885*

Mr. Holt's arguments fell on silent ears, but in time if England and the other developed countries still failed to embrace insects as a food, the snail found its slow and methodical way to the dinner table when France muscled its way to the world's culinary lead. In some areas of France today, the molluscs are starved for a week or longer to eliminate any toxins or unpleasant taste that might be in the flesh because of what the snails had eaten. In other regions, they are put on a diet of thyme or other herbs to flavor them. And then they are made into a broth; simmered inside their shells with white wine, or garlic butter, a chili-flavored gravy, and chives; shelled and cooked with a white roux using butter and flour, or garlic-flavored mayonnaise and bernaise sauce; or sprinkled with salt, pepper, thyme, and crushed fennel, then grilled. Served with farmhouse bread and red wine.

In Laos and northeastern Thailand, apple snails gathered in the rice paddy during the rainy season are simply boiled and served with a dipping sauce of pounded garlic, chilis, fish sauce, and coriander leaves. Traditional sticky rice is the usual accompaniment.

If these and numerous other snail recipes have found favor, the slug remains, as it was for Ms. Fisher, at the bottom of the food chain as well as on anyone's list of desirable mealtime treats. It may be said that, lacking the pleasing, symmetrical shell, the common garden and sea slugs are, comparatively, somewhat unattractive. But so are many other foods "on the hoof," including the crab, the lobster, the oyster, and, for that matter, the chicken.

In fact, the only significant difference between a snail and a slug is the shell. While most molluscs are invertebrates whose bodies are protected by a hard shell, the slug remains in the same scientific classification, along with squids and octopuses, but has no protector armor. There are more important similarities. Like the snail, the land slug dines on vegetation, usually at night, thus it, too, is regarded as a pest. While the sea slug, resembling its air-breathing cousin closely, feasts on coral or other animals in the sea.

If the land slug has failed to draw a hungry audience, the capture and cooking of the marine slug has a long and exuberant following, from China and Japan to the Eskimos of the frozen north. There are some visual differences between the two. Land slugs appear in many colors, from red to gray to yellow to black, and while they vary in size according to species and age, most sea slugs are black or gray and are far larger, weighing as much as two pounds.

Over time, it also has received some poor notices, dating back to a pre-fifth century fragment of a Chinese work called *The Canon of Gastronomy*, where it was called *hai-shu*, or "sea rat" and was described as "looking like a leach, but larger." In time, its status improved and it came to be called *hai-shen*, or roughly, "ginseng of the sea," as it was believed to have the same restorative properties. So popular was the sea slug in China, the emperor sent huge fleets as far as Africa and Australia in search of an adequate supply. In what is now Sri Lanka in 1415, a war was fought over the lowly slug, when the local king ordered the fleet away; in response, the Chinese dispatched an army, captured the king, and continued to harvest the sea and its shores.

One of the reasons for its lionization and renown was its supposed ability to enhance male virility, a reputation explained, perhaps, by the fact that it has a long, thick, muscular form that swelled to the touch. A document surviving from 16th century China reported that when the slug was not available, "take the penis of a donkey and use it as a [gastronomical] substitute."

In 1913, a woman named Elie Hunt was interviewed in her native Kwakuitl language in what is now Alaska, recounting the details of how the sea slug was caught and cooked. The hunter, always a man, waited for low tide, when he paddled his canoe over the tidal pools and captured the plentiful animals with a forked stick. "He takes the sea slug, takes his knife, and cuts off the neck. Then he squeezes out the insides, and he throws it down hard into his canoe, saying as he is throwing it down, 'Now you will be as stiff as the wedge of your grandfather'."

Back on shore, the slugs were steamed for two days, then boiled over an open fire. Because the water of the slugs almost always boiled over, the Kuakkuitl woman said, the man threw handfuls of dirt from the floor of the house into the water, the only way to halt the boiling over. They were then washed a final time and served as is.

Today, the sea slug—sometimes called a "sea cucumber," again because of its shape—generally is dried and soaked for several days, then boiled in several changes of water until its original spongy texture returns. The slug is praised by nutritionists, if not for its aphrodisiacal properties, for its zero level cholesterol, saying, also, that pound for pound, it has four times the protein of beef.

Because it is fairly tasteless, but known for its satisfying crunch—similar to bamboo shoots or jellyfish—when eaten, the Chinese usually cook it with chicken, pork, seafood, or vegetables, or add it to a soup. The Japanese sometimes eat them thinly sliced and raw in vinegar at sushi bars.

As for the garden slugs, the ones that Ms. Fisher found so off-putting, they may be simmered with several changes of water to remove the slime before being arranged on a slice of toast with a mushroom cream sauce, garnished with sesame seeds.

The House of Snails

If there is a center of snail gastronomy, it is at the Maison de l'Escargot, a firm established in Paris in 1894. It sells what its owner, Christian Bernard, calls "luxury snails" collected by hand in the wild in Burgundy and Alpes.

Some 200 kilograms of the little creatures begin their journey to the French capital alive by truck. Upon arrival, they are sorted according to size and placed for three week in boxes in a cold room, so they can completely empty their gastrointestinal tracts. Finally, they are repeatedly machine-washed in twenty-five kilo batches, then cooked, the butter, fresh garlic and herbs being added just before serving.

France doesn't have a monopoly. There are 116 edible varieties and more and more of the snails eaten in France, Italy, Germany and Austria come from farms or eastern Europe and Turkey. Among the most praised are the giant *Utala vermicula*, from Africa, whle companies in Indonesia and Taiwan market the *Achatilna fulica*, usually in pieces.

"I would never touch a snail from a snail farm," says Mssr. Bernard. "They have no taste." For him it is a tragedy that so many restaurants present their customers with frozen farm-raised snails. "Pieces of rubber with the taste of margarine," he sniffs.

Worms

As I was growing up in the United States, I remember that when someone felt rejected and angry they told their parents, "I'm gonna go eat a worm!" I suppose they figured that by making such a perilous threat, the parent would give in. It never happened. And I don't know anyone who actually ate a worm, either.

Today I listen carefully when someone says that worms may be the meal of the future, or at least part of it—along with other life forms I once never thought were edible. I know now that worms are good to eat and so numerous as to be an answer to the food shortage that soon the entire world may face.

Like too many other great foods, worms have an unfortunate reputation, at least in the language and culture that shaped my childhood, when girls were made of "sugar and spice and everything nice" and boys were made of "worms and snails and puppy dogs' tails." Later in life, I heard people insult one another by calling out, "You worm!" And to use dubious means to accomplish or escape something was to "worm your way" into or out of it. The only positive thing I can think of referred to ambition and reward: "the early bird gets the worm."

When I was growing up, worms were what you put on a hook when you went fishing, captured in the early morning after a rain, when the "nightcrawlers" were still sliming around in the rectangle of crab grass we called our front yard. Later, in biology class, I learned that they were the earth's great composters and recyclers, transforming decaying organic matter and everyday dirt into worm "castings"— excrement, if you want to be frank—turning the soil over like tiny underground ploughs, giving the soil valuable nutrients. In just one acre, I learned, there could be a million or more worms, eating ten tons of vegetation a year, turning over tons of soil. Gardeners and farmers welcomed earthworms like sunshine and rain.

It is for such reasons that a sizeable earthworm industry exists today. All over the world, small businesses are selling worms by the bucket for what is called "vermicomposting." Just throw some of the critters into a box with some dirt, add lawn clippings and the kitchen garbage—apple cores, coffee grounds, that sort of thing—and the worms will quietly turn it into rich potting soil. There's not even any smell. Or, just add them to your garden and besides adding nutrition, they leave tunnels behind to let in air and water.

There also are dozens of entrepreneurs selling start-up kits and instructions telling how to join their ranks. The idea is: you buy some worms and "bins," or propagation boxes, that serve as "farms," then just sit back with a can of beer, watch the sunset, and let the worms reproduce. Then you sell them, either by mail (the post office and most couriers accept them), in a shop, or door-to-door in your neighborhood, although that last choice may get you some odd looks.

As desirable as this creature may be to farmers, home gardeners, and fishermen, very little credit has yet been given in the developed world to the earthworm as a food, and a shame it is, too, because earthworms are seventy to eighty-two per cent protein (the scientific findings vary) and the taste is pretty good, as well. Worms have always been only one step away in the human food chain via birds and fish, and in the case of Australian Aborigines, New Zealand's Maoris, and some Chinese, it was and is a direct food source.

It should be understood, by the way, that many creatures called "worms" are not. Mealworms, for instance, are larvae that turn into beetles, as are the "worms" in bottles of the popular Mexican booze, mezcal. Earthworms, on the other hand—and there are about 6,000 species—are found in all regions of the world except in deserts and frozen areas.

Like larvae, worms should be purged before eating, an easy task: just put them in a container of moistened corn meal for forty-eight hours as soon as you catch them or receive them live in the morning post. Then they can be washed and cooked right away, or washed and frozen for later use. To wash worms, rinse them vigorously in cold water, then blot dry on paper, removing any that have died. (They're the ones that aren't moving.)

Most often, worms are boiled or baked. Two pots of boiling water are used, transferring the worms from the first to the second after cooking for about fifteen minutes, then boiling again for another fifteen minutes—to remove the mucus. More boiling is okay if any mucus remains. To bake earthworms, they must be frozen first (so they won't wriggle off the baking pan), then defrosted and put on several layers of paper toweling on a baking sheet. Thirty minutes later, yum.

The baked worms may be eaten as snacks, perhaps with some salt and other seasoning; ground into a meal for use in a cake or bread; or included in any other dish that calls for meat. The Maori in New Zealand, the Aborigines in Australia, the Aztecs in Mexico, and other primitive peoples usually baked them over a fire or in the sun, then pulverized them for use in a simple bread or stew. *The Worm Book* by Loren Nancarrow and Janet Hogan Taylor (1998) takes a more modish approach, suggesting recipes for Vermicelli with Earthworm Meatballs (adding earthworm flour to ground beef), Oatmeal Earthworm-Raisin Muffins, Earthworm Meatloaf, and Caramel Earthworm Brownies. In another book, *Urban Wilderness: A Guideboook to Resourceful City Living* (1979), the author, Christopher Nyerges, suggests coating the worms with flour, browning them in butter, adding bouillon and simmering, then mixing in sauted onions and mushrooms, and covering with sour cream.

And...they are cheap. If you don't have any in your yard or don't feel comfortable wandering around the public park or school yard after dark with a bag and a flashlight, there are dozens of sources where you can get up to a thousand large ones for only US$25, while snack-sized "cups" of twenty-five go for about a dollar.

So far, the worm has not made many inroads as a food. In time, a dish called *Soufflé Ver de Terre*—*ver de terre* is French for earthworm—may show up on a restaurant menu, but for now, at least in the developed world, only a few are championing the wriggler's edibility. In Butler, Pennsylvania, in 1998, for instance, students in an eleventh grade class fried worms, coated them with chocolate, took deep breaths, closed their eyes and swallowed as part of an experiment in alternative food sources.

"I did it 'cause it was cool," said Knoch High School student Josh Murdoch. "It's really not that bad."

Another Odd Critter to Behold

The earthworm is a strange creature and that may explain, at least partly, why so many humans continue to think it's only good for bait and putting nitrogen back into the earth. The front end and rear end are hard to differentiate. They are slimy, moisture playing a key role in their survival. Although their gastrointestinal system is comparable to a human's—mouth, esophagus, intestine, anus, etc.—the worm has no legs, brain or lungs, but has five "hearts." It also is capable of producing sixty per cent of its body weight per day in urine.

In addition, some species of nightcrawlers can regenerate themselves when cut in half, occasionally creating a worm with two tails or two heads. There's one species found in South America that is eight feet long, making it clear why a movie starring Fred Ward and Kevin Bacon called *Tremors* is about huge, man-eating earthworms. Names like Red Wiggler and European Nightcrawler don't help lighten the image, either. Finally, worms have both male and female reproductive organs, making them hermaphroditic, although it still takes two to make a baby worm.

A History with Twists and Turns

Worms have been around for about 120 million years and weren't always shunned by society. In Cleopatra's time, Egyptians believed they were sacred and Socrates, usually credited with knowing what he was talking about, called them "the intestines of the soil." Charles Darwin studied them for nearly four decades, saying, "It may be doubted whether there are many other animals in the world which have played so important a part in the history of the world." He even wrote a book about them, *The Formation of Vegetable Mould Through the Action of Worms With Observations on Their Habits*. Why is it that academics have such a hard time with titles?

Loren Nancarrow and Janet Hogan Taylor write in *The Worm Book*—now there's a title I can live with—that most earthworms were killed in North America during the last ice age and that they were reintroduced by early European settlers in the 17th and 18th centuries. "Most worms arrived in the soil clinging to the roots of favorite plants brought to settle the new land," they said. "The settlers' ships also used soil as ballast, and this was off-loaded at ports once it was no longer needed. The soil contained many earthworms, which gradually spread out from the many ports. Some farmers, after seeing plants in the port cities do better with the earthworms, deliberately introduced the earthworms to their land."

Earthworm Patties

1 1/2 lbs ground earth worms (purified)	2 tablespoons soda water
1/2 cup butter, melted	1 egg, beaten
1 teaspoon lemon rind, grated	1 cup dry bread crumbs
1 1/2 teaspoon salt	2 tablespoons butter
1/2 teaspoon white pepper	1 cup sour cream

Combine earthworms, melted butter, lemon rind, salt, and pepper. Stir in soda water. Shape into patties and dip in beaten egg, then in bread crumbs. Place in heated butter and cook for 10 minutes, turning once. Place patties on hot serving dish. Serve with heated sour cream on top.
—*Courtesy, Matthew Stewart, The Incredible Edible Wild*

Fish Eggs

I joined the Japanese women squatting at the ocean's edge at low tide, reaching cautiously into the tide pools to lift sea urchins from the bottom. For every dozen gathered, each of the women seemed unable to resist eating one. The sea urchins—in Hawaii, where I lived at the time—were at the largest only three inches in diameter, each one a fragile dome covered with spines that looked like the pincushion my mother had in her sewing kit, with all the pins reversed and standing on end, sharp ends pointing out. To step on or handle a sea urchin was painful, and their harvest was an activity defined by caution.

The women were gossiping, watching the sea for incoming waves, carefully turning the urchins over, the spiny top held in a gloved hand, to open them from the bottom with the unprotected fingers of their other hand or a knife, deftly breaking the invertebrate's shell, extracting the digestive system to get at the orange genital glands and eggs attached to the top of the shell. This was the edible portion, called the coral. They then raised the broken shells to their mouths and sucked the eggs into their mouths. They gave one to me, along with a protective glove. I mimicked their opening ritual awkwardly, but was able to get to the eggs. The taste carried the tang of salt, mixed with a hint of iodine. The texture was similar to caviar. As it should have been. These, too, were eggs from the sea.

The women were showing me how to harvest the small, spiny creatures that they would serve, raw, that night to their husbands with the customary sake after work, or balance on fingers of moist rice, a kind of sushi (called *uni*). But the roe tasted so good fresh from the sea, sparkling with brine, the women couldn't resist. They had to eat a few. Me, too. It was like eating affordable caviar.

The sturgeon that swim in the Caspian Sea, adjacent to Russia, the fish that produce the "real" caviar today may soon be declared a threatened species because the worldwide demand has overwhelmed the number of fish. (More about caviar in a minute.) If this is so, and the supply can't meet demand, or regulations cut back the capture of the fish, urchin roe could take up some of the commercial slack. It's an expensive delicacy for what is, usually no more than a canapé, but compared to the least expensive caviar, urchin roe is a bargain. There are about 700 species of sea urchin in the world and all are delicious. And both the males and females bear edible eggs.

It's best to use the roe within twenty-four hours and to keep it refrigerated until used. Served in a sushi bar, atop the ubiquitous nugget of rice, or on a whole grain cracker with finely chopped onion, lime juice, salt and pepper—as is popular in Chile—it is the perfect hors d'oervre. The classic recipe in Japan calls for *kanten* (agar-agar), which is processed from sea vegetables, not animal protein, to be added to the eggs. It jells more firmly than conventional gelatin, although that may also be used. This makes the dish more economical, while holding the crumbly eggs together, preventing them falling off the rice.

It may also be turned into a main course. In South America, the urchin, or *erizo*, grow large—some species up to ten inches in diameter—and are cooked in omelets and other dishes. In France, where they are called *oursins*, or sea eggs, they may be boiled in seawater and eaten with the fingers. The eggs can also be crushed into a paste to flavor sauces, soufflés, and to accompany seafood. A paste called *neri uni*, sold bottled at most Oriental groceries, may be blended with eggs to make a glaze for boiled fish. (Never, ever, use caviar for this.)

The legend and lore surrounding caviar, the eggs of the sturgeon, goes back to at least to the days of Aristotle, who wrote about Greek banquets that ended with a trumpet fanfare introducing a heaping platter of caviar garnished with flowers. The Persians called the eggs the *Chav-Jar*, meaning "cake of power" and, later, in England the sturgeon was called the Royal Fish of England when King Edward II decreed that all sturgeon caught had to be given to feudal lords.

But it was in Czarist Russia where caviar hit its zenith. Nicholas II taxed sturgeon fishermen what amounted to a total of eleven tons of top-grade caviar each year. So passionate was the Czarist appetite, the favored species, the sterlet sturgeon, is virtually extinct.

A hundred years ago, caviar was plentiful, not only in Europe, but also in waters near North America, where along the eastern seaboard it was set out on the bars in saloons much the way peanuts and popcorn are today, a salty snack that was believed to increase the patrons' thirst. Until the 1900s, the United States produced 150,000 tons a year, mainly in New Jersey. So common was it in some waterways—for example the Delaware and Hudson Rivers, a serving of the best caviar was bargain-priced at five US cents, while increased production in Europe drove the price down, in France, to forty centimes for a kilo (2.2 pounds), little more than the cost of a loaf of bread.

But all good things don't last and as the number of sturgeon rapidly dropped, and the source of the prime caviar, the Caspian Sea, was isolated by two world wars, the price of the eggs went up again, until only the wealthy could afford them.

This is when much of the ritual was instituted, in the same way that the etiquette of drinking wine developed. For the connoisseur, chilled caviar was never mixed with chopped egg, onion, unsalted butter, or sour cream—although they could be on the side—and always was presented either with toast points (or blini) or a bland, unsalted cracker. It was never served with a metal spoon, as it was believed this would contaminate the flavor; instead, spoons made from bone, tortoise shell, or mother-of-pearl were used.

The preferred drinks? Frozen vodka to honor the Russian heritage, of course, or a very dry champagne, or when the caviar snobs wanted to go slumming, a sparkling or a dry white wine.

There was also argument about "grades" of caviar. Beluga, produced by the largest species, was regarded by many as the best, thus was the most expensive. This was light to dark gray in color with large granules and a delicate skin. Osetra caviar with smaller grains a dark brown to a golden yellow in color has its champions, too. While Sevruga, a product of the smallest sturgeons, which are most prolific and give small gray eggs, is the cheapest.

There is, in fact, a fourth grade, "pressed" caviar, a thick, marmalade-like spread that is made from the ripest and broken eggs by pressing them in cheesecloth to remove the moisture. Some say the result is too salty, but many caviar fanciers insist it is the best.

While most who can't afford it, or don't like the saltiness (in much the same way that anchovies and other salty foods are shunned) or reject the "idea" of eating any eggs that don't come from a chicken, caviar is dismissed.

Yet, in the Caspian Sea and some Russian rivers, until the end of the 1990s it continued to be a major industry. Here, the sturgeon were caught in large nets and the females of egg-bearing age were stunned by a blow to the head with a wooden club. They were then taken ashore, where they were given another knock and cut open. The egg sack was removed and the "berries" were rolled gently across a grate to separate the eggs by size. After washing, a gentleman known as a "Master Salt Blender" graded the caviar and salted it, depending on the quality of the eggs and the final product desired. The salt acted as a preservative and curing agent, causing the eggs to become firm. Borax sometimes was added for the European market to give them a softer, sweeter finish—in the U.S., borax was regarded as an undesirable additive—and after all excess liquid was removed, the eggs were packed in lacquer-coated tins. The caviar usually was pasteurized for longer shelf life, and sold in jars.

By 2001, sturgeon catches had collapsed, falling thirty-fold over the past twenty years, mainly because of over-fishing. CITES, the international organization that protects rare wildlife, threatened to blacklist caviar exports altogether in Russia, Kazakhstan, and Azerbaijan, the three big Caspian producers and the three countries agreed to halt fishing, while Iran was regarded as having fairly effective harvest management. In the years following, poachers and legal fishermen who suddenly found themselves to be illegal continued to feed the market. Bottom line: the price of caviar went through the roof and a tin of the eggs that cost US$100 in Moscow cost ten times that in London.

For those who like fish eggs, and cannot afford caviar, there are numerous alternatives besides the urchin. (Technically, roe refers to the reproductive glands of both the male and female fish; the eggs are called "hard roe," the sperm or "milt" of the male "soft roe.") Salmon roe, the large bright red eggs from the Atlantic salmon, is prized for its decorative qualities as well as its flavor, while the golden whitefish produces tiny yellow eggs with a delicate taste that are used primarly as a garnish. The eggs of the cod (often smoked), grey mullet, tuna, mackerel, carp, and lumpfish may also be used. In Japan, the roe most commonly served in a sushi bar, after *uni* and *ikura* (salmon roe), are *tobiko* (flying-fish roe), often served with the bright yellow yolk of a quail egg on top, and *masago* (the roe of capelin, a kind of smelt), while *kazunoko* (herring roe) is prized as a traditional New Year's dish.

As with sea urchin—and the caviar snobs with their dry toast points and mother-of-pearl spoons be damned—fish eggs go well with dozens of dishes. They can be used as a topping on scrambled eggs or wrapped into an omelette, mixed with sour cream and used to stuff baby red potatoes, stirred with softened butter to top grilled or poached fish, added to egg salad, or used as a garnish with beef tartare, broiled oysters or clams, cold soups and open-faced cucumber sandwiches.

Finally, there are the red-orange eggs found in pregnant female crabs. In some parts of the world, the eating of female crabs is banned and those captured must be returned immediately to the sea to insure a continued crab population. In other areas, the eggs are so cherished that in markets the females have a portion of their abdomens cut away to show the presence of roe. Not surprisingly, they command a higher price.

Sea Hedgehog?

The food encyclopedia *Larousse Gastronomique* offers five recipes for what is called, in France, a "sea chestnut" or a "sea hedgehog." In all, urchin eggs are the key ingredient, added for its rich taste—the champion flavor in a hearty soup with green crabs and rockfish, in an omelet, in a sauce with butter and eggs for fish, in a purée with holandaise sauce that is used to fill puff pastries, and in a mixture of diced tomato, chopped shallots, peeled shellfish, heavy cream, whipped butter, cognac and white wine, which is returned to the empty, cleaned urchin shells and baked. Sprinkled with chervil leaves.

Served with a good French wine, of course.

CHAPTER THREE
birds

ONE OF THE MOST COMMONPLACE protein sources in the world today is a bird—the chicken, a domestic fowl that is easily digested, lending itself to preparation in hundreds of enticing ways, from soup to chop suey to paella to McDonalds and KFC. Other feathered species are popular as well—including turkey, duck, goose, and guinea fowl in the farmyard category, and among the numerous game (or hunted) birds, grouse, quail, partridge, snipe, woodcock, pheasant, and wild duck.

There are many more species that find their way to the dinner table today less frequently, or at least in limited distribution and geography. Ostrich and emu, for example, are just now winning an audience outside Australia and South Africa, and while song birds are a common dish in much of Asia, Africa, Latin America and parts of the Mediterranean, elsewhere they are virtually overlooked.

Birds have much to offer as food. The meat has less fat than mammal flesh and it is rich in proteins and B vitamins. Birds also are everywhere to be found, many of the plumper species usually in abundance, so numerous in some areas that they are regarded as pests. The smaller birds offer far less meat than is found in domesticated fowl, but if the game is young, the strong, fragrant aroma of the flesh more than compensates. Because so many are small, the bones (even the heads) often may be consumed as well, depending on how they're cooked.

Although wild birds have a culinary history that goes back to when the first human figured out a way to catch one and make it a part of the meal—something to fill in when mammals were unavailable—

they play a relatively small role in much of the world cuisine. Today, birds are regarded as something to watch hop around on the lawn, sing in the trees (or in cages), and lend a beauty to the world that can only come from their inimitable ability to fly. What's not given full credit, is that they're also a delicious treat.

Birds are also valued for their eggs, a perfectly balanced food, fairly low in calories, providing all the amino acids essential for human nutrition, and easy to digest, although they contain a high level of animal fat, which is found mainly in the yolks. What makes an egg "strange?" It is in what happens to it on the way to the mouth. Some are half-way hatched before serving, so that there are little bird embryos inside. Others are, by a simple process turned green or black.

Odder is a dish called bird's nest soup, made from the gelatinous saliva of an Asian swallow or swift. Peculiar not only because of the material from which the soup is made, but also because, like jellyfish and shark's fin, by itself it has no taste. And we have talked yet about rooster wattle and testicles, duck beak and web.

I rush to such food's defense, if for no other reason than to praise imagination. In a time when chicken is cooked to its lowest culinary denominator and becomes, as one writer expressed it, "the new standard for an American 'dining out' experience"—and this turns into one of America's major exports (after Mickey Mouse, Elvis, and Coke), it is abundantly clear that we've distressingly lost our way. The fast food joints are giving birds a bad name.

Balut

Back in the 1990s, Ray Bruman was an American with a site on the World Wide Web called "Ray's List of Weird and Disgusting Foods." In his introduction to a long list, he says, "I have a theory that many (all?) cultures invent a food that is weird or disgusting to non-initiates as a sort of a 'marker.' The kids start out hating it, but at some point they cross over and perpetuate it (perpetrate it) on the next generation. Then they nudge each other when foreigners gasp."

That sounds like balut to me.

Balut is, or are, sixteen- to eighteen-day-old duck or chicken (traditionally duck) embryos. They are eaten by opening the narrow end of the egg in much the same way a soft-boiled chicken egg is opened. Some aficionados add a sprinkle of salt before sucking out the mush and juices. This is the easy part of the experience. Next you carefully remove the remaining shell, revealing the unborn bird, veins, bones, eyes, beak—a scrawny little thing that looks precisely like what it is: a wet, warm, feathered fetus. More salt may be added, with perhaps a spritz of vinegar, then you just pop the little critter into your mouth and chew, little bird feet and all. Yum. Or so the connoisseurs insist.

While in Manila, I hired a taxi to take me to the balut capital of the world, a neighborhood called Pateros, once a rural suburb, now a part of the city. On the way, I asked my driver if he ate balut.

"Every time I make love to my wife, I eat balut," he said, giving me the thumbs-up sign. "Have five children. Pregnant with number six!"

Pateros became the center of the egg embryo universe many years ago, before it was incorporated into metropolitan Manila, when it was home to many duck farms. As urban sprawl overtook the neighborhood, the duck farmers moved away, mostly to provinces in the north. They still provide the eggs, but to avoid the long commute in heavy traffic, the freshly laid eggs are trucked to Pateros for processing and easy distribution once they are ready to eat.

Following instructions from someone selling balut on the street, we went to an address on Pateros Avenue and walked down a driveway past an ordinary clapboard home to a structure in the rear about the size of a large garage, which it might once have been. Five wooden boxes filled the room, measuring approximately three feet in height, five in width, and twenty in length, separated by narrow aisles. Each of the containers, looking like large, deep planter boxes for growing vegetables, was filled to the top with rice hulls, except for a dozen duffle-bag-sized holes in each box lined with burlap. These holes were filled with eggs and on top was a burlap bag also filled with husks, forming a sort of lid, replicating, more or less, the dark, warm comfort of a laying mama duck. Light bulbs in the low ceiling and a total lack of ventilation pushed the temperature well above 100°F. Men stripped to the waist bathed in sweat told me that some processors used mechanical incubators which made for better working conditions, but, they insisted proudly, balut produced in this "natural" manner had a better taste.

On the floor was a primitive sort of light box, with egg-sized holes. A hundred-watt bulb inside permitted the men to take an egg and hold it in the hole and "x-ray" (their term) the eggs on the ninth day of incubation to see that the semila, or "life of the egg," the embryo, then a shadow in the center, was forming on schedule. The eggs also are moved from one hole to another, as the ones near the bottom are warmest and the transfer allows them to develop evenly.

Not all the eggs do so and they are put aside to be boiled. Then, after sixteen to eighteen days—the duck normally would hatch in twenty-eight days—the remaining eggs are removed from their nests and rushed to markets and street vendors all over Manila, where they are kept warm in lined baskets and sold for about twenty-five US cents apiece, starting when the bars close, with sales picking up again in the morning when they serve as a quick and easy breakfast. They also are standard fare at train and bus stations.

I asked how many eggs the men in this garage produced. One of the men said, "40,000." Weekly. And this was one of dozens of similar operations.

Originally believed to have been introduced to the Philippines by Chinese merchants, when Filipinos migrated to other parts of the world, they have taken their cuisine with them, so it is now possible to buy balut from Hong Kong to Canada. In fact, a balut farm in California now exports some of its product to the Philippines, where it has been well received, just as some California wines made from cuttings from Europe find grudging approval in France. (It should be noted, apologetically, that like many other things from the US, the American eggs are larger.) The duck embryo is also a treasured dish in Vietnam, where it is called *ho bit long*.

Not all of the eggs

Most balut in the Philippines is sold on the street by vendors and eaten as a between-meals snack, served with a folded piece of paper containing the salt. However, with the arrival of upscale restaurants and trendy nouvelle Philippines cuisine, some menus are now offering balut in specially prepared dishes. It also is prepared as an appetizer, rolled in flour, fried, and eaten with a vinegar and chili dip, or baked in a crust with olive oil or butter and spices. A pricey restaurant in Manila's financial district, Makati, prides itself on its Balut Bisque and I heard but never was able to track down reports of balut being used in a paté and a soufflé.

I confess that however much I pride myself on my sense of culinary adventure, I don't like balut, although I think that has more to do with the crunch than the taste. Perhaps it helps to keep your eyes closed. M.F.K. Fisher was probably right when she said that if we didn't start early enough, some foods may never be embraced. After my visit to where most of Manila's balut was incubated, in Pateros, my driver suggested we give the local treat a try right there on the street. When in Manila with a cab driver, as the old saying about Rome sort of goes, you do what the cab driver does. He loved it and I silently promised myself that I'd never eat balut again.

I didn't want any more children, anyway.

Ostrich & Emu

Some years ago, while staying with a family in Capetown, South Africa, I found myself alone in the kitchen, foraging for something to eat. I opened the refrigerator door and saw, for the first time, an ostrich egg. It was about the size of an American football, somewhat fatter in the middle and rounded at the ends, and it occupied nearly half an entire refrigerator shelf. Before the day was out, it became the centerpiece for a meal, an omelet for ten, equal to about twenty chicken eggs. I was impressed. (As much by the rather bland taste as the necessity of using a heavy wooden mallet to open it.) In the 1970s, the ostrich was not commonly regarded as a protein source, at least not outside its usual habitats, mainly in Australia and South Africa. Times have changed.

I'm drawn to ostriches. Like many people, I'm attracted to the physical oddities in the animal world. Giraffes, duckbilled platypuses, elephants, that sort of thing. Animals that look like they've been made out of spare parts for several species, or are too large to be practical or believable. They appear to be Mother Nature's private jokes, like dinosaurs and bats. Ostriches, with their long, skinny necks and legs, their bulky bodies covered with feathers, and such big adorable eyes, must be liked as well as gaped at. Is it not for this reason that Big Bird is such a favorite character on television's *Sesame Street*?

That said, the ostrich's image in much of the world is that of a long-legged, long-necked, cowardly creature that sticks its head in the sand to avoid confrontation. This impression may be based on when the bird is resting, it sits on its haunches and extends its neck so it can look out for danger. This means all anyone sees from a distance is the ample bulk of its body with a head held close to the earth. In fact, the ostrich is not cowardly and can be quite aggressive, and when a bird up to eight or nine feet in height weighing as much as 300 pounds, with a ground speed of up to forty miles an hour in short sprints, takes a disliking to some intruder into ostrich territory, that someone or something is best advised to escape by any means available, preferably by horse or car. The *Guinness Book of Records* calls it the world's largest and fastest bird. Its egg is also the largest.

The ostrich, or *Struthio camelus*, originated in the Asiatic steppes during the Eocene Epoch, forty to fifty million years ago, and once ranged through much of Asia, Europe, and Africa. Ancient Egyptians trained them to pull carts and over 2,000 years ago, the Egyptian queen Arsinoe rode an ostrich with a saddle. Teams of ostriches sometimes were used in Rome to pull chariots.

The ostrich's history as a food is long, going back to the days of Roman empire, when strange foods—even for the time—seemed to be almost mandatory cuisine for emperors. Vitellius, considered the greatest glutton in all history by Robert Ripley, the world-famous collector of oddities, was known to favor ostrich brains, alongside the livers of parrot fish and the tongues of nightingales.

More recently and commonly, and certainly more affordably, the ostrich has been captured, butchered, and cooked by the Aborigine in Australia and the Zulu in South Africa. (The latter group's tall, ferocious warriors also included the feathers as part of their battle dress.) Until modern times, these birds were never farmed, but killed in the wild, usually with spears and traps.

Ostrich farming really began in the last half of the 19th century— when Charles Darwin praised the meat—and by the early 1900s, spread from South Africa and Australia to Algeria, France, and the United States when there was a demand for the plumes used in feather dusters, as decorations on expensive women's hats and feather boas, and as accessories on showgirl costumes. Sally Rand, a famous fan dancer, star of the vaudeville and music hall stages in Europe and America in the 1920s through the 1940s, performed naked using a large ostrich feather fan to mask her nudity from the audience.

When the feathers—and fan dancers—eventually went out of style, so did ranching. Today, it's back, big-time, and not just for the feathers, but largely for the leather and meat. When diners around the world began to look for low-cholesterol alternatives to beef, ostrich farms popped up from China to Holland to Israel to North America. By 1997, there were approximately 70,000 birds in Australia. The same year, just two years after China imported its first eight birds, there were 400 farms across twenty provinces, with a total population of about 80,000. While South Africa was home to more than a quarter of a million and the United States boasted 10,000 ostrich farmers with as many as 500,000 birds, located primarily in the South and Southwest where the climate and environment most closely resembled their natural habitat. Even in wintry Canada, there were thriving (heated) ostrich ranches in almost all the provinces.

Ostrich, as well as rhea and emu, are called ratite, the name given to large, flightless birds. In Australia, the emu, the world's second largest bird, used to roam throughout that island continent, but now is limited to Western Australia, although its picture appears on the national coat of arms. In South America, the rhea lives on the open grassland from Brazil southwards. One more flightless bird is the cassowary, a much smaller bird with shorter neck that makes it look like a cross between a small ostrich and a turkey, found in Papua New Guinea. All are eminently edible, but it is the largest of the birds that has found the greatest commercial success as a protein source.

Of the three, the emu is far and away the leader in this long-legged gastronomical race. In Australia alone, from 500 breeding chicks in 1985, the Australian flock in 1995 was estimated at more than 470,000, far outdistancing the ostrich in numbers, sometimes appearing on restaurant menus, there and elsewhere, as ostrich merely because its bigger relative was better known. When travelers returned home and said they'd eaten emu, friends didn't know what they were talking about, but when they said they'd had an ostrich steak, "Wow!"

How this happened is a tale in modern day marketing. In a report in Ostrich News in 1993, the owners of the Day-O Ranch in the United States said they were intrigued when asked to invest in "a 400-pound chicken that has red meat that tastes like a cow, but with less fat, cholesterol, and calories than chicken or turkey; a fourteen- to twenty-square-foot hide that brings $40 to $50 a square foot wholesale for boots, briefcases, wallets., etc.; feathers for dusting new cars and computer components; and lays a three-and-a-half-pound egg that equals twenty-four chicken eggs." But when told how much it cost to buy a pair of breeders, they laughed and bought a Christmas tree farm instead. Later, as the market for meat, oil, leather, and feathers increased, they changed their minds and now Day-O is one of the many farms spreading the ostrich gospel on the Internet.

By the early 1990s, ostrich became the investment flavor, or curiosity, of the week, in the same way that people once invested in mink and chinchilla ranches for the anticipated profit from the sale of furs. In 1993, ostrich breeding farms were selling a pair of chicks to start-up farmers for US$600, two three-month-olds for $2,000, and two adult breeders for $25,000! In 1994, cost of a breeding pair of emu was even higher, as much as $100,000!

Though start-up costs were high, it was pointed out that a healthy female ostrich, on average, could lay up to fifty eggs a year in captivity and that the birds were ready for slaughter at around a year old. With the meat selling at premium prices, profit seemed assured. In New Zealand, one new rancher named his first two birds Cash and Flo.

However, patience was required, along with the beginning bank account. "You need to wait two or three years for a good return," Raymond Lam, managing director of Global Ostrich Investments, Ltd., told me in 1997. His was one of several companies that sold ownership of birds that were raised on farms in Australia—the idea being that investors owned the birds and let the farmers do all the work, everyone reaping a share of the profits when the birds began to reproduce.

The concept of buying what might thus be called "ostrich futures" was not without its critics. Chas Dale, the general manager of the Australian Ostrich Company Ltd., in a phone interview disparaged the scheme. He told me that his company, formed by a non-profit ostrich farmers' association to market the leather and meat, would accept the $4,000 to $5,000 it believed a pair of proven breeders was worth, but warned that some investment companies charged the investor double that figure, or more.

"We believe the market will grow slowly," he said, "and part of the reason is that the meat is expensive. We're emphasizing the health aspects. We're targeting up-market restaurants that will offer it as a superior meat. When you order lobster, you expect to pay for it. It's the same with ostrich."

Mr. Dale was right and when the market grew too slowly for some investors, the cost of a pair of breeders dropped to about half in just three years. But interest in the industry continued to grow. Meat started appearing on selected restaurant menus worldwide, and then in supermarkets in large cities. The distinctive tan hides with the evenly spaced dark dots were made into boots, shoes, belts, wallets and purses, seventy per cent of the leather going to Japan. Ostrich oil became an ingredient in cosmetics, shampoo, and drugs. The feathers were discovered to be free of static electricity, so that when you brushed something with them, the dust was cleaned off completely, consequently were used on cars before they were spray-painted and in the assembly of computer disks to brush away dust before the two sides were joined.

The meat market was given a further boost when "mad cow disease" crippled the European demand for beef in 1996. In the search for alternative protein sources, ostrich was one of the big winners. It looked like beef and tasted like beef and was "mad cow" free, although a spoil sport in Thailand's Public Health Ministry warned that the bird could be a carrier of fleas that caused a deadly fever. Because of its lower interior and exterior fat deposits, it ranked lowest in calories when compared in a study to eighteen other meats, including pork, rabbit, chicken, and duck. Ostrich flesh also was higher in "good" cholesterol levels and lower in the "bad" cholesterol count. And a drumstick could weigh as much as fifteen pounds.

For a time, British Airways served ostrich medallions in its first class cabin and today, ostrich is offered in upscale restaurants from Dallas to London to Singapore, for as much as US$55 for a top loin or tenderloin plate. Once upon a time, ostrich (and emu and rhea) were cooked simply, chopped into steaks and roasted on a spit over an open fire. Those days are gone, along with the feather boas and hats. Now, the bird is served like any other gourmet meat. The Australian Ostrich Co. Ltd. distributes a glossy brochure full of recipes that includes such treats as (take a deep breath) Coriander Green Curry Ostrich Served with Cardamom Scented Rice and Cucumber Riata... and (take another breath) Bengal Five-Spiced Ostrich with Moroccan Couscous and Tomato Salsa.

How could anyone resist?

Coriander Green Curry Ostrich

100 gram ostrich fillet, diced
100 gram butter
5 onions, diced
1 clove garlic, crushed
1 tablespoon green curry paste
1 tablespoon sambol
3 lime leaves, fresh or dried

1 bunch coriander, chopped
400 ml natural yogurt
1 cucumber, finely diced
1 kg long grain rice, washed and
    drained
5 cardamom pods
10 pappadams

Melt butter and sauté onion and garlic until transparent. Add ostrich fillet and simmer over low heat until lightly browned. Add curry paste, sambal, and lime leaves and simmer covered for 2 hours or until tender. Stir in coriander.

Combine yogurt and cucumber and refrigerate until required.

Place rice and cardamom in a large saucepan and cover with twice the volume of cold water. Bring to the boil and simmer covered for 15 minutes or until water is absorbed and rice is cooked.

Moisten pappadams in water until slightly softened and cut into strips. Deep-fry in hot oil until crisp and golden.

For each serving, spoon approximately 200 gr of ostrich curry over cardamom rice and garnish with pappadam strips. Serve accompanied by 50
ml cucumber riata.

—Courtesy, Australian Ostrich Company Ltd.

Rooster Comb,Wattle & Testicles, Duck Beak & Web, Chicken Feet & Odd Eggs

I first encountered rooster comb and wattle in northern China at a
lunch hosted by the owners of a marble quarry, who'd just sold a million dollars worth of statuary to an American hotel developer. I was
traveling with his son, who was doing the buying, while researching a
book about the hotel that was to be used by the developer as a corporate Christmas present and sold in the hotel rooms. (This is the same
guy who chickened out with me when we encountered warm snake
blood in Taipei.)

Once negotiations were complete—a two-day process—good
manners called for the Chinese businessmen to host a lavish meal,
what turned out to be a five-star lunch served in a zero-star environment, an eight-hour drive from Beijing. The walls and floor of the
restaurant bore the abuse of decades, the furniture was nondescript,
and everything smelled of cigarettes, but in the parking lot were the
Mercedes Benzes of the local Communist party leaders and stacked to
the right of our plates were packs of Long Life cigarettes, signs that we
were honored guests dining in the town's best eatery. The supply of
rice whisky was unlimited and we were expected to drink at least one
shot of it between every course, of which there were multitudinous.

Many courses into the meal, I vaguely remember a stir-fry with an
ingredient I couldn't identify, either visually or by taste. It was
explained, when I asked, rooster comb and wattle, the red fleshy deco-
ration from atop a male chicken's head as well as beneath his loud
mouth. Just as the randy rooster was "strong," taking care of a host of
hens, our host said, I would be made "strong" by eating his wattle.
"Strong" is a word you hear attached to a lot of odd foods in China.

This is not the only odd poultry part that shows up in Asian meals,
and in a few other places unoffended by gastronomical experimentation. (In France, for example, cocks' combs are bled and skinned, marinated in olive oil and lemon juice, then skewered, dipped in beaten
egg, sprinkled with fine bread crumbs and fried in clarified butter.

Those French always do something elaborate.) In fact, there are many poultry parts that might be called Barnyard Foul.

The most unusual must be a rooster's testicles. No need to explain why they're consumed, except to say that they are popular in both China and France, which probably says something rude about both countries. I have only seen photographs of the jars and the globes therein contained seemed much larger than a rooster could carry around comfortably. Which may be why he crows. Calvin Schwabe's wonderful *Unmentionable Cuisine* (1979) suggests cooking turkey testicles, peeling them like Concord grapes, then breading and frying them.

There are many other chicken parts that Euro-Americans find a bit strange. My Thai-Khmer wife Lamyai just looooooooves to chew on chicken feet, the part of the bird below what I consider the bird's flesh line. The market for this marginally nutritious snack is Asian, once again, but also is found in other undeveloped or poorer neighborhoods where the economy is such that nothing even remotely digestible is discarded. Essentially, it is the soup in which the meatless but gelatin rich extremity is cooked (with other ingredients and stock) or the batter and oil in which it is deep-fried that surely holds the appeal. That, or the primeval joy that comes with gnawing on something, a sop to hunger enjoyed in the manner in which a poor dog savors a bone.

Duck beak and web seem even odder to me than feet, although of course the web is a part of the duck's feet. Dishes including these also come from my wife's northeastern Thailand, where the beak is deep-fried and the web is sliced and peeled, then cooked until tender and added to a salad that might also accommodate a similarly crunchy accompaniment like jellyfish. Once again, it's the gelatinous texture that contributes as well to soups and braised dishes.

Many intriguing things also are done to eggs. In Arabia, they're fried in olive oil and sprinkled with mint or marjoram and green onion. In the Philippines, they're pickled and fertile ones are allowed to turn into embryos. (See chapter on Balut.) Former U.S. President Richard Nixon liked them scrambled, with catsup, perhaps the strangest thing I've heard yet, anywhere. Even when it comes to what follows.

The first thing you have to know about Thousand-Year-Old Eggs is that they only look as if they were found in some long-dead Chinese emperor's tomb. (A thousand years would date them to the Song Dynasty, 960-1126.) This is accomplished by soaking duck or chicken eggs (duck is preferred) in a heavy salt solution with lime, lye, and tea leaves for about three months, then coating them with a paste of clay, lime, ashes, and salt and burying them in the ground for at least two months, during which time the whites turn dark green and become somewhat cheesy and the yolks will go yellow or black. The Thais call them "horse piss eggs," but that is to deride a food that actually has an enticing texture and taste. However peculiar the color scheme, the flavor is delicious, reminiscent of over-ripe Camembert, and they go well with pickled Chinese vegetables or ginger.

An even larger market exists for "Salted Eggs," again most often duck. First, the super-saturated solution of salt is created by adding salt to warm water until salt no longer dissolves in it. The uncooked eggs are then placed in a crock or large jar, covered with the salty water, and set aside for at least two weeks and up to a month and a half. Calvin Schwabe believes that the "secret to good salted eggs" is to add a cup of gin to every gallon of water. The longer the immersion, the saltier they become, of course, and probably also the drunker. Before serving, the eggs are hard-boiled and, if sold in markets or on the street the shell usually is dyed red so buyers won't be surprised when they get home.

Salted eggs may be peeled, quartered and eaten with hot rice or congee, a rice porridge that is a popular breakfast dish, again principally amongst Chinese. They also may be sliced, added to cut tomatoes, and served with sliver of preserved ginger root, sprigs of fresh coriander or basil, and green onion. If a salad dressing is used, it should be light, or just a little oil and vinegar, or olive oil by itself.

And then there is something called The Monster Egg. I first spotted the recipe for this in the estimable *Larousse Gastronomique* and since have seen variations in many other texts, though I am skeptical that such a dish was often prepared. The recipe calls for twelve to twenty-four eggs, two clean pig bladders—one of them small, the other large—and a very large pot for boiling water.

The eggs are broken and the whites are separated from the yolks. The yolks are then beaten and tied up inside the smaller bladder and boiled in a pot until hard. Once cool, the solid ball of yolk is removed, the unbeaten whites are placed into the larger bladder, and into this the ball of yolk is placed. (Reportedly, it will float to the middle automatically.) The larger bladder is then tied tight and boiled until the white hardens. After a second cooling, the gargantuan egg is removed and sliced.

With a straight face, no trace of irony, *Larousse* suggested eating it cold sprinkled with vinaigrette or browned in the oven with bechamel sauce.

Duck Webs in Oyster Sauce

5–6 duck webs
1/2 broccoli
2–3 Chinese dried mushrooms,
    soaked
2 ginger roots, peeled
2 scallions
2 tablespoons rice wine (or sherry)
1 tablespoon soy sauce

1/2 tablespoon sugar
1 teaspoon salt
1 star anise
2 tablespoons oyster sauce
1 teaspoon sesame seed oil
1 tablespoon corn starch
    (corn flour)
4 tablespoons oil

Remove the outer skin of the duck webs; wash and clean well. Crush the ginger root and scallions.

Heat up 2 tablespoons (30 ml) oil; toss in the crushed ginger root and scallions, followed by the duck webs. Stir a few times. Add rice wine or sherry and soy sauce. After 5 minutes or so, transfer the entire content to a sandpot or casserole. Add sugar, a little salt, star anise, and a little stock or water. Simmer gently for 3 hours.

Just before serving, stir-fry the broccoli or greens with the Chinese dried mushrooms, a little salt and sugar. Place them on a serving dish, then arrange the duck webs on top of that. Meanwhile, heat a little oil in a sauce pan, add oyster sauce and sesame seed oil. Thicken with cornstarch mixed with a little cold water; when it is smooth, pour it over the duck webs and serve. Serves 6.

—*Chinese Regional Cooking by Deh-Ta Hsiung (1979)*

Small Bits Stew

Cook together in a mixture of olive oil, wine, and garum, capon testicles, some small fish, tiny meat balls, suckling pig sweetbreads, leeks, and mint. Add pepper, coriander, a little honey, and more wine. Thicken with pieces of flour and oil.

—*Ancient Roman recipe in Unmentionable Cuisine*
by Calvin Schwabe (1979)

Songbirds, Pigeons & Doves

I'm an early riser, usually up before dawn, and on the morning of my first visit to Hanoi I noticed something odd: there were no birds singing. I looked out my hotel window. I saw no birds. Well, I thought, maybe it's the neighborhood. All day, I continued to look for birds on the street and in the trees, but I didn't see any. At the end of the day, I asked someone why there appeared to be no birds in Hanoi.

"We ate them," she said, matter-of-factly.

There are many foods that often are called "survival" foods and I suppose the birds of Vietnam's capital fell into that category, just as rats did in Paris during the Revolution and again during World War Two, and in various places during times of famine people ate tree bark and grass or anything else they could find. When I visited Hanoi in 1992, Vietnam had only recently emerged from the embargo imposed by the United States and during that twenty-year period, the country experienced extreme poverty and deprivation, when food, along with just about everything else, was scarce. So of course the Vietnamese ate the birds in the trees.

This is a story with a happy ending. Most people in Hanoi now have enough to eat, the birds have returned, and my mornings there sound like mornings anywhere else. At the same time, Hanoi is a city where you can order a delicious entré of pigeon, dove and a variety of songbirds in restaurants too numerous to count—birds that are frequently farm-raised. Birds have returned to the "legitimate" menu, leaving "survival" behind.

A somewhat different story may be told about Cyprus, where millions of warblers were killed annually to satisfy not hunger but tradition. There, in hundreds of tavernas, small birds called *ambelopoulia*, caught while resting on a flight from Europe to the warmer climes of North Africa, were marketed as delicacies—plucked, cooked, and pickled and usually sold by the jar, eaten whole with the exception of the beaks. Ornithologists said as many as twenty million were being trapped each year, leading to legislation making the consumption of the birds a criminal offense. To no avail, one of the protestors against the law was a man who asked, "Have you seen the Cleopatra movie with Liz Taylor? They made reference to pickled *ambelopoulia* from Cyprus in that film, which were given as gifts to Rome and to Alexandria. Have you no respect for tradition?"

Over the millennia, bird-catchers have supplied the gourmand and peasant alike with a wide variety of birds known not only for their splendor and song, but also for their succulence. The ancient Greeks hunted wood pigeons, jackdaws, owls, and seagulls, importing flamingos from Africa, while the Romans stuffed wild boar with thrushes before roasting. In 16th century France, doves were cooked with other birds—curlews, wood pigeons and egrets among them—

and, according to *Larousse Gastronomique*, "were more highly prized by some than beef, veal, and pork." Tits, lapwings, warblers, curlews, plovers, thrushes, robins, finches, sparrows, larks, and jays—all made wonderful meals across England and the European continent.

Remember the children's rhyme about "four and twenty black-birds baked in a pie" that dates back to the 19th century? Even the noisy crow was cherished in soups and stews. (Perhaps inspiring Tokyo Governor Shintaro Ishihara in 2000 to suggest Japanese citizens reduce the flocks of crows by eating them.) Of course, the most popular wild birds for eating have always been the larger game birds—heron, duck, pheasant, grouse, and among the smaller ones, quail. But the song birds, the ones that did not greet the Hanoi dawn a few years ago, have long been welcomed at meal time and they are served in many parts of the world today.

In much of rural Southeast Asia, small rice birds known for their silky gray feathers, part of the sparrow family, are grilled until crisp and eaten in one or two bites, head and all. In 1995, a group of Australian Aborigines revived a centuries-old yolla bird industry that once harvested one million birds during the annual five-week season, offering a range of new products from health pills to paté. About the same time, some 400 blue peacocks were introduced to the press in Yunnan province in China by a private company that said it planned to increase the number to 20,000 by 1999, with an eye to the gourmet market. While in Spain and elsewhere along the Mediterranean, birds were still caught by small boys and sold, strung together in garlands, by black-clad old women at the entrance to villages.

"When the birds are cooked with the powerful aromatics so beloved of the Mediterranean palate," Elisabeth Luard wrote in *European Peasant Cookery* (1988), "there is not much difference in flavor between the farmed and the wild." She was talking about quail, but said it was the thrush that she had in mind when she included in her book recipes for Grilled Small Birds, Stewed Small Birds, and Small Bird Paté. She said she made the substitution because her book was published in England, where the thrush was protected. In other European countries and North America, the bird existed in great numbers.

Birds usually are caught in cages, or when they are molting and unable to fly, baiting them with grain. They are prepared in much the same way as animals, though they are usually plucked and cooked with the skin on instead of being skinned, the feathers to come off just before cooking time and never after. Fred Smith, a popular TV chef known as the Frugal Gourmet, warned that carrion eaters could be prone to infection, lice and ticks, and said that they, along with old crows, blackbirds and parrots, were best boiled. While young specimens could be stuffed with herbs and fruit and roasted. Fish-eating birds, he said, don't keep fresh longer than a day and should be skinned to avoid a fishy taste.

Many birds taste like what they eat, their delicate flesh flavored by juniper berries, grapes, or other fruit, and along with their relatives the blackbirds they may be prepared in the same way as quail—grilled (broiled); sautéed in butter (and served on a bed of rice pilaf); braised with grapes; stuffed with ham, truffles, forcemeat or chicken livers, or a mixture, and roasted on skewers; poached and glazed; jellied; in a casserole dish (sprinkled with brandy just before serving); made into a light paté; or cooked in pies and terrenes.

Of all species of small birds, pigeons and doves may be the most commonly eaten, in part because they have existed in such great numbers over so much history and geography. Pigeon stew was enjoyed in ancient Egypt and in imperial Rome, where chefs clipped the birds' wings or broke their legs, then fattened them on chewed bread before cooking. During the reign of Louis XIV in France, it was fashionable to serve pigeon in a stew with peas. While menus for ordinary households in 18th and 19th century Europe and America frequently called for "potted pigeons," a sort of casserole, and "*palpatoon* or *pupton* of pigeons," a kind of hot paté.

Today, cage-raised pigeons under a month old, called squabs, may be found in Chinese poultry markets in many large cities, and commonly in Asian ones, frequently sold alive. Bruce Cost in his book *Asian Ingredients* (1998) noted that "plucking them is a hassle—unlike a chicken you can't scald them to loosen their feathers." (Although he said chilling them for a few hours in a refrigerator tightened the flesh, so there was less danger of tearing during the plucking process.) Once cleaned and dressed, the author said, they could be seasoned and roasted, grilled, or fried, Chinese-style, or like duck, seasoned and steamed or fried. "At around one pound apiece," said Mr. Cost, "they're an ideal size and have many times the flavor of a Cornish game hen." When grilled or roasted, *The Oxford Companion to Food* suggests protecting the breast with strips of bacon.

Ms. Luard credits the Belgians for being excellent gardeners, numbering the Brussels sprout and Belgian chicory among their contributions to the vegetable markets of the world, but it is the battle between the sower of seed and those the farmer sees as seed-stealers— the birds—that inspired a recipe in her book where pigeon was cooked with the gardener's vegetables.

Pigeon eggs are a cherished food, as well, but here the price is dear, both in the retail cost to the customer, who may have to order the eggs in advance—you rarely see them in shops—and to the birds themselves, who lay only two eggs a year, and if both are taken, sometimes stop laying. Like eggs of other small birds, such as quail, usually they are hardboiled and added to other dishes.

A final word about pigeon. The birds that proliferate in urban areas—called "street squab" in some cities—belong, like the song birds of post-war Hanoi, in the survival category. In London in 1996, there was a small scandal when more than a thousand pigeons disappeared from beneath Admiral Lord Nelson's imperious nose atop his statue in Trafalgar Square. The birds, which perched in and around Nelson's towering column, were as much a part of London's life as the ravens at the Tower of London. Well, it turned out that two bird-snatchers were scooping up the tourists' feathered friends in batches of thirty or forty at a time and carrying them off in a large box. One of them, a seventeen-year-old named Jason Lidbury, when arrested said he had caught at least 1,500 pigeons in various London locations over six months and sold them for US$3 apiece. To restaurants? Mercy, no. To people who raced pigeons as a hobby, a popular English pastime. He said.

Pigeons raised on farms for restaurants are plumper and cleaner than street pigeons, of course, and if prepared properly taste somewhere between chicken and fish. Some that I've eaten in Asia were fried to a delicious golden-brown, with enough fat sticking to the skin to keep the meat succulent. The birds were surprisingly meaty—I've had other small birds that seemed to be mostly frail skeletons—and flavorful enough to indicate they had not been subjected the kind of hormonal tampering that produces the large, bland chickens available in most markets.

Technically, there is little scientific difference between a pigeon and a dove, except that the dove generally is regarded as smaller. In fact, some say the rock dove, still thriving in parts of Europe, is the ancestor of all modern species of pigeon. There are several varieties of dove today, many taking their names from their appearance, such as the ringed, collared, and spotted doves, describing feather patterns and coloration. The mourning dove, so named for its plaintive cry, is the most plentiful game bird in North America today and is usually found on farmlands, cleaning up the grain left behind by modern harvesting machines.

2,000-Year-Old Flamingo

One of the classic cookery books of all time is *The Art of Cooking*, commonly called *The Roman Cookery Book*, which was written during the first century by Gavius Apicius. Although modern editions of the book appear to have been expanded and much changed over time, his instructions for the preparation of flamingo may still resemble the original text:

"Pluck the flamingo, wash, truss, and put it in a saucepan; add water, dill, and a little vinegar. Halfway through the cooking make a bouquet of leek and coriander and let it cook [with the bird]. When it is nearly done, add defrutum [must or wine reduced by a half or more by boiling] to give it color. Put in a mortar pepper, caraway, coriander, asafetida root, mint, rue; pound; moisten with vinegar, add jericho dates, pour over some of the cooking-liquor. Put it in the same saucepan, thicken with corn flour, pour the sauce over the bird and serve."

Flamingos used to be seen in large flocks along the southeastern United States, but now are nearly nonexistent in the American wild and are seen only in zoos. They continue to thrive in large numbers in South America and East Africa.

Parrots, Parakeets, & Cocatoos?

Yes. Many of these high-flying tropical birds with their wildly colorful plumage are now threatened by smuggling activity in South American jungles, to satisfy demand from pet shops in Japan, Australia, Europe and North America. But it is not for their vibrant good looks and export value that they are cherished by the indigenous peoples of the Amazon. There, the birds are cooked in a stew or grilled on an open fire, the brilliant feathers then used for personal adornment.

Richard Thomas Orlando Bridgeman Bradford, Earl of Bradford, in 1985 published a collection of odd bits of this and that in *The Eccentric Cookbook*, including a recipe for Parrot Pie, although the list of ingredients called for a dozen parakeets, the smaller cousins of the bird for which the dish was named. After dressing, they were to be layered in a pie dish with undercooked slices of cold beef, rashers of bacon and sliced hard-boiled eggs, then baked. Sufficient for five or six persons, he said, and "seasonable at any time."

Quoting *The Oxford Companion to Food*: "One can find traces of such dishes as parrot pie in early Australasian cookery books, but they attracted only lukewarm praise and were often the subject of jokes [cook a cockatoo with an old boot in boiling water until the boot is tender, then throw away the bird and eat the boot—that sort of thing.]"

Finally, an incident in 1995 in Israel made it clear that parrot was regarded, at least by some, as a serious meat. In case you missed the story, two Thai gentlemen living in that country were deported after it was discovered they had eaten nearly the entire contents of a local children's zoo. When arrested, they admitted they had devoured forty parrots, four goats, and two love birds.

Pigeons with Bacon

4 young pigeons
2 oz/50 g butter
Salt & pepper
Winter savory
4 oz/100 g fat bacon

1/2 lb/250 g small onions
1/2 lb/250 g carrots
1 lb/500 g small potatoes
1 small cauliflower

Pluck, draw, and wipe the pigeons. Put a knob of butter in each, worked with salt and pepper and the savory, chopped fine. Cube the bacon and sweat it in a casserole until the fat runs.

Meanwhile, peel the onions (tiny ones are the best and can be used whole) and chop them. Peel and slice the carrots. Scrub the small potatoes. Divide the cauliflower into small florals.

Preheat the oven to 375°F/190°C. Turn the birds in the hot fat until they sizzle. Tuck all the vegetables around them and add 2 tablespoons of water. Sprinkle with salt and pepper and a little more chopped savory. Bring swiftly to the boil. Cover tightly, sealing down the lid with flour and water. No steam must be allowed to escape.

Stew in the oven for an hour. Unseal the lid at the table. The gardener has his revenge. No other accompaniment but good Belgian beer.

—*Elisabeth Luard, European Peasant Cooking*

Birds' Nest

Trial and error must explain the way many edible things were discovered to be edible. As in: "Oh, that little round thing on that bush over there looks cute, I think I'll eat it." Then, if the courageous or foolhardy caveman or cavewoman who ate it didn't get sick or die, word spread that this little round thing, or berry, might be considered food.

In this manner it must be that a lot of strange stuff got moved from "what the hell is that?" to "oh, boy!" After all, how delicious do snails, oysters, even chickens look? You can't help wondering how it was that they, along with other foods—frog's legs, shark's fins, ants, and so on—ever found their way to the world's dinner plate.

One of the most puzzling may be birds' nest soup. How, I wonder, did anyone ever climb to the top of a dark Asian sea cave, look at a bird's nest made largely from saliva that was stuck to the side of the cave, and say, "Hey, I bet that messy piece of housekeeping would make a yummy soup"? One may also wonder why anyone today would be willing to pay a small fortune for a bowl of it.

Birds' nest soup is one of the true culinary enigmas, a high-priced delicacy that is made from the nests of swifts, found in bat-filled caves in Southeast Asia. The nests are made of seaweed, twigs, moss, hair, and feathers glued together by the birds' saliva and the spawn of small fish. Is this something you want to pay up to US$300 a bowl for, elbow to elbow in a noisy Hong Kong restaurant?

Why so expensive? Well, first of all, it's considered by many to be an aphrodisiac, a word—some say myth—that is driving many animal species to the edge of extinction. For centuries, Chinese have given their children the soup, believing it will help them grow. Others consume it to improve their complexion and defeat lung problems, or as an all-purpose tonic.

In addition, its cost is a status symbol: take the boss out to dinner and buy him a bowl of this gluey stuff and it just might move you up a notch in his estimation of your value as an employee. Factor in the physical effort and risk involved in harvesting the limited crop of nests—and the shooting wars being waged over the caves where they are found today—and it is no mystery why the dish is the soup world's most expensive as well as the most mysterious.

There may be no answer to the question why birds' nest soup is believed to be a sexual supplement. Rhino horn, at least, resembles an erect penis, more or less, and, for some people, it is not an impossible reach to think that tiger penis soup might convey the strength and stamina of what *The Guinness Book of Records* calls the most dangerous man-eating animal on earth. Why the nests of birds that, just before their breeding season, feed on gelatinous seaweed which makes their salivary glands secrete a thick, glutinous spit, with which they construct their nests, should be added to anyone's list of aphrodisiacs cannot be fathomed.

So be it. There are tens or hundreds of thousands, perhaps millions, of people—most of them living in Asia or born of Asian heritage, and mostly men—who think birds' nest soup is good for your sex life, general health, and social status. That is reason enough to make this dish one of the most exalted.

The impact on the environment, and survival of the birds, is debatable. Some harvesters insist they have protected the species from extinction by collecting nests only after the baby birds have fledged. But there are many who take the nests early, whether or not there are eggs or chicks in them.

So no one knows how many swiftlets and swallows remain. According to a World Conservation Union estimate, the demand for nests has reduced the population by a third. The Convention on International Trade in Endangered Species (CITES) has asked all countries in the region to conduct more scientific research in order to promote the sustainability of the harvesting through management programs. The birds are not considered endangered yet, but few studies have been instigated. Attempts by conservationists to gather data on the bird's habitat have encountered resistance and claims that the trading companies are doing all the research that is necessary; and to allow outsiders to enter the caves would disturb the birds, frightening them and ruining business. One can't help wondering why the actual removal of the nests doesn't do the same thing.

Besides, as in Thailand, regulation of nest harvesting is not in the hands of the Forestry Department, whose job is to oversee wildlife. The responsibility goes instead to the Finance Ministry's Revenue Department, whose job is to collect fees and taxes, and it is believed by conservationists that that is a very large pile of you know that, who say the enormous profits surely inhibit chance that such a survey or a review of harvesting practices ever will be made.

In other countries the situation is no different. In Indonesia, for example, no real effort at all has been made to study the subject.

The origin of nest harvesting is unclear. Dr. Yun-Cheung Kong, professor of biochemistry at the University of Hong Kong, says nests have been part of the Chinese diet for 1,500 years, as good a guess as any. He also notes that early in the Ming Dynasty (1368-1644 AD), a Chinese admiral made seven voyages through the "Southern Ocean" and it's believed that one of his missions was to find new sources for the nests, although no documented record has been discovered to confirm this. However, histories of the region show that fleets of Chinese junks sailed the same waters yearly during the 18th and 19th centuries, not only to deal in nests, but also in pepper, shark's fins, and other items of exotic gastronomy for culinary and medicinal use at home.

An account of the nest-gathering appeared in 1928 in a book published in Sweden, *Forest Life and Adventures in the Malay Archipelago*. It was written by Eric Mjoberg, who was one of those wanderlusts drawn to the remote corners of the world and determined to share their experiences with the stay-at-homes, a sizeable publishing niche during the early 20th century. He said the nests at that time appealed largely to "the almond-eyed sons of the Celestial Empire," a racist remark also typical of the period. He added that the natives he met in Borneo paid a yearly tax to the Raja of Sarawak for the right to collect the nests with "four-branched, spear-like implements—fixed to a handle several yards in length—and provided at the top with a lighted candle-end. Holding fast with his left hand to the ladder, [the collector] gives the nest a poke with his long tool and loosens it from its support, then hauls it down, takes if off the spiked fork and lays it in a rattan basket fastened around his waist."

The harvesting methods haven't changed. Only the fees, and earnings, have gone up. Today, in Thailand, in the caves of the Rangnok islands, located near the Malaysian border, the Rangnok Laemthong Swallow Nest Company Ltd. has had a monopoly on the collection of nests since 1958. This company, headquartered in Bangkok's Chinatown, in 1994 was granted a five-year concession for which it paid Thailand's government nearly five-and-a-half million US dollars, a concession that was renewed before the expiration date, extending its monopoly through 2003. The amount paid this time was not revealed. It is believed to be twice the previous figure, counting in all the "commissions" paid for the continued exclusivity.

The search for the nests usually begins in March, when the birds begin mixing their regurgitated spittle with other handy building materials, a process that may take two to four weeks to create a nest that looks like half a tea cup and is afixed to the roof or wall of a cave. The collectors for Rangnok Laemthong insist they do not harvest any nests until the eggs have hatched and the chicks have left the nests, but the extraordinary high price paid for the newest nests has thrown the claim into doubt. It is at this time that they are the most translucent and least contaminated by bird droppings and feathers, thus they sell for as much as US$2,000 a kilogram. There are two other harvests, in May and August, by which time the quality of the nests has fallen, but even by the end of August, the price may start at $700. These prices then double or triple when sold to Hong Kong, Singapore and to Chinese restaurants in Europe and North America.

Rangnok Laemthong and companies in other areas—in Java, the

Moluccas, Borneo, and Myanmar—argue, logically, that it is in their best interest to preserve and protect the birds, thus insuring future sales. However, it's no surprise that in a region where income is minimal, the nests represent temptation for those who have no regard for the survival of the species, only their own. The first nests often are gathered even before eggs are laid—which actually is permitted as the adult birds then build another—but later, eggs and baby birds often are thrown away, which is illegal. While the poachers, some of them former company employees who know the cave locations, routinely bribe the armed guards by making them partners in the late-night theft.

The guards patrol the islands with automatic weapons and over the past few years, many poachers as well as innocent fishermen seeking shelter from storms have been killed. In 1992, ten were gunned down in one incident in Thailand and in 1994, more than twenty men were shot. Villagers who saw the bodies said one of the men was found with a Buddha image in his mouth—the victim having put it there, hoping to ensure his safety—while others were lying with their hands together in the *wai* posture, as if knowing they would be killed. The gunmen were found innocent by the Thai judicial system, claiming self-defense.

Many nest gatherers, legal and illegal, also have fallen to their death from the flimsy bamboo climbing ladders. Yet, the risk has not deterred the Dyak tribesmen or Moluccan aborigines or descendents of Muslim Thai fishermen from pursuing the trade for hundreds of years, even though what they are paid represents a tiny percentage of the harvest value. Seasonal nest gatherers in Thailand are paid a monthly salary of about U$80–100, supplemented by an additional $100 for each of the three annual seasons, while long-time workers may earn a bit extra. It is telling that the guards are paid more, about $110 for each season, with subsequent bonuses of $140 per harvest. In a region where subsistence fishing may offer the only alternative, such income is considered excellent.

Birds' nests have occupied a prominent place in Chinese cuisine and medicine for centuries, but all the nutritional studies indicate that it's a waste not only of nests (and birds), but also of money and lives. Although the untreated nests have been found high in a water-soluble protein—fifty to sixty per cent of volume that could promote cell division within the immune system, a good thing—it's also been discovered that preparing the nests for consumption removes all but a fraction of one per cent. The gluey stuff also contains small amounts of calcium, potassium, and phosphorus, but not in sufficient quantity to do any good, so claims about the soup treating and preventing illnesses is now regarded, officially, as bunk. In 1998, the Nutrition Research Institute at Thailand's Mahidol University compared bottled bird's nest soup with eggs and milk. Twenty-six bottles of the soup costing about $100 offered the protein found in one egg, priced at six cents, while thirty-six bottles were required to match the protein in a fifteen-cent carton of milk.

Such negative notices apparently have little effect. Those who consume the revered soup have not changed their minds about its value, as if to say, "That bowl of soup cost a fortune, so it must be good for me." Such is the value that both buyer and consumer may attach to tradition, or superstition.

Nor is there any agreement in the manner of preparation. There isn't even any accord on how the dried nests should be soaked before cooking. Bruce Cost in his book *Asian Ingredients* (1988), describes a series of soakings and pluckings and simmerings that almost challenge shark fin in their preparation. And this is before the actual cooking begins, when a variety of ingredients—from minced chicken and egg white, to ham and wine, to chrysanthemum petals and lotus seeds—are added for flavor and texture. Mr. Cost described a soup that was baked in a pumpkin, another that was steamed with rock sugar. Another source tells of an elegant recipe called Phoenix Swallowing the Swallow, calling for a chicken to be stuffed with birds' nests and double-boiled in a porcelain pot to produce a clean consommé. Still another suggests soaking the nest in hot water for several hours, then, when the strings of the nest begin to unravel, some vegetable oil is added; the goop is then stirred and more hot water is added, bringing the oil and impurities to the top. This process is repeated several times and the noodles are then boiled in chicken or beef stock, along with rice or vermicelli. It all sounds like too much work to me and it's no wonder that the soup is rarely prepared at home and is left to the kitchen staff in expensive restaurants.

Birds' nests may, of course, be purchased in Asian groceries and Chinese herbal shops, where it costs upwards of US$300 for a small packet weighing about an ounce—making it, literally, worth it's weight in gold. With so much money changing hands, it is no surprise that a common crime in Hong Kong is the burglary of shops that sell nests, while some street vendors sell phony nests made from karaya gum, a harmless plant extract, while back in the gathering grounds of Thailand a large black market has developed for nests that have either been stolen or skimmed from the official count.

Also for sale in shops today are a number of products claiming to contain birds' nest, among them an eight-ounce can of liquid manufactured in Hong Kong whose ingredients also include water, sugar, and white fungus. No ingredient percentages are given and the expiration date that was supposed to be printed on the bottom of the can that I bought was missing.

Until 1950, China was the biggest importer of the nests. Today it is Hong Kong (now, of course, officially a part of China), in 1997 consuming about 100 tons (worth US$25 million) annually. Chinese communities in North America rank second, accounting for about thirty tons. The soup is offered throughout Asia, as well as in cities around the globe, wherever there are Chinese restaurants and rich fools who believe it is good for them, or their libidos.

CHAPTER FOUR
insects, spiders & scorpions

"HISTORICALLY IN GLOBAL TERMS, eating insects has been the norm for human beings. It is only in the western world, and in recent times, that it has been viewed as a strange or even revolting practice."

Thus begins an essay about "Insects as Food" in *The Oxford Companion to Food*, arguably the best gastronomic encyclopedia.

Insects have played an important role in the history of human nutrition in Africa, Asia, Australia, and Latin America, and were an equally important resource for the Indians of western North America, who, like other indigenous groups, expended much organization and effort in harvesting them. Spiders and scorpions have contributed much to the world's cuisine as well, and although they are from another scientific order, I include them here because they and insects seem to look alike and elicit the same response from most diners in the so-called west.

In Euro-America, most may regard these creatures as emergency food to ward off starvation; that's what they're called in United States Army and England's SAS survival manuals. Millions more disagree, including insects—in the larva, cocoon, pupa and adult stages—and other creepy-crawlies as a planned part of their diet throughout the year or when certain species are seasonally available. In fact, the Yukpa people of Colombia and Venezuela prefer some traditional insect foods to fresh meat to such a degree that when mopanie caterpillars (larva) are in season, the sale of beef is seriously affected. While in some countries in Africa, the enjoyment associated with eating caterpillars is so commonplace, it appears in children's rhymes and songs.

For many in the developed world, insects are viewed as a culinary curiosity and while it is true that in some cases in undeveloped or still-emerging countries, people eat insects out of necessity, generally speaking it is the abundance, accessibility, nutritional value, and taste that makes insects popular as food, and not the threat of starvation.

Of the more than 800,000 species described by entomologists, thousands play a role in the human diet. Some of the more important groups include grasshoppers, beetle grubs and adults, ants and termites, moth and butterfly larvae and pupae, crickets and cicadas, bees and wasps, and flies, all of which get some attention in the following chapters.

In Mexico, where many Indian tongues include no separate word for insect, people consume at least 308 species. Insects comprise as much as two thirds of the animal protein eaten in parts of southern Africa. The Thais fix a zesty hot-pepper sauce with ground-up water bugs. In Cameroon, a dish for special guests is palm grubs with salt, pepper and onion, cooked slowly inside a coconut. The Nepalese squeeze live bee larvae through cloth and fry the resulting liquid like scrambled eggs. In Venezuela and Laos, giant tarantulas are a tasty snack. On and on.

Kevin Krajick argued in 1994 in *The Food Insects Newsletter*, published quarterly by the Department of Entomology at the University of Wisconsin, that while the eating of insects "has never gained global acceptance, partly because ancient hunter-gatherer methods limit harvests...a growing number of scientists and businessmen [now] want to make insects a main course for the masses, using industrial-scale cultivation. According to recent studies by Third World entomologists, this most plentiful of creatures—rich in food value and agricultural potential—could substantially cut malnutrition in poor countries.

"The study of edible insects is a growing speciality: African and Asian researchers are documenting insects' role in human diets and pushing governments to promote them. Analyses of Mexican and African food species show that some contain sixty or seventy per cent protein, carry more calories than soybeans or meat, and offer vitamins and minerals lacking in plant-dominated Third World diets."

In the developed world, entomophagy—as the eating of insects is called, scientifically—is still largely a matter of fad. Trendy Australian restaurants serve witchety grubs along with emu steak and European and North American zoos hold annual insect cook-offs and buffets with celebrity chefs (as fund-raising events). Tequila-flavored lollipops containing an embedded beetle "worm" sell as fast as they can be distributed by their California manufacturer. Even Jay Leno had a good time with a presentation of insect foods by entomologists from the University of Iowa. Despite this high-profile exposure, deep-fried grasshoppers, ant egg salad, and mealworm bread are not replacing more traditional protein on many Euro-American dinner tables. Yet.

The odd thing is that we're all eating insects already. The Food and Drug Administration (FDA) in the United States and similar regulatory agencies elsewhere all permit a startling number of "insect parts" in a given weight of packaged food because it is impossible to remove all of the insects during processing, especially in plants. For example, the FDA allows about 450 insect fragments per kilo in wheat flour, a staple used in dozens of foods, from bread to hot fudge sauce.

Some time in the future, the aversion to eating insects in the developed world may change, either because of a need for new protein sources, or when this or other reasons make it clear that big money can be made from their sale. Dr. Gene DeFoliart, former editor of *The Food Insects Newsletter*, wrote in 1992 that if insects "become more widely accepted as a respectable food item in the industrial countries, the economic implications are obvious. They would form a whole new class of foods made to order for low-input small-business and small-farm production. International trade in edible insects would almost certainly increase."

And, by the way, guess which insect gets mentioned most often as the protein source of he future. Get ready. It's the cockroach.

* *Food Insects Newsletter, Department of Entomology, 1630 Linden Dr., University of Wisconsin, Madison, WI 53706; a contribution of at least US$5 is requested to be placed on the mailing list; back issues sell for $1.50 each.*

New York Entomological Society Centennial Banquet
Wednesday, May 20, 1992

At the Bar
Crudite with Peppery Delight Mealworm Dip
Spiced Crickets and Assorted Worms
Buttered *Hor D'Oeuvres*
Waxworm and Mealworm and Avocado California Roll with Tamari
  Dipping Sauce
Wild Mushrooms in Mealworm Flour Pastry
Cricket and Vegetable Tempura
Mealworm Balls in Zesty Tomato Sauce
Mini Bruschetta with Mealworm Ganoush
Worm and Corn Fritters with Plum Dipping Sauce

Buffet
Chicken Normandy with Calvados Sauce
Rice Pilaf
Roast Beef with Gravy
Roesti Potatoes
Mediterranean Pasta
Melange of Vegetable Ragu
Mesclun Salad with Balsamic Vinegrette
Assorted Seasoned and Cricket Breads and Butter

Dessert Buffet
Lemon Squares
Chocolate Cricket Torte
Mini Cannoli
Peach Clafouti
Cricket and Mealworm Sugar Cookies
Sugar and Tea

Grasshoppers

Entomophagists—students of insects as food—generally concede that next to ants, grasshoppers are the most popular six-legged edible bug, with a cuisine dating back at least to Old Testiment times when, it is reported in Leviticus (11:22), that four bugs were an approved part of the ancient Hebrew diet: "Even these of them ye may eat; the locust after his kind, and the bald locust after his kind, and the beetle after his kind, and the grasshopper after his kind." Inasmuch as grasshoppers and locusts are essentially the same, at least in modern times, that gives this creature three out of four holy stamps of approval. (It was not specified what beetle was approved.)

Grasshoppers are found worldwide, wherever any vegetation grows, and range in size from one to five inches in length. The young, called nymphs, are similar in appearance to the adult, but wingless. (It is the adult that is eaten.) Some species undergo seasonal color changes, from green to red or brown, and some males make chirping noises like their cousins the crickets, by rubbing their spindly, barbed legs against other parts of their bodies.

Mostly, over time, the locust has been known as a pest. Agricultural journals are full of stories of migratory swarms so vast and destructive they make many Hollywood disaster films seem tame. In fact, *The Guinness Book of Records* calls the desert locust whose habitat is the dry and semi-arid regions of Africa, the Middle East, through to Pakistan and northern India, "the most destructive insect in the world." This arbiter of superlatives goes on to say "this short-horn grasshopper can eat its own weight in food a day, and during long migratory flights a large swarm will consume 20,000 tons of grain and vegetation a day and bring famine to whole communities. In the U.S., a swarm that once swept across Nebraska was reported to be 100 miles wide and 300 miles long—nearly half the size of Nebraska itself—and, in some places, nearly a mile high. In Ethiopia one huge concentration destroyed sufficient cereals in six weeks to feed a million people for a year."

The fight against such insect odds is not an easy one. The hordes of hungry hoppers that invaded Utah in the mid-1800s, for example, threatened to destroy the Mormon settlement at Salt Lake City as well as Indian villages in the region, prompting the Indians to counter-attack in an interesting fashion. Carleton S. Coon, in his book, *The Hunting Peoples*, told a story about a group of Indians who dug trenches a foot wide and a foot deep and thirty to forty feet long, covering the trenches with a layer of the dry grass on which the insects were feeding. Villagers then spread out in a line, beating the 'crickets' toward the line of trenches with armloads of grass. The insects hopped and crawled into the trenches, when the Indians set fire to the grass held in their hands and scattered it over the grass in the trenches, killing, and at the same time cooking, the locusts with the heat and smoke. The women then removed the toasted insects from the trenches by the handful, and carried them in baskets home.

Other Indians dug a hole four or five feet deep and ten to twelve feet wide where grasshoppers were in abundance, then encircled an area up to several acres in size, the hole in the center, driving forward and beating the ground with sticks, in effect herding the creatures to the center, where they jumped into the hole and were captured.

The Indians ate the locusts, of course, while the Mormons prayed for help (history does not indicate any Mormon ate a single insect), finally getting it when seagulls in the Great Salt Lake region began to feast. Today, a large statue of a seagull decorates the Utah capitol grounds. Other pioneer Americans did eat locusts, boiled in salted water, then cooked with cut-up vegetables, butter, salt, and vinegar and served as a stew, a soup, or over rice.

Why modern Euro-Americans don't include the locust in their diet is a mystery. Surely there's much history. Pliny the Elder, ancient

Rome's greatest naturalist, said that they were much eaten by the Parthians and Herodotus, the Greek historian, described the method adopted by the Nasamones of powdering locusts, then baking them into cakes. Over millennia, in Crimea, Arabia, Persia, Madagascar, Africa, and India, they were cooked in various ways—merely fried with their legs and wings plucked off; boiled, turning red like miniature lobsters; curried; and whatever other fashion suited local tastes.

The indigenous tribes of California held feasts when they swarmed, soaking them in salt water and cooking them in clay ovens, eating them straight away or pulverizing them for later use in soup; so, too, their descendants today. In Africa, they're eaten raw, fried, roasted, boiled, jellied, mashed into a paste, cooked in salt water and dried in the sun, or boiled like shrimp and served with couscous. In many parts of Asia, they have been a culinary staple for more than a thousand years and may now be purchased inexpensively from street vendors from Bombay to Bangkok to Beijing, usually deep-fried. In Japan, they're marinated in *shoyu* (soy sauce) and fried in a little oil.

Most commonly, locusts are consumed in Asia as a snack rather than as part of a larger meal or as an ingredient in other dishes. I've eaten them on several occasions, in much the same way popcorn or peanuts are consumed with beer, the vendors often showing up in neighborhoods where there are several working class bars. The crisp outer portions and legs are crunchy and taste much like anything else that has been deep-fried, the softer insides creamy in texture and mildly sweet.

And, as mom always used to say—except in this case it's the *Journal or Appropriate Technology*, in an article in 1996, saying they are good for you. High in protein (with between forty and fifty per cent, compared to a steak's fifteen), low in fat, rich in minerals (calcium, phosphorus and iron) and vitamins (B2 and Niacin).

A quiet warning may also be appropriate. Grasshoppers sold on the street nowadays are not harvested by people patiently driving them into trenches, setting fire to roast them naturally, but may be killed with chemical pesticides. Of course, other chemicals and preservatives and who knows what are present in more traditional foods, so it remains the decision of the individual diner whether this should be a factor in deciding yes or no, just as it is with any other food.

Some people say it's also a good idea to remove the wings and legs before eating, because they get stuck between your teeth. Same thing happens with popcorn with me.

Clockwise from top: **Figure 26.** Brown-rumped, or edible-nest, swiftlets nest 500 feet up a sheer wall of the Gomanton caves in Sabah, Borneo. The nests, woven purely from the birds' saliva, adhere to the surface of the rock, enabling the birds to inhabit locations which are difficult for predators to reach—but not impossible for man! **Figure 27.** Birds' nest as savory dumplings wrapped in caul. **Figure 28.** A partly shelled Filipino balut reveals the partly formed embryo. Feathers, head, and beak are all distinct, but with the texture of the egg white.

Figure 29. Mealworm salad in cucumber cups—artfully arranged for a cocktail party—are prepared with peeled, cored cucumbers, and filled with lightly fried mealworm, chopped shallot, bell pepper, coriander leaf, and chives.

This page, from top: **Figure 30.** A Thai girl bites into a crisp-fried grasshopper. **Figure 31.** Honeypot ants in the "larder" chamber.

Facing page: **Figure 32.** A dish popular throughout Laos and northern Thailand, the large white eggs of the red ant known locally as *mot som,* or "sour ant," can be steamed, cooked in a curry, or made into a spicy salad. Part of their appeal is the texture—in the mouth, their delicate skin pops open to reveal a creamy texture like soft Camembert cheese.

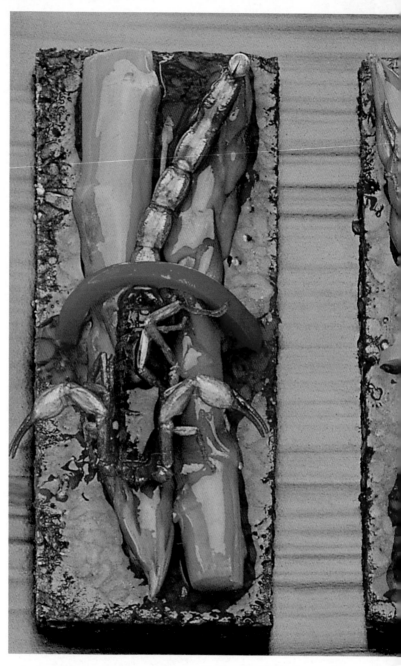

Figure 33. To prepare scorpion and asparagus canapés, the scorpions are first deep-fried until crisp, while the asparagus spears are boiled in the normal way for five minutes. These are both arranged on slices of pumpernickel and decorated with thin strips of bell pepper. Each canapé is then carefully coated with vegetable aspic and chilled in the refrigerator until the aspic sets firm.

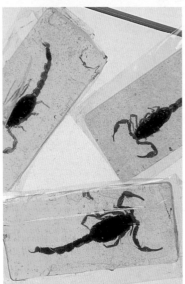

This page, clockwise from top: **Figure 34**. Their feet tied with rubber bands, live water bugs known as *maengda*, fresh from a Thai market, will be pounded into a spicy dip, then relished for their perfumed aroma and flavor. **Figure 35.** Bamboo grubs—known colloquially as "fast cars" because of their rapid crawling ability—are fried with a little garlic by a Lisu hill-tribe woman. **Figure 36.** Scorpion candy, available by mail from the Nevada W & S Corporation.

Facing Page: **Figure 37**. Tarantulas, deep fried with salt and pepper, are a specialty of the small town of Skuon, about two hours' drive north of Cambodia's capital, Phnom Penh. Villagers collect the arachnids from their burrows, taking care to avoid the poisonous fangs (which are trimmed with scissors before cooking begins). The spiders are properly cooked when the legs are crispy but the thorax still retains its moist, gooey interior texture. The experience of eating bears some resemblance to that of a plate of soft-shell crab.

This page, from top: **Figure 45.** The beginning of *tom praedt*, or "ghost soup," a Thai dish in which the fry of freshwater mullet are placed in cold water with the chopped hollow stems of the water convolvulus, or morning glory as it is also known. The water is slowly heated so that the fish seek shelter in the cooler stems. They are trapped there, and the cooked stems are thus stuffed with fish. If the water were already hot, the fry would naturally try to escape and not think of entering the stems. **Figure 46.** Live lobster sashimi, called *odori-gui* in Japanese, from the words "to dance" and "to eat." In its preparation, the unfortunate creature is re-assembled artfully at great speed, so that it will still be moving when it reaches the diners' table. Part of the tail is inverted and replaced as a kind of tray for the flesh, which has first been removed and sliced.

Facing page: **Figure 47.** Black pudding, as blood sausage is known in the North of England, freshly made at a butcher's shop in the mill town of Todmorden.

This page, from top: **Figure 48.** In a village in Vietman's Phu kanh province, *nuoc mam*—fermented fish sauce—is still made in the traditional way and allowed to mature in wooden barrels. **Figure 49.** A fad that arose in Japan during the booming economy of the 1980s—gold-leaf sushi—became an over-priced specialty of some restaurants. Since gold is inert, in these quantities it has no biological effect on the human body, good or bad.

Fried Locusts with Salt

1 lb 1–2-day-old locusts
8 oz groundnut oil or butter
1 pt water

Vinegar
Salt to taste

Remove the limbs and wings and place locusts in a heavy pan with the salt and water. Simmer for about half an hour, until they are soft. Then boil until the water evaporates, lower the heat, and stir in half the oil or butter. Cook over a low heat until the insects are crisp. Spritz with vinegar and add salt.

Grasshopper Paste

1 lb 1–2-day-old locusts
1/2 lb peanuts or cashews

Vegetable or peanut oil
Salt and pepper to taste

Limbs and wings may be left on. Deep-fry in oil and drain when crisp. Then grind in a mortar, adding more oil and nuts until a paste the consistency of peanut butter is produced. Or, dry in the sun and add oil sparingly as the locusts are ground together with the nuts. Store in a jar and use as a spread for sandwiches or crackers.

—Collected by author in Thailand, 1998

Ants & Termites

I once ate chocolate-covered ants, when I was in college in the early 1950s, when you could find them in jars and tins in specialty shops. It was a sort of fad in the United States at the time, usually purchased as a sort of gag gift, if you'll forgive the pun.

I had no idea at the time, of course, that in many parts of what was then called the Third World—in Africa, Asia, and Latin America—ants were a valued source of cheap, fresh protein and a regular part of the local diet. Now I know. I live in that part of the world—Thailand—and there is a restaurant not far from my Bangkok flat that has Sweet Vegetable Curry with Ant Eggs on the menu. And just a few weeks ago as I write this, I had lunch at a restaurant in Singapore that offered Crispy Black Ants on Shredded Potato and Vegetable.

At the same time, I know from personal experience that in parts of "upcountry" Thailand (outside Bangkok), ants, along with a number of other insects show up at mealtime regularly. It was during one of my first visits to the Jankaeo farm in northeastern Thailand that I had my first ant salad. Insects—the Thai word is *malaeng*—are much appreciated in that part of the country and whenever insects of the order *Hymenoptera* are in season, they show up on the lunch and dinner plate. I'm now married to the senior Jankaeo daughter and the dish she served that day included black ants in a spicy rice—left to cool after stir-frying—topped with a small handful of live red ants collected from a nearby mango tree just minutes earlier. I had to dig in fast, lest the salad escape my plate.

Of all the two million or so insect species, ants likely are the most popular—that is, their consumption is the most widespread. Perhaps this is because they are virtually everywhere on the planet, from the tropics to the arctic regions, and they are plentiful. It is unusual to see only one or two, unless they are scouts in search of something, which, if found, means that in minutes there will be hundreds more in orderly attendance, forming bridges out of their own bodies to cross a stream, building mud homes taller than a man, waging well-planned wars and carrying their dead home in their teeth, marching across kitchen cabinets, inviting themselves to picnics, and crawling up pantlegs.

There are 5,000 or so species and all are prolific, as hungry as they are industrious, and always, always numerous. Many claim that ants are the best organized species on earth (certainly more organized than anyone I know)—living in colonies, abiding by strict rules and divisions of labor, always accommodating the group, and humbly serving their queens. Ants also have served a medicinal need for man, with one species used 3,000 years ago in India to close wounds; the live ant was held in position to bite the skin, whereupon the jaws locked and the rest of the ant was pinched off, leaving the jaws intact, and so on with other ants until the cut was sealed. More recently in China, the Nanjing Jinling Ant Research Healing Centre developed Chinese Ant King Wine on the basis of an ancient recipe and modern discoveries concerning the medicinal qualities of ants. It says the wine is effective in treating rheumatism, strengthening muscles and bones, boosting the immune system, and preventing senility.

It may be in Colombia where the ant is at the center of a contemporary insect cuisine. Here, in the jungle in late spring and early summer, what the locals call the "big-bottomed ant" crawl from their earthen catacombs for a rare look at the sun. Waiting are peasants who rush them to the roadside marketplace, where they are sold either live or cooked, bringing about US$6 for a kilogram—about as much as can be collected in a morning, producing more than double the income that might be earned for an entire day harvesting another crop. In this region, many buses have ants painted on their sides and lottery shops are called "The Little Ant." In one town, prominently displayed in the mayor's office, is a statue of an ant.

Ants get no such official recognition in Thailand, but in the poor northeastern part of the country where my wife and I have our home, they play such an important role in the cuisine there are restaurants that have much of the menu devoted to them. One is Satow Wan near Surin, where duck soup—including the bird's liver, meat and blood— is served with hundreds of the local red ants floating on top. This part of Thailand, closely identified with the culture and cuisine of neigh- boring Laos, also is known for a dish called *larb*, a crumbly sort of paté of beef or pork with fiery chili peppers and uncooked, chopped onions. Ants are included in the recipe at Satow Wan when *larb* is made from minced catfish. Ants also are added to curries and stir-fried with vegetables and served with rice. The ant eggs may also be steamed in banana leaves with minced pork, pounded shallots, chopped green onion and hen's or duck's eggs, seasoned with salt, black pepper and fish sauce.

The ants used most often in Thailand, as well as in Laos and Cambodia, are red ants that live in large mounds above ground, which are shoveled and thrown into the air. The ants separate from the dirt and are scooped into paper bags and transported to restaurants and local markets, where they sell for about US$1 a kilogram. Other species in the same region live in nests in trees and are collected in a long-handled net, the ant-catcher dumping both ants and eggs into a bucket half-filled with water. The ants drown, making it a simple mat- ter to separate the eggs and edible winged females.

Of all the edible ants, one of the most interesting may be the para- sol, or leaf-cutting, ant, so called because they cut out pieces of leaves and carry them back to their nests, where they chew the greenery into a sort of mulch, lining their chambers. Fungus grows on the mulch and the ants eat the fungus. These ants, in turn, are eaten by most of the Indians in the Amazon Basin and by others in Central America. The winged females are collected as they swarm from the nest by the thou- sands on their mating flights during the early part of the rainy season. They are easy to collect as they leave their nests at dawn and can be drawn to a wood fire and caught in a basket. The part eaten is the abdomen, which when roasted tastes like crackly bacon.

Other ants taste like a tangy honey. These include, in Australia, a favorite of the Aborigines called the honeypot ant. Workers of this species gather honeydew from other insects, feeding it to fellow worker ants. They, in turn, store the sweetness in their stomachs and serve as a sort of larder from which other ants later dine. These helpless ants with their greatly swollen abdomens are kept in underground chambers, ready to regurgitate some of the nectar when solicited by hungry workers. These subterranean nests may be six feet deep, but once discovered by the Aborigines, are easily dug out. Usually, the heads are pinched off and the remainder is eaten raw.

The honey ant serves a similar role in dry areas of the Western and Southwestern United States, where they collect the sweet sap that oozes from large swellings, or galls, on oaks and other trees. Again, the "honey" is stored in the ants' abdomens and once found, the insects are popped into the mouth like a berry or small grape.

Other ant species are considered delicacies, as well. In Mexico, pupae of two species called *escamoles*, are on the menus of urban restaurants. They have a delicate flavor and are usually served fried alone or with black butter, or cooked with garlic and onions. Rural people who collect *escamoles* by digging them from their underground nests sometimes earn more during the collecting season than many rural workers do during an entire year.

People who study the eating of insects—entomophagists—believe ants are one of the true bug feasts. The formic acid in some species pretty much disappears when they are boiled or fried, while other species, including the ever-present black ant, have a semi-sweet flavor eaten raw and may be used to sweeten tea. They may also be crushed and used to thicken and add protein to stews and soups and fried with eggs. Like many other insects, they are rich in protein, low in fat, and high in phosphorus, but only include trace vitamins.

Termites are a different species, but many look like ants with wings and they share many characteristics. They build tall homes made of mud, they consume paper and wood, they are prolific, and they are captured when they swarm and eaten soon thereafter. As is true of winged ants, termites are attracted to light and may be collected by placing a bowl of water under a light source. When I lived in Hawaii, some joker suggested an almost effortless way to get rid of the pesky critters was to turn on the swimming pool lights after dark. The termites are attracted to the light and drown and in the morning all you have to do is scoop them up with the pool net. Of course, you have to have a swimming pool and a taste for chlorine, if you have dinner in mind.

The most widespread consumption of termites is in Africa, where they are a highly regarded food in nearly every sub-Saharan country. So common are they in the markets, some longtime expatriates from the developed world are among the enthusiastic customers.

In his classic study *The Hunting Peoples*, Carleton S. Coon told a story about the harvesting of termites in pygmy Africa, where each man in the village staked out his own termite hill for later harvest. Then, as the swarming season neared, the villagers probed the mounds to see how high the insects had risen, so that they could be there when they emerged. Next, trenches were dug around each hill and a roof of leaves was erected over the top, so that when the termites began to swarm, they banged into the roof and fell into the trenches. The women collected them in covered baskets, serving them alive at the soonest mealtime, boiled or roasted, or ground into a paste. When boiling, the oil that rose to the surface of the water was put aside for cooking and used as a pomade, mixed with red wood-powder.

Mr. Coon said the insects were so numerous the women scooped them up in baskets. This is not unusual. When termites swarm, they have been known to darken the sky. Tropical termite queens can produce between 8,000 and 10,000 eggs a day and some Australian queens are believed to lay as many as three million a year. African queens, who may reach the size of a large potato, the world's largest termite, may lay 100 million in her lifetime. So this is hardly an endangered species, and every category in the colony is tasty and nutritious, including the eggs and queen.

Like ants, the taste for termites is not new. An analysis of digestive remains from a prehistoric dig in Mexico shows the residents of the region once ate winged ants and termites (also water flies and grasshoppers). Roasted, inch-long queens with swollen backsides are sold on the street in Colombia today, a custom that dates back to pre-colonial times.

One of the most avid proponents of termite cuisine is Frances L. Behnke, who wrote in her *Natural History of Termites* (1977) that the insects "destroy wood, distill an acid that eats through lead, manufacture liquid that will dissolve glass, spread a substance that will rust metal, allowing them to bore through it. Yet, they are good to eat." Like ants, they can be eaten as a snack—roasting removes the wings—and ground up for use as a flour for bread, oil for cooking. Ms. Behnke said chicken fried in termite oil tasted as if cooked in butter.

Another enthusiastic advocate was the late Laurens van der Post, the South African writer (and, late in life, a sort of guru to Britain's Prince Charles) whose book *First Catch Your Eland* (1982) is regarded as one of the finest about African food. He wrote that the taste for termites "existed all over Africa and is not to be despised if one is hungry in bush or jungle." As a child growing up in South Africa, he said he knew it as "bushman's rice" or "rice ants" because of their color and size. "They had a sharp tartaric flavor and, when fried, even in tinned butter, went down well with roast venison," he said. "In fact, some of the capitals of Europe today, specially prepared termites are on sale in tins and the Japanese in particular have developed a liking for them."

Termites, uncooked, taste sort of like pineapple and are higher in protein than an equal weight of chicken, fish, or beef. (Someone once counted the number of termites it took to equal a kilogram. 60,000.) They also are a rich source of fat, thus high in calories. Gene Defoliart wrote in the *Bulletin of the Entomological Society of America* in 1975 that a hundred-gram portion of fried termites "would go a long way toward meeting the daily requirement of sixty-five grams of protein recommended by the USDA and supply a nice ratio of protein to fat calories. One can even visualize that the chitlin which constitutes five to ten per cent of the dry weight of insects would provide sufficient 'roughage' to help maintain the intestinal tone." While in Indonesia, older men eat the queens, believing they will strengthen their failing bodies and make them feel young again.

To listen to the humor, no picnic is complete without ants. In time, they may not only be invited, but prepared at home and brought along with the rest of the lunch nesting in the Tupperware.

Ant Eggs Steamed in Banana Leaves

1 cup ants' eggs (the eggs of the
    red ant, known in Laos as
    mod som, the 'sour ant')
Minced pork, including some fat,
    a quantity the size of a betel nut

2 hen's or duck's eggs
3 small shallots, pounded
Ground black pepper, salt and
    fish sauce
Chopped spring onion leaves

Mix together the minced pork, the pounded shallots and the hen's or duck's eggs. Sprinkle with salt and fish sauce. Add the ants' egg after washing them clean. Taste and check the saltiness. Then add the ground black pepper and the chopped spring onion leaves and mix thoroughly.

Wrap the mixture in pieces of banana leaf, making 2 packages, and secure these with bamboo or coconut-stem pins. Steam them in a steamer. When cooked, open the packages and transfer the contents to a platter and serve.

Termites a la Bantu

1 pt termites   Salt (if available)
1 teaspoon vegetable oil

Remove wings and spread on a flat stone in the sun to dry. Smear pan or stone with oil and spread dried termites upon it. Toast over hot coals until almost crisp. Sprinkle with salt. Eat like popcorn immediately or store for future use—they can be stored for months.

—Insect Fact and Folklore

Bees & Wasps

Lamyai and I had built a house on her family's rice farm in northeastern Thailand, where I was reading late one afternoon when she came running and called, "Papa, Papa, come looking!" I followed along to another home on the property, occupied by one of her sisters and her family. There, I found Muapon, the sister, admiring a beehive that her husband Mein had just cut out of a tall tree in the nearby woods. Several other family members were gathered around, looking much like a group of children in the West might've appeared as if they'd just stumbled upon an abandoned ice cream vendor's cart. Together, Muapon and Mein were carefully extracting the bee larvae from the neat, papery compartments that bees use as residences and for storing honey.

One by one the nearly formed bees were dropped into a bowl, while the younger ones were set aside on a plate for immediate consumption. Muapon offered me the plate and I popped one into my mouth. It had a creamy texture that tasted a bit like honey, as was appropriate.

Once all the bees were removed, they were divided and sent to three different country kitchens, where fires were soon heating oil in which the insects would be fried and eaten hot, passed around in a bowl like popcorn or chips.

Insects were a protein staple as well as a treasured snack in this part of Thailand, as they are in many parts of the world. Crickets and ants and grasshoppers and other six-legged creatures were more common. Bees were a special treat.

Bees—and their cousins, the wasps—play an important role in the world's culinary history and, in tropical areas, still provide protein for millions. Probably if they didn't have such a threatening image—they sting, after all, and Hollywood and the media have painted a menacing picture of so-called "killer bees"—perhaps more of us would be including them in our diet, too. The poison in the sting is basically a protein that disassembles at high temperatures. The stinger softens and the insect is rendered harmless. And not only are they tasty, they're nutritious, in the adult, larvae, or pupae stages. Bee pupae contain eighteen per cent protein and are a rich source of vitamins A and D.

Gene DeFoliart, professor emeritus in University of Wisconsin's entomology department and the founding editor of *The Food Insects Newsletter*, thinks that despite the stigma of the sting, the bee has an excellent pubic image and thus could be a "valuable tool in reshaping attitudes towards insects as food." It is, he says, associated with pleasing activities like "flower-visiting, nectar-gathering, pollination, honey and candle wax production and is super-clean compared with many of the animal foods that we eat."

He goes on to say that bees are higher in protein and lower in fat than beef and have no crunchy cuticle as is the case with some other insects used as food, perhaps making it somewhat more palatable for those who don't like their food to make a lot of noise when it's eaten, or have to peel away the hard carapace and pick off the legs before eating. "It could," Mr. DeFoliart asserts, "become an interesting, high-priced gourmet delicacy."

Another champion of entomophagy, the eating of insects, is Tom McRae, the former chief scientific officer in the entomology department of the University of Queensland in Australia. He says that bee larvae are frequently eaten raw in China by bee keepers while servicing their hives. "I find bee larvae eaten while alive, like oysters, to be quite delicious with a sweet creamy taste," Mr. McRae wrote some years ago. "When fried and served salted with a dusting of paprika, they make the perfect cocktail savory and as a paté they are equal to anything in your local delis. It is said that in czarist Russia, the landowners received the honey at season's end, while the serfs got the brood comb. Guess who got the best of the deal."

Mr. McRae also recommends adult bees. Find a friendly beekeeper or catch them yourself, he says, and kill them by placing them in the freezer for at least half an hour. "Wash well in several changes of water, but wear rubber gloves, as dead bees can still sting. Dry on paper toweling and throw a cup of them into an onion mixture. Add red wine, season with salt, pepper and a pinch of mixed herbs, try a little tomato paste, if you like. Use a dash of brandy in the final few minutes [of cooking with a small amount of oil in a pan]."

There are about 10,000 different kinds of bees (some of them stingless) and 17,000 different wasp species. The most popular, no surprise, is the honey bee. The expression "busy as a bee" is well-known, but that doesn't even come close to describing the bee's industriousness. A good hive—in nature, not in the domesticated boxes fancied by bee farmers—may have as many as 30,000 bees and produce up to sixty tons of honey in a single season, the color and flavor varying according to the flowers from which the nectar came. (Another amazing fact: the bees in one hive can fly 75,000 miles, combined, just to get one pound of nectar.) Most of it is consumed by the bees themselves, by other animals—can anyone forget the image of Winnie the Pooh with his honey pot?—and by humans, of course. And some is stolen by wasps known as "suicide raiders," because so many are killed by the bees guarding the hives.

In industrialized nations, the keeping of "domestic" bees, called apiculture, is practiced primarily for honey, with other commercial products of the hive being beeswax, pollen, royal jelly, and venom, used for treating people with severe sting allergies. Throughout the tropical world, however, human populations enjoy not only the honey, but also the bee brood (the larvae and pupae). Thus, as Mr. DeFoliart notes, "honey bees might be thought of as the invertebrate equivalent of dairy cows, which are valued not only for their milk but also their meat."

Adult bees also may be put into soups and stews instead of or as a supplement to meat, and used to make "bee wine" by adding a couple of dozen corpses to a bottle of rice wine, then putting aside to age. (For at least a month; many Asians don't give aging the importance it's given in the West and in Vietnam near the China border where I drank some, I was told it was finely aged. Two months!)

In Brazil, more than fifty bee species are eaten, eight of the stingless variety being semi-domesticated or to some extent manipulated as a "mini-livestock." In Mexico, at least eight species are cultivated in clay jars near the walls of houses and in small hollowed out trunks of dead trees. In Colombia and Venezuela, bee brood is so important that the Yukpa people's name for it is *wano*, the term also used to describe all types of honey. From Zaire in Africa to Thailand and elsewhere in Southeast Asia, the brood is harvested along with the honey. While in Australia, the honeybag bee, a stingless variety, has been consumed for millennia by the ever-resourceful Aborigines, who would catch a bee that was feeding on nectar, then affix a small leaf or flower petal to its body to set it loose. The bee would always fly straight home and the attached leaf or petal would slow the bee's progress and make it easier for the hunter to follow.

Wasps (yellow jackets, hornets, mud daubers, etc.) play a smaller role in the world's culinary history, perhaps because they are so aggressive and, unlike bees, can sting repeatedly. (The bee leaves its stinger—and much of its abdomen—in the victim and dies.) But like the bees, they are numerous—there may be 4,000 yellow jackets in one of their distinctive ball-shaped, paper-like nests—and they are all edible. Wasp's nests are raided by Aborigines in Australia, using bundles of burning grass to smoke them from their hives, while people in Japan's Nagano province prize the pupae of wasps. Preparation follows the methods for bees.

Bee Grubs in Coconut Cream

50 bee larva	1 cup coconut cream
1 small onion, sliced finely	Pepper to taste
6 citrus leaves	

Marinate grubs, onions and citrus leaves in coconut cream with pepper. Wrap in pieces of cloth and steam. Pour over steamed rice. Can serve 4–8.

Spiders & Scorpions

The first time I ate a scorpion was in a highly unlikely setting, a very nice restaurant in Singapore just a two-minute walk from the fashionable Raffles Hotel. As you enter the Imperial Herbal Restaurant, the first thing encountered are glass display cases containing deer antler and dried penises and behind that, a full-sized herbal pharmacy.

This pharmacy, and restaurant, also has a resident Chinese herbalist, Dr. Li Lian Xing, a thin, sincere gentleman of seventy-plus years who migrated from Tianjin in northern China. The restaurant is one of the earliest business ventures in Singapore involving a corporate partner from China, the Tianjin Traditional Chinese Medicine Group Corporation. Dr. Li is the firm's official representative. His job? To "diagnose" customer ills and imbalances, then suggest certain dishes or drinks from the menu that may help.

After being seated at one of the tables—there were pink tablecloths and fresh flowers—the waitress suggested I meet the good "doctor" before ordering. He took both of my wrists and checked my pulse. After a moment or two, he released my wrists, said I was in excellent health, and suggested a glass of the deer penis wine.

Returning to my table, I noticed that the wine was one of the most expensive drinks (of several) available, so I scanned the rest of the menu. It included a variety of rather conventional Chinese dishes for luncheon or dinner guests who might wish to be seen in the place, but not want to try the house specialties. These included Braised Superior Sea-Cucumber and Bull Pizzles (penises) with Chinese Yam, Crispy Black Ants on Shredded Potato and Vegetable, and Deep-Fried Drunken Scorpions with Asparagus. At US$3 per scorpion, how could I resist? I was told they were small, so I ordered several.

The "drunken" part of the dish meant the scorpions had been marinated in wine, after which they were deep-fried until crisp, while the asparagus spears were boiled in the usual way for five minutes. The two disparate ingredients were arranged on slices of pumpernickel and decorated with thin strips of bell pepper. Finally, each canapé was carefully coated with vegetable aspic and chilled in the fridge until the aspic was firm. In all, it made for a rather attractive sight, while giving the diner as he or she bit into it the softness of the bread, the crispness of the al dente asparagus, and the crunch of the scorpion.

I have a theory that you can eat just about anything—perhaps including your smelly socks—if it is fried in oil until it is crisp, then coated with something tasty or served with a tangy dipping sauce. That meal proved to me that at least it is true for scorpions. And, yes, you eat them whole, tiny claws and pointed tail, too. No worries: the cooking neutralizes the critter's poisonous tendencies.

I asked about my meal and was told that one of the species harvested in Singapore was the black scorpion, a dark, glossy creature that reached six to eight inches in length and was found in public parks. The spotted house scorpion was smaller and more venomous. I don't know which I was served, except that they were awfully small, under three inches from claw to stinger, same size as the scorpions sold by street vendors in Thailand, Laos, and Cambodia, which are deep-fried and sprinkled with salt; a vinegar splash is optional. One other way to eat a scorpion, available to everyone with a postal address: a company in Texas sells sugar-free toffee flavored candy that contains a real scorpion "cooked and prepared carefully."

Spiders are eaten more commonly than scorpions, most frequently by Indians in South America, the Bushmen of southern Africa, and the Aborigines in Australia. While in China and other parts of Asia they are regarded not only as food, but also medicine. Some believe that ten years is added to the life of someone who eats spiders. For common contagion, people in Old England—the word comes from Old English spinnan, to spin—were advised to carry a spider in a silk bag worn around the neck or in a nut shell in the pocket. Live spiders were also rolled in butter and swallowed, or eaten in molasses, or rolled in a cobweb and taken like a pill.

All spiders are "venomous" in the sense that most of them possess a pair of poison glands, the toxin used mainly to paralyze or kill their prey. However, of some 50,000 different species, only a couple of dozen are known to be dangerous to humans. The notorious black widow spider—for which novels, movies, and murderers have been named—found in America, Europe, and Australia, can paralyze breathing muscles, killing the victim by suffocation. Bites from other dangerous spiders can cause pain, blisters and local swelling, chills, muscle cramps, nausea, vomiting, fever, and loss of sight.

Still, most spiders are harmless and several make a lovely meal, even some of the more "threatening" ones. One such is the tarantula, also famed in humankind's scary fiction and film. It's bite is painful, but it will strike only if threatened and it can only knock out a mouse. People, generally, don't like spiders and in Venezuela this one may have a leg span of twenty-five centimeters (ten inches) and an abdomen the size of tennis ball, which I guess puts some people off.

Paul Hillyard, in his *Book of the Spider* (1995), said the Piaroa Indians twisted off the abdomens using a leaf (to avoid touching the poisonous hairs) and squeezed the contents onto another leaf which was folded over and tied, then placed on the hot coals, while the rest of the spider was merely thrown onto the coals. When it was cooked, the large fangs were detached and put beside the body, to be used as tooth-picks! The white flesh found inside and the meat in the legs tastes a bit like prawns. In Laos and Cambodia, the tarantula is toasted on a bamboo skewer over a fire and served whole with salt or sliced and mixed with chilis. The crisp body is then broken open and the meat is sucked out in much the same way a crab is consumed. The eggs of the female are considered a delicacy.

If you're starting with live spiders, remove the fangs with scissors. Then strangle the hairy arachnids by placing a finger over the thorax and squeezing. Wash, toss in a mixture of sugar, salt and monosodium glutamate. Deep-fry some crushed garlic in oil, adding spiders when the garlic gives off a good smell. Cook until the legs are crisp. The abdomen, considered the best part in Cambodia, will still be runny. Raw they taste like something between (if you can make the leap) almonds and the marrow of chicken bones.

In this part of Asia, as in many other undeveloped areas, foraging is a way of life and anything that crawls or flies will be served with the daily rice and greens. So it's not unusual to see women beside the road and at transport cafes bearing trays piled high with hairy, two-inch arachnids on wooden skewers. Passing motorists are the primary customers, paying, in 1997, the equivalent of about twenty US cents, for a brochette of four with fiery green chilies.

Spiders and scorpions differ from insects in several ways. They both have four pairs of legs, no antennae, and no wings. By contrast, all insects have three pairs of legs, one pair of antennae, and many adult insects have one or two pairs of wings. Spiders and scorpions are also meat-eaters, subsisting on insects, while insects feed on nearly anything organic: plants, animals, wood, garbage, etc.

The thing they do share is dinnertime. If it's your dinnertime, it could get you a place in one of the restaurant trends of the new millennium: daredevil gastronomy.

Cockroaches

Question: What is worse than finding a cockroach in your sandwich?
Answer: Finding half a cockroach.

This simple joke captures the way most people feel about this lowly insect, but there are some people who say we'll all be singing a different tune not so long from now. In time, some scientists and nutritionists insist, cockroaches will be turned matter-of-factly into a tasty, healthy paste that may be spread on slices of bread like peanut butter or perhaps cooked with pasta in a casserole. In time, we are assured, this bug will be regarded not as an unsightly pest, but welcomed for the fact that it's three times as protein-rich as chicken and tastes like shrimp. As David George Gordon put it in his book, *The Compleat Cockroach* (1998), it is time to "step into a world that until now you've stepped on." Entomologists and imaginative chefs say we'll even come to like it.

How can this be possible? It may not be so difficult as it seems. First, of course, we must put aside unfortunate images of a cockroach scuttling across our kitchen floor or down a dark, damp alley and know that worldwide there are about 4,000 species, only twenty-five or thirty of which have any form of pest status, scientifically. We must acknowledge that the rest are no more than merely a suborder of *Dictyoptera* called *Blattodea*, just another group of six-legged insects, living unmolested and unhated as innocent members of the earth's fauna, many of them clean, peaceful and gentle enough to make great pets.

It was with this in mind that a page appeared on the Internet called "The Care of Cockroaches," offering hints on housing (including heating and bedding), feeding, and breeding. There's also a Cockroaches Home Page, created by the Blattodea Culture Group, formed in 1986 to "promote the study and culture of cockroaches on a worldwide basis," an organization that publishes a regular newsletter containing species reports and other related articles, while promoting a "policy of free distribution of excess livestock between members."

We must also consider the fact that there have been in the past and are now many peoples and cultures in the world who called, or still call, the cockroach food, a delicious snack or main dish.

Surely, only a few of these people live in what we call developed countries. Without doubt, even if Nicholas Cage ate one in a movie (*Vampire's Kiss*), eating a cockroach in Europe or North America is the place where even the most adventurous diners quickly draw the line. (Cage, by the way, afterward said it was the dumbest thing he ever did, not because he minded doing it or because it tasted awful, but because the press and his fans wouldn't let him forget it, years later still asking, "Did you really eat that cockroach?") It may safely be assumed that when cockroach products are introduced to the market, it will require a prodigious and inventive advertising and public relations campaign to make them welcome at the dinner table.

First, let's meet the meal. Cockroaches have been on the earth for at least 250 million years and are, in some odd ways, quite advanced. For example, cockroaches have "compound eyes," each one made up of 2,000 individual lenses, in contrast to human eyes which have only one apiece. The hairs on their legs give them their sense of touch, their antennae their sense of smell, and two little hairs on the rear end act like a motion detector, so that when something tries to sneak up on a cockroach from behind, the slightest movement alerts the insect to move in the opposite direction, fast. A cockroach mouth can smell as well as taste. And its skeleton is on the outside and shed several times as the insect grows. They can hold their breath for forty minutes and seventy-five per cent of their time is spent resting. The world's largest, a resident of South America, is fifteen centimeters long and has a wingspan of thirty centimeters.

Cockroaches don't date. When a female cockroach wants a mate, she produces an odor (a pheromone) that excites male cockroaches. Some females mate only once and are pregnant for the rest of their lives. Some species produce seven egg cases containing up to forty-eight eggs each. Although the creature may not live longer than 140 days, if all offspring survive, one female can easily have over 35,000 descendants in a year.

A cockroach also can live for a week with its head cut off, because its brain is not located in its head like ours, but is spread throughout its body; death in such a circumstance usually comes from thirst, or perhaps from running blindly into a wall.

Entomologists, the people who study insects, believe that our long relationship with cockroaches probably began with them serving as food, a plentiful protein source readily available in any hut or cave. Later, when we began storing food for the winter, their numbers seemed to multiply and they became constant companions.

Now, here's a small surprise that flies in the face of popular belief. Never in the cockroach's history has it been associated with a specific disease, as has the flea and mosquito, taking the blame, respectively, for plague and malaria. Even so, because cockroaches frequent dark, moist places, we tend to think of them as dirty and in some way infected.

I digress, because none of this has anything to do with eating cockroaches. It is with good reason that we should not eat the roach found in our homes or city streets. It's the other 3,950 species, bugs we rarely and maybe never encounter, that may be the meal of our future, satisfying a rapidly expanding world population's need for food that is outgrowing our ability and space to produce it. Put simply, the protein derived from cattle is probably the least efficient in the history of husbandry, with too many acres denuded of forests to provide the supermarkets and fast food outlets of the world steaks and hamburgers. On the other hand, as anyone knows, a zillion cockroaches can be raised—happily—in a shoebox.

A facetious comment, of course. The cockroaches regarded as the protein source of the future will not be harvested from shoeboxes, but likely from cockroach "farms." These insects will be fed approved food and surely will have to undergo the same regulation and inspection systems in place for other food animals. In time, the cockroach may even achieve a level of acceptance where no one will sue a restaurant for finding a cockroach part in a salad. In time, there will be cockroach salads! I do not jest.

No one is sure where the word "cockroach" comes from, by the way. Some say it is a variation of the Spanish word *cucaracha*, which in

1624 was rendered as "cacarootch" by Captain John Smith in what is now the United States. He was quoted in a document surviving from that time as saying, "A certain India Bug called by the Spaniards as Cacarootch...creeping into Chests they eat and defile with their ill-scented dung." Ever since, the cockroach has gotten bad press.

Except once, when back in the 1920s a fictional cockroach named archy every night jumped across the typewriter of Don Marquis, a columnist at the *New York Evening Sun*, chronically missing shift key and punctuation marks, as he told vengeful two-legged vertebrates to keep their place. Remember, archy said, cockroaches had seniority, for "insects were insects when man was only a burbling whatisit."

Beetles

I'd already eaten ants, termites, grasshoppers, and silkworm larva when I first watched Nittaya Phantachat casually consume a bag full of what appeared to be huge cockroaches while drinking a beer in Bangkok. I was wrong about the species—they were water bugs, called *mangda* in Thai, the largest of the true bugs, reaching three inches in length—but at the time it didn't matter. I watched, both fascinated and repelled, as she removed the carapace (the hard outer shell), the wings and the legs to get to the edible bit in the center.

Ms. Phantachat worked as a chef and I assumed she knew what she was doing when it came to food. She told me that the Thai liked to eat the beetles marinated in fish sauce, roasted over a fire, steamed, pounded, and added to chili paste. She said it gave the paste a pleasant aroma.

All that said, when she offered me one, I blanched. Simultaneously, I knew my moment had come, there was no escape. Fortunately, I'd had a few beers by then, as well; it helps at such perilous times. As she dissected another water bug, I followed her lead, awkwardly picking off the outer bits, then placed what remained inside my mouth, simultaneously biting down as I pulled it out, precisely as if eating an artichoke leaf.

"Hey!" I said, grinning foolishly. "It tastes sort of nutty."

"Good for you," my friend said. She wasn't congratulating me. She was talking about my health.

Most beetles are good for you and according to A.D. and Helen Livingston's *Edible Plants and Animals* (1993), all 250,000 species are edible, offering protein in both the larva and adult stages, eaten either raw or cooked. Most of the beetles I've encountered were being sold by street vendors in Southeast Asia and were either deep-fried or steamed. Most in the adult stage are somewhat nutty in flavor—although I know a Thai woman named Meo who is so practiced at this she insists that she can identify the plant the bug had been eating before it was caught and cooked.

It was Meo's friend Richard Lair who introduced me to (take a breath) buffalo dung beetles, a frequent part of his diet when he lived with elephant trainers in the jungle in northern Thailand. Named for their peculiar habit of burrowing into freshly deposited water buffalo dung, Mr. Lair said they were collected in the morning and left until the evening when the beetles re-emerged. The beetles were left overnight in a bucket of water to allow them to rid themselves of the ingested dung. They were then soaked in water for two to three hours until clean, then thrown into a covered pan and fried without oil with a little salt.

"The noise of their running inside the fry-pan is off-putting to some," Mr. Lair said, grinning devilishly, "but it doesn't last long."

The larva of beetles are consumed in far greater quantity than are adults, and usually are eaten raw, roasted, or fried—from the aboriginal lands of Australia to the rice fields of Asia to the jungles of Africa and South America to the desert of northern Mexico. They also have a long culinary resume, going back to prehistoric times. According to Pliny the Elder, who published the thirty-seven-volume *Natural History* in 77 A.D., the ancient Roman fatted grubs on flour before eating them; the noted gourmet Lucellus had stag horn larva fed for months on wine and bran before his chefs roasted them. More recently, grub eaters included North American Indians, the Aztecs in Mexico, the Maori in New Zealand, and natives of the West Indies during Christopher Columbus's time.

One of the most popular today is the yellow meal worm, often used as food for reptiles, thus it can be purchased from pet stores, biological supply dealers, aviary owners, and bait-and-tackle shops, or raised at home in an aquarium. The adult, a hard-shelled beetle, may lay as many as three hundred eggs in her two- to three-month lifetime. Small, tough-skinned larva hatch from the eggs and grow to about one inch long, when they may be eaten raw or cooked.

Stephanie Bailey, entomology extension specialist at the University of Kentucky, offers helpful hints on the Internet, urging buyers of mealworms to put them on a diet of bran or corn meal before consumption to purge them of impurities. After washing, she said, they could then be cooked or frozen for later use—baked in an oven and ground into a flour for bread, or used as thickening in a soup or stew.

Sometimes larva are mistakenly called "worms." One of these is the so-called sago worm, a favorite in Indonesia, where they are sold live in the open markets and served roasted or in a sort of stew in small, out-of-the-way restaurants catering to local diners. The sago worm gets its name from its home, the sago palm, a tree cultivated in the tropics that at the end of the 17th century was one of the most popular sources of starch in the developed world, used for garnishing veal or chicken, for thickening soup, and for making soft rolls. Today in Europe it is only used for thickening and to make puddings, but from Papua New Guinea to India it is still used in a vast variety of dishes, from fritters to ravioli to jelly. As for the larva, who offer the same pulpy taste, outside the tropics, they haven't been properly introduced.

Oddly, the sago worms are harvested "by ear." Collectors roam the forest and when they find a downed tree, they thump on the trunk as if knocking on a door, then stoop to listen. If they hear worms moving around inside, they hack away the tree's outer shell with machetes and claim their meaty reward, which is then eaten uncooked on the spot or taken back to the village for the evening meal.

In West Africa, another palm weevil is the most widely used. A cookbook on Cameroon cooking, *Le grand livre de la cuisine camerounaise* (1985), described a recipe for "coconut larva" as "a favorite dish offered only to good friends." Coconuts at the half-hard stage are emptied of their milk, refilled with the larva and condiments, then re-capped and cooked in water.

Different species of the same beetle family appear in Southeast Asia and the Western Pacific, as well as in Colombia, Venezuela, and Paraguay, where they are farmed in a process that Gene DeFoliart of the Department of Entomology at the University of Wisconsin calls "semi-cultivation."

"The cultivation and harvest procedures vary slightly from one region to another," he wrote in *Biodiversity and Conservation* (1995), "but, basically, palms are cut down and the logs left lying in the forest with the expectation that larvae will be ready to harvest from the decaying pith one to three months later."

Mr. DeFoliart has suggested that palm worms, which grew up to four inches in length, could be promoted as "traditional cuisine of gourmet quality, the kind of delicacy that could be promoted as tourist and urban fare by the best restaurants throughout the tropics and subtropics, and eventually, maybe, even as an item for export." So far, no one has taken his challenge seriously.

And so it goes around the world. The "banana grub" is found in many tropical areas in fallen banana trees. The larva of the long-horned beetle, reported in much of Southeast Asia, Sri Lanka, and Papua New Guinea, are cooked in coconut milk. (Hunters may find as many as one-hundred grubs in a single, rotting log.) The larva of the rhinoceros beetle is eaten in India, Myanmar, Thailand, and the Philippines. Bamboo grubs—known colloquially as "fast cars" because of their rapid crawling ability—are fried with a little garlic in much the same area. The tiny flour beetle, sometimes found in the home flour sieve, are the same insects consumed avidly from South America to the Middle East to India, where they are mixed with other insects into an appealing paste. Fried and roasted cockchafer grubs are eaten in France, or made into cockchafer soup. Metallic wood-borers and June beetles are prized in Southeast Asia because they carry with them the taste of their own diet of tamarind, persimmon, plum, mango and custard apple tree leaves. And so it goes.

It seems appropriate to close this chapter with a note about what may be the grub that may be best known in the West, the white maguay worm, larva of the hesperiid, a beetle that hatches out of large cactus in Mexico—found, by the time it reaches the Euro-American's tongue inserted into bottles of tequila, the alcoholic drink that is made from the same desert plant. In the United States, where until recently more tequila was consumed than even in Mexico, a test of manhood involved swallowing it with a shot.

Today in Mexico, this "worm" is appearing as an exotic *hors d'oeuvre* in expensive restaurants, an essential part of *alta cocina*, Spanish for haute cuisine. As a writer for the *Los Angeles Times* put it, "What Wolfgang Puck did for the pizza, these chefs are doing for tacos, cactus leaves and worms." The crunchy, brown larva also are being stuffed into tacos and washed down with a "designer" tequila that may cost as much as US$1,000 a bottle. Thus, Mexico's 3,000-year-old gastronomic heritage, once shunned by the middle and upper classes, is now becoming hip.

Finally, for entomographers with a sweet tooth, a sugar-free tequila flavored lollipop with a real "worm" inside is available by mail.

Rootworm Beetle Dip

2 cups low-fat cottage cheese	1 tablespoon parsley, chopped
1 1/2 teaspoon lemon juice	1 1/2 teaspoon dill weed

2 tablespoons skimmed milk	1 1/2 teaspoon Beau Monde
1/2 cup reduced calorie mayonnaise	1 cup dry-roasted rootworm
1 tablespoon onion, chopped	beetles

Blend first 3 ingredients. Add remaining ingredients and chill.
—Courtesy, Entomology Department, Iowa State University

Roasted Cockchafer Grubs in Paper

Salt and pepper the grubs and roll in a mixture of flour and fine bread crumb. Wrap in parchment baking envelopes well-buttered on the inside or in aluminum foil. Bake in the hot ashes of a wood fire.
—Unmentionable Cuisine by Calvin Schwabe (France)

The Galloping Mealworm Gourmet

Tom McRae, ex-chief scientific officer of the Entomology Department of Queensland University in Australia, wrote to me (1998), saying that mealworms are "the basis of many of my recipes," and offered a recipe for paté.

Fry a finely chopped onion in butter until soft and transparent, but do not brown, he said, then add minced garlic to taste, 2 cloves, and fry a little longer. Then add a cup of live, clean larvae and simmer for 5 minutes and pass the contents through a sieve into a second pot and return to the heat, stirring frequently, until the liquid is substantially reduced and the mixture thickens. Allow to cool and refrigerate in jars until needed. Do not freeze.

Mr. McRae also suggested a mealworm dish with booze. The creatures were purged and washed as usual, then coarsely cut with kitchen scissors, and added to a mix of finely chopped onion and garlic, with a liberal dash of white wine. Season with salt, black pepper and a pinch of mixed herbs. For that final gourmet touch, he said, put in a dash of Curacao, Cointreau, or Grand Marnier in the final few minutes of cooking. To be served with rice.

Crickets & Cicadas

What do crickets and cicadas have in common? Well, they're really quite different, although both have six legs and are reputed to have good "voices," and for me that's enough to let them share a culinary duet.

Both are popular snack foods in the Orient, but in the so-called developed world, for a variety of reasons, they are shunned. Not only do most Euro-Americans decline to eat any insect, when it comes to a cricket, there seems to be a lot of cultural baggage that gets in the way. Pinnochio's best friend, and conscience, was a cute little fellow named Jiminy Cricket, after all, and for hundreds of years, a cricket chirruping in the home or barn has been considered good luck. As for the cicada, the bug that clings to the trunks of trees and make a loud chattering, buzzing sound during the mating season, for many they're just too unattractive to eat, resembling, as they do, large cockroaches, measuring up to three or four inches long. Such folks just don't eat cartoon characters, magic charms, and anything that looks like a cockroach.

Crickets are much smaller than cicadas, with approximately 1,500 species ranging in length from under a quarter of an inch up to two inches, and all have outsized rear legs like grasshoppers designed for jumping. Mostly, they like to sing in warm, dry places (the hearth is a preferred "stage"), and in many cultures, most commonly in China and Japan, people have kept crickets in small, finely crafted cages as pets. Such a cage played a small but key role in the film *The Last Emperor*, with a cage hidden in cushions by the emperor as a child and retrieved by him as a defeated old man.

Mostly, crickets are found in and near homes, barns, or other buildings. And while some consider them pests—they are known to chew or damage silk, woolens, paper, fruit, and vegetables—many are deliberately raised at home, either for song or for food. The Entomological Society of Michigan at Michigan State University suggests that you grow them in a "large glass container with a screen cover. Place three to four inches of dry sand in the bottom and put three small shallow cups (about one-half inch high) on the sand. (Sea shells or inverted lids from small jars work well.) To one cup, add water and a cotton ball so the crickets won't drown. Keep it wet. To the second, add slightly moist (not wet) sand for the egg. Place small bits of food in the cup, not on the sand. Crickets eat almost anything, but very small nymphs prefer soft food such as banana, apple, or lettuce. Dry dog food is good for the larger crickets. Add some crumpled paper for hiding places. Discard dirty food and clean the jar occasionally to keep it free of mold."

In years past, crickets were raised to fight, once a traditional pastime and the object of much gambling activity in China. In some Asian cities today they are still sold on the street in bamboo cages, but more often they are collected or raised for food. Filipino farmers flood fields to capture crickets as they rise to the surface; they are then cooked and may even be found on restaurant menus, after being boiled in vinegar and fried in butter. In Vietnam, they're mixed with shelled peanuts and fried in lard, then served as a condiment. In Thailand, they may be cooked in a curry or in coconut cream and spices wrapped in banana leaves, although my Thai family tends to take the easy route, frying them lightly in a wok, with a sprinkling of salt before snacking. In Africa, the cricket is collected from tunnels beneath the earth and roasted over a fire or hot coals.

After capturing crickets—with nets as they fly around lights at night or by pouring water into their holes—they should be kept alive and in a refrigerator to slow their movement. This will make washing them easier. Or, they may be kept alive for a few days and fed apple slices to flavor them. After dry roasting, or cooking them in a pan, you may want to remove their legs and wings before eating, although if they are deep-fried, the entire bug will be edible, crunchy on the outside with a soft mid-section. The females are most favored when they're fat with eggs.

Another hint about eating crickets (and other bugs) comes from the Montegnards of the Central Highlands of Vietnam, where they would be put in a container with a two-inch-wide strip of oil painted on the inside around the jar near the top. The oil kept the crickets inside the jar and in the following day or so they would empty their intestinal tracks, the apparent cause of some bitterness in the flavor. After they were then "clean," they were dumped into a cloth bag which was then hung by a fire to dry (cook) slowly, or left in the pot and heated over a slow fire. When dried, they were munched as a snack or used in rice meals.

In classic (haute cuisine) insect cookery, crickets probably are the most frequently encountered and nowhere more prominently than in the premier guide to insect recipes, *Entertaining with Insects* by Ronald L. Taylor and Barbara J. Carter (1992), whose home-tested recipes include Cricket Crisps, Cricket India, Cricket Rumaki, Cricket Patties Claremont, Chirping Stuffed Avocados, Cricket Louis, Hot Cricket-Avocado Delight, Cricket Pot Pie, Pizza Hopper, Tempura Cricket with Vegetables, and Jumping Melon Salad. The tops of the tomatoes may be sliced off and after the pulp and seeds are scooped out, they are filled with humus and two fried crickets, garnishing with slices of green chili.

Another kind of cricket treat is marketed by a company in Texas. This is the Cricket Lick-It, a translucent Creme de Menthe flavored lollipop that contains a real cricket. Health conscious diners should know that the item is sugar-free.

In Homer's time, the Cicada was a popular theme for poets, both for its music and its taste. Aristotle wrote of the Greeks eating the pupae, or chrysalids, as well as the females heavy with eggs. Cicadas are less commonly eaten today, but no less cherished in many areas. Oddly, the creatures spend most of their lives—up to more than a decade—underground, emerging to mate. The males, producing their din by rapidly vibrating a drum-like membrane located on each side of the body, die soon after impregnating the females.

There are 2,000 species, most of them tropical, although they are found in temperate parts of the world as well. In Japan, the seasonal buzz is often so loud, it competes with the roar of traffic, heralding their addition to selected restaurant menus, usually during the hot season from March to April. Even in the larger cities, tree trunks may be so thick with them they can be harvested by the shopping bag in just a few city blocks.

In rural areas, as the sun sets, an ultraviolet or blue light bulb will attract the large flying bugs, which then can be caught in a net. They may also be hunted by holding a lamp under a tree, shaking the tree, then collecting them as they fall to the ground. Frequently, the males are discarded—because of what some claim is a slightly offensive odor—and the females may be eaten raw, fried, roasted, or skewered on a bamboo stick over an open fire or grill. Most often, throughout Asia, they are steamed, and after the hard carapace, or shell, is removed, eaten as a snack or served with cooked vegetables.

The tender, nutty meat may also be pounded in a mortar or mixed in a blender with chopped red chilis, diced onion, garlic and sufficient lemon or mango juice to form a thick paste. It may then be spread on crackers or bread, with sliced onion added as garnish.

Chocolate Chirpie Chip Cookies

1/2 cup dry-roasted crickets	3/4 cup brown sugar
1 1/4 cup flour	1 teaspoon vanilla
1 teaspoon baking soda	2 eggs
1 cup butter, softened	12 oz chocolate chips
3/4 cup white sugar	1 cup chopped walnuts

Preheat oven to 375°F. In a small bowl, combine flour, baking soda, and salt; set aside.

In a large bowl, combine butter, white and brown sugar, and vanilla; beat until creamy. Beat in eggs. Gradually add flour mixture and insects, mixing

well. Stir in chocolate chips. Then drop by rounded measuring teaspoon-fuls onto an ungreased cookie sheet. Bake for 8–10 minutes.
—*Courtesy, Iowa State University, Dept. of Entomology*

Butterflies & Moths

During my first visit to Thailand, I stayed in a small village where I was introduced to an older woman who was sitting beside a wood fire outside her home. On the fire was a pot of boiling water and in the pot, floating, were what appeared to be a dozen or so yellow worms. One at a time, she removed them from the water with a bamboo stick, then with her fingers she began to pull a golden thread from them. These were silkworm cocoons, also called pupae, or chrysalids, the almost adult stage of the mulberry moth, which hold an extremely fine fila-ment up to a thousand feet long. It is from such basic beginnings, dresses, shirts, suits, neckties, and various accessories are made.

Once she had exhausted the pupae's silk supply, the woman held the small golden corpse that remained up to my face and opened her mouth, her way of telling me to do the same. Thinking I might offend her if I refused, I did as she asked. I was happily surprised. It tasted like corn and I ate two more. Later, I learned they were regarded as a quick and easy tidbit for the villagers, much cherished by the children and sometimes added to stir-fried dishes with vegetables. Rarely were they discarded and, in fact, in Thailand, China and other Asian coun-tries where there was a silk industry—but not in Italy—the worms were collected and sold commercially and boiled, steamed, baked, fried, or roasted, depending on locality and individual preference.

In China, they are pickled with salt or softened with water and fried with chicken eggs in an omelet or simply fried with diced onion and a thick sauce. In Thailand, where in 1987 the Thai Ministry of Public Health included silkworm pupa on a list of local foods that could be used in supplementary food formula developed for malnour-ished infants and pre-school children, they are fried and ground into a coarse powder which is then added to curries and soups. In Vietnam, they're boiled with cabbage, seasoned and served as a soup. From South Korea, they are exported in tins and sold in Asian groceries as far away as the United States. They may also be dried in the sun, pre-serving them for later use.

Today there are many countries with silkworm farms—stretching from Asia to Italy—but a few hundred years ago, the silkworm center was in China, where, according to Marco Polo, the pupa were sold in the markets of Hangzhou, the capital of China during what we now call the Middle Ages. At the end of the 19th century, the French missionary Pére Favaud, as quoted in *Larousse Gastronomique*, wrote that he witnessed and participated regularly in the consumption of silkworm chrysalids in China, describing them as an "excellent stomach medicine, both fortifying and refreshing and often a successful remedy for those in poor health."

Pupa represent one of three stages of the immature moth or butterfly: the eggs and larva being the earlier stages of the insect's life, with most eggs looking like, well, tiny white eggs, and the larva being what is commonly called a caterpillar. All three—eggs, larva, and pupa—have a long and delicious history.

Lepidoptera comprise a major order with species of about eighty genera in twenty families used as food, not only in Asia but in sub-Saharan Africa, where, in some areas, the large, spiny mopane caterpillar (the larva stage of a giant silk, or emperor moth) is so popular that when they are in season, crawling all over village and jungle trees, the sale of beef and other protein meats is seriously affected. One company in Botswana with retail outlets in Johannesburg, sold what it called Mopani Worms (the word is spelled variously), turning a profit its first year, 1983, selling them dried in large bags, much like any other dried food.

Found mainly in the bushveld from Mozambique and Zimbabwe to Namibia and South Africa, where village women collect them in the early spring, often popping one into their mouths after deftly pinching out the pungent-smelling insides. Later, the women stew them with tomato, onion, and a wild spinach-like green, or fry them, then sprinkle them with salt and lemon juice. Leftover mopane may be dried in the sun. Any way they are prepared, South African government researchers claim that just twenty of the protein-rich caterpillars will satisfy an adult male's entire daily requirement for calcium, phosphorus, riboflavin, and iron.

Gene R. Defoliart of the University of Wisconsin's Department of Entomology and the former editor of *The Food Insects Newsletter*, writing in *Biodiversity and Conservation* (1995), said they were "a feature on the menus of some small city restaurants and the trend appeared to be spreading." He also noted that mopane could be eaten like peanuts at cocktail time, with or without a sour cream dip

The monopane are not alone. According to Prof. Defoliart, food use of lepidopterans reaches its maximum in Africa, "where more than twenty species are consumed in some countries." And they are not only tasty, they are good for you. There were, he wrote, "some twenty-three species of caterpillars analyzed by nutritionists who found that the crude protein content averaged more than sixty-three per cent, compared to beef's meager eighteen per cent. The calorie count was about the same—200 to 300 per hundred grams for beef, depending on the fat level, and 265 for moth larvae—but where beef contained about fifty-eight per cent water, the caterpillars came in at a dry four per cent. Thus, as noted by one entomologist, moth larvae are "good if you want to get into body building on a budget."

The consumption of butterflies and moths has a long history, dating to prehistoric mealtimes, but usually has eluded the blessing of the modern Euro-American. In *Swiss Family Robinson*, the account of a family shipwrecked and stranded on an island, published in 1813, moths were presented as a safeguard against hunger. In 1885, when Vincent M. Holt published a treatise called *Why Not Eat Insects*, he took that story and altering it to his own argument, lobbied enthusiastically to put moths on the menu. Alas, in vain.

Mr. Holt further said that "The Hottentots," a term used to describe natives of Africa at the time (politically incorrect nowadays), as "collecting and carrying [caterpillars] in large calabashes to their homes, where they fry them in iron pots over a gentle fire, stirring them about the while. They eat them, cooked thus, in handfuls, without any flavoring or sauce. A traveler who on several occasions tried this dish, tells us that he thought it delicate, nourishing and wholesome, resembling in taste sugared cream or sweet almond paste."

At the same time Mr. Holt was waxing so eloquently in England, in the Cascade and Sierra Mountains of North America, Indian tribesmen harvested the large caterpillars of the pandora moth. "The full-grown caterpillars measure from two to two-and-one-half inches in length and are as fat as an index finger," wrote the author of *Insect Fact and Folklore*. "Normally, these caterpillars live on the pine trees, far out of reach, but in order to pass into the pupal stage they descend in great numbers to burrow into the soil. Just before this takes place the Indians build fires under the trees and stupefy the caterpillars by the smudge. This causes them to loosen their hold on the trees and fall to the ground where they are collected in baskets. They are then prepared as food by being dried over a bed of hot ashes or by being boiled in water." These moths are rarely, if ever, eaten in North America today.

Of all the moth larvae, likely it is the Australian witchetty grub that has found the most exposure to western tongues and tastes.

Australian natives, known as Aborigines, have eaten many different insects for uncounted thousands of years. Dr. Ron Cherry in *Cultural Entomology Digest* (1995) claimed that they were the "most important insect food of the desert." The grubs were collected by digging up the roots of the acacia bush (also known as the witchetty bush), and chopping them to obtain the grubs within. "Ten large grubs," Dr. Cherry said, "are sufficient to provide the daily [protein] needs of an adult."

Witchetty grubs are part of what is now called "bush tucker," once denigrated by city folk, but now a key ingredient to tourist cuisine. Once upon a time, they were eaten raw or cooked in ashes and now they are prepared according to contemporary tastes, roasted and served with a frosty can of Foster's lager, or stir-fried with vegetables, served with kangaroo steak. "Tucker trips" are among the most popular expeditions for both domestic and overseas visitors throughout Australia's tropical north and the Outback around Alice Springs, where people pay an absurd amount of money to hunt and sample these larvae live.

The Aborigines, like the stranded Swiss Family Robinson, also feasted on Bogong moths, harvesting them in large numbers during the winter months from the caves and rock crevices of the Bogong Mountains. By cooking them in hot sand or stirred in hot ashes, they burned off the wings and legs. The moths were then sifted through a net to remove their heads, kneaded into balls and roasted in open fires, or ground into a powder and with water made into a paste that was cooked into bite-sized cakes.

Obviously, a single moth or butterfly, or larvae from either one, will not fill an empty stomach, nor even an hors d'oeurve make. Some effort must be made in the harvesting to reap sufficient food. Yet, in parts of southern Africa one person can pick about twenty quarts of a single caterpillar species in a day if the bush is rich, and seven days' picking, if all are sold, can earn the equivalent of a month's salary for a general worker.

Pickers and traders today may travel more than a hundred miles during the regulated season, in November and December, the opening intended to ensure that the caterpillars are large before harvesting, the closing date to ensure that there is enough "seed" for the next season. However, pickers arrive in such great numbers that officials now consider the pickers rather than the caterpillars a larger threat to the national forest because of the damage done to trees and undergrowth. It also is difficult to enforce the closing date.

As noted by one entomologist in *The Food Insects Newsletter*, "People find it very difficult to stop picking this sweet relish!"

'A plump baked moth'

"I think it is in the *Swiss Family Robinson* that there is a clever account of some travellers, wandering at night through a forest by torchlight, being greatly annoyed by huge moths, which repeatedly extinguished the torches by their suicidal love of light. However, annoyance was turned to joy when, tempted by the appetizing smell of the toasted moths, the hungry travellers ventured to satisfy in part their hunger with the suicides, which they found as excellent in flavor as in smell. From what I recollect of the tale, I believe this was quite a fancy description, probably founded on the real habits of the natives which had been observed by the travelled author of the book. I well remember that, on reading that account, my youthful imagination reproduced without effort the appetizing smell of a plump baked moth; but it did not occur to me then to try such a tid-bit. Lately, however, I have done so, to find the dream of my childhood fully realized as to the delights, both in taste and smell, of a fat moth nicely baked. Try them, ye epicures! What possible argument can be advanced against eating a creature beautiful without and sweet within; a creature nourished on nectar, the fabled food of the gods?

"Most of the commoner moths which flit in thousands by night, around our fields and gardens, have nice fat carcasses, and ought certainly to be used as food. Why, they are the very incarnescence of sweetness, beauty, and deliciousness; living storehouses of nectar gathered from the most fragrant flowers! They, too, voluntarily and suggestively sacrifice themselves upon the altar of our lamps, as we sit, with open windows, in the balmy summer nights. They fry and grill themselves before our eyes, saying, 'Does not the sweet scent of our cooked bodies tempt you? Fry us with butter; we are delicious. Boil us, grill us, stew us; we are good all ways!'"
—*Vincent M. Holt, Why Not Eat Insects. 1885*

Fried Silkworm Chrysalids

After the cocoons have been spun, a certain number of chrysalids are taken and grilled in a frying pan, so that the watery fluid runs out. The outer coverings come away easily, leaving behind a quantity of small yellow objects that resemble a mass of carp roe.

These are fried in butter, fat or oil, and sprinkled with stock. After cooking them for 5 minutes, they are crushed with a wooden spoon and the whole mass is carefully stirred so that nothing remains at the bottom of the pan. Some egg yolks are beaten, in the proportion of 3 to every 100 chrysalids, and poured over them. In this way, a beautiful golden yellow cream with an exquisite flavor is obtained.

This is the way the dish was prepared for the Mandarins and the wealthy.

On the other hand, the poor people, after grilling the chrysalids and removing their outer coverings, fry them in butter or fat and season them with a little salt, pepper, or vinegar, or even eat them just as they are, with rice.

—*Pere Favaud*

Flies

According to aficionados, the dragonfly is a wondrous beast with a history that pre-dates the dinosaurs, an exotic beauty that sends those who eat them into cries of ecstacy as they catch them in their nets.

The ordinary fly, on the other hand, elicits not praise and nets, but curses, smelly sprays, sticky strips of paper hung from the ceiling, and rolled-up newspapers.

Both are good to eat, in the larva as well as the adult stage. Fly larva? Isn't that...aren't they...maggots? Alas, it's true. But the maggot is unfairly maligned. The high protein content makes them especially desirable in areas where more conventional protein choices are limited. A report by the Zinhua News Agency in Beijing put the protein content at fifty per cent, and claimed that the low-fat oil produced was effective in preventing heart disease.

"Some term other than 'maggot' should probably be coined for muscoid fly larvae when discussed as food," Gene DeFoliart wrote in *The Food Insects Newsletter* in 1994. "The natural habitats with which many of these species are normally associated conjures up rather unsavory connotations."

It is true that maggots and adult flies have a curious diet, at least by human standards. In fact, they will eat nearly anything, meat that's beginning to go bad, rotting fruit and vegetable matter, other insects, sucking whatever they find through what might fairly be compared to a syringe. (No adult fly can chew.) They then fly about, landing here and there, cleaning themselves and, it cannot be denied, spreading germs.

But as is true with cockroaches and many "loathsome," disease-spreading creatures in the insect world, not all flies are bad news. Flies are one of the major successes of the insect world, with at least 60,000 different species surviving happily just about anywhere, even in Antarctica. The common house fly is the one that humans see most often and with good reason it is to be shunned. It is always advisable when eating insects to get them as far from humans as possible, in order to avoid pesticides and other contaminants so often associated with human development.

And so it has always been, with most stories about eating flies associated with indigenous groups in undeveloped areas. For example, snipe flies frequently laid their eggs on vegetation hanging over streams, where the females soon died. As more and more laid their eggs, the masses of insect corpses soon grew large, inspiring the Modoc Indians of California to dam the stream with logs, then shake the bushes, causing the dead insects to fall into the water. When the bodies reached a hastily constructed dam downstream, the Modocs merely scooped them out.

"As many as a hundred bushels a day could be secured in this way," according to *Insect Fact and Folklore*. "The Indians used a basket to dip the flies from the water and to carry them to their ovens, where they were cooked. They were not taken out of the oven immediately, but were allowed to cool gradually. The Indians called this dish '*Koochab-bie*.' When cold, it was about the consistency of headcheese and was firm enough to be cut into slices with a knife." The Modoc Indians are long gone, but lake flies are still cherished in tropical Africa and mayflies are caught for food in Mexico. And the role of such insects in diet is now being studied by entomologists in several American and European universities.

Significant research also has been done into using fly larvae from the soldier fly to grow edible protein for livestock. University of Georgia entomologist Craig Sheppard estimates that the waste from a large commercial chicken farm (minimum of a 100,000 birds) seeded with soldier fly eggs will produce sixty-six tons of animal feed larvae in five months. They can be cooked, dried, and mixed in with conventional animal feeds.

Similar preparation of fly larvae will do for us as well, even that found on decomposing meat. The meat is placed in a box with openings in the bottom corners. Containers for collecting the larvae are placed under the openings, the larvae crawl to the corners and fall into the containers. Once captured, they are washed in cool water, then cooked. They may be stir-fried with vegetables, added to fried rice with onions and chilis, or boiled and made into a stew or soup. They also may be roasted or grilled.

Near the Arctic Circle, a species of botfly deposits its eggs on the backs of caribou. When the eggs hatch, the larvae tunnel through the skin to feed, and as they grow in size, swellings that look like boils appear. When the larvae are full-grown, they emerge through the skin and fall to the ground where they hatch. The Dogrib Indians in northern Canada, who raised caribou as beasts of burden as well as a food, learned to squeeze the swellings, forcing the mature bot to fall out. Usually, they were eaten alive and when a mature caribou was slaughtered, they were left alone and cooked along with the meat.

Maggots also are eaten in Africa, dead or alive, when other large animals were found to be infested while butchering. Common through much of Asia is a kind of maggot fried rice, a variation of the one-dish meal, making use of leftover cooked rice, dry-roasted maggots, chopped garlic, sliced peppers, seasoned with fish sauce, soy sauce, sugar, shallots, spring onions, and coriander.

Dr. Ed Dresner wrote a letter to *The Food Insects Newsletter* (1994), telling how he came to eat Oriental fruit fly larvae while working on a control program in Hawaii. "I and most of my hiking companions ate the fruits enthusiastically, not discriminating because of larval infestation," he said. " My impression is the larvae made the fruit a little less tart." While Tom McRae, retired chief of scientific research for the Entomology Department of the University of Queensland in Australia, said in a letter to me that adult fruit flies were easily cultured in huge numbers, "so are an excellent bulk source of insect protein." Kill by freezing, he said, then wash and dry, and cook in a skillet with finely hashed onions, butter, and a pinch of ground ginger.

Fly larva, sold mainly as food for pets, are also bargain-priced— just US$5 for 500 by mail, a thousand for $7.50, delivered live to your door.

If maggots are easy to collect or purchase, flies are not and most of those available commercially today are of the wingless variety, sold by pet shops for feeding reptiles.

Dragonflies are hard to catch, too, but highly prized. They begin life underwater, clinging to a reed and consuming protozoa, even tadpoles and tiny minnows. At the end of a year, the nymph crawl out of the water onto a stem of a plant and dry off, as the wings and legs emerge. In another two to five hours, the creatures will be airborne and in search of a meal. Prey is caught in full flight and they are known to eat as many as 300 mosquitoes and other small insects a day.

Most are caught in nets, but because the dragonflies have a habit of sitting on the end of a stick or reed over the water, some hunters will put a sticky substance on the perch that catches them like ordinary flies on fly-paper. In Bali, where dragonflies are a special treat, hunters go out with long sticks "baited" with a gummy substance, and after picking off their legs and wings, add their catch to a pounded mixture of coconut paste, fermented fish paste, garlic, chilis, tamarind juice, basil leaves, ginger, and the juice of a lime. This is then wrapped in banana leaf packets to make a common dish known as *pepes*.

Some dragonfly hunters raise the nymphs at home in aquariums. In prehistoric times, their wingspan equaled that of a modern hawk or large crow, but today's 5,000 or so species are far smaller, thus one or two will not go far toward filling an empty stomach

An Aeronautical Impossibility

Members of an organization called the Dragonfly Society of America, whose members organize safaris with large butterfly nets, marvel at the speed and elusiveness that characterize the creatures. With the sharp eyes of a skilled predator and aerobatic talent that the US Air Force admires and has tried to figure out, it is no wonder that they're called "mosquito hawks" and that the poet Alfred Lord Tennyson described them as "living flashes of light."

Aeronautical engineers are flying them through windtunnels and hooking them to strength meters, trying to figure out how they can go from zero to thirty miles per hour and then stop on a dime in a blink, hover like a hummingbird, and dart right, left, backwards and upside down in a manner that defies conventional flying theory. Of course, they've had three-hundred-million years to develop, and those same engineers, following similar logic said it was impossible for the bumble bee to fly because they were too heavy for their wings.

The Amazing Isan Bug-Catcher

I was struck first by the ingenuity of the device, and then by its efficiency and low cost. It was a contraption—the perfect word!—for capturing *malaeng* (insects), considered a basic protein source in northeastern Thailand where my family lives. Such gifts come seasonally and in the Spring of this year, there were two kinds, one to feed the chickens, the other for us. My wife Lamyai said she learned how to build the device from her papa.

First, she took a ten-foot length of two-inch bamboo, cut from the undergrowth nearby, and to it she nailed a piece of corrugated iron measuring about three feet wide by four feet long, salvaged from a pile of trash left behind when some of the roof of her mama's cookhouse was repaired. To this, she affixed a fluorescent tube—the only true out-of-pocket expense—running lengthwise. Then she dug a hole about thirty feet from the house and stuck the bamboo pole into it, iron on top and tilted backwards at a slight angle. Picture a huge flyswatter, or spatula, stuck into the ground, handle first.

At the base of the gadget Lamyai now placed a large container, a quarter filled with water. Sometimes she uses a barrel-sized ceramic water jar, other times a big plastic washtub. And nearby she piles up some dirt, covering it with one of those big rattan baskets Asians place on top of chickens to keep them from escaping. (Bear with me, all this will make sense soon.) An electrical cord is then stretched from the fluorescent tube to the house and plugged in after dark.

What happens next is amazing, or at least it is to me. Lamyai's been catching insects as protein since she was a child, so she was more-or-less non-plussed, but when the tube was turned on and hundreds of insects appeared, an airborne river of buzzing bugs, drawn by the light, and started slamming into the metal and sliding down the iron grooves into the container of water below, I laughed. It was hilarious. For the first time in my life, I wanted one of those home video cameras. Thailand's Funniest Farm Videos.

There were two kinds of insect seduced by this crude technology. The most numerous were hard-shelled black beetles of varying sizes, the smallest slightly bigger than the head of a pin and called "stink bugs" because when you crush one between your fingers it's not just a bad smell, it's like having all the air sucked out of your lungs and replaced instantly with the an odor that goes unidentified because you're so busy slapping at your nose and jumping up and down and cursing and gasping for breath. These are the ones for the chickens!

The *malaeng* catcher also attracts crickets, I'm happy to report, and being larger in size and perhaps better at escape and evasion techniques, when they smack into the iron, they are only stunned and manage to escape the watery death below and flutter to the ground, where they scramble to the pile of dirt, into which they burrow immediately. The basket is there to keep the fifty or so free-range chickens that Lamyai has from getting to the crickets in the morning before we do.

We come out of the house at cock's crow and look into the water jar, where bugs are swimming around rather nervously. I thrust my hand and arm into the jar through at least eighteen inches of bugs! Imagine a cold soup of beans with legs. Lamyai called for the chickens, emitting a loud, whooping cry that ended in a series of clucks that brought the chickens running. They got fed first.

Then we began digging for the crickets, throwing them into a bucket to be washed and afterward fried in oil. Salted lightly and terrific, I discovered, with beer.

CHAPTER FIVE
plants

PLANTS ARE MIRACLES that come from a combination of sunlight, water, and dirt (or no dirt if they're grown hydroponically), and they come in hundreds of thousands of varieties. Or to put it in technical terms, they are multi-cellular organisms that produce food from sunlight and inorganic matter by photosynthesis, with rigid cell walls containing cellulose. Most, but not all, are edible.

In fact, one of the chapters in this section is titled "Poisonous Plants," which explains how some foods must be processed in a prescribed way to remove the threat (or at least most of it) or consumed only in the minutest quantity. One wonders how such things were discovered and why anyone bothered to try when so many got sick or died in early experimentation. For example, some manioc is deadly when left uncooked, yet today it is one of the world's top carbohydrate sources, after it has been properly prepared.

Historians believe that, traditionally, it was the women who gathered the plants, while their burlier mates went out to hunt mammoth and other large game. "Hunting was a flamboyant business—the drama of the chase and the return in triumph are still enshrined today in the ceremonial of many primitive tribes—whereas gathering depended on quiet patience and the kind of perseverance that was continuous rather than (as with hunting) sporadic," wrote Reay Tannahill in her classic *Food in History* (1973). "But though there might be little excitement in the task, the foodstuffs women collected were more than just supplementary to meat. When the hunting was poor, they were what everyone depended on."

So much so, that modern agriculture developed before the domestication of animals, with the cultivation of wild wheat and barley in what is now called the Middle East. Gathering still plays a significant role in many parts of the undeveloped world, but elsewhere farming is dominant, and plant life continues to play a monumental role in the human diet—even our meat sources depend on it.

As is true in other sections of this book, the plants considered here generally are ones that may be valued in one part of the world, but are denigrated or ignored in another. Some, like *keluak*, a fruit found in the Caribbean, is actually banned from import into the United States, because it is regarded as life-threatening; the durian from Southeast Asia is forbidden by many airlines and hotels because its strong odor is considered offensive; and the noni fruit is thought to taste so awful it needs an ice cream chaser.

Another, cactus, has been associated for millennia in some areas or with specific groups such as native Americans, gaining only a small following outside those populations, perhaps because of their spines, and while flowers are turning up nowadays in the spring mix in numerous supermarkets, most people in the so-called west still regard them as something decorative rather than delicious or good for you, and algae and seaweed are, well, slimy or rubbery to the look and touch, cherished in one area, ignored in another.

In the 1960s and 1970s, accompanying a sort of back-to-nature movement nurtured by the hippies and a newfound interest in organic foods and medicinal herbs, wild plants as food attracted more attention. Books by Euell Gibbons, most notably *Stalking the Wild Asparagus* (1962), and others became bestsellers. Niche markets developed and something called the "health food store" became a commercial generic. Thus, many new plant foods found unprecedented commercial success.

Some are included here, among them seaweed—an essential ingredient in Japanese cuisine—and algae, the one-celled green scum seen in watery environments that has been turned into a food supplement called spirulina.

Add plant life generally thought to be survival food (grass, bark, and sap, etc.) and throw in hallucinogenic vegetation and slather a piece of toast with a thin layer of tongue-twisting Marmite or Vegemite, the stuff made from yeast left over from the manufacture of beer.

The produce section of my local market never looked so interesting.

Universal Plant Edibility Test

The following sounds like a lot of work—it is!—but that's because it comes from the *US Army Survival Manual* as republished in 1994 as "a civilian's best guide for toughing it, anyplace in the world...a must for campers, hikers, explorers, pilots, and others whose vocation or avocations require familiarity with the wilderness or out-of-doors..."

1. Test only one part of a potential food plant at a time.

2. Break the plant into its basic components—leaves, stems, roots, buds, and flowers.

3. Smell the food for strong or acid odors. Keep in mind that smell alone does not indicate a plant is edible.

4. Do not eat for 8 hours before starting the test.

5. During the 8 hours you are abstaining from eating, test for contact poisoning by placing a piece of the plant part you are testing on the inside of your elbow or wrist. Usually 15 minutes is enough time to allow for a reaction.

6. During the test period, take nothing by mouth except purified water and the plant part being tested.

7. Select a small portion of a single component and prepare it the way you plan to eat it.

8. Before putting the prepared plant part in your mouth, touch a small portion (a pinch) to the outer surface of the lip to test for burning or itching.

9. If after 3 minutes there is no reaction on your lip, place the plant part on your tongue, holding it there for 15 minutes.

10. If there is no reaction, thoroughly chew a pinch and hold it in your mouth for 15 minutes. DO NOT SWALLOW.

11. If no burning, itching, numbing, stinging, or other irritation occurs during the 15 minutes, swallow the food.

12. Wait 8 hours. If any ill effects occur during this period, induce vomiting and drink a lot of water.

13. If no ill effects occur, eat 1/2 cup of the same plant part prepared the same way. Wait another 8 hours. If no ill effects occur, the plant part as prepared is safe for eating.

It is further recommended that all parts of the plant be tested, as some plants have both edible and inedible parts. Nor is it to be assumed that a part that proved edible when cooked is also edible when raw.

It seems so much trouble, it'd be easier to starve.

Poisonous Plants

When Sam Sebastiani Jr., a member of one of California's most prominent wine-making families, died in 1997 after eating mushrooms gathered near his home, the media went mad about mushrooms. Someone whose fortune and fame was founded in the growing of grapes had been felled by another plant. It was as if Henry Ford had been run over and killed by a Buick while jay-walking. How ironic—and how stupid—people said. While newspaper and television reporters dashed into the forest with their camera crews to photograph mushrooms.

Mushrooms, a type of fungus (a plant with neither chlorophyll nor flowers), have a reputation that most of them don't deserve. Nearly all are not only edible, but have greater food value than green vegetables. Consequently, dozens of varieties are staples in every supermarket produce section. On the other hand, some are deadly, the most infamous of these being members of the mushroom family collected by Sebastiani and his friends, the *Amanita*. The *Amanita* comprise a genus of mushrooms containing a few species remarkable for their toxicity. There are many edible *amanitas,* but eating the wrong one can bring on cholera-like diarrhea, dehydration, vomiting, abdominal pains, delirium, cramps, or, as the young wine-maker discovered, death by liver and kidney failure.

The odd thing is that many people felled by this mushroom didn't mistake it for an edible cousin: they knew that this was the mushroom made famous by Lewis Carroll in *Alice in Wonderland*, and they ate it deliberately. Mr. Carroll's wonderland, after all, was the result of eating the distinctive red caps with the big white polka dots, wasn't it? And if you didn't eat too many...you went on a wonderful trip. Yes? Yes. Many plants have been eaten over the centuries in order to get high and several of them have proved deadly when consumed in too great a quantity. (See chapter on Hallucinogenic Plants.)

The *Amanita,* along with a basket full of other mushroom varieties, is just one of many health- or life-threatening plants that are consumed as food, several of them matter-of-factly. The difference is, that even when cooked, some of the mushrooms can kill, while proper processing of several other poisonous plants renders them safe.

Some may reasonably wonder how such dangerous foods were discovered not only to be edible, but also palatable and, in many cases, nutritious, too? How long did it take to develop such long, complicated preparations as are sometimes required to make a toxic food safe? How many culinary pioneers, out of ignorance or curiosity, fell over dead or got sick before the proper preparation was discovered? (In a phrase, how many cooks were spoiled by the stew rather than the other way around?) History rarely answers such questions. These dishes were not created overnight; they evolved. However it happened, through perseverance, or possibly dumb, blind luck, someone eventually created from a dangerous plant a food that found its way into an exotic and cherished delicacy, or, in one instance, one of the world's most important sources of starch, the manioc. (Back to the mushroom in a minute.)

Manioc, also called the cassava and in Latin America the *yuca* or *mandioca*, is a white, starchy tropical tuber native to Brazil that was established as far north as the West Indies by the time Columbus arrived, then quickly spread to Africa and Asia, where it is now an essential food staple. It is also the most common poisonous plant, the one eaten over the greatest expanse of geography and by the largest number of people. It is easily grown in hot, humid environments, resists drought and insect pests, requires little cultivation, and provides a valuable source of carbohydrates for peoples who have difficulty raising other crops. In the west, it's used to make tapioca, a starch used for puddings and thickeners. When I was growing up in the United States, my brother and I called the little starch globules in the bowl of tapioca we sometimes got for dessert "fish eyes."

Although there are many varieties there are only two main categories: bitter and sweet, and it is the former that is life-threatening, in its uncooked state containing lethal amounts of linamarin which releases hydrocyanic acid, more commonly known as cynanide.

Commercially, manioc generally is processed within twenty-four hours of harvest to halt the loss of starch. First, it is washed to remove dirt and impurities, then it is peeled and rasped to reduce the flesh to a thick, coarse mixture of pulp, juice, and starch called a slurry. Next, it is exposed to sulphur dioxide gas or a sodium-bisulfite solution to prevent discoloration and retard bacterial growth. Then the juice is extracted in much the same way soap is removed from clothing in a laundry, by repeated rinsing in clean water. Finally, the starch is dried with hot air, and sifted. The result is manioc flour, used to make cakes, soups, stews, and bread.

In some areas, patties are cooked until crisp, in others they are only lightly toasted, leaving them soft and pliable. Pieces are then torn off, boiled fish paste is spread on top, and they are served like open-face sandwiches.

The leftover juice may be boiled and used as a thickening for soups. Additional boiling and sweetening in the sun produces what is called casareep, which is used as a flavoring that is especially popular in British Guiana, where it appears in virtually every dish, and in the West Indies, where it is the foundation of that country's celebrated pepper pot.

The root may also be roasted like a potato, with the extreme heat removing the poison. Alternatively, the root may be peeled, cut into quarter-inch slices, and dried in the sun for two or three days, then stored for later use. (Frequently, it may be seen drying on rural highways or urban sidewalks. I've seen the former in Vietnam, the latter in China.) When needed, the washing, grating and juice removal process is identical to that described above.

Finally, of course, manioc may be fermented to produce an intoxicating beverage. (Is there any botanical product in the world that can't be turned into booze?) The home brew—it hasn't been manufactured commercially, yet—is produced in a manner that has gone unchanged over centuries. The sliced and grated tuber is fermented in water, with some chewed root added to assist the process. The liquor is then stored in gourds.

Another poisonous plant is the ackee, a bright red tropical fruit not recognized as edible in most of the places where it is grown—in parts of Central America, as well as in Antigua, Trinidad, Grenada, and Barbados. More ominous, its import into the United States is banned. Yet, it is a sort of "national dish" in Jamaica and to visit this Caribbean nation without eating it is akin to visiting Japan without consuming sushi or Kobe beef.

And, it will kill you, if its poison is not neutralized carefully.

So why do people eat it? For the same reason they eat anything, because it tastes good, and, for some foreigners visiting Jamaica because the whiff of danger gives ackee dishes an added thrill. Disarming the fruit is easy: all you have to do is wait for the fruit to ripen, then boil it. It is when it is not ripe, or eaten uncooked that you are playing Jamaican roulette.

Most often, it is consumed at breakfast with salted, dried fish, usually cod, though other fish such as mackerel may be used. Just bring the fruit to a boil in water for about ten minutes, simmer it down with the fish (or cooked bacon), cut-up onions, peppers, tomatoes, and seasonings, then serve with fried dumplings or roasted bread fruit (a tropical starch fried, baked or roasted like a potato), put on a Bob Marley record, and pour yourself a cup of Blue Mountain coffee laced with a tot of Jamaican rum.

Ackee is believed to have come to the Caribbean from West Africa on a slave ship in the 18th century and its scientific name, *blighia sapida*, comes from Captain William Bligh, who took the fruit to England in 1793, one of his many important botanical contributions that were, later, overwhelmed by a famous disciplinary problem in the South Pacific called mutiny.

Here's another poison-on-a-plate special, a Southeast Asian food that is deadly if eaten in its natural state, the *buah keluak*, whose very name translates as "the fruit which nauseates." In fact, it is not a fruit at all, nor a nut, as many of its champions insist. It is the soft interior of a hard seed case about the size of a small egg found within the fruit of the great kepayang tree. In its uncooked state, it is used in the Indonesian jungles to coat spear and arrowheads for hunting, a clue to its deadliness.

Yet, with the appropriate—and somewhat peculiar—preparation, it is transformed into a delicacy that many call the "truffle of Asia." Usually it's found in a thick curry or stir-fry called *ayam buah keluak*, or chicken with *keluak* fruit. This is a cherished part of the cuisine of the Peranakan, the "native-born" Chinese who have lived for generations in Singapore, Malaysia, and Indonesia.

Its danger lies in the prussic acid contained within the flesh, a poison that can be removed only by burying it in the ground with ashes for at least thirty days and preferably for double that. It must then be soaked in fresh water for one to two weeks, with frequent changes of the water. Finally, it is boiled in hot water for ten minutes before opening each seed with a cleaver to see if the meat inside is moldy. One bad seed will spoil the dish and they must be removed. (How, I ask again, did anyone discover such a process to make this strange food edible?)

Connoisseurs argue over the ways to cook any special food, and so it is with *buah keluak*. Some eat the somewhat bitter flesh straight from the shell, once it has gone through the long burial and soaking process. Others prefer to scoop out the black meat and blend it with chopped pork, fish, prawns, salt and pepper, then stuff it back into the hard seed case before cooking. It may then be added to a chicken curry that contains chopped onions, ginger, lemon grass, chili, the skin and juice of tamarind, and a paste of mashed candlenut which provides the required stickiness.

One final note: the flesh of the *buah keluak* is black and it dominates the dish, so if you think you might be squeamish about eating anything black, Singapore is also famous for its fried rice.

Finally, we return to Mr. Sebastiani and his final mushroom harvest. The fungus Mr. Sebastiani is thought to have eaten was an *Amanita Muscaria*, known as the "death cap" mushroom. It is the cause of ninety-five per cent of mushroom poisonings worldwide, fatal in one out of every three cases. Toxins in its cap destroy the victim's liver and kidney by rupturing the cells.

At the time of his death, Mr. Sebastiani was one of three victims of *amanita* poisoning awaiting a possible liver transplant at the University of California Medical Center in San Francisco. Several of his relatives had volunteered to be donors for a partial liver transplant (in which part of the donor's liver is grafted onto the patient's liver, and the healthy liver often helps the damaged cells to regenerate), but a transplant was ruled out because his body was too heavily infected.

Titanic Tapioca

In 1972, tapioca pudding threatened to sink a freighter off the coast of Wales when fire started in lumber stacked in the upper holds. The water thrown onto the flames by firefighters seeped down to the lower holds where 1,500 tons of tapioca pellets from Thailand were stored. The water swelled the tapioca and heat from the flames began to cook it. Fire fighters said the ship's steel plates could have buckled if they hadn't reached the shore quickly, where some 500 truckloads of tapioca pudding were hauled away to the local dump.

Rhubarb Fool

In researching this book, I was also surprised to discover that another meal from my childhood was potentially dangerous: rhubarb, which usually arrived at the table in my house as rhubarb pie, one of many ways the red celery-like stalks can be used in a dessert. Recipes spooned up from the pages of such magazines as *Bon Appétit, Gourmet,* and *House & Garden* magazines include such mouth-drooling choices as Rhubarb-Raspberry Jam; Lemon Ice Torte with Strawberry-Rhubarb Sauce; Scandinavian Rhubarb Pudding; Rhubarb and Pear Compote; Rhubarb Tart; Rhubarb, Onion and Raisin Chutney; Strawberry-Rhubarb Cobbler with Cornmeal Biscuit Topping; and something called Rhubarb Fool.

The latter dish may carry the most weight (as a warning perhaps), if not the greatest number of calories. Because only the stalks of this buckwheat family member are edible and care must be exercised when harvesting to leave out the leaves and roots, which contain oxalic acid. Even the stalks, carefully culled, are unusually tart, needing sweetening from a sugery fruit, as the recipes named imply, or generous amounts of sugar. For good reason the ancient Greeks called it "the vegetable of the barbarians," and deer, who will eat almost anything, give it a pass. It doesn't just make your mouth pucker, it turns it inside out.

Flowers

In Hawaii, where I lived for a number of years, it was common in a hotel restaurant to see an orchid decorating a plate of fresh fruit, a sandwich, or a salad. It was something to give the tourists a small touch of tropical exotica, purely decorative. Many of the tourists had never seen orchids before and, thinking them part of the dish, ate them. Poor dears.

Garnishing a plate of food with uncooked blossoms and sprigs of fresh this and that is common and while many of the floral and green decorations, like parsley, are nutritious and edible, the orchid is not. In fact, most orchids don't taste very good. They don't even have much of a scent, contrary to what a lot of novelists say in their poorly researched books; for the most part, they are odorless, as well as sort of bitter. The diner is not the fool in this tale. The chef or restaurant manager is. No one should ever put anything on a plate that is not meant to go into the mouth.

Many blossoming plants are not only palatable, they add surprise and zest to a meal and elegance to a dinner party that guests likely won't forget. They also offer nourishment. The custom of eating flowers began at least 5,000 years ago, when the Chinese began to consider herbal medicine and food as having the same origins (and flowers were an essential part of both), and continued right through history. The Roman chef Apicius sprinkled brains with rose petals, added sweet marjoram blossoms to an assortment of hashes, and made a sauce with safflower petals. The great 19th century French novelist Alexandre Dumas, author of *The Three Musketeers* and *The Man in the Iron Mask*, created a recipe for herb soup *á la dauphine* containing marigold flowers. Today? Even some supermarkets in America include a few flowers in their produce section, not far from the artichokes and broccoli. (Which are also flowers.) As is true of many foods unknown or rejected in Euro-America, the pretty part of the plant recently has found a niche market.

In considering the ethnology of eating flowers, botanists discuss only the blossom itself. For example, the seeds of the sunflower are of no interest to them, but should someone sauté the buds with butter and lemon juice and then garnish the dish with fresh petals, the scientists will reach for their knives and forks.

The number of flowers and their culinary uses seem almost countless and a newcomer to flower cuisine may wonder where to start. In one of the best recent books on the subject, *Edible Flowers: From Garden to Palate* (1995), the author, Cathy Wilkinson Barash, reccomended a "Big Ten," based on taste, versatility, and ease of cultivation: the calendula (a member of the marigold family), chives, day lily, mint, pansy, rose, sage, signet marigold, squash blossoms, and nasturtium. Of these, mint, sage, and chives might be called somewhat commonplace. But how many in Europe and the US put any of the others on their plate recently?

I ate my first nasturtiums in the 1960s, when my wife and I followed the back-to-the-earth crowd and bought a farm in California, where we planted and nurtured a garden about an eighth of an acre in size, adding a bed of nasturtiums near the compost heap to mix with chervil, oil, and lemon juice for a salad based on a recipe we saw in a book by Alice B. Toklas, the companion to Gertrude Stein who was better-known during the 1960s for her recipe for hashish brownies. (A food made from another flowering plant entirely, and not unfamiliar to some of our neighbors at that time.)

Ms. Toklas was not alone in her appreciation of the nasturtium. The Greek historian Xenophon reported that this ornamental plant was eaten by the Persians about 400 B.C. Louis XIV of France cultivated them in his garden, as did Thomas Jefferson, who used the flower as a seasoning. Even Dwight D. Eisenhower, not known for his gustatory sophistication, had the White House chef put nasturtiums in vegetable soup.

The name is Latin, combining two words, *nasus*, for "nose" and *torquere*, "to twist," the nose-twister, for its tangy fragrance and peppery taste. Some compare the flavor to capers, thus it is no surprise that Ms. Barash offers recipes for salmon with nasturtium butter or nasturtium vinaigrette. The flower may also be added to cloves, peppercorns, and garlic to produce a spicy vinegar, or stuffed with cream cheese. Most commonly, they are used whole as an accompaniment to salads, vegetables, pasta, and meat dishes.

Better known but also under-appreciated as a food is the rose. No other flower is wrapped in more legend and history. It's petals were used to make early Catholic rosaries, the white rose regarded as a symbol of the Immaculate Conception, the red representing Christ's blood. The same two roses were flown on flags of opposing armies in the War of the Roses. Today, songwriters call the rose the ultimate symbol of romance, a dozen of which, with long stems, may cost as much as dinner for ten and last just a little longer than the meal before wilting.

The rose is also one of the tastiest and most versatile flowers in the kitchen when and if it ever gets there. The fresh petals can be made into rose water, dried petals into rose tea. The petals may also be used to season butter; flavor ice cream (a favorite treat in India); make jelly, syrup, and jam; like the nasturtium, flavor a vinegar or vinaigrette; and bring fragrance to salads and vegetables. The buds can also be used in summer puddings or as a condiment when dried. The more fragrant roses offer the most flavor and the darker ones usually have the strongest taste. So it must've been a combination of the two that went into the sauce made with roses in the movie *Like Water for Chocolate* (1992) that sent everyone into a frenzy.

If you've ever eaten Chinese hot and sour soup, you've eaten the dried petals of the day lily, as it is one of the key ingredients. The name comes from a blossom that blooms only a single day, but it has been eaten for thousands of years in China, where it is cultivated as a cash crop for export around the world. New York City imports over more than two tons of the dried petals each year, nearly all of it sold in Chinatown.

The use is not confined to soups. The flowers can be cooked with duck, pan-fried with pork and onions, wrapped into pancakes, sautéed alone as a vegetable, and stir-fried with chicken or shrimp. The buds may also be dusted with flour, dipped in a batter and deep-fried, then served with an avocado dip, or blanched and frozen for up to eight months, allowing almost year-round use.

The calendula is the marigold's botanic name, derived from the Latin *calens*, meaning the first day of the month. Christians called it "marygold," honoring the Virgin Mary, because it was thought to be ripest during holidays. The signet marigold is generally agreed to be the tastiest of the large group, when bruised giving off a lemony scent. Enjoyed for their bright color, they once were called a "poor man's saffron," dried and powdered and used as substitute for that expensive condiment.

Early this century, the dried petals were sold in country stores, "out of a wooded barrel by ounce" as were other herbs. Leona Woodring Smith writes in her book, *The Forgotten Art of Flower Cookery* (1973), that "our great-great-grandmothers left us many recipes using marigolds in buns, rice stews, cakes, broths, 'drinkes,' pickles, and 'possets and pottage.' Dutch chefs famous for their soups and stews acknowledge the marigold as their secret ingredient. Many wine and cordial recipes today use marigolds as the base." As versatile as the rose, the fresh petals can be cooked with quiche or eggs, and added to a custard, biscuits, or a sandwich spread, while the powdered petals can be mixed with flour, butter, cheese and egg yolk and baked on a cookie sheet.

Pansies offer a taste reminiscent of grapes if the petals are used, of peppermint if the entire blossom is added to salads and Italian dishes. Sage, mint, and chives are well known as herbs; the point is to use the flowers, not just the leaves. I've watched large yellow pumpkin blossoms being harvested by hill tribe villagers in Vietnam to cook with maize and garden greens. Xu Jian Chu of the Kunming (China) Institute of Botany told me that 150 different flowers were eaten in Yunnan province, among 1,200 plant species used country-wide for food and medicinal purposes.

Ancient Chinese folk lore insists that if you add one chrysanthemum petal to a glass of wine, gray hair returns to its natural black. The blooms of borage , cornflower and dianthus add brilliance to a soup or punch. Banana flowers, hanging in dense clusters in a purple pouch beneath the fruit, may be cooked and eaten like a vegetable or boiled and served cold with salads. Violet, lavender and honeysuckle add a sweet flavor to salads or desserts. Mustard flowers lend a spicy taste to casseroles. Boiled rice cakes made from the powder of glutinous rice are stained yellow with dried, powdered camellia petals. Numerous blossoms are "crystallized"—dipped in beaten egg white, then in superfine granulated sugar and dried—to decorate pastry or eat like candy. (Martha Stewart suggested them for wedding cakes.) Dandelion heads are made into coffee and wine, the latter winning appreciative fame in Ray Bradbury's reminiscence of his Ohio childhood that took the drink for its title.

Varieties of chamomile, jasmine, hibiscus, butterblossoms, gardenias, carnations (pinks), geraniums, gladiolas, peonies, primroses, johnny-jump-ups, orange and apple blossoms, sunflowers, tulips, gladiolus, hibiscus, daisies, and yucca blossoms, to name just a few more, are nutritious and tasty as well.

This does not mean that you can just buy some flowers at the local florist or nursery, or reach over your neighbor's fence when it's dinner time. Not all blooms are edible and, in fact, many of the pretty things are toxic, including azalea, buttercup, several types of lily, rhododendron, morning glory, sweet pea, and hyacinth. It is also important to note that virtually all commercially available flowers likely have been heavily sprayed with pesticides and some have been hybridized to where there is only beauty left and little or no taste or nourishment.

B. Rosie Lerner, a consumer horticulture specialist at Purdue University in the United States, offers a few more words of caution: "On your first trial, go easy on the flowers. Eating too many blossoms can lead to upset tummies, diarrhea and stomach cramps. You might want to start out using flowers as a garnish and sample the flavors before trying more daring culinary delights. Or sprinkle a few flower petals over a salad to add color and flavor."

She also suggests picking flowers in the morning or late afternoon when water content is at its peak, unless they're to be dried, then midday is best. "Choose only those blossoms that are free of insects, disease or other damage. Do not harvest from plants that were treated with pesticides, unless the product was labeled for use on edible flowers and the harvest restrictions have been followed. Gently wash the blooms in water to remove dirt and allow to drain on paper towels. Once harvested, [most] flowers will not keep long—even when refrigerated—so plan to serve within a few hours of harvesting."

The best advice comes from the chef who said that the key to happiness was to make time to stop and smell the roses...then eat them.

Dandelion Wine

2 qts dandelion blossoms, without stems	1 lemon or lime, cut into slices
1 1/2 lbs sugar	1 tablespoon brewer's yeast
1 orange, peeled and sliced thinly	2 qts water
	1 pc toast

Place blossoms in a bowl and cover with boiling water, stirring, then cover with a cloth and leave for 3 days, stirring occasionally.

Strain into a second vessel, add the rind of the orange, lemon and sugar. Boil slowly for 30 minutes, then leave to cool.

Add yeast spread on a piece of toast and let stand for 2 days, then put into a dry cask, well sealed. Leave for 2 months, then bottle.

Nasturtium Soup

1 qt chicken stock	1 1/2 tablespoon chopped onion
8 nasturtium flowers, chopped	1 sprig parsley
8 nasturtium leaves, chopped	Salt and pepper to taste
Additional nasturtium flowers & leaves	1/2 cup chopped celery

Combine all the ingredients except the last and bring to a boil, stirring constantly. Turn down the heat and let simmer for 6–8 minutes. Strain and serve immediately.

Garnish each serving with a pinch of finely chopped nasturtium leaf and a single blossom. Tuck a leaf and a fresh flower onto the soup plate at the side of the bowl before serving. Serves 4–6.
— *Leona Woodring Smith, The Forgotten Art of Flower Cookery*

Noni Fruit

It was one of those two-page magazine advertisements, what is (or used to be) called a "double truck," where the first page sets up the message and the facing page delivers it.

The first page showed an ugly, bumpy green (orange when ripe) lump with the label "Noni fruit" and below it the words, "Cures hangovers, kidney complaints, gastric ulcers, cramps, senility and pain. Tastes disgusting."

On the opposite page there was a picture of a pint of ice cream and the words, "Häagen-Dazs. Pralines and Cream, Ingredients: pralines, cream and caramel. Cures the taste of Noni fruit."

Why, I asked, as I have frequently asked in writing this book, would anyone willingly eat something that either stank or tasted "disgusting"? There are two likely answers: (1) it was a taste acquired in childhood (see chapters on fermented food, durian, and Marmite), or (2) it was supposed to do something good for you (of a medicinal nature, usually having to do with sex).

Among the health fads to sweep America in 2000, and then encompass much of Asia and the Pacific, one of the strangest was an appetite for noni products. That's what the Polynesians call the fruit they come from and it flourishes from Hawaii to Thailand. In the Philippines it's variously known as *apatot, bungudo, bankoro,* or *nino.* Malaysians call it *mengkudu* and in Thailand it's simply *luk yor,* Thai for "praise," its auspicious name taken to bless the property where it was grown with the admiration and respect of others. The tree's fruit, leaves, root, trunk, and branches have been used for several purposes, including food, medicine, and dye. *Hormok bai yor* (minced fish steamed in noni leaves) is a popular Thai dish and noni juice, along with powders and pills, is now being marketed worldwide.

And what a great marketing success it is. With a sales pyramid scheme pioneered by Amway and Nu-Skin, in the United States, where Morinda and Nature's Sunshine Products were the two main companies selling noni juice, sellers were required to buy a case of four 945-ml bottles of juice a month for about US$150 (after signing a non-disclosure agreement about the deal). Each seller than recruited other distributors, from whom he or she got a cut of the subsequent sales of the stuff, after it was cut and sold in smaller bottles. Those distributors in turn recruited others, usually at hotel seminars. Obviously, the lower your position on the pyramid, the less the original distributor gets, but it is also true that such campaigns soon saturate the market-place, leaving the last ones recruited with dreams quite unfulfilled.

It wasn't long before the fad exploded in the United States—the main producers are Utah-based and Mormon-owned—and then after spreading across the Pacific and into Southeast Asia, people began farming the plant. As Asian food processors got into the game, the price began to come down and the fruit and its leaves began appearing in greater volume in markets and from street vendors. While the leading American manufacturers continued their recruiting scheme.

So what's it supposed to do? Is there any truth to the claims alluded to in the ice cream ad? According to a couple of U.S. food scientists and a Hawaii biochemist who helped spark the craze, noni contain a substance called proxeronine and the enzyme proxeronase, which react in the stomach to form xeronine, an alkaloid which they insist aids cells function, producing therapeutic results. So far, there are no hard facts, only the hype and hyperbole, along with wild claims on the Internet.

In Thai traditional medicine, *luk yor* is described as a "hot" food or medicine and suggested to counter aliments believe to be the result of a lack of heat or "fire energy" in the body—for example, colds, asthma, coughs, allergies, and some types of paralysis. *Yor* also is supposed to help with digestion, easing gas in the bowels. Women of child-bearing age are encouraged to eat the fruit as it is believed to improve blood circulation and skin complexion.

The simplest, if most difficult, way to eat the stuff is raw, adding salt or honey to take away some of the bitterness. It may also be used as a substitute for papaya in *som tam*, the salad known for its fiery chili peppers. Jams and jellies are another popular way to get the fruit down, mixing it with sweet berries.

Just like any fruit, noni has Vitamins A, B and C and anti-oxidants, so it's consumption is harmless for most people. A high incidence of potassium may make it risky for people with kidney ailments and Food and Drug Administrations from the U.S. to Thailand all warned buyers that it was not a "medicine," as some sellers insisted, but only another faddish "food supplement" (like spirulina, wheat grass, bee pollen, and a hundred other "miracle cures").

Usually the concentrate is mixed with other fruit juices because in its unadulterated form, the ripe noni and puree tastes awful and the smell is reasonably compared to rotten cheese.

Perhaps the man in Manila who wrote a caption for a photograph of two women vendors had it right when he said, "The bitter fruit…supposedly cures a wide variety of diseases, including cancer, AIDS, and street hawker poverty."

Grass, Bark, Leaves, Wood & Sap

Sounds like survival food to me, the stuff you eat just before you turn to dirt or die. And for many, that's what it is, or has been.

We've all read stories in the press about how severe drought in North Korea and elsewhere forced humans to eat bark, leaves, and grass because that was all there was. I do not wish to take anything away from the tragic needs of such people, but there is a lesson here for many of us.

Much of our diet starts with grass. Sheep turn it into lamb chops. Cattle turn it into hamburgers and T-bone steaks. Goats turn it into milk and cheese. Why, I wonder, can't we eat grass as well? Go right to the source, eliminate the middleman (or cow).

The answer, of course, is that we can. But we must be selective. Getting down on your knees in the garden or park to chomp on the joined stems and bladed leaves that characterize this common family of plants will not satisfy. In its natural state, most grass tastes awful and that so many herbivores have multiple stomachs says a lot about its digestibility. (Although most of the world's breads and cereals come from cultivated plants that evolved from grass, including wheat, millet, rice and maize.)

Still, there are grasses that not only are edible, but also relatively tasty. The *US Army Survival Manual*, a handbook that tells you how to live in the wild if your plane gets shot down, says, "There are no known poisonous grasses, so you should consider wild grain as an important emergency food source. Grains are edible raw, but roasting or boiling improves the food quality."

There also are some seeds from ordinary grasses found around the house or farm that may be ground and made into nutritious bread. These include common barnyard grass and that old enemy of the manicured lawn, crab grass, so named, I guess, because it sends out lateral stems that take root, permitting the grass to "crawl" across the lawn like a crustacean. It once was called "crop" grass, when its seeds were ground into flour or eaten as a cereal or as an alternative to rice. It is still eaten in parts of Africa.

In fact, before the rise of agriculture, collecting the seeds of wild grasses is believed to have led to the beginning of cereal cultivation in West Asia, the Mediterranean, the Sudan, and Ethiopia, and probably in China, too. As Carlton S. Coon pointed out in *The Hunting Peoples*, the technique for harvesting the wild seed was uncomplicated: "They did not reap the grasses, but simply walked through the stand, each woman holding a basket in one hand and a stick in the other. She would place a handful of stalks against the edge of her basket, and beat the seed into it with the stick."

The blades of some grasses themselves are edible, of course. But I do not enthusiastically endorse all of them, however good nutritionists insist they are for you. Two of the best known are wheat grass and barley grass. Before they undergo the reproductive cycle that creates the seed, or grains, the grasses contain about the same vitamins and minerals as dark green vegetables. When grasses are harvested at a young age, they have a different chemical makeup from their adult counterparts. Unfortunately, this is one of those times when what's good for your body doesn't do much for your mouth. Back in the 1960s, my then-wife grew wheat grass in pots in the kitchen window and liquefied it in a food processor, along with other things in an attempt to make it palatable. It didn't work. What it did do was turn my tongue and teeth green. This may explain why barley grass—another health faddist's delight—is sold in powder and capsule form, and rarely grown on a window ledge.

There are three more grasses that grow wild in Europe and North America that are not generally regarded as very appetizing, although they have a long culinary history. One is elk grass, which flourishes from California north into Canada and sometimes is called bear grass or squaw grass or, because of the thousands of little flowers that adorn a central stalk, bear lily, pine lily or fire lily. Indians and early settlers in the region roasted the large roots for food.

Another with several aliases is quack grass, also called couch grass, witch grass, and dog grass, the latter because dogs eat the flowering spikes and leaves to settle their upset stomachs. Herbalists have used the leaves to make a tea that is taken for urinary problems and the rhizomes may be ground into a flour or roasted and used, much like chicory and dandelion root, as a somewhat bitter coffee substitute. Quack grass, its most common name, grows to a height of about four feet throughout much of North America and Europe.

The third is the distinctive foxtail grass, named for its thin, cylindrical top containing long hairs that give it the appearance of a miniature bushy tail. This one is found not only in Europe and North America, but also in open sunny areas, along roads, and at the margins of fields in western Asia and tropical Africa, where it sometimes is grown as a food crop. The grains may be eaten raw, but are hard and, like most grains, somewhat bitter unless boiled.

Another is water bamboo, or wild rice, a perennial aquatic plant that grows wild in Asia in brackish or fresh water pools and marshy areas. It is neither bamboo, nor rice, but has a resemblance to both. The edible part is the swollen base of the stem, generally harvested in the spring and summer and used in a variety of dishes to absorb other flavors, because its own flavor is mild. During late summer and fall, the husks may be collected, dried, and parched; the rice inside is removed, boiled or roasted, then ground into flour for making small cakes that are fried or grilled over coals.

A cousin of this "wild rice" grows in North America, where the Indians so valued the plant that one tribe named itself for it; the *Menomin*, or "wild rice men," lived mainly on the grass that grew in the shallow lakes. Michael A. Weiner wrote in *Earth Medicine-Earth Foods* that the Indians prepared the food by "parching the seeds in a receptacle for a short while over hot coals. The rice was stirred constantly to keep from burning. When cool, the husks were beaten off and the seeds winnowed. The parched seeds were then boiled in water and eaten with blueberries or maple syrup or used for thickening soups. Like the commercial variety, wild rice swells with boiling, sometimes increasing in size from three to four times during cooking."

Finally, there is the common reed, found in any open, wet area throughout most of the temperate regions of both the Northern and

Southern Hemispheres. This is a tall, coarse grass that grows to twelve feet, with gray-green leaves and large, feathery clusters of brown flowers that droop and wave in the breeze. All parts of the reed are edible raw or cooked. The new stems maybe boiled or, before the flowers appear in the early summer, beaten into flour.

There are many barks that are edible, too, as recommended in England's *SAS Survival Handbook*, where no fewer than eleven families of trees are considered to be a source of edible and nutritious bark—"best in the spring, when the sap has started to flow." In other words, it's best if your plane is shot down in March, April, or May.

"Choose bark from near the bottom of the tree or from exposed roots," the *SAS* guidebook advised. "Peel it back with a knife to reveal the inner layer. This is mildly sweet and can be eaten raw—but can be made more digestible by long boiling, which will reduce it to a gelatinous mass. It can then be roasted and ground for used as flour." Or as a thickening for soups and stews.

The handbook's eleven edible barks are slippery elm, basswood, birches, aspens, tamarack, poplars, maples, spruces, willows, pines, and hemlocks.

Many indigenous groups have eaten bark quite matter-of-factly. American Indians ate birch bark raw, shredded and cooked as noodles or dried it and ground it into flour for making bread. The Zuni tribe boiled and pounded the inner bark of the piñon tree into a mash, shaped it into cakes and baked them in a clay oven or pit; the result was so hard it had to be boiled in water to soften it, but it could be stored for months. So, too, with the larch tree, found in sub-arctic parts of North America, Europe, and Siberia. The Siberians used the bark to make a broth, North American Indians to boil a tea.

The gums and resins of trees also have a long gastronomical history. With some trees, when cut, sap seeping out on to the bark hardens into a lump. If this is soluble in water, it is a gum; if not, it is a resin. Both are nutritious, rich in sugars and mineral salts. A few have medicinal properties, in their hardened state all are good firestarters, and some Native Americans enjoyed chewing it. It is, in a way, the tree's "blood," as edible or drinkable as the blood of most animals, and can be prepared in as many ways.

Maple trees, of course, are known for the value of their sap. Mostly this goes into the production of sugar and syrup, a substantial industry in North America. Edible sap also comes from birch, hemlock, mesquite, and pine trees, although they don't contain as much sugar as the maple. It may all be eaten raw or boiled.

The leaves of some trees are edible, too, although the *US Army Survival Manual* recommends only three, the acacia, baobab, and sassafras. There are many more, including spruce, willow, and hemlock, as well as a number of evergreens, pinions, pines and spruces among them. The thin leaves, or needles, of the evergreens may all used to make tea. The sassafras is a common tree in eastern North America that grows at the margins of roads and forests. The young twigs and leaves can be eaten fresh or dried, or added to soups. Dig the underground portion of this small tree, peel off the skin, and let it dry, then boil it in water to prepare sassafras tea. The young leaves, flowers, and pods of the acacia, found in most tropical regions, are edible raw or cooked.

The young leaves of the baobab, a tree with an trunk so thick (up to ten meters in diameter!) that it may be hollowed out and used as a human dwelling, are also edible. It grows in savannas in Africa (where dried and powdered baobab leaves are called lalo and used for making bread) and in parts of Australia, and on the island of Madagascar. Most often the young leaves are added to soups and stews and cooked as a vegetable. The baobab also has a large, gourd-like fruit, sometimes called monkey bread, with a pulp that can be made into a refreshing drink.

Willows, long a favorite browse for deer, are the first sources of Vitamin C to appear through the snow in the spring and the young leaves can be eaten raw, best in a salad with other greens. The leaves can also be boiled or steamed and eaten as a vegetable.

The general rule when eating leaves is to use only young ones, which are, like most animals, birds and many other creatures, more tender and more easily digested before they reach maturity.

Finally, in a few species the wood of the tree itself is edible. The sassafras has been mentioned, where the young twigs may be stripped and chewed or boiled to make tea. The same is true of the juniper, found in sunny areas in North America and northern Europe, across Asia to Japan, and in the mountains of North Africa, and the birch, although the twigs must be steeped in hot water and not boiled, as the higher temperatures removes the desirable wintergreen flavor.

The trunks of two palms tell another tale. The best known, and most important, of these is the sago palm, a native of the Indonesian archipelago. This is used to produce a yellowish flour that is essential to the local diet in the remoter islands; on the Moluccas Islands, sago, not rice, is the staple food. Sago is also exported to other Pacific locations and to Europe.

The trunk of the tall buri palm in coastal areas in the East Indies also contains a starch, which is edible raw, cut into chewable chunks. It may also be chopped, dried and ground into a flour that can be formed with water into patties, which then are grilled or fried. The very tip of the trunk, hidden away in the large, fan-shaped leaves, is also edible raw or cooked, and is usually boiled like a vegetable.

Slime? Sublime!

It's not a pretty sight, this gunk called Methocel. Developed by the Dow Chemical Company, its early use was as a thickener for putty and drywall mud. Twice, Dow considered halting production. Then along came Don Coffey, a newly minted PhD in food science, who was hired to cook up some new recipes. Today, it may be found in some 400 foods, from frozen pot pies to whipped toppings, as well as pills, paints, shampoos, and special effects for Hollywood. (Dinosaur sneeze in *Jurassic Park*, Wampa drool in *The Empire Strikes Back*.)

What appealed to the young Coffey was that, chemically peaking, the stuff reacted to heat the opposite of plastics that got thinner. Methocel had a sticky layer that broke free when the molecules were heated, bonding together to form something that looked like cooked egg whites. Then, as it cooled, it turned into a tasteless, odorless, and calorie-free oozing slime that could be used to thicken soups, sauces, and gravies. It now may be found in such foods as Burger King onion rings, Hidden Valley Ranch salad dressings, Marie Callender pot pies, Progresso soups, and Twinkies.

So what is it, really? Chemicals are used in the manufacturing process, but the end product is all-natural wood cellulose, the chief constituent of the cell walls of plants, more commonly known for its use in making paper and textiles.

Marmite & Vegemite

For only a little longer than it takes to read this book, I was one of those food faddists who cluttered the landscape in the early 1970s, eating tofu burgers, subsisting for days on trail mix and herbal tea, and growing wheat grass in a tray in my kitchen window to blend into horrible drinks. It was during this period that I discovered in what we then called "health food stores" a canned sandwich spread from Australia called Vegemite.

"What's this?" I asked the clerk, a woman in a tie-dyed smock who was munching a carob bar.

"Think of it as peanut butter from Australia," she said. "It's rich in thiamin and pantothenic acid and, dig it, vegemite has lots of the B vitamins and you know what they do for your nerves. It has a strong smell and taste, but it's also good for your eyes and your digestion and your skin. How many jars do you want?"

I was wearing a tie-dyed shirt myself in those days, so I purchased a jar and, at the woman's earnest suggestion, took it home for a test drive as a sandwich spread. (On seven-grain bread, of course.) On the way, I read the list of ingredients: yeast extract, salt, malt extract, natural flavor. It sounded simple enough.

Well, rich in vitamins it might have been, as many of my foods were in those golden days, but it had a peculiar, purple-brown-verging-on-black color, a smooth, sticky texture that reminded me of the grease that accumulated in the engine of my Volkswagen van, and an odor that filled the kitchen with an invisible cloud that even the wheat grass didn't like. I wondered if I'd bought a bad batch. No, I told myself, the woman said it was "strong," so I took a knife and as if it were peanut butter, spread a thick layer on a piece of bread and bit off a chunk. I had not yet heard it compared to a "canned stool sample," but I knew at that moment why such a likeness was not only possible, but reasonable. Imagine: anchovies, fermented to bring out the taste of salt.

Express this point of view in Australia, where Vegemite is as revered as the koala bear and Foster's lager, and you may get thrown onto the barbie next to one of Crocodile Dundee's shrimp. In Australia, and wherever else in the world that Aussies gather, Vegemite is something akin to a national dish, the subject of fierce and lethal loyalty. Say anything negative about it, or make an ugly face while trying to choke it down, and expect to get clubbed with Down Under's famous digereedoo, a sort of aboriginal baseball bat.

A quick and easy way to understand how dedicated some Australians are to this food is to log on to the Internet, where I was referred to more than 1,000 documents, a resounding majority of them on a Vegemite chat line, praising the food, answering pleas from Aussies overseas ("Anyone know where I can find Vegemite in Edmonton, Canada; I'm in withdrawal and need it urgently"), or defending it from its critics. There also were a number of messages urging Vegemite lovers to use it to play practical jokes, suggesting you wrestle someone to the ground and force a full tablespoon of the stuff into his or her mouth, or when going to a job interview, smearing some of it on your hand so that when you shake the interviewer's hand...well, you get the level of fervor and humor in all this. One can't help wondering if the stuff stunts one's (mental) growth.

The way the official history goes, in 1922, a young Australian businessman named Fred Walker asked one of his chemists, Dr. Cyril Callister, to start a series of experiments with the yeast and malt grunge that was left over from the manufacture of beer at the nearby Carlton & United Breweries. There was a product from England already on the market, called Marmite, made from the same by-products and Mr. Walker wanted some of that market for himself, and he wanted the product to be homegrown.

Well, the stuff tested out rich in vitamins and so on—just as I was told fifty years later—and soon there was a sandwich spread in a limited number of Australian markets called Parwill. (A play on words. Mar mite, Par will. Get it?) Reconsidering, Mr. Walker held a contest to name the new spread and Dr. Callister's paste became "Vegemite." Packaged in cylindrical jars and advertised as a "pure vegetable extract," initially it was promoted as a children's food with an advertising jingle that began:

> We're happy little Vegemites,
> As bright as bright can be,
> We always eat our Vegemite
> For breakfast, lunch, and tea.

Despite its dubious taste and smell, and the simplicity of the jingle, the product caught on and by the time Australia was invaded by the Japanese at the beginning of World War Two, it had become a staple at home and subsequently in the kits of Australian servicemen fighting alongside their British cousins from Europe to the Sahara to Burma and Malaysia.

The war ended and with the Japanese gone, Australia's favorite spread was available in great supply again. In time, Mr. Walker's company was bought by Kraft, the American food giant that manufactures it to this day. Kraft also sells packaged cheese slices with Vegemite. Aussies say that cheese and Vegemite go together like peanut butter and jelly. (The addition of Vegemite to the cheese turns the cheese sort of gray.) And, I was told, the Vegemite was always, always spread very thinly—my mistake; I piled it onto the bread half an inch thick— because "goodness goes a long way."

Another sandwich recipe: spread Vegemite on one slice of bread, honey on the other, and put cheese in the middle to create an Australian Sweet and Sour Sandwich. Some also like to toast the spread and cheese slices under the griller (oven or toaster). Most Vegemite is consumed in this fashion, in sandwiches, but, of course, it may also be added to casseroles, stews, and so on.

Today's Vegemite contains the same old yeast and malt extracts, sea salt, potassium chloride, caramel color, niacin, thiamin hydrochloride, riboflavin, and whatever "natural" flavors that may survive. Not long ago, in a bid to appease health enthusiasts, the salt content was lowered from ten to eight per cent.

Marmite has a longer history, first developed and marketed in Great Britain in 1902. I give Vegemite first priority now only because it was the odd, dark spread that I tasted first (while living in Hawaii); Marmite came, and went, later.

Marmite is a registered trademark of CPC International Inc. at Burton-on-Trent in Surrey, using yeast from the Bass Pale Ale brewery in the same neighborhood. Variations bearing the same name are manufactured by other companies in other parts of the world, usually following a slightly different recipe. Some add wheatgerm extract, others different herbs and spices, a few sugar and caramel. (Purists say the sweeteners make a "weak" or "sissy" Marmite, totally unacceptable to die-hard fans of the Real Thing.) In New Zealand, it is made by the Sanitarium Health Company, a name that its owners, Seventh Day Adventists, will enjoy my refrain now from making easy jokes. The breweries usually pay Marmite to remove the yeast from their factories, the opposite way it works for most recycling.

Marmite's name is puzzling, because its origins are in France, not always England's favorite European pal. According to *Larousse Gastronomique*, the last word on all things French and culinary, *la marmite* is a metal or earthenware covered pot with two handles, with or without feet, depending on whether it's used for cooking in a hearth or on the stove. The capacities are huge, up to 500 liters or 100 gallons. The word marmite is derived from an Old French word meaning "hypocrite," applied to the cooking pot because its contents were concealed, and leading me again to keep my mouth shut. A picture of the stewpot was on the original earthenware jar containing the stuff and is on the glass jars today.

So why are so many people so faithful? Like other foods relished in other parts of the world—balut in the Philippines, haggis in Scotland, durian in Southeast Asia, and so on—Vegemite and Marmite and other similar spreads (Promite, Bovril, etc.) are a love it or hate it proposition and it appears incontrovertible that being fed the stuff at an early age is almost a requirement to continue eating it into adulthood. Mark Wearing, the company's plant manager, told no less than the New York Times, "Our research shows that if you haven't been exposed to it by the time you're three, it's unlikely you'll like it."

Yet, an incredible number do. The Brits—who also are known to enjoy dishes called Bubble and Squeak, Toad in the Hole, and Spotted Dick—buy twenty-four million jars every year and it is, quoting the Times again, enshrined as "a national symbol right up there with the royal family and the Sunday roast."

"The fact that no foreigner has ever been known to like it," the Times concluded, "simply adds to its domestic allure and its iconic status as an emblem of enduring British insularity and bloody-mindedness."

Seaweed & Algae

I love the stuff. It's slimy and sometimes rubbery and frequently looks like scum. It is not a pretty sight. Yet, when you pull it from the coral reef or shoreline rocks, to smell and taste it is to return to the sea from which, scientists say, we all came, when, perhaps, it was a primary slice of our daily gastronomy.

I'm talking about seaweed and algae, the numerous one-celled or colonial organisms that contain chlorophyll and flourish in aquatic environments.

In some parts of the world, seaweed is eaten so matter-of-factly, no resident of the region even thinks about it, let alone calls it unusual. I lived in one of them, Hawaii, for many years, gathering several varieties from the ocean, routinely including the slippery leaves in my soups and salads and cooking it with vegetables. For me, seaweed was, and is, not a strange food. I now live in Asia, where the same thing can be said. Yet, for the majority of the planet it remains stuck in the category of "weeds," and thus is, if not inedible, at least undesirable.

Seaweed is not a "weed" in the sense that it is a nuisance and has no popularly perceived value. A large number of the genera known as "algae" are highly prized, and for good reason. The three general types—blue-green, brown, and red—find their way onto our tables and into our mouths in soups and sweets, wrapped around balls of rice called sushi, thickeners, emulsifiers, stabilizers and food supplements, or eaten by itself.

The Chinese may have used it for medicinal purposes as long as four to five thousand years ago, when reportedly it was prescribed for goiter, bronchitis, abscesses, and intestinal troubles. During the Middle Ages, monks ate an algae jelly as a stomach remedy. These early endorsements were not misplaced.

In many parts of the world for millennia, seaweed that washed ashore was raked into the soil where crops were grown, especially where there was an absence of soil (the seaweed was mixed with sand) or where the soil was poor. In 17th Century Ireland, real estate near the shore was worth up to sixty-five per cent more, not because of the view but because of the advantages of access to seaweed and its use in agriculture.

Today, it's regarded as an ideal companion for space travel. Writes Lucy Kevaler in *The Wonders of Algae*, an authoritative study of the subject published in 1961, "Many kinds have only one cell—no root, no stem, no leaves, and no flowers. But it's their very simplicity that makes them ideally suited for use in spaceships. All they need to make them grow is water, light, the carbon dioxide breathed out by the space pilots, and the nitrogen and other minerals that can be gotten from the men's daily wastes. Algae grow with incredible speed, so that a small cargo could continue to produce oxygen all the way to Mars and back."

Ms. Kavaler, writing later in the *Woman's Day Encyclopedia of Cooking* points also to the geographical spread of this most primitive of plants—fossils go back some two to three-and-a-half billion years showing no basic structural change—saying, "Wherever you go, you will find some form of seaweed: in the cold ocean off the rugged coasts of New England or Scandinavia, in the warm Pacific bounding California or Hawaii, in the Indian Ocean, in fresh-water ponds. There are giants nearly a mile wide and several miles long, tiny blobs, thin ribbons, leafy clusters, tangles of threads, delicate fernlike growths. In the shallow waters near shore one finds green, yellow-green, blue-green, and brown seaweed; dimly seen in deep waters lie dark-red and purple ones, waving their fragile, beautifully wrought leaves." This is the seaweed's boast: it's versatile and it's everywhere.

A growing number of scientists and food economists predict that in the next century, it finally will have its day in court, or, rather, in kitchens around the world, as one of the most important food sources, one of the answers to world hunger. It's well known that these "vegetables from the sea" can grow both taller and closer together than vegetables grown in soil and for that reason alone the yield per acre is far greater than any a land farmer might expect. And, there is no waste. At least half of every other vegetable or grain is discarded; only with algae, can all of the crop be used, as there is no inedible root, leaf, or stem.

There are some 30,000 species of algae—constituting seventy per cent of the earth's biomass and providing eighty per cent of the planet's oxygen, two facts little known—and, of course, not all of it is edible. However, as Ms. Kavaler notes, "there are so many wholesome varieties that almost every nation living on the sea has found ways of making seaweed palatable. A visitor to Edinburgh a hundred years or so ago would surely have heard street vendors crying 'buy dulse and tangle,' referring to a sweetened seaweed mixture with a taste similar to peanuts. British whalers gathered the leafy 'laver' and it was virtually the only fresh vegetable they ate during their prolonged voyages. In parts of Wales it retains its popularity to this day Among the Irish one can still find old men who cling to the timeworn custom of chewing dried dulse or crannogh in place of tobacco."

From the time when the scum of algae was scooped off still waters by primitive people in Africa, Mexico, and Britain and made into bread and a type of pancake, to when American Indians living along the eastern and western seashores ate "sea lettuce," to the present day, when a wide variety of products made from algae are sold as a "natural" diet supplement in expensive food boutiques, seaweed has been consumed. Agar-agar is an extract of seaweed from the Indian and Pacific Oceans that comes in strips, in loaves, and powdered form. When dissolved in water over a low heat, it blends with the water, and on cooling sets to a jelly, and is commonly used in puddings, ice cream, pies, jellies, candy, and canned soups. In grocery stores, look on the labels of such foods for the words alginate, alginic acid, and carrageenin.

When Spanish explorers came to the New World in the 16th century, they found the Aztecs diet of maize, beans, squash and a mysterious blue-green scum that was scooped from the surface of Lake Texcoco, near where Mexico City is today. The Aztecs called this protein-rich substance *tecuitlatl*. Today, it is known as spirulina, a freshwater algae that contains sixty per cent protein, making it one of the best building blocks for muscles. By comparison, uncooked meat contains twenty-seven per cent protein and soybean thirty-four per cent. It also offers generous amounts of vitamins A to E, as well as calcium, iron, sodium, and magnesium, and so is cultivated nowadays in California, Hawaii, Taiwan, Thailand, and Japan.

In no other part of the world have algae and seaweed been, nor do they continue to be, more popular than they are in Japan, where some say the consumption represents as much as ten per cent of the national diet. Two kinds of seaweed are basic. The first is *konbu*, or kelp, the large brown algae that is a key ingredient in *dashi*, the soup stock that in turn is the basis of miso, as well as tempura and sukiyaki sauce. It also is used to season rice and vegetables, and is cut into strips and made into small baskets which are fried and served with cooked vegetables. One chef suggests cutting it into small pieces and baking it with navy, pinto or kidney beans. Other cooks delight in pickling it with ginger, vinegar, and *shoyu*. Kelp's main purpose is to enhance flavor; in fact, it was from kelp that monosodium glutamate (MSG) was first extracted by the Japanese. But it also is consumed as a vegetable, simmered with chicken, or cut into thin strips and sautéed or as a salad vegetable.

The second is nori, the purple seaweed that is dried and powdered or pressed into paper-thin sheets and used for wrapping sushi or fish, and in either powdered or flaked form is added as a condiment sprinkled over sauces, soups, salads, grains, cooked vegetables,and garnishes. It may also be roasted until crunchy and eaten as a snack. Once opened, packages of nori can be kept in the freezer in a closed plastic bag or tin; the sheets defrost instantly and may be re-frozen many times. Nori powder or flakes should be kept on a dry shelf, away from direct sunlight and heat, keeping in mind that the aroma fades in a few months; in all cases, rubbing the flakes between your fingertips just before use brings out the aromatic best.

There are many other varieties, eaten in widespread parts of the world, depending upon tradition and availability. In Japan and Korea, wakame is eaten fresh in the spring; elsewhere in the world it is sold dried, soaked and then quickly cooked in soups or added to other salad vegetables. Irish moss, found on both sides of the Atlantic Ocean, is boiled in soups or added to vegetables in the United Kingdom. Red warm-water seaweed accounts for a portion of the local diet in the South Pacific. Freshwater algae found in green, jelly-like globules about the size of marbles, is dried and used in soups in China and in parts of Europe and America.

Despite its worldwide availability and adaptability for use in a wide variety of dishes, seaweed remains an uncommon—and to some, strange—comestible. Nonetheless, inroads are being made. A typical champion of seaweed as food in the west is Larch Hanson, an avowed conservationist who operates the Maine Seaweed Company in the United States. In a booklet, *Edible Sea Vegetables of the New England Coast: A Forager's Guide*, he describes ways to harvest, store, and prepare dishes using half a dozen of the most common types (nori, kelp, sea lettuce, Irish moss, dulse, etc.), as well as ways to prepare it for the table. Hanson, who sells seaweed by mail to those who don't wish to harvest their own, or cannot, suggests two books that contain many more recipes, *Cooking With Sea Vegetables* by Peter and Montse Bradford, and *Complete Guide to Macrobiotic Cooking* by Aveline Kushi.

Miso Soup with Kelp

Cut a 5-inch piece of longicruris kelp (a quick-cooking kelp; you may substitute saccharina kelp) into bite-sized pieces. Soak 1/2 hour. Add to 1 quart of water and bring to a boil. Add cut vegetables from yang to yin: carrots, onions, celery, greens. Turn off pot when veggies are tender. Soften 2 teaspoons miso in a bit of stock and add.

Baked Beans with Kelp

Soak 2 cups of beans (navy, pinto, kidney) overnight. Drain and rinse. Place in a stovetop-to-oven pot and simmer 15 minutes with water to cover. Cut digitata kelp (similar to Japanese kombu, which may be substituted) into small pieces and add cover. Place in oven at 350°F for 1 hour. Add 1 diced onion and bake for 30 minutes more. Mustard may also be added for extra zip. Be sure to watch the water level...too little water will give dry beans; too much water and the beans will not develop the "gravy." Other vegetable additions include burdock, carrots, celeriac, shitake mushrooms, celery, Italian parsley, summer savory.

Nori Tempura

Batter: Combine 1 cup whole-wheat pastry flour, 2 tablespoons arrowroot, 1 cup water, pinch of salt. Keep cool until ready to use. Heat 2–3 inches of safflower oil in a wok. The oil is ready when batter dropped into the oil sinks and rises quickly. Break off small bite-sized pieces of nori, dip them in the batter, then into the hot oil. Fry until golden brown and keep warm in a 150°F oven. Make a dipping sauce with 1 tablespoon tamari, 1 tablespoon water or kombu stock, 1 teaspoon mirin, and a touch of grated ginger.
        —*Larch Hanson, Edible Sea Vegetables of the New England Coast*

Hallucinogenic Plants

"Would you like your pizza happy or very happy or very, very happy?"
    It was mealtime in Phnom Penh. You couldn't buy ganja by the

bushel at the Russian Market any longer, and the government insisted that it'd stopped all the cops and military from growing the stuff for export, but from 1994 until at least 2003 there were as many as five pizza restaurants along the city's riverfront where the key word in the name of the place was "happy."

The first was Happy Herb's, so called not because ganja was a herb, but for its American chef, whose name was Herbert. By 2003, the cook was long gone, but the smiles on the menu remained. I had a friend who lived in the Cambodian capital who said he ate at Herb's once and it was two days before he recalled where he'd parked his car.

On a recent visit to Phnom Penh I visited Happy Phnom Penh Pizza, close by the Foreign Correspondents Club. Here, the thirty-something, English-speaking and affable Chann Hour, owner-manager, offered a menu that included twenty-five different pizza choices. Chann also invited me into the kitchen, where he produced a jar that once contained Nescafe instant coffee and now was full of ganja. He explained that he processed the stuff in a food processor and then ran it through a flour sifter to produce a uniform powder. A circle of dough was pulled from a fridge and lathered with tomato sauce. Chann then sprinkled the ganja on top—lightly, moderately, or generously, following the degree of happiness selected by the customer—and added cheese and other ingredients. The pizza was then baked in the usual fashion, the heat activating the Tetrahydro-cannabinol, or THC, releasing the stuff that gets the diner buzzed.

The consumption of marijuana and numerous other psychotropic plants to get high and/or for religious reasons—and often for the added taste, or the oil made from seeds—has been enjoyed for more than five millennia and seems to be on the upswing again today, as a worldwide campaign of suppression led for more than fifty years primarily by the United States now seems to be faltering. For the traveler today—and for many stay-at-homes, depending on where you live—a wide variety of hallucinogenic substances are being added to meals matter-of-factly, as legalization and decriminalization gain favor and the harmlessness, or benefit, becomes more widely recognized. (Or, rather, that the fears engendered by governments appears to diminish.)

Most popular of these are the strains of the Cannabis sativa, a leafy plant thought to be native to North and South America but farmed in China from 3000 B.C. and now grown virtually everywhere except in the Arctic and Antarctica (where of course it may be cultivated indoors under powerful lamps). Mainly, the plant's tough fiber has been used for rope and cloth; during World War Two, many American farmers were actually told to grow it for the war effort.

The ancient Greeks ate fried hemp seed and, according to *The Oxford Companion to Food*, it has continued to be used as a food "until the present day in Poland and parts of Russia, where oil pressed from the seeds is used for cooking. The seeds (*asanomi*) are eaten in Japan in fried tofu burgers." This use is non-hallucinogenic, however.

Cannabis is also made into "narcotic" foods such as the hash brownies popularized in the 1960s when *The Alice B. Toklas Cook-book*, a memoir of Paris in the 1920s, found a new generation of readers. Alice and her companion, Gertrude Stein, would've been proud to know Mary Jane Rathbun, who came to be called "Brownie Mary" for the pastries she took to patients of San Francisco General Hospital, discovering they were especially popular and helpful on the AIDS wards; in the 1990s, she was instrumental in getting medicinal use of marijuana legalized in California. Mary died in 1999 at the age of 77.

Most places in the world, ganja is consumed not for relief from pain, but for fun or religious purposes. The holy sadhus of India seem to smoke it constantly, but it's also a key ingredient in a variety of dishes that are sold legally, mostly in yoghurt drinks and desserts. The Rastafarians in Jamaica also attach religious significance to its use. In the Netherlands, there are ganja coffee shops. In Morocco there's a candy called *majoun*. In parts of Southeast Asia, ganja, chili peppers, and other seasoning such as galangal and lemon grass (chopped and fried in a pan just long enough to activate the THC; remove from the heat at the first sign of smoke) may be pounded into a paste and added on request to soups and curries in small restaurants when the customer is known. Cookbooks are sold through the mail.

One of these, *Cooking With Ganja*, is a sixty-eight-page handbook packed with recipes, published anonymously in England in 1998. The author, identified only as "Eric," warns cooks and consumers that by "eating cooked ganja or hash, you will certainly become more stoned and for a lot longer than you would from smoking the same amount." He also suggests disguising the strong taste and odor—the latter was what got "Brownie Mary" arrested several times, when the smell of baking permeated her apartment building—by combining it with other strong flavors: chocolate and coffee, fresh herbs and spices and strong alcohol, such as dark rum, brandy, or red wine. Some recipes are redolent of the East—Sacred Ghee, Bhang Paste—while others have the Western taste in mind—Peanut Butter Cookies, Veggie Burgers, Asparagrass Soup, and Pizza Maryjane. There's even a section for microwave cooking.

Most of the recipes call for "cannabutter"—melt butter in a pan, add powdered ganja, and stir for half an hour over a low heat—or "bhang paste"—boil leaves in water for five minutes, squeeze out water and grind the grass in a mortar with a little milk. The result is added to all recipes and may be stored in a fridge.

A final word about ganja and the diet. For most, it increases the appetite, a factor that helped AIDS patients, whose disease and its medical treatment generally caused them to lose weight. For others, it often increased appetite to the point where it was a good idea not to go to a food market while stoned.

A variety of other native plants play a role in modern gastronomy:

MAGIC MUSHROOMS: The best known is Fly Agaric, the mushroom that created Alice's Wonderland, is discussed, tragically, in the chapter on poisonous plants, but the most popular are other species that have less threatening effect. A report by a jungle botanist, Richard Schultes, was published in *Life* magazine in 1957 under the title "Seeking the Magic Mushrooms." Thus the small, dried fungi with the long stems came to the United States, soon to be promoted for its active ingredients psilocybin and psilocin by Timothy Leary, one of the high priests of the American drug culture of the 1960s. Schultes did his collecting in the region stretching from southern Mexico—where the mushroom was used by Indians specifically to create hallucinations—to Amazonia, where he remained for fourteen years, recording thousands of "new" plants, some 2,000 with medicinal value. Use of the mushrooms for the "psychedelic" effect dates at least to the Spanish conquest and representations of the mushrooms in stone in Guatemala go back to between 200 B.C. and 300 A.D. There is evidence of mushroom cults in Mexico in the 16th century forward.

From the 1960s onward, the mushroom began sprouting in other parts of the world, literally on the slopes of Maui's Mt. Haleakala, where cattle manure enriched the volcanic soil, eventually finding its way to Amsterdam where it was sold in what were called Smart Shops with names like Conscious Dreams, Magic Valley, and Inner Space. In 1999, Dutch courts decided against outlawing the marketing of fresh mushrooms, while limiting sale of dried ones that were brewed into a heady tea.

PEYOTE: The religious use of peyote, or *Lophophora williamsii*, is permitted for members of the Native American Church, a pan-tribal religion derived from the practices of native peoples who inhabited what is now southwest Texas and northern Mexico. For other Americans, it's considered a dangerous drug.

The 300,000-member peyote church, as it's sometimes called, dates back to the 19th century. Members usually consume it in a tea or in powdered form and don't report feeling a high, but rather a period of intense spiritual reflection. Thus, it was no surprise when it, too, was embraced by the longhaired, tie-dyed throng to whom Leary preached. Many at the time thought of it as "Mother Nature's LSD."

Because the bitter taste was well known, when my wife and I decided to give the little cactus buttons a try in 1973, we washed the small, pale green fruits thoroughly and threw them into a blender with some strawberry yogurt, believing that, as Mary Poppins said, a little bit of sugar helped the "medicine" go down. Soon after consuming the awful goop, I found myself in the yard, puking. Weird (and sometimes sensual) hallucinations followed, as did a suicidal mood. I never tried them again.

KAVA: This calming yet stimulating drink has long been made from the root of the *Piper methysticum* for use in cultural and religious ceremonies throughout much of Polynesia, especially in Fiji, but also in Tonga, Samoa, and to a lesser degree in Hawaii. In Fiji, it is regarded as a ceremonial libation, but in the U.S. and elsewhere it's just another one of those "herbal remedies" or "dietary supplements" that don't have to meet the usual standards of safety and purity specified in the federal Food, Drug and Cosmetic Act. It also has been suggested as an aphrodisiac useful during rituals of tantric yoga when there is a need to control thought and visualize creatively as a means of preventing orgasm.

Its reputation as a natural alternative to muscle relaxants and anti-anxiety drugs have made kava capsules and tablets a popular herbal remedy in much of the west, although there have been cases of arrests for driving under the influence in California. One judge discharged a man accused of drinking twenty-three cups of kava tea and another case ended in a mistrial when jurors said not enough was known about the tea's effects.

True enough, but Germany, Switzerland, Australia, France, Canada, and Britain have taken action ranging from warnings to removing kava products from the market. While in the U.S., the Food and Drug Administration has linked the root's consumption to liver problems. It's also warned that habitual chewing of the root eventually will destroy tooth enamel. If that weren't enough to worry about, the dried root is traditionally chewed by a circle of village women, who spit into a communal bowl, passing it around until the bowl is full; the belief is that this releases more powerful resins resembling narcotics. The bowl is then offered to village men or, in recent years, curious and courageous visitors.

Ganja Crisps

4 oz unsalted butter
4 oz Stilton cheese, crumbled
4 drops Tabasco sauce
1 oz poppy seeds
1/2 oz ground ganja leaves
   or 1/4 oz ground ganja buds

2 oz blanched, chopped
   almonds
4 ox plain flour
1 egg, beaten
1/8 oz hashish

Beat butter and cheese together until creamy, add finely ground ganja and mix in well. Add the almonds, flour, 1/2 egg, and Tabasco sauce, beat until smooth. Roll into a log shape about 1 1/2 inches in diameter and wrap in cling film. Leave in fridge for 1 hour, then cut into thin slices and place on a lightly greased baking tray. Brush with the other half of the beaten egg, sprinkle with poppy seeds, and bake 15 minutes at 200°C/400°F, until crisp and golden. May be kept in freezer. Makes 25 crisps; 2–3 enough for one person.

—*Cooking with Ganja, "Eric" (1998)*

Kava Coconut Drink

1 ounce kava powder
10 ounces water (or coconut milk)
1 tablespoon lecithin

2 tablespoons coconut or
   olive oil

Blend until the liquid takes on a milky appearance. Serves 1 or 2.

Durian

Pity the poor durian, a tasty Southeast Asian fruit. Not only is it unattractive, it stinks. Many hotels won't let you take it to your room. For most, it's a restaurant taboo. It's widely banned from taxis, buses, and ferries and Singapore Airlines will confiscate any durian brought aboard by a passenger. In Singapore's subway system, there are signs showing a durian set in a circle, with a red slash through the center, meaning just what that symbol means when it proscribes smoking, spitting, and all the other things that are taboo in that squeaky clean city-state. In January, 2003, durians in the cargo hold of an Australian airliner led to a full-scale security alert and evacuation of the plane as baggage handlers feared they faced a possible terrorist threat.

It's the odor. It is, as many have said, something that tastes like heaven, smells like hell. One writer called it "the limburger cheese of fruits." Even fine chefs say it has an odor somewhere between rotten onions and stale cheese. Others have compared it to "carrion in custard" or say it's like "eating ice cream in an outhouse."

Well, maybe. The durian, which takes its name from the Malaysian word *duri*, meaning thorn, is little known outside Asia, and it does have a pungent bouquet. To smell a ripe durian is unforgettable and to walk past a street stall piled high with them in, say, Singapore, Bangkok, or Kuala Lumpur, is nearly overpowering. On a warm day, it's possible to smell a durian vendor from a block or two away. Yet, its flavor is delicious and despite its redolence—which strengthens as the fruit ripens—it commands a fine price, easily competing with more fragrant fruit.

Some say it's an acquired taste, or one you have to be born into, much as you must certainly be from the Philippines to enjoy balut, from China to savor fish maw, from the U.K. to fancy Marmite. It is a fruit you either love or hate. I've eaten it many times and my reaction is that it's neither as delicious as its fans say, nor as smelly as its detractors insist. Unless it's over-ripe. Then I side with Singapore Airlines.

Despite all of Singapore's rules regarding where you can and can't take a durian, that city has a restaurant, the Four Seasons, that devotes an entire section of its menu to durian during the high season (May to August), while another, Durian House, located in the trendy Clarke Quay, sells only durian, offering durian pudding, durian milkshakes, durian juice, durian mousse, durian bean curd, durian sago paste, durian moon cake, durian-flavored sticky rice, durian candy, durian cake, durian puffs, durian pancakes, durian ice cream, durian noodles, and—for those who wish to sneak some of the stuff onto the plane—tubes of durian paste and cans of durian fruit, candy, and juice that have been "smell-free vacuum packed."

A native of Malaysia, the durian has been cultivated for hundreds of years, on trees that grow to over 100 feet in height, making harvest of the fruit problematical. Waiting for the fruit to fall is the easy way, but also dangerous should you strolling below. It varies somewhat in size and shape, but generally it is as big as an American football—making it one of the largest fruits in the world—and its hard green rind is covered with sharp thorns, giving it the appearance of a medieval instrument of war, the mace, where a ball covered with metal spikes was affixed to the end of a pole and used in hand-to-hand (or, perhaps, hand-to-head) combat. It's not a pretty sight.

The tree may take as long as fifteen years after planting to bear fruit, compared to only three years for mangoes and other popular tropical fruits, so many farmers don't want to bother. Deforestation in Thailand, Malaysia, and Indonesia is also threatening the crop, at the same time that demand for it continues to grow. In Hong Kong, it's become a status-symbol gift among the wealthy, so much of the fruit grown on remaining plantations in Southeast Asian countries is now being exported. Cathay Pacific flies at least a hundred tons of durian from Bangkok to Hong Kong during the high season, daily! In Beijing, they may cost as much as US$50 apiece. Even in Thailand, one of the leading grower nations, a large fruit may command the same price if it's from Nonthaburi, the province just north of Bangkok; connoisseurs say that's where the very best are grown.

There is no end to the praise. Alfred Russel Wallace, a Victorian-era naturalist who did as much to advance the theory of selection as his contemporary Charles Darwin, said the durian all by itself was "worth a voyage to the east." In 1999, *Reader's Digest* called it "the monarch of tropical fruit, His Majesty, King Durian."

Inside the fruit, which may weigh as much as twelve pounds, are five or more oval compartments containing a cream-colored, custardy pulp with smooth, cream-colored seeds the size and shape of large Brazil nuts. Durian may be eaten raw with the fingers by itself as a snack—as is common on the streets in many Asian cities and villages, after it has been whacked open with a cleaver—or consumed with rice and sweetened with sugar and cream. It also is preserved with sugar or salt and cooked as a vegetable. In Indonesia it's made into a fruit jelly with coconut milk. The seeds may also be eaten, boiled or roasted over an open grill like chestnuts.

Warnings are given about eating durian while consuming alcohol. Some, misinformed, say it can be lethal. The more realistic say the combination may induce sound sleep. But still there is an apocryphal story, as told by one news wire service, about "the fat German tourist who devoured a ripe durian, followed by a bottle of Thai Mekong rice whisky, then took a hot bath and exploded."

In 1996 in Thailand a condom manufacturer began marketing

durian-flavored condoms. The government was not amused. Saying it affronted a cherished part of Thailand's agricultural heritage and industry, the condom was banned from future sale. In 2003, the durian-flavored condom made a comeback, so to speak, in Indonesia, where it was introduced as an aid in the government's fight against AIDS. In the Philippines, however, when a similar campaign was introduced, there was quite an uproar because many assumed it promoted oral sex.

There is, among some, a belief that the durian has aphrodisiacal powers, perpetuated by the folk saying, "When the durians fall down, the sarongs rise up."

This hasn't been studied, let alone proved, but it probably doesn't hurt sales. No matter how foul the smell.

Durian Ice Cream

1 qt vanilla ice cream	1 can durian

Place ice cream in the refrigerator to soften about 10 minutes while preparing the durian. Drain juice from durian and reserve the juice to add to pineapple juice, orange juice, or as a topping over ice cream. Puree the durian in a food processor, blender, or mash well with a fork. Place softened ice cream in a large bowl, add durian puree, and blend. Repack and freeze. For best flavor, use as soon as it hardens or within 1–2 days.

Cactus

I swear this is a true story, the simple moral of which is to remove the thorns, or spines before eating. This seems an odd thing to say. After all, most animals are skinned or at least the hair is removed, ducks and chickens are plucked, fish are scaled, and porcupines, presumably, are de-quilled before consumption. But I had a friend once who saw a cow on the open range in the southwestern United States, munching on a prickly pear, the cactus that looks like a lot of green Mickey Mouse ears stuck together in a random pattern. (It has brilliant flowers blooming along the edges of the pads in spring or summer, followed by succulent, fleshy fruits, usually red or yellow.)

"I hear cactus tastes pretty good," he said.

I nodded my assent and asked if he'd like to take some back to the cabin for lunch. We began to harvest some of the flat, oval fruit and younger pads, or leaves, using a knife, carefully dropping them into a small knapsack. My friend glanced back at the cow—who was also looking at us, and still chewing—and, apparently figuring what worked for the cow would work for him, he took a bite out of one of the leaves, failing to avoid the spines, piercing his lip.

"Cactus especially tastes good with blood," I said. "You damn fool."

My friend was right in one respect. Cactus usually is eaten raw, but only after it is peeled, which removes the spines to which the cow seemed totally oblivious. There are many ways to remove the glochids, or spines: by swatting the fruits with small, leafy branches while they are still attached to the adult plant, by rolling the fruits and leaves on the ground while wearing heavy gloves, or by wiping with a damp, rough towel. (Leather gloves are recommended, but even they are not impervious; some harvesters insist on using tongs when detaching the leaves from the plant.) Then cut off a slice from the bottom and top, make an incision lengthwise, and peel.

Inside is the gooey, sweet pulp that has been a part of the human diet—according to ethnobotanists—for about 9,000 years. You can also cut the fruits lengthwise in half and scoop out the pulp with a spoon, seeds and all, sprinkling the cacti with lemon or lime juice. Or, you can pick out the seeds and roast them for snacking, or dry them in the sun and grind them into a flour-like meal for cooking bread. The seeds may also be made into an oil. The fruit and leaves can be dried for later use, for making jellies and candy, and, with small effort, brewed into a low-alcohol drink.

The question is: now that several edible species, notably but certainly not exclusively, the prickly pear—generally regarded as the tastiest—have spread from their native North, Central and South American origins to parts of southern Europe, North Africa, the Middle East, Hawaii, Australia, and parts of Asia, why aren't more people eating them? The plant may also be cultivated easily in gardens at home, and in pots, another reason to ask the question. If the home gardener wants a low maintenance food crop, cactus is it. Just put it in the sun and forget about it. You don't have to water it very often; occasional rain or fog will suffice.

So far, few farmers have taken the simple challenge. In the Negev Desert in Israel, however, Yosef Mizrahi, a professor at Ben-Gurion University of the Negev, and a team of horticulturists started breeding, cultivating, and marketing cacti in 1996, believing that eventually they will be a viable, acceptable cash crop. The Kalahari Desert's Mongongo tree, India's desert apple, and the Moroccan Argon tree are among the more than eighty wild, fruit-bearing cactus plants and 1,500 hybrids that that have been domesticated in the professor's orchards, with shipments going mainly to specialty markets in Europe.

There are about 250 species of prickly pear alone, all of American origin, so much of the lore is American Indian, giving it an alternate name, "Indian fig." (The French snootily call it *figue de barbarie*.) Navajos harvested the spiny pads with forked sticks, the Apaches used wooden tongs. Usually it was peeled and eaten raw, but it was also dried for later use. Sometimes it was ground with dried venison and fat, producing a dish that could be scooped up with the fingers or eaten as a spread on coarse bread. The Indians also roasted the unpeeled pads—the cooking removed the spines—or used them as an emergency source of water by peeling the "figs" and chewing the raw pulp for its high moisture content. The young leaves also were peeled, sliced, and boiled like beans, or fried in fat or oil with other vegetables.

The lowly, but nutritious cactus still isn't eaten often in most areas where it grows, but it is consumed here and there in small, increasing quantities. In Mexico and the Southwestern U.S., the young stem segments (cladodes) of the prickly pear are sliced or diced and cooked with green vegetables, onions, chili peppers, cheese, eggs, spices and herbs to make fillings for tacos. They also may be added to salads, and chopped for omelettes. Park S. Nobel, author of *Remarkable Agaves and Cacti*, (1994), suggested harvesting the cladodes when they were a few weeks old, when under twelve inches in height and had no spines, using a potato peeler or knife to remove the small knobs where the spines would later grow.

"Simmer until tender, about ten minutes, in roughly one-third their volume of water with salt and sometimes onions, garlic and cilantro," he wrote. "If any sticky material remains after cooking and draining, rinse with cold water. They taste like gherkins or green peppers, with a texture between string beans and okra."

In many parts of the American southwest and Mexico, where the cactus is called nopal and the food is known as nopalitos, a significant cactus industry has developed in recent years. This has put canned cactus in Mexican food stores as a vegetable, and candies and jams in tourist shops and supermarkets.

A cactus is a plant of the family *Cactacae*, green, fleshy, with typically leafless joints, very spiny, and remarkably resistant to drought.

Besides its value as a food, several Indian tribes attached religious significance to the plant—using it to physically whip their new chiefs to imbue them with great power and luck in hunting. They also placed pieces of cactus at the corners of a new house "to give the house roots." In China, it is called the fairy's hand and is considered unlucky for pregnant women, although widely eaten otherwise. It's also found in salads in Greece, North Africa, and the Middle East.

Especially valued for its moisture, cactus sometimes provides the only source of water in a semi-arid or desert environment. Besides the prickly pear, there are three other species offering such relief. The pin-cushion cactus, a round, short, barrel-shaped plant covered with spines, is one; just slice off the top and dig in. Another is the Cereus cactus, a tall, thin plant with ridges running lengthwise, sharp spines, and protruding fruits. All parts are edible and for water, again all that's necessary is to break off the stem and scoop out the pulp. The third is the saguero, sometimes called the "monument" or giant cactus because of its size; the central stem may be up to two feet in diameter and as tall as fifty feet, with branches that grow out at right angles and then turn upwards, as if a large green man were holding his arms up while being held at gunpoint.

The saguaro is about as close as the cactus world comes to an endangered species, with a range that includes only southern California, Arizona, and swath of northern Mexico. When it was more plentiful, the Indians considered its sweet, red fruit a special treat and made jams and fermented syrup from it. They also dried it for later use in a gruel.

As for my friend with the cactus in his mouth and bleeding lips, I explained that the spines were there to discourage precisely what he had done.

"But how do cows get away with it?" he asked.

"They don't," I said, "They're just hungrier than you are." And only slightly dumber, I thought to myself.

The Cactus That Ate Australia

The prickly pear was introduced in Australia in 1839 to provide natural hedges as an aid to ranchers, to control the movement of cattle without having to erect fences, expensive to put in place, costly to maintain. The plant quickly went wild in parts of Queensland and New South Wales, creating barriers over six feet tall, and by 1925, over sixty million acres of land had been bullied into submission by the hardy cactus and in half this area, no other plants would grow. How did the Aussies handle the problem? Did they take a hint from history and start eating it? No. They imported a South American caterpillar to eat it instead.

Cactus Juice, Jelly, Syrup & Wine

"Now's the time to dig out those kitchen tongs and a plastic 2-gallon bucket. Remove the ripe fruits with the tongs. Fill the bucket with fruits. Now wash those fruits with a garden hose. Allow the water to spill over...you'll want to wash the fruits twice. Allow the water to spill onto a plant that needs a drink. Dump the fruits into a large kettle and add 2 quarts of water. Bring this to a boil and then stab the softened fruits with a fork. This punctures the skin and allows the juice to escape. When the fruits are soft, they can be mashed with a potato masher. Dump the mashed fruits into a colander and allow them to drain.

"Now strain your juice through 3 layers of cheesecloth. You are now ready to venture into making cactus jelly, cactus syrup, or perhaps cactus wine.

"Here's a never-fail method of making cactus jelly. To 1 quart of cactus juice, stir in 4 cups of sugar. Bring this to a rolling boil and stir in 2 packages of powdered pectin. Slowly bring this to a boil and then remove it from the stove. Allow this to cool and then pour it into plastic containers. Now freeze those containers. When you remove them and allow them to thaw, you'll have jelly.

"If, for some strange reason, your jelly fails to gel, the worst you'll come up with is cactus syrup. Cactus syrup is great on pancakes, waffles, or ice cream. Cactus syrup is made the same way as cactus jelly, only use 1 package of pectin for each quart of juice.

"To make cactus wine, add 8 cups of sugar to a gallon of cooled cactus juice. Now stir in 1 package of yeast. Pour the juice into a gallon jug and cap it lightly. Now store the juice in a cool, dark place, like a closet. It'll be ready to drink in 1 month.

"Warning: if you screw the cap down tight, the jug will blow up in your closet, causing you mucho grief and embarrassment."
—*Courtesy, David L. Epperle, Arizona Cactus, 1994*

CHAPTER SIX
leftovers

Quite literally, "leftovers" are what remains after everyone has consumed as much as he or she can eat. This is the extra food that may be warmed up—perhaps spiced up as well—and served another day. The holidays of my childhood were memorable not only for the main feast, but also for the succeeding meals comprised of the leavings of the original gorge, when, for example, a Thanksgiving banquet with all of the trimmings was followed by a couple of days of turkey soup and sandwiches.

So it is, I'm sure, in all places and was at all times. Back when humans gathered around an open fire in caves, one can be sure the entire saber-toothed tiger was not consumed at one sitting, even if shared with friends.

Similarly, this section is comprised of stories and recipes and other oddities that were left over when I finished the other ones. Mainly, these are tales of fact and fancy that didn't fit more clearly defined categories, or crossed too many boundaries to be stuck under one or another of them.

For instance, all manner of animal and vegetable matter is fermented on its way to being called a food. Fermentation plays a significant role in the world's alcohol intake, but at the same time it produces several odd foods.

As does the widespread and imaginative use of blood. Vampires are not the only ones to enjoy this ruby food.

So, too, with "fake food," a category where vegetables pretend to be meat and sugar can be duplicated with a secondary school chemistry set.

Another chapter considers a practice that is no big deal in Asia but in the developed world is called barbaric—eating something that's still alive. I confess that I've done it.

Additionally, there are two chapters about inorganic substances, from the top and bottom of the economic ladder: glittery precious metals and ordinary clay and dirt.

Finally, there are, believe it or not, chapters on Dumpster Diving (the salvage of discarded food); Sex and Food (mainly aphrodisiacs); Road Kill (more salvage); and Excrement (no explanation required).

Blood

"You shall not eat flesh with its life, that is, its blood" are words I read as a youth in Genesis, the first chapter of the Old Testament in the *Bible*. Blood was interpreted as "the life" in many other religious texts as well—including Islam's *Koran*—and therefore banned, leading butchers to bleed their animals as they slaughtered them, and many cooks to remove any blood that was left by soaking the flesh in cold water and salting it.

There was also the matter of the 17th century Romanian king Vlad Dracul, alias Vlad the Impaler, better known to the readers of Bram Stoker as Count Dracula. When I was growing up, blood-sucking vampires had been a staple in fright fiction and movie-making for more than a century, more recently through the novels of Anne Rice and numerous big-budget Hollywood films.

Actually, scholars think the first "vampire" was a female, a countess named Elisabeth de Bathory, a vain woman from a prominent Hungarian family who in 1604, slapped one of her servants, causing some blood to splash onto her skin. After wiping it off, she believed that her skin was whiter, less wrinkled. Thus, she concluded that if she could take regular baths in a virgin's blood, her fading beauty would return. Before she was done, and an act of parliament was passed for her arrest, she was thought to be responsible for the death of as many as 650 young women, to drain them of their life-giving blood.

Such tales have not done much to cast the subject of blood, and its consumption as a drink or food, in a positive light. In fact, long before Vlad Dracul and the dreaded countess appeared in the history books, blood had been accepted as a valued source of protein as well as a curative for ills, a means of postponing aging, and a pre-Viagra boost to virility. In fact, for many early civilizations, fresh animal blood was consumed routinely.

In Marco Polo's vivid account of the Mongol armies, he said each of the riders had a string of eighteen horses and they traveled "without provisions and without making a fire, living only on the blood of their horses; for every rider pierces a vein of his horse and drinks the blood." The theory was that a horse could afford to lose a pint once every ten days, enough to keep the rider going and not impair the animal's health or strength. At the same time, the Mongols were saved the trouble of finding food in a strange and barren land, and did not have to gather scarce fuel for fires, which would have been seen for miles, alerting their enemies. Thus, blood was not only nourishing, but also the perfect survival food.

Even before the Islamic bans, the Arabs formed patties of camel hair and blood, cooking them over an open fire. Later, in the area south of what is now called the Gulf of Aden, and farther to the south in present-day East Africa, wandering tribes would survive on a diet of fresh blood and milk from their cattle, a practice the independent Masai in Kenya and Tanzania continue to this day. While others, in the upper Nile region, prefer the blood boiled or allow it to coagulate, then roast it in the coals of their cook fires.

In Europe, too, blood was cooked and eaten or drunk matter-of-factly in some quarters, ignoring all religious and literary prejudice. In Ireland, a cake was made by sprinkling salt on a layer of coagulated blood, adding another layer of blood, sprinkling more salt, and so on, until a block was formed which was then cut up into squares. Scandinavians still prepare a goose blood soup, calling it *swartsoppa*, or black soup. In Poland, blood from poultry, game, or pigs is eaten with rice, noodles or fried crouton, thickened with a puré of chicken livers. French cooks use blood as a thickening agent, frequently for ragouts and always in certain chicken and rabbit casseroles, where the blood is simmered briefly, then added to the dish just before serving. The latter dishes are called *en barbouille*, meaning "the smear," which describes the effect they have on the diners' lips.

In Victorian England, blood was believed to prevent tuberculosis and was consumed by the glass, by women as well as men, at the neighborhood slaughterhouse.

Even as far back as the 17th century, a traveler in Ireland noted that the peasants "bleed their cows and boil the blood with some of the milk and butter that came from the same beast; and this with a mixture of savory herbs is one of their most delicious dishes." A version of this today is called *drisheen*, a king of black pudding, or blood sausage.

According to *Larousse Gastronomique*, black pudding is one of the oldest known cooked meats, dating from ancient Greece. Today, it is served with apples and mashed potatoes, while "in France there are as many types of *boudin noi* (black pudding) as there are pork butchers. Although the *boudin de Paris* traditionally contains equal portions of blood, fat, and cooked onions, these can vary widely; butchers may use a range of different seasonings and add fruit or vegetables, aromatic herbs, milk, cream, semolina, crustless bread, etc."

French colonialists took the dish around the world and in 19th century Louisiana in the United States, known as Acadia, it became one of the great delicacies. Since the annual slaughter of pigs came during Advent, the *boudin* was usually saved for the Christmas holidays. The Cajuns, as the Acadians came to be called, slaughtered a pig, collecting the fresh blood immediately, adding salt and stirring to prevent coagulation. Fresh pork lung, heart, and neck were cut into large pieces and simmered for three hours. After cooling, the meat was cut into small pieces and minced, returned to the cooking liquid with chopped onions, pepper and spices, and brought to a boil, when the blood was poured through a sieve. A small amount of flour was added, the whole thing was simmered for another hour, stirring frequently. The sauce was then poured over a meat entré or added to meat and vegetables in a stew or soup.

It is in Scotland, where along with haggis, blood pudding and blood pudding sausages have attained the status of what might be called the country's unofficial, official "meat." There are records going back to the 16th century, when, according to *The Household Book of Lady Grisell Baillie*, there were dishes called "Scots collips wt marow and black pudings about them." Another writer of the time noted while writing about one of the judges of the Courts of Session that "with puddings, a great deal of anchovy toast, and plenty of good claret, his Lordship happily managed to overcome his domestic difficulties."

Even today in Scotland they rarely skimp on the blood and up to three quarts may be mixed with raisins, sugar, assorted nuts and chestnuts (pounded), rice, oranges (including the rind), and figs, blended and baked in individual casserole dishes. Other recipes add to each quart of pig's or ox blood a half a pint of milk, a pound of shredded suet or pig fat, a large handful of oatmeal, and plenty of minced onions, pepper and salt, all of it shoveled into a length of washed intestine tied off at the ends to form the sausage, which is then cooked in the usual manner or hung for a later time. (See separate chapter on Haggis.)

And so it goes around the European continent. In Poland, blood soup is called *tchernina* and in Hungary, blood fritters are made from frying sliced onion in fat, adding slices of congealed goose, duck, or pig blood, seasoning with salt and paprika, serving with boiled potatoes and a salad. Germany is known for its *blutwurst*, another sausage, made from pig's blood, calf's or pig's lung, and diced bacon, seasoned with cloves, mace, and marjoram.

In Asia, blood is not only cherished as an invigorating drink, but also as a hearty food. Thailand's northeastern region, called Isan, is noted for many innovative dishes, including beef noodles mixed with fresh cow's blood. Isan cooks also use pig's blood in curries and fish maw soups, and when barbecuing spare ribs, while in the jungle in northern Thailand, elephant *mahouts* (trainers) may begin the day with a glass of wild boar's blood, congealing from the previous day's kill.

At a weekend hill tribe market in Vietnam near the China border, I watched blood from pigs, cattle, and dogs being stirred together and poured into boiling water, then once it had coagulated, removed, cooled, and cut into one-inch cubes, to be served to hungry shoppers with rice. I was surprised to find that what looked like reddish brown cubes of tofu were crunchy. And, of course, they were extemely rich, tasting like jellied organ meat.

Now, about those blood drinkers in the United States. I confess I have no more than a few newspaper articles with headlines like "Interview With a Vampire," inspired by a book called *Something in the Blood*, written by two Texas journalists and published in 1996. The authors claimed there were about 8,000 "vampires" in the United States at that time who regularly drank blood, human when it was available. One of them, Cyne Presley, a thirty-eight-year-old security guard in El Paso, Texas, apparently told the writers that she drank up to a pint of blood two or three times a week, a habit she said started when she was a child, sucking the cuts and skinned knees of her friends. (A part of the let-mama-kiss-it-and-make-it-well school of nursing?) "I love blood," she told the Los Angeles Times. "I hunger for it. I get this comfortable feeling when I drink it. It's like I'm coming home."

Where does Ms. Presley get her supply? No, not the neighborhood blood bank. Frequently, she said, she still used friends who let her puncture the fleshy part of the inside of an arm with a needle or razor. She then gently sucked the blood out. She said she rarely had trouble finding a donor, but occasionally would settle for blood from a cow, obtained from a butcher where she shops.

Of course, there are risks. Hepatitis B and the HIV virus are transmitted by human blood. (Which is why Ms. Presley drinks only her friends.) And once word gets out that you drink human blood, it could affect how people react and parents might not want you around their children. The Texas resident said she had received threats from people who wanted to put a stake through her heart, while others asked if she slept in a coffin.

Enough. Surely, the two journalists who wrote about Ms. Presley and the other (mostly unnamed and unverified) 8,000 "vampires" were not serious. This was a spoof, yes? No one is talking and Ms. Presley cannot be found.

However, including blood in the human diet—cow's blood in this case—is serious business today in Brazil, where an experimental food supplement is being praised as a possible solution to the worldwide spread of malnutrition. Called Prothemol, it's primary ingredient is cow's blood. In poor regions, where government and relief agencies do not have funds to provide the needed groceries, Brazilian nutritionists in 1996 began distributing a yellowish, odorless, flour-like substance made from plasma, dried egg white, Vitamin A, and flour. This is dissolved in food or in sweetened beverages.

"Our children needed proteins containing the essential amino acids that the human body does not produce, but are necessary for development and growth," said Dr. Naide Teodosio, a professor of physiology at the Federal University of Perambuco. "We had plenty of it at no cost and we were wasting it."

A Glass of Blood

"The Marquise had gone from doctor to doctor—seeking out the celebrated and the obscure, the empirically-inclined and the homeopathic—but at every turn she had been met with a sad shake of the head. Only one of them had taken it upon himself to indicate a possible remedy: Rosaria (the Marquise's daughter) must join the ranks of consumptives who go at dawn to the abattoirs to drink the lukewarm blood freshly drawn from the calves which are bled to make veal.

"On the first few occasions, the Marquise had taken it upon herself to lead the child down into the abattoirs; but the horrid odor of the blood, the warm carcases, the bellowing of the beasts as they came to be slaughtered, the carnage of the butchering...all that had caused her terrible anguish and had sickened her heart. She could not do it.

"Rosaria had been less intimidated. She had bravely swallowed the luke-warm blood, saying only, 'This red milk is a little thick for my taste.'"
—Jean Lorrain, *The Glass of Blood*, 1890

Blood & Milk, More or Less Massai Style

3 pts cattle blood	1/2 pt milk
1 small onion, chopped (optional)	4 oz butter
Salt & pepper to taste	

Separate the liquid blood from the coagulated lumps. Cook the onion in half the butter until brown, then add the combined milk and blood, cooking over a low heat, stirring regularly to prevent sticking. Add more milk as needed if the mixture becomes too thick. (Thicker than, say, mushroom soup.) Add the remaining butter, salt and pepper, cover and simmer for 10–12 minutes. Serve hot over rice or in a bowl with bread for dunking.
—*Various local cooks, Kenya, 1972*

Live & Almost Alive

"What's the strangest thing you ever ate?" is a question I get asked all the time. I'm inclined to say peanut butter, because it looks like you know what and sticks to the roof of your mouth. But I know that isn't what the curious are looking for. They want a story.

The tale I tell is about a food that is not so much "strange" as it was "difficult." I have mentioned elsewhere my refusal to drink a glass of freshly drained serpent's blood in Taipei and my reluctance to bite into a steamed waterbug in Bangkok, both finally overcome. Of all the other things I've tried, the hardest to swallow—or, rather, to put in my mouth at all—was a live and writhing shrimp.

It happened in Honolulu many years ago when I accompanied a friend to a sushi bar. This was back when Japanese imports—even cars and television sets—were not so commonplace, before Toyota and Sony became household epithets in the offices of Ford and RCA. My friend had been to Japan many times and he spoke "fluent sushi," meaning he knew the Japanese words for eel, sea urchin, roe, various species of tuna, and other vaguely identifiable protein slices placed artfully on thumb-sized lumps of rice flavored with vinegar. Nearly a third of the Hawaii population was of Japanese heritage and the islands were a favorite holiday destination for residents of Japan, so the fiftieth American state represented a sort of beachhead in the sushi invasion that followed those of the appliance and vehicle manufacturers.

My friend and I had been working our way through the sushi menu, tossing down those thimble-sized cups of hot sake that make you think you aren't really drinking very much, when he announced it was time for the Ultimate Sushi. He said something to the sushi chef, who grinned at me and then reached into an aquarium that was on a shelf nearby, extracting two small, live shrimp.

His movement was economical and swift. He put two finely formed lumps of rice in front of him, deftly peeled the live crustaceans, placed them atop the rice, then squeezed a little lime juice over each, causing the little creatures to wriggle and thrash about in what I presumed was extreme displeasure. My friend picked up his tiny treat and popped it into his mouth, chewing delightedly. In a demonstration of courage divined in rice wine, I did the same. The difference is I don't think I chewed, I swallowed.

In the last ten years or so, eating live protein—mainly seafood, although not exclusively, as we shall see—has become almost fashionable, not only in China, Korea, and Japan, where it seems to be most popular, but in selected restaurants in major cities well scattered across the planet including some in the squeamish United States. The argument is: if fresh is good, can anything be better than "live"?

The idea surely is barbarian and cruel, if we are to listen to animal rights activists. (Has anyone yet taken up the cause of the sushi shrimp?) I remember seeing a movie where in an exercise in proving one's manhood, a live lobster was placed on a table, then whacked in half with a cleaver. The man who was being tested was expected to grab the front part of the lobster that was still scrambling to escape and dig out its flesh and eat it. Lest we shrug and say, "Well, that's Hollywood," a couple of years ago there was a trendy restaurant in Manhattan called Sushi Samba that served—yes!—a $29 lobster that was still moving.

Logic demands that we ask: is it any more humane to kill the food in another room before serving it? And is it more humane to cook it first?

Eating live seafood banned

SYDNEY—A diner who watched in horror as people at a nearby restaurant table tore pieces from a live crayfish and ate them will soon be spared such sights by a new law against eating live seafood.

Cyrina Holland, 18, was out for a celebratory meal with her boyfriend. Confused by an item on the menu—which offered diners the chance to "check the cray dance," she asked her boyfriend to explain.

"He pointed to the table behind me and there was a crayfish cut in half and walking around the table," she said. "It was alive, and they were going after it with their chopsticks."

She said the crayfish's tail had been stuffed with rice and noodles, but the body was still alive and the diners were breaking off its legs. "That was a complete turnoff—there were a lot of people in there and they were watching that table very strangely."

The couple left the restaurant in disgust shortly afterwards. Holland contacted the Society for the Prevention of Cruelty to Animals, but found that crustaceans were not covered by animal welfare laws. In Australia, the state of New South Wales passed legislation this year providing a sentence of up to two years' jail for anybody serving live fish or seafood.

—*Associated Press, July 31, 1997*

Of course, this is nothing new. Eating surely arrived in the history of civilization before cooking did and likely some of the early meals were so fresh as to be still breathing, flipping, or wriggling. For hundreds of thousands of years, the evolving human ate his or her food raw, before the first deliberate use of fire and it is reasonable to assume that some of the just-speared fish, for example, became lunch before they had gasped their last.

More recently, in the 1920s, there was in the U.S. a fad where male college students demonstrated their manliness by swallowing live goldfish. (In the syndicated cartoon by Robert Ripley, *Believe It or Not!*, it was reported that Phil Turco of Madison, Wisconsin, swallowed 339 goldfish in two hours! Believe it or not.) But this is not what we're talking about here. Today, there is a more widespread fashion, where people go to fancy restaurants and pay substantial amounts of money to eat something that hasn't been cooked. This is a boon for the restaurants. They don't have to hire a chef, only someone who knows how to fillet a fish without killing it, so that it may be served while still flopping on the plate, but boneless.

In a recent issue of China Youth Daily, it was reported that in both commercial establishments and at home on special occasions "consuming living animals is the latest fad to flaunt affluence and the belief that living creatures are healthier than those already slaughtered." The story of eating the brains of a live monkey has already been told in another chapter. If that weren't enough to consider vegetarianism, there is another dish called Three Screams, a incredible tale that I later had confirmed by a friend from China. For this, several hairless, newborn mice were washed, rolled wet in spicy condiments, and served in some sort of basket from which they couldn't escape. Pick up a wiggling mouse and dip it into some flavoring when it will emit the first cry. Stab it with a knife or fork and it will scream again. Bite into it and the little thing will give its third cry as it says farewell to the world.

Whatever the response to eating live food, the custom cannot be ignored. Throughout much of the world, even today, a variety of insects, both adults and in the larvae stage, are consumed soon after being captured, described elsewhere in this book. In Thailand, where I now live, I have watched people snatch water spiders from the surface of a pond, popping them into their mouths for a snack. Even the *US Army Survival Manual* recommends the just-caught, uncooked larvae of locusts, ants, and termites as a nutritious, high-protein survival food. Millions in the so-called Third World agree.

Richard Lair, an American who lived in the jungles of Southeast Asia with elephant *mahouts* (trainers) for years at a time, says the experience changed his eating habits in a major way: there is nothing, save perhaps for elephant, that he says he won't now eat. When I asked him what the oddest food was that he'd ever encountered, he told me about a couple of Chinese dishes (others subsequently insisted they were Japanese) that used rather common ingredients; it was the manner of preparation that was unusual.

"You put a pot of water on the fire or stove and once the water is hot, you dump in some cubes of tofu and a couple of dozen live baby frogs," he said. "The frogs will swim to the tofu and cling to it because it's cooler than the water. They die still holding on to the tofu and after both tofu and frog are cooked, you extract them from the water carefully and serve them with vegetables."

This introduces the "almost live"—or, as Mr. Lair puts it, the "very recently deceased"—category of food. There are several similar stories, again placed in Asia, the part of the world's geography where most who live elsewhere probably believe people will eat anything. In one story, tiny live fish were dumped into a pot of hot water along with vegetables with internal chambers that had been cut to expose the cavities, such as lotus root or small green peppers. The fish swim into the holes seeking the same relief sought by the frogs on the tofu, where they, too, will be cooked, ready for the chopsticks to follow. With a nice chili dipping sauce.

Another variation on the same theme called for adding live baby eels to boiling water with larger blocks of tofu. The eels wriggle into the tofu, where they are cooked, after which the tofu blocks are removed and chopped before serving.

> ### *Raw Food Risks*
>
> Meat not cooked through to 160 °C holds some risk.
>
> Undercooked pork can contain parasites such as tapeworms, or transmit illnesses that can lead to cysts developing in the brain.
>
> Undercooked chicken likewise should always be avoided.
>
> Beef can contain tapeworms.
>
> Raw fish carries the risk of acute bacterial infections such as dysentery. Lung fluke is common across Asia. Also be wary of packaged sushi.
>
> Shellfish are the most dangerous because they feed on whatever is in the water and are susceptible to a number of viruses and algae blooms.
>
> Freshwater fish are next because of their exposure to human waste. Deep seawater fish, such as tuna, are the safest.
>
> If you want more information, check the US Centers for Disease Control and Prevention web site at http://www.cdc.gov/ncidod, or the Center for Food Safety and Applied Nutrition at http://vm.cfsan.fda.gov/
> —*Adapted from Asian Wall Street Journal*

Fermented Food

Bill Peterson traveled widely and willingly went along with many of my suggestions about foods to order, but he was not a gastronomical experimenter at heart, and now he was complaining.

"I just don't understand," he said, "how the same process can produce so many good things to drink—beer, wine, and whisky—and also so much bad food."

An American who had tried ostrich fillets in Australia and one grasshopper in Thailand, where I live, was talking about fermentation. I laughed and asked which ones he'd tried. "After all," I said, "if it weren't for fermentation, we wouldn't have bread and cheese."

"Alright, okay, but I'm talking about some of those things you eat in Asia—the fermented fish sauce, the hundred-year-old eggs, *kim chee*, stuff like that. I have to admit it, I don't even like yogurt or sauerkraut."

My friend is not alone. There are many who think the only thing to do after mistakenly putting a fermented food in their mouths is to wash out their mouths with...well, something fermented.

Fermented food and drink are solids and liquids that are prepared so that micro-organisms or enzymes (a natural part of the food or added, like yeasts, molds, and bacteria) change the properties of the food. The goals include a better taste or texture and an increased shelf life for the product of the biochemical change. For example, all the different types of cultured milk have evolved from the fact that fresh milk rapidly deteriorates, and a controlled fermentation with lactic acid bacteria provides the time to get it distributed widely and safely without losing nutrition or taste.

Another reason is to make food which are hard to digest in their original state, such as wheat and soy beans, digestible by converting them into digestible ones like bread.

Some, like my friend, say the process doesn't just alter the taste and texture, it twists it, damaging the food's original appeal, figuratively as well as literally. Many visitors to the region where I live, Southeast Asia, will consume the fermented fish sauce that is so essential to local cooking if you don't say anything, but if you administer a sniff test first, they make a face and call it "rotten."

In a way, they're correct, of course. In Thailand it's called *nam pla*, or "fish water," and in Vietnam, *nuoc mam*, in Laos, *nam pa*, in Cambodia, *tuk trey*, in Burma, *ngan-pya-ye*, and so on. All these neighboring countries—whose leaders bicker at other levels as well—boast that their brands are best, although it is Thailand that exports the translucent, brown sauce in the largest quantity. All are produced by packing fish—sometimes shrimp—into barrels or pottery jars with salt, leaving the food to ferment for at least a month, after which the liquid is collected and bottled. (Some insist the fermenting process should last several months and Pichai Fish-Sauce Co. Ltd., Thailand's sales champ both inside and outside the country, keeps the stuff deteriorating for a full year.) Few Southeast Asian meals are considered complete without it. It takes the place of salt and is, in a way, what soy sauce is to the Chinese and Japanese. But more pungent.

It is the outsider, like my friend, who thinks fish sauce difficult. A Jesuit missionary in the 18th century, Nicolas Gervaise, noted in his journal that *Thai kapi*, as it was then called, "has such a pungent smell that it nauseates anyone not accustomed to it." Even as recently as 1997, Annabel Jackson-Doling noted in *The Food of Vietnam* that *nuoc mam* "in its purest form has a strong smell and incredibly salty flavor which renders it an acquired taste for non-Vietnamese. Vietnamese rarely expect a foreigner to enjoy the taste, but are delighted when one does."

There also are some solid fermented foods in Asia that command attention. In Laos, *padek* can best be described as fish sauce with chunks of the fermented fish still in it, along with some rice "dust" and husks. *Padek* has an odor so pungent that the large pottery jar holding a family's supply usually is kept out on the verandah. Phia Sing, writing in *Traditional Recipes of Laos*, said that most *padek* was home-made: "The real thing is not available in the west, but jars of fermented fish from the Philippines are one acceptable substitute. And I was once told that the Lao bride of an Englishman, on being offered canned anchovies for the first time, exclaimed: 'But this is *padek*—rather salty *padek*, but good!'"

In Thailand, again, there is a dish called *pla ra*, the second word meaning "mold" or "fungus," which should give the diner a clue. In the words of David Scott and Kristiaan Inwood, authors of a small book about Thai food called *A Taste of Thailand*, this is a fermented fish dish that recalls the "accumulated stench of putrifying corpses, abandoned kennels, dirty feet, stagnant bilges and fly-blown offal," an exaggeration, certainly, but not much of one, at least to many westerners. It is made by packing gutted and scaled freshwater fish into sealed earthenware jars with salt, adding a fine powder made from fried rice in a few days, after the fish have begun to "rot." It is ready to eat in a week, although, once more, connoisseurs prefer a longer fermentation time.

As key as such foods and sauces are to their respective countries, it is possible to cook Southeast Asian cuisine without using them. Not so in Korea, where *kim chee* (or *kimchi*) has attained the status of "national dish" and is impossible to avoid or turn away, as it served with just about everything and not to eat it is regarded as a gross insult. A general term given to a group of fermented vegetable foods, *kim chee* is characterized by its sweet-sour carbonated taste, quite different from sauerkraut and other fermented vegetables found in Europe and North America. It was devised to keep vegetables edible through the long, cold winters in the northern part of the Korean peninsula, yet even with the modern development of greenhouse agriculture and a year-round supply of imported vegetables, the dish remains a part of nearly every meal. Although there are about 150 different kinds of *kim chee,* the most popular involves salting chopped Chinese cabbages and/or radishes, then washing them, adding spices and seasonings (powdered red pepper, chopped garlic and ginger, sliced green onion, salt, and sugar), and letting it all sit in a cool place for a few days to ferment. Served at room temperature or slightly chilled with rice and meat dishes. Another Korean delicacy, salt-fermented oysters, dates back 600 years and is believed not only to relieve fatigue and treat anemia, but also to contain the spirit and wisdom of one's ancestors.

In Hong Kong and Japan, fermented tofu is a specialty and fermented soya bean "cake" called *tempe* or *tempeh* is widely consumed as a meat substitute in Indonesia. In the Philippines, a variety of dishes are made from salted and fermented anchovies and tiny shrimps, called *bagoong.* While in China, small black soybeans are preserved in salt before being packed into cans or plastic bags, producing such a pungent food it must be soaked in warm water for half an hour and then finely chopped before being used, usually as a flavoring for fish or meat dishes. Some cereals are also fermented in India and parts of Africa, where a long shelf life would otherwise be impossible due to a lack of refrigeration.

Asia and Africa have no exclusive on aromatic fermented food. It's found just about everywhere and, in fact, can be made from nearly anything, although seafood dominates. In Alaska, the Inupiat and Kobuk Eskimos traditionally catch sheefish with hooks made from bear teeth and ivory through holes in the ice in winter, or seine for them in the summer when they swim upriver to spawn. The rich, oily flesh and roe of the twenty- to thirty-pound females (who may drop as many as 350,000 eggs each!) are preferred over the smaller males, but whatever the catch brings is buried ungutted in a leaf-lined pit, where it ferments (decays) in its own natural juices for several weeks. It should come as no surprise that the aromatic result is known, colloquially, as "stinkfish," which usually is eaten raw.

A similar dish, called lutefisk, or lye fish, is prepared in Norway and Sweden and served in December at the height of the culinary calendar. This tradition dates at least to the 14th century, when freshwater fish such as trout, char or grayling were caught in mountain lakes in August and September, then wrapped in birch bark and buried. The fish remained underground until the first snow, when they were dug up, rubbed with salt and packed tightly belly up in covered wooden containers. Today, the fish are stored in a similar fashion aboveground for about three months, then re-hydrated in a strong alkaline solution for several days until the fish is soft enough for a finger to be pressed through without meeting resistance. Caustic soda generally is used, but documents dating back to the Middle Ages tell that the original solution was made from the ashes of the same tree used for wrapping, birch. After soaking, the fish is rinsed for several days in running cold water before steaming or poaching. The result is a translucent, golden fillet with a stiff-jelly consistency. Oddly, the taste is surprisingly bland and usually is brightened with a choice of sauces.

In Russia, southwestern Asia and eastern Europe, *kefir* dates back many centuries to the shepherds of the Caucasus Mountains who discovered that fresh milk carried in leather pouches fermented into an effervescent beverage. In Germany, sauerkraut made from shredded, fermented cabbage, is served with pork knuckle or sausages, as important to the German diet as potatoes and beer. In the United States and elsewhere, cucumbers are fermented in brine to become dill pickles and fermented cider is served as a slightly alcoholic drink. In Greece, pickled olives are a treat with ancient roots. Pickled eggs are a traditional in England. Yogurt, a fermented milk product that originated in Turkey, is now produced in numerous brands and flavors, and when plain it is often sweetened with sugar to disguise its sour bite.

So far as my friend Bill is concerned, just about all of this food stinks.

Food & Drink

Fermentation serves us in many ways. Besides increasing the variety of our menus along with the shelf life of foods—without using chemical preservatives, an important point for many—fermented food offers a high level of living enzymes. During the process of fermentation, complex proteins, starches, and fats are broken up into simple compounds that are easily assimilated by the body with minimal digestive effort. Research also shows it can inhibit certain bacteria that cause diarrhea, which kills one out of every ten children in developing countries (through dehydration), a key factor behind a World Health Organization program to use fermentation as a technique for the preparation and storage of infant food.

As for the unusual or pungent taste and smell? One thing may be assumed by all—that many of these fermented foods go down well with a distilled, alcoholic beverage made from a fermented mash of various ingredients including grains and other plants. Whisky, gin, vodka and rum are among the most popular. Others include, in alphabetical order, aquavit, arrack (made from sugar cane in Sri Lanka and other tropical countries), bourbon, brandy, malt liquor, mezcal (the Mexican favorite), okolehao (more sugar cane, from Hawaii), scotch whisky, and tequila.

> Add to the list ale, lager, wine and champagne, beverages created by feeding sugars and nutrients in solution to yeast, which return the favor by producing carbon dioxide gas and alcohol.

Sunflower Seed Cheese

(Any other raw seed or nut may be substituted, including pumpkin, pine seeds, walnuts, pecans, and almonds, or any combination.)

Method: In the evening, put about 1 pound (depending on how much you wish to make) of raw, shelled seeds or nuts in a large bowl and cover with pure water. Add enough extra water to cover the seeds by at least 1 inch. Do not use chlorinated water, for it will kill the enzymes and prevent fermentation. Leave the seeds to soak overnight.

Next morning, drain the seeds through a colander. In a blender or food processor, put one cup of soaked seeds plus 1 cup of pure (unchlorinated) water, and blend well. Pour the purée into a large bowl. Purée the rest of the seeds the same way, adding 1 cup of pure water per cup of soaked seeds, and pouring the purée into the same large bowl.

Leave the bowl of puréed seeds uncovered on a table or counter in the kitchen to ferment naturally. Depending on weather, this takes from 4–7 hours. The hotter and more humid it is, the shorter the fermentation time. When ready, the surface will become a bit puffy, and the "whey" (water) will have separated from the "curd" (purée) on the bottom of the bowl. There will also be a slightly sour smell, something like yogurt.

Line a large colander or sieve with a piece of cheesecloth (or any sturdy but porous cotton cloth). Pour the fermented purée into the cloth, and let it drain over a bowl by itself for about 30–45 minutes. Then, pull the corners of the cloth together and twist the purée inside the cloth, squeezing out as much additional water as possible. Scoop the drained, fermented purée into a plastic container, cover tightly with a lid, and store in the refrigerator. It will keep about one week.

To serve: Scoop out as much as you wish to use into a bowl. About 1/2 cup is sufficient for 1 person. Add: good quality sea salt, ground black pepper or cayenne, 5–6 finely chopped green onions (scallions), 3 tablespoon extra virgin olive oil. You may also experiment with other seasonings, such as garlic, and various spices, but the combination given above is our favorite.

Blend well with a spoon or fork, then scoop into a smaller bowl for serving. It may be used as a spread for bread of toast, as a dip for chips or vegetable sticks, as a stuffing for halved avocados or tomatoes, or eaten straight with a spoon. You may also form it into small balls, then cover them with cooked brown rice and squeeze in your palms to form larger rice balls, heat briefly in the oven and serve.

—*Dan Reid, author, TheTao of Health, Sex and Longevity (1989)*

Fake Food

In Singapore, I went to a vegetarian restaurant in the Geylang district, traditionally the home of the city's Malay, Arab, and Indonesian communities. The restaurant was, as expected, a clean and well-lighted place, with plastic lace tablecloths under round slabs of plexiglass. That should've been my first clue about how "real" the food would be.

Of course, it wasn't my first visit to a vegetarian restaurant—the Good Earths in my past cannot be counted on the fingers of my hands—but it was the first time I deliberately ordered and ate fake meat. I'd seen "vegetarian chicken" and "vegetarian beef" on what were called "health food restaurant" menus before, but I always selected a fresh salad, or perhaps a vegetable curry instead.

Why, I wondered, did vegetarians do this? Were these dishes created for the converts, the former meat-eaters who now ate only veggies? However deep their current conviction, did they still miss the taste of flesh? (Just as some reformed smokers chewed nicotine gum?) I also wondered what the ersatz meat tasted like? Did it really taste like beef or chicken? Was it good for you? I ordered a dish of all-vegetable chicken legs.

Guess what? It tasted like chicken—a phrase that runs like a tide through this book, I fear—but it didn't feel like chicken. I don't care how you cook or flavor what is called in the trade "textured vegetable protein," it only approaches what is being copied, and for me is never convincing. Yet, there is a market for this stuff, in specialty stores, by mail, even in traditional groceries and supermarkets. One mail order catalog recently offered a new product, "all-vegetarian smoky bits, ready to eat as is. Great for salads, dips, soups, omelets, or anywhere you want a bacon flavor without using animal products." A pound of the stuff cost US$9.95, five pounds just a little over double that.

Many such meat substitutes are made from the soya bean, a plant that is used all over the world to produce oil and flour and as a food-stuff in various forms for both livestock and humans. Tofu, a staple in Asian cooking that dates back to as early as the 2nd century in China, is prepared from beans that have been soaked, reduced to a purée, then boiled and sieved, and, finally, jellified by the addition of a coagulant. As early as the 6th century in Japan, it was called the "meat vegetable" because of its high protein content.

To me, the motives for vegetarianism appear rooted in a search for good health or good karma. This assumes that you believe that flesh and its by-products are best eliminated from your diet for dietary or philosophical reasons. So that a bowl of vegetarian "chicken" broth can satisfy your need to revisit your non-vegetarian past—and savor the taste of chicken—without threatening your health or belief system. Vegetarians argue that the flesh of many animals is harmful for humans—and there is a lot of scientific evidence to support this—or that too much natural forest is being destroyed to create pasture land or grain to feed grazing animals or that you shouldn't kill something that has "feelings."

I have no disagreement with much of this philosophy. Still, I am puzzled by the ardent fervor for that which is fabricated from artificial or bogus ingredients, however healthy they may or may not be. In an advertising campaign aimed at slowing sales of Pepsi Cola, Coca Cola called itself The Real Thing. Food I'm talking about now is the opposite. The Not Real Thing. The Kitchen Counterfeits. Strange food, indeed.

Not all imitation meat is made from soy, as were the "chicken legs" I ate in Singapore. Gluten, described by one mail order source as a "low-fat, easy-to-use meat substitute," is a protein derived from wheat, popular for centuries in Asia and sometimes called *seitan*, the Japanese word for cooked gluten. "Unlike textured vegetarian protein, which comes pre-shaped in various sizes, you can shape gluten into whatever shape or size you need for your favorite recipes, even giant roasts or mock turkey!"

Pass the gluten and cranberry sauce, please.

Meat-like flavors and alternatives are not alone in the fake food industry. When some dieticians and health experts decided butter was dangerously high in cholesterol, manufacturers of margarine and other butter proxies prospered. So, too, manufacturers of all the low-fat spreads now standing side-by-side on market shelves with mayonnaise (thought to contain too much cholesterol-rich egg yolk), made from liquid safflower and soybean oil, food starch, cellulose gel and other thickeners and emulsifiers.

What of all the synthetic casings for sausage that've replaced sheep's or pig's intestine? What of mock turtle soup, which is made from the meat from a boiled calf's head? How about all the "crab-like" crab, that is made entirely of fish scraps that are jelled and streaked with a red dye? How far from reality do the many modern additives take food—the coloring agents, preservatives, permitted antioxidants, flavorings, mineral hydrocarbons, emulsifiers, and stabilizers?

The concept of fake, or "alternative," foods is not new. During the Napoleonic wars, in the early 1800s, when the British blockade of continental ports cut off supplies of cane sugar from the West Indies and Southeast Asia, the sugar beet began to take its place. That was, of course, real food, just another real source for real sugar. Yet it seemed to point the way to the near future, when, in 1860, a food technologist named Hippolyte Mege-Mouries was commissioned by the French navy to find a cheap replacement for butter, a substitute that contained beef suet, minced sheep's stomach, chopped cow's udder (I'm not making this up!) and a little warm milk, steeping this in warm, alkaline water. Voila! The first butter substitute. So pleased was Napoleon III, he gave the inventor a factory in which to produce the stuff and soon enough a taste and market for what was called "butterine" soon spread to America, where it was regarded as a way to turn organs normally discarded by slaughterhouses into profit. By 1876, the US was exporting more than a million pounds of butterine to the UK.

Over the years, of course, the recipe changed along with the name, as manufacturers learned how to "cream" the artificial product, how to mature it with micro-organisms similar to those used in making real butter, and how to utilize vegetable oils, and add vitamin concentrates. The manufacturers of real butter fought back, predictably, and they are still fighting. But even aggressive advertising campaigns failed to stem the synthetic tide, as margarine, once made from animal fat, now could be manufactured from a single vegetable oil or a blend of them, such as sunflower, safflower, and soya bean.

Time marched (and stomachs grumbled) inevitably on and there were similar developments in the sugar industry. Sugar once was a luxury only the rich could afford, in Persia and ancient Arabia. The West didn't even know about sugar until the 9th century when it was introduced by the conquering Moors. At that time, it came in large loaves that were broken apart and ground into a powder in a mortar. In time, of course, all that changed and when too many people decided they were consuming too much of it, some began looking for substitutes.

One of the first artificial sweeteners actually was discovered by accident in Baltimore in the 1880s by Johns Hopkins University scientists, developed in their lab something they called "saccharin," which was said to be 300 times sweeter than sugar and soon, with the addition of an "e" at the end would enter the popular vocabulary as anything "cloyingly sweet or sentimental." Later still, some said that although it offered the advantage of containing only eight calories per teaspoon, it gave foods a bitter aftertaste when cooked, and, oh yes, it might be carcinogenic.

In the late 1960s, German scientists formulated something called Acesulfame-k, or Ace-k, approved by the FDA in America in 1988; it was claimed to be 200 times sweeter than sugar and it had no unpleasant aftertaste. It was composed of carbon, nitrogen, oxygen, hydrogen, sulphur, and potassium atoms.

This is food?

Solid argument can be made in support of some ersatz food and drink, explained by scarcity or other pragmatic reasons, as when sugar beets took the place of sugar cane, and during World War Two, when shipping lines were interrupted in the Atlantic between South and North America, cutting the supply of coffee beans, and the somewhat bitter chicory plant found a new market. Nor was it practical to transport real eggs to the military in a battlefield situation (think of the breakage!), thus—when I was in the U.S. army, anyway—we were fed a powdered egg substitute called Starlac that only slightly resembled eggs in appearance or taste.

As humans began circling the earth in rockets, space itself became another factor dictating a variety of radical alterations and substitutes. Space capsules are cramped by weight limitations, so there was not much room for food storage. The solution? Make food smaller by dehydrating it, cutting the weight in half by removing the water. Water used to re-hydrate the food came from the capsule's fuel cells, mixing hydrogen and oxygen with electricity.

In the early days, space food was not very palatable and astronauts in the Mercury program were given bite-sized, freeze-dried cubes and semi-liquids in aluminum toothpaste-type tubes. They found the food unappetizing, had trouble re-hydrating the freeze-dried foods, disliked squeezing the tubes, and had to chase crumbs from the bite-sized cubes to prevent them from fouling instruments.

In time, things improved. In the Gemini launches, the bite-sized chunks were covered with an edible gelatin to reduce crumbling and re-hydration was improved when water was injected into the food packs through a nozzle with a water gun and the contents were kneaded until moist, then squeezed through a tube into the astronaut's mouth. It still seemed largely fake.

The Apollo program introduced hot water, which made the food far more attractive, if still short of delicious, and the Skylab with its hugely increased room actually gave the space jockeys a table and chairs equipped with foot and thigh restraints that let them "sit down" in space to eat. Now the astronauts ate off metal trays with built-in warming units and used utensils held magnetically to the trays. They also had sufficient storage area to accommodate a freezer for steaks and a refrigerator for chilling fruit and beverages.

Contrary to what some people think, food in pill form has not been given the astronauts.

Meanwhile, back on planet earth, Robert Kok, an agricultural engineer at McGill University in Montreal, Canada, said in 1994 that he wanted to build a factory to raise insects in "true industrial quantities"—10,000 tons a day—for processing into familiar forms, like simulated hamburger or chicken breast. Kok said that in the crowded, hungry planet of the future, a hundred factories could supply much of the world's protein, replacing mammal livestock. To demonstrate what could be done, he prepared and served the press a meal that included a tent-caterpillar meat loaf and some flour-beetle hot dogs. He described the hot dogs as being "every bit as bad as the real ones."

Most startling of all are three developments in the late 1990s, when the US Food and Drug Administration approved two new "food" products for sale to the American public, and soon, of course, to the world. Johnson and Johnson began marketing a new, no-calorie brand of artificial sweetener that tasted like sugar, was claimed to be 600 times sweeter, yet passed right through the body without leaving any telltale fat or cellulite. How was that possible? Scientists changed sugar's molecules to make the sweetness more intense, but not allow it to be absorbed. Sucralose, as the product was called, could be used in almost every kind of processed food, from soft drinks and ice cream to baked goods, jellies, and the tabletop sugar bowl. It was also ruled safe for diabetics, to whom a significant number of low-sugar "specialty foods" are marketed.

At the same time in Thailand, researchers at King Mongkut's Institute of Technology developed an artificial egg yolk for those concerned about the real one's high cholesterol. The ingredients included egg white (acceptable to cardiologists), protein extracts of soybean and wheat vegetable oil, and carrot juice, the latter presumably to give it color. The ingredients were mixed and boiled in a stainless steel tube, the result then wrapped in egg white. The finished product looked like a boiled egg except for the cigar-like shape, which probably would present a marketing problem.

The third innovator to weigh in was Proctor and Gamble, the American company that owns Frito Lay, introducing something called olestra, using the brand name Olean (pronounced oh-LEEN), in corn and potato chips. What the hell was Olean? Fake fat. It tasted like fat, and it cooked like fat. Yet, the body could digest it, so it, too, passed right through the gastrointestinal tract, leaving no ugly calories behind. A snack-sized bag of potato chips with olestra had fifty-five calories—about the same as a rice cake—instead of the usual 110, and all fifty-five were from the potato.

Now all we need is a fake potato. Stay tuned.

Plastic Chewing Gum?

Will someone tell me what a "non-dairy creamer" is? (The ingredients listed on the packets vary from place to place, but all seem to contain glucose syrup, "edible vegetable fat," "approved emulsifiers" and a variety of sodium, potassium and phosphate this-and-thats.) Is coffee made from dried and roasted chicory or dandelion root still coffee? When you take all the fat out of milk, is it still milk? Are Cheez Whiz and Velveeta really cheese? Even chewing gum, originally made from chicle, the sap of a Central American tree, is now being made with PVA (polyvinyl acetate, a plastic) plus artificial flavors, colors, and sweeteners.

The Ultimate Fake Food

The idea behind fake food is to create something that both looks and tastes like the real thing. There is one other "food" in this category that looks real, but is never eaten: *kappa-bashi*, the three-dimensional models of Japanese dishes displayed in restaurant windows to entice passers-by. Originally carved by skilled artisans from wax, most now are manufactured largely from plastic.

There are similar food facsimiles worldwide. How many phony bunches of grapes and bananas have you seen arranged in a basket on someone's living room table? Similarly in Thailand what appear to be quail eggs in tiny nests are in fact a sugary confection made with the same attention to convincing detail that characterizes Thai fruit and vegetable carving that turn those edibles into believable "flowers."

Gold & Silver

Gold has been the symbol of power and wealth for millennia, associated with the sun god Ra in ancient Egypt because of its sunlike color, with the throne in the time of China's first emperors, with victory in early Greece, with art and personal ornamentation in all these places and times in history, as well as in pre-Columbus Mexico and Peru.

More recently, it became the most readily accepted medium of exchange for goods and services, and starting in the 19th century was used as security for much of the world's paper currency, leading to an international gold standard. The passion for this rare metal did not diminish, even when the gold standard was abandoned. Although some twenty per cent of the world's production is put to industrial use (gold conducts electricity and is used in microchips and satellites have been layered with gold foil to keep off excessive heat from the sun), a whopping eighty per cent is still used either for art and jewelry, or hoarded as a personal safeguard against hard times.

With so much value attached, is it any wonder, then, that gold and its less expensive but still "precious" cousin silver found their way onto the gourmand's dinner plate or suspended in what are believed to be health-giving drinks?

The use of gold and silver is not new, dating back at least to the 15th century when gold leaf was used to ornament sweet pie that had been blanched with walnuts and wetted with saffron water. Elizabeth Raffald, a resident of Manchester, England, in the late 1700s who was known for her elaborate jellies, used clear "Blomange" to fill two fish molds which then were gilded with foil, laid in a soup dish and covered with clear calf's foot jelly so thin they could "swim" in it.

During Japan's economic boom, in the late 1980s and early 1990s, when that country's rich delighted in finding new ways to spend a small fortune on a meal, the newest fad was food garnished with real gold. Mainly in Tokyo and other large cities, restaurants began sprinkling or wrapping gold leaf around all sorts of delicacies to excite the Japanese palate, serving omelets and curries and ice cream with tiny flecks of gold mixed in. One establishment offered "longevity noodles" made of Korean ginseng soup, noodles, and gold flakes. The flakes or thin wafers of gold leaf also were used to brighten up traditional dishes like sushi, using the gold instead of the traditional, dry seaweed to wrap the rice. Washed down with gold sake, of course.

"This fad was initiated by restaurant owners who found out that gold flakes are a convenient means to enhance the value of their food and drink," a manufacturer told a Reuters reporter in 1992. "Restaurant owners felt they could draw potential customers' attention at relatively low cost, since gold flake appears to have more volume than its actual weight."

How is this possible? First, bars of gold are mechanically pressed into strips about 100-millionths of an inch thick and cut into pieces measuring one-quarter by one-half inch. These pieces are then placed on translucent paper and stored in an ox-hide pouch to preserve the heat so important for the beating to follow. Locked into place with strips of bamboo, these pouches are then hammered by strong young men using heavy metal sledges. After up to six hours of pummeling, the leaf will have increased twelve times in size and is now so thin as to almost tear if you look at it.

The flimsy pieces of gold are finally turned over to young women who cut them into small squares or strips with knives made of bamboo. Metal scissors cannot be used because the gold will stick to metal. The rooms must be sealed to keep away wind, and no air conditioning is permitted because the gold will shrink in cool temperatures. At last, the small pieces are packed in thin paper and sent to the restaurants (or, more commonly, to temples and shrines in Buddhist countries, where they are rubbed onto images for luck).

"Gold flake is so thin, we had problems wrapping the sushi in it when we started," said Seiichi Ohmura, owner of a restaurant in Chiba near Tokyo, whose menu in 1992 included a wide range of gold-garnished foods, "but we've got the knack now." He said he sold three or four dishes of gold sushi a day at 5,000 yen, then worth about US$40 a plate.

An almost identical fad occurred in South Korea in 2001, when restaurants and coffee shops served fish, pork, coffee and liquor sprinkled with gold dust to customers who believed it helped clear their bodies of waste material. A serving of ten fish with the "special seasoning" retailed for about US$1,500 until the Korea Food and Drug Administration imposed a ban under a good hygiene law that allowed gold only for coloring beverages and sweets. "We have decided to take action as various kinds of expensive food containing gold are so widespread," said an official of the KFDA, "that it is stirring up public resentment against the rich."

If the Japanese taste for gold weakened along with the national economy in the late 1990s and the Koreans were forbidden or eat it, there is now a growing market for both gold and silver as a "cure" for everything from asthma to depression to cancer and they consume it daily. Jim Powell reported in the magazine *Science Digest* in 1978 in an article titled "Our Mightiest Germ Fighter" that "thanks to eye-opening research, silver is emerging as a wonder of modern medicine. An antibiotic kills perhaps a half-dozen different disease organisms, but silver kills some 650. Resistant strains fail to develop. Moreover, silver is virtually non-toxic."

Technically, such products are not true foods, but categorized as "food supplements," the all-purpose euphemism for products that are reputed to be healthy, without government approval, and most are marketed in alternative "health food" distribution systems and by mail. Dozens of companies in the United States now sell gold and silver, either separately or in combination, in colloidal form, that is, ionically suspended in distilled water.

The first colloidal gold was produced in 1857 by Michael Faraday, the famous English scientist better known for developing the first laboratory model of an electric generator and inventing the electric motor. Today, some manufacturers blend the gold and silver with rhodium, iridium, and platinum, or package it as a gel with aloe vera, the plant whose sticky interior frequently is used to treat burns.

None of this is cheap. A four-ounce bottle of colloidal silver and gold, equal to about a third of a can of soda, usually costs more than US$20, the same amount of the mixture that also contains the other metals almost three times as much. As a cost-saving service to customers, some companies market Colloidal Silver Generators for home manufacture. They sell for $99 and up.

If self-medication is not your strong suit—like many others, I usually content myself with aspirin and alcohol, not necessarily in that order—perhaps it is better to mix these precious metals in the food. The use of silver leaf in India is fairly common, although understandably it's an extravagance that frequently leads to aluminum being used instead. The silver, called *vark* or *varaq*, is used to decorate various foods, especially in Moghul cuisine and in the more prosperous cities, such as Mumbai and New Delhi, the best thing for a hot summer's day is ice cream with silver flakes.

Not even Baskin-Robbins or Ben and Jerry offer this one.

There also is a brandy-based liqueur called Goldwasser, flavored with caraway seed, orange peel, and spices. Its name, which translates from German as "gold water," comes from the fact that it has minuscule flecks of gold leaf suspended in it. A similar drink, dating back to the 18th century, was called "The Golden Cordial" and was a blend of brandy, alkermes, oil of cloves, sugar, spirit of saffron, and gold leaf, two leaves to every bottle.

Looking for something for the kids? A firm in the United States markets lollipops with gold leaf inside.

The Ore-ganic Harvest?

Scientists at Massey University in Palmerston North, New Zealand, in 1998 in an article in *Nature* magazine, said they had found a way to make plants soak up gold from ore. Although they were suggesting a new way of mining the precious metal, the report of Christopher Anderson, Robert Brooks and their colleagues made it clear the discovery could, in time, spill over into kitchens and onto dinner plates.

They said the approach, called phytomining, already was used for recovering nickel and for removing pollutants like lead and mercury from the soil. In their new findings, the New Zealand team said that Indian mustard and chicory plants that grew in pots of ore for a week contained about twenty parts per million by weight, when the leaves and stalks were harvested and dried.

While this mining technique is not regarded as commercially viable when compared to more traditional recovery methods, the produce potential is obvious. The ore-ganic food fans will love it.

Finally, a recipe published in 1995 in *Gourmet*, the American magazine, may offer more appeal. This was for Gold-Dusted Bourbon Pecan Balls, calling for unsweetened cocoa butter, confectioner's sugar, vanilla-wafer crumbs, roasted and finely chopped pecans, honey, and bourbon, along with the gold powder.

Sugar, booze and gold. The straight world's answer to sex, drugs and rock and roll.

Dirt

I've always thought that eating dirt would be the last resort, something you did when there wasn't even any grass left, nor leaves remaining on trees, nor even any bark. In fact, I never even considered eating dirt at all, except when I was a toddler making mud pies in the garden. So it was with great surprise when I discovered that eating dirt, the soil beneath our feet, the ground we walk on, had a long and impressive history, that it even had a scientific name: geophagy, meaning, I suppose, eating the geography.

Besides making mud pies, I knew that children commonly ate dirt when they were little because at age one to three they tend to put everything in their mouths as an aid to identification. I'd also seen photographs of people returning to their homelands after a long absence or ordeal (such as war), kneeling to kiss the ground. I knew that chickens and ostriches didn't have teeth, so they ate gravel to aid digestion of their food. And I knew that worms ate dirt, enriching the earth when it passed out the other end. But geophagy was a new one for me.

But not a new one for human kind. Now I know that people have been doing just that for millennia, by choice! Not because they were starving and there was nothing else to eat, but because it offered them something as a legitimate food source.

I made my discovery when researching acorns and I read in *Edible Plants and Animals* (1993) by A.D. and Helen Livingston that "...certain Indians mixed clay with acorn meal [at a ratio of about one part clay to twenty parts meal by weight]. The clay was said to make the resulting bread sweet, and to make it 'rise' like yeast." I further learned that eating shards of pottery in India was popular in the 19th century. Water poured into the thin clay cups assumed a pleasant taste and odor and once emptied would be broken by the women and eaten.

A University of Mississippi professor in the US, Dennis Frate, who has studied dining on dirt, told a writer for the *Columbus Ledger-Enquirer* in Georgia in 1997 that the practice was first noticed around 40 B.C., when Greeks prescribed a variety of clays to combat a number of illnesses. "Almost every major population has been observed eating dirt," he said.

Mr. Frate admitted there was a down side, however. "There have been documented cases of bowel compaction caused by this," he says. "I've conducted a chemical analysis of the soil in our area and found no reason for not eating dirt, but that doesn't mean that I condone it."

Other scientists went further, actually enthusing over the value of eating dirt. Researchers Susan Aufreiter, a laboratory analyst at the University of Toronto in Canada, and William Mahaney, a York University geography professor, published their findings in 1997 in *New Scientist* magazine and the *International Journal of Food Sciences and Nutrition*, both published in England, saying that chemical analysis showed a light, yellowish soil used as survival food in China was rich in iron, calcium, vanadium, magnesium, manganese, and potassium, all of which would be in short supply in times of famine.

The same wide-ranging study also showed that in Zimbabwe, the natives ate the red soil from termite mounds for digestive complaints; careful analysis revealed that the termite soil contained kaolinite, the principle ingredient in the popular diarrhea remedy, Keopectate. The clay was also rich in iodine and iron, two elements whose scarcity was "responsible for a lot of [nutritional] deficiency diseases," Ms. Aufreiter said. When the termite clay was eaten, "these elements go into solution in the acids of the stomach, [improving] the odds...that your body can absorb it, and that's nutritional." Another sample, taken in North Carolina in the U.S., also was found to contain iron and iodine. While in Thailand's rural province of Si Sa Ket, a region with unusually salty soil, villagers chew salty earth as a snack.

Looking back, Ms. Aufreiter and her colleagues noted that the Romans made medicinal tablets from soil and goats' blood, that the Germans in the 19th century spread fine clay on their bread instead of butter, and that in some West African countries today pellets made of termite clay are sold as a digestive remedy, a practice that spread to the US during the days of the slave trade, remaining in some pockets of the American South today, where usually it is taken by pregnant or lactating women who say it helps settle their stomachs. According to Peter Farb and George Armelagos in *Consuming Passions: the Anthropology of Eating*, (1980), this is a response to a need for calcium and other minerals.

Some Indian groups in the Amazon eat blocks of clay with their meat. It's also well known that lime—not the fruit but the white or grayish calcium oxide that is used in mortars, plasters, and cements and as a fertilizer—is an ingredient in the Mexican dish posole. The great Spanish explorer Cabeza de Vaca wrote in his memoirs that the Indian tribes in what is now central and south Texas and northern Mexico processed mesquite beans for human consumption by mixing them with earth and water. So, too, in India, where the shards of earthenware vessels are crushed in sandalwood oil, made into pills called *mitti*, another form of dirt ingested by pregnant women.

"At this time, their taste changes," said the agent for the Mexican manufacturer. "Ask any lady who is in the family way. They want different things to eat. Some ladies eat tamarind, others may eat non-vegetarian, even though usually they are totally vegetarian. But normally, they eat earth. That is why this product was invented. The smell of this is like the first drops of the monsoon on the hard earth."

So, can anyone just go into the woods or garden, scoop up some dirt, and expect to derive any nourishment from ingesting it. Not likely. "You can't go around eating topsoil," Ms. Aufreiter said. Many organic food markets and restaurants around the world have adopted the name Good Earth, but that didn't mean all earth was good for you. To obtain quality clay for medicinal purposes, she suggested visiting reputable shops.

Nor is it a good idea to assume dirt-eating is widespread in the American South, a region that some outsiders said was so poor and peopled by so many ignorant people, they ate dirt. Humorist Roy Blount Jr., a Southerner, got so fed up with Yankees making such rude remarks, he began distributing fictitious recipes he swore were legitimate, for example, for "blackened red dirt," Cajun style.

For a time in the mid-1990s, it was possible to buy one-pound bags of dirt in Atlanta shops. It says on the package that it's a novelty item and "not for human consumption." But that didn't stop piles of the stuff being sold along with other, more recognized produce. Only US$1.19. Visiting conventioneers bought lots of it.

The Case of the Coffin that Ended Up Inside the Man

Actually, there seem to be two kinds of dirt eaters, those who eat it for nutritious reasons and those with a rare medical condition called "pica." Often they are children who seem addicted to eating non-nourishing items such as dirt or clay. Doctors say the child usually starts foraging between age one and two years, sometimes because of a lack of warm parenting, or a delay in intellectual development. The same child may also be seen eating paint from the walls of the home. A medical examination is urged.

Pica is not just about eating dirt, by the way. It's about eating any non-food items, and the medical history books are full of odd cases about people— adults as well as children—eating hair, chalk, glue, even their socks. There was a case in the United States where a twenty-two-year-old woman was eating about half a sock each evening. She told doctors she'd been eating her clothing since she was a teenager. Another recent report told of another twenty-two-year-old, this one a man in China, swallowed up to fifty stones a day from a supply used to make roads. He explained that the habit began when he was ten and experienced an epileptic seizure while tending the family's goats. To diminish the pain, he said, he swallowed pebbles and his discomfort went away. A similar case, also in China, in 2003 concerned a man who started eating pebbles when he had a belly ache as a twelve-year-old and at the peak of his addiction gulped down as many as ninety stones a day, consuming an estimated three tons over a nine-year period.

There are two others who earned a strange sort of immortality by eating non-food items. The first was called "The Human Ostrich" by Robert

Ripley in one of his syndicated cartoon panels, *Believe It Or Not!*, published in 1937. So named because ostriches are believed (erroneously) to eat anything, Edmond C. Nickels reportedly consumed 607 objects ranging from several dollars in pennies, nickels, dimes and quarters, to nails, screws, watch parts, chains, and street car tokens. He died of pneumonia in 1934, three years before Mr. Ripley made him famous.

More recently, in the 1996 edition of *The Guinness Book of Records*, under the heading Medical Extremes, Michel Lotito, a forty-six-year-old man from Grenoble, France, known as Monsieur Mangetout ("Mr. Eat Anything"), was said to have been eating metal and glass from the time he was nine years of age. "Gastroenterologists have x-rayed his stomach and described his ability to consume two pounds of metal per day as unique," *Guinness* said. "His diet since 1966 has included ten bicycles, a supermarket cart (in four and a half days), seven TV sets, six chandeliers, a Cessna light aircraft, and a computer. He is said to have provided the only example in history of a coffin (handles and all) ending up inside a man."

Dumpster Diving

Can anyone who's seen the 1978 movie *Animal House* ever forget the scene where John Belushi as the guitar-bashing, beer-can-smashing Bluto Blutarsky eats garbage? Mr. Belushi catapulted to international fame in this film (following several years of stardom on television's *Saturday Night Live*) and some thought it might trigger a new campus fad: eating garbage.

It didn't happen. Fraternity members may be known for being led around by their noses, and frequently by other protuberances, but this time they chugged another beer and said no. Too bad, because what one man calls garbage, another may call a hearty meal. Garbage—discarded food—has an ugly reputation that may be ill-formed.

Ask Lars Eighner, a writer who survived three years as an Urban Scavenger, pulling many of his meals from Dumpsters. In an article for *Harper's Magazine* in 1991 that was revised for a book named for his dog, *Travels With Lizbeth*, published two years later, Mr. Eigner said that while living as a starving writer and then traveling from Texas to California and back as a homeless person, he discovered that those large metal trash containers found behind markets, in malls, and outside apartment buildings were the supermarkets of the poor, not only a source of sustenance but also a bazaar of surprising quality and variety.

Eating from Dumpsters—Eighner capitalized the word because it was trademarked by the Dempster Dumpster Company or Knoxville, Tennessee—"is what separates the dilettanti from the professionals," he wrote. Of course there was some risk, as there is whenever we open our mouths, even in nice restaurants. Even so, Mr. Eighner claimed that eating safely from one of these bins only involved three principles: "using the senses and common sense to evaluate the condition of the found material, knowing the Dumpsters of a given area and checking them regularly, and seeking always to answer the question 'Why was this discarded?'"

The safest food, he said, came from cans or in the original packaging, the latter being "not so much a positive sign as it is the absence of a negative one." He had few qualms about eating dry foods such as crackers, cookies, cereal, chips, and pasta, "if they are free of visible contaminates and still dry and crisp," along with raw fruits and vegetables with intact skins. He cautioned that cans should make a hissing sound when opened, establishing the validity of the vacuum seal, and said even if produce had bad spots, usually they could be cut away.

Often timing was a key factor. For the pizzas that started him diving, he showed up just after the shops closed, following final inventory, when home delivery pizzas that were rejected (for being cold or a variety of other reasons) finally were discarded; they were still cold, but all the ingredients were "fresh." University neighborhoods were another excellent source at class break, when students cleaned out their cabinets and refrigerators, thinking the stuff might spoil during the holiday; the end of term or year offered another bonanza. (Drugs, porn, and alcohol also turned up in the collegiate trash when parents were expected, say, for Dad's Day or Homecoming.) Visiting Dumpsters regularly was another priority, Mr. Eighner said; arrive early and there was nothing there, arrive late and your meal had been hauled away.

"My test for carbonated soft drinks is whether they still fizz vigorously," he wrote. "Many juices or other beverages are too acidic or too syrupy to cause much concern, provided they are not visibly contaminated. I have discovered nasty molds in vegetable juices, even when the product was found under its original seal; I recommend that such products be decanted slowly into a clear glass. Liquids always require some care. One hot day I found a large jug of Pat O'Brien's Hurricane mix. The jug had been opened but was still ice cold. I drank three large glasses before it became apparent to me that someone had added the rum to the mix, and not a little rum. I never tasted the rum, and by the time I began to feel the effects I had already ingested a very large quantity of the beverage. Some divers would have considered this a boon, but being suddenly intoxicated in a public place in the early afternoon is not my idea of a good time."

There were, of course, foods to avoid, including poultry, pork, game, egg-based foods, and unfamiliar foods that were often found in ethnic neighborhoods.

Despite the care taken, Mr. Eighner said he still got dysentery at least once a month. (As happens in many Third World or "developing" countries, even when eating in "good' restaurants; only in the developed West is it a big deal.) Other hazards were bees harvesting donut glaze, cats that didn't like being interrupted at their meals ("especially thrilling" when Mr. Eighner had his dog along), and biting ants. He also came to resent the scroungers collecting recyclable cans because they tended to stir everything up and ruin a lot of otherwise edible food. And, he confessed, he usually gained weight when diving because he often ate as if he didn't know where his next meal was coming from, and consumed a lot of junk food because he hated to see edibles go to waste.

"I do not want to paint too romantic a picture," he cautioned. "Dumpster diving has serious drawbacks as a way of life." The warning out of the way, however, he said he liked the "frankness of the word scavenging."

"I live from the refuse of others. I am a scavenger. I think it a sound and honorable niche, although if I could I would naturally prefer to live the comfortable consumer life, perhaps—and only perhaps—as a slightly less wasteful consumer, owing to what I have learned as a scavenger."

Eighner was not alone in his scrounging, nor do the Dumpsters of today go unvisited. I live in Asia, where a large proportion of the population scavenges one way or another, in both rural and urban environments. Is there any place on earth nowadays where we don't see people rummaging through trash containers for a recyclable that can be sold or something to be eaten on the spot?

As is well known, in Mexico and the Philippines and elsewhere, there are, literally, mountains of garbage serving as a "home" for the indigent who sort through the mess for something useable, saleable, or edible.

And as more and more markets and apartment buildings invest in more and more Dumpsters, and the gap between the rich and the poor accelerates, there may soon be queues forming.

For many, garbage is a way of life, and of living.

Road Kill

Q: How many rednecks does it take to eat a possum?
A: Two. One to eat and one to watch for traffic.

Buck Peterson surely laughed if he heard this simple joke, but he probably hated it, because it speaks poorly about a subject dear and close to his heart, or at least to an organ near it, his stomach.

Mr. Peterson is the author of three books championing the modern Urban Scavenger who travels roadways wherever wild life encounters the internal combustion engine, fatally. The result is called "road kill," a highly under-rated and much denigrated food source. The first slender volume, *The Original Road Kill Cookbook*, published in 1985, like his subsequent offerings, was written tongue-in-cheek, but he assures me that when he talks about "ditch dining" and "yellow-line yummies," he's deadly serious.

He may go for the easy laugh in creating recipes called Windshield Wabbit, Curbside Cat, Dumbo Gumbo, Asphalt Armadillo, and German Shepherd Pie, yet he insists that the recipes are legitimate.

Mr. Peterson, a native of Minnesota—known for its numerous and careless deer—and now a resident of Wisconsin, who has published books about hunting and fishing of a more mainstream nature, talks in his road kill guides about the advantage of "shopping" with a minivan or pickup truck over a subcompact or sports car, both for killing power and the ample room for the dead animals in the rear. He additionally recommends roadside parks for dining for the availability of running water, "filet" (picnic) tables, and large garbage cans for disposal of unwanted parts. Yet, he believes, fervently, that by writing such books, he is performing a public service.

"All my books on the subject are intended to lower the readers eyesight to the animal level and to take some responsibility for our actions. Of course, no real animals were injured in the execution of my books. And all the recipes work."

Mr. Peterson surveyed both domesticated and wild animals (most are the latter), from large (bear, elk, deer, antelope, moose, reindeer, llama, camel, cow, horse, even elephant) to small (squirrel, raccoon, possum, porcupine, armadillo, turtle, dog, cat, even skunk and rat). Gravel Goose and Datsun Duck and other birds also get his attention, and all are, in a phrase, fair game.

He does not say, however, that if a driver comes upon a dead animal or bird or reptile on the road, it may be scooped up and taken away and eaten without caution. If the creature has been dead for a while, the driver should keep on going, as meat spoils quickly, especially in a warm climate. The roadside shopper should also know how to "field dress" a just-killed animal. The vital organs must be removed, the animal skinned (or plucked), the meat butchered and cleaned, the cuts to be eaten immediately or refrigerated as soon as possible. The salvage of road kill should be left for those who are hunters, he said. "They know how and when, much like survivalists."

"I hunt white tail deer in Wisconsin," Mr. Peterson told me, "and it's typical that one-fourth to one-third of the rental car fleet in the part of Wisconsin I hunt has cars being repaired by what the industry calls 'deer/car interaction.' These repairs are not just for head-on collisions but for repairing side panels where does and bucks ram blindly during their romantic (or unromantic) chases from their trails to ours.

"The papers I've read on the subject are very technical and used to support some sort of fencing/ramps/tunnel solution to large animal road kill. Typically, these solutions are too expensive for the sponsoring agency and large animal road kill is considered collateral damage in our rush to pave through their former domain. This attitude fits with developers' absolute resistance to hire wildlife biologists in the planning of their housing/commercial developments. What typically happens is a developer will level a fine piece of white tail habitat and leave small greenbelts as eye candy and tout Bambi sightings as a perk living in his housing boxes—the development called Deer Ridge (Hollow) Estates. It all gets crazy when whatever deer that stay around eat all of the soccer moms' and dads' rose bushes and the large predator cats come to play. For those trapped in the Disney world of animals, the wild kingdom becomes even wilder.

"There are exceptions, of course. On the north edge of the Olympic Peninsula in the state of Washington, biologists have collared resident elk that carry a device that when close to the road triggers a flashing sign and this effort has reduced road kill significantly. Elk, of course, act a little differently than white tail deer and certainly antelope. But this experiment has been a noticeable success."

Inevitably, many readers of Mr. Peterson's books and of what I am writing here will not take us any more seriously than the guy who wrote the redneck joke. However, I live in Asia, where road kill is both ordinary and acceptable. My first trip to Cambodia in 1993, when the United Nations was supervising that country's first election, a UN driver hit and killed a water buffalo on a rural highway, reporting the incident to his supervisor when he returned to Phnom Penh. His boss sent him back to give the owner money and upon arriving, the villagers invited him to join them in eating the beast. This sort of thing is not unusual. In much of South and Southeast Asia, elephants are having "interactions" with trucks and trains on a regular basis. Which would you prefer: to eat a slice of roasted trunk, which is considered a treat, or to dig a grave big enough to hold an SUV?

Mr. Peterson has not been the only writer intrigued by the gastronomy of highway kill. Tim Dorsey in 2002 went for a regional market, writing *Florida Roadkill*. Presumably, similar books could be or have been written about almost anywhere.

The most notable author on the subject was the late John McPhee, a longtime *New Yorker* writer whose numerous non-fiction books made him one of the most admired practitioners of the New Journalism that flourished in the 1960s and 1970s. In a long article titled "Travels in Georgia," published in 1973, he drove along miles of back-country road with a zoologist named Carol Ruckdeschel and Sam Candler, a conservationist who was the great-grandson of the pharmacist who developed and at one time wholly owned the Coca-Cola Company. Both worked for the Georgia Natural Areas Council and for several weeks, McPhee accompanied them as they examined and ate road kill—they called it D.O.R., for Dead on the Road—while taking a detailed wilderness inventory. No surprise, there were several unforgettable scenes.

For example: "I lived on squirrel last winter," McPhee quoted the zoologist as saying. "Every time you'd come to a turn in the road, there was another squirrel. I stopped buying meat." A couple of pages later, Ruckdeschel added, "People don't make sense. They hunt squirrels, but they wouldn't consider eating a squirrel killed on the road."

Another time, they found a weasel and roasted it over the glowing coal of a wood fire. "'How do you like your weasel?' Sam asked me. 'Extremely well done,' I said. Carol sniffed the aroma of the roast. 'It has a wild odor,' she said. 'You know it's not cow. The first time I had bear, people said, 'Cut the fat off. That's where the bad taste is.' I did, and the bear tasted just like cow. The next bear, I left the fat on.' The taste of the weasel was strong and not unpleasant. It lingered in the mouth after dinner. The meat was fibrous and dark. 'It just goes to show you how good everything is,' said Carol. 'People who only eat cows, pigs, sheep, chickens—boy, have those people got blinders on! Is that tunnelization! There is one poisonous mammal in the United States: the short-tailed shrew. And you can even eat that.' Sam built up the fire."

In the weeks that followed, during which time they toured the river where *Deliverance* was filmed and met the governor of the state, Jimmy Carter, they came upon king snake, blue jay, sparrow hawk, wood thrush, raccoon, catbird, cotton rat, fox squirrel, nighthawk, box turtle, loggerhead shrike, cottonmouth, cat, and dog.

"D.O.R. gray squirrel," wrote McPhee. "'We could eat him,' Carol said. 'We've got enough food,' said Sam."

I confess I've never eaten any road kill, but I don't think I'd hesitate if I had Buck Peterson or one of McPhee's friends along.

More Road Kill Disrespect

Another early jokester to enter the affray was Robert Roswell, who operated Roadkill Cafes in Louisiana and New Hampshire. Diners were invited to bring their own road kill to the restaurants and then the kitchen staff would "cook and baste the little critters to everyone's delight."

Dishes on the menu—but unavailable as it was all contrived for the laughs—included Center Line Bovine ("Tastes real good, straight from the hood"), The Chicken ("That didn't cross the road"), and Flat Cat ("Served on a shingle or in a stack"). The same rhyming gag format also offered but didn't deliver Rigor Mortis Tortoise, Poodles N Noodles, and Road Toad *ala Mode*.

Mr. Roswell decorated his cafes with photographs of real road kill and of dishes allegedly made from it.

Buck's Three-Eyed Dead-Eyed Gitya-Up 'N Go Swamp Stew

1 possum
1/4 lb salt pork
1 cup pearl onions, peeled
1 cup sweet red peppers,
    chopped and seeded
2 8 oz cans black-eyed peas
1 cup favorite dressing
2 tablespoons bacon and/or
    sausage drippings

1/2 cup coffee
1/2 cup water
2 tablespoons white flour
1 teaspoon coarse salt
1/2 teaspoon dried red peppers,
    finely chopped
Salt and pepper to taste
Redeye gravy

Preheat oven to 325°F.

Prepare redeye gravy in a saucepan. Using low heat, mix drippings with white flour. Whisk until mixture is smooth. Stir in coffee and water. Season with salt and pepper and set aside.

Skin, gut, and clean the possum, then rub coarse salt and red peppers into meat. Stuff possum with 1 cup of your favorite dressing, onions, and sweet red peppers, sewing up possum the same way you would a turkey. Thinly slice the salt pork and lay strips across the back of possum. Place the possum in a roasting pan and bake for 20 minutes or until tender. Remove from oven and let stand.

Heat peas according to label directions.

Slice possum and arrange slices on preheated plates with a serving of peas and cover with heated redeye gravy. Serve with white lightning.
—*Adapted only slightly from Buck Peterson's International Roadkill Cookbook*

Sex & Food

Besides water and air, the only two things essential to humankind's survival are food and sex. So it is no surprise when they are mixed, or, rather, intermingled—both are or can be quite sensual, one inevitably leading to the next, or occurring simultaneously. Can anyone conjure up an image of life in imperial Rome or, more recently, in Czarist Russia without food and sex being conjoined in gooey excess?

Let's begin at the beginning and talk about food and seduction. Some believe that kissing stems from mouth-to-mouth feeding. And is not the prelude to sex frequently a "romantic" dinner with something foolish to drink? Remember the scene in *Tom Jones* when Albert Finney and Susannah York shoved succulent medieval meat into each other's mouths? Hey, even *Lady and the Tramp* had a food/sex scene, before those little canines did you know what.

Chocolate is another sex-starter. "I have done things with Mackinaw Island fudge of which I'm not proud," says a friend. How many chocolate bars bought sex during World War Two? Even Mama Cass looked delectable, almost Playboy-esque, in that famous poster from the 1960s picturing her in a tub of chocolate syrup.

Consider, too, all the wondrous ways that sex is used to sell something edible? Many bakeries offer cakes and other pastries that look like mammalia and genitalia—sold at premium prices, too. Modern sex boutiques offer with their dildos and salacious lubricants such items as penis-shaped gummy bears and pasta, cookies that look like breasts, and edible undies. Do you recall the billboards in the 1960s for a popular pizza chain that asked, "Have you had a piece lately?"

Then, when we finally get down to it...there's food as a sexual partner or accessory. Here we move into somewhat kinky areas where bananas and cucumbers stand in for absent penises and the Japanese, ever the sexual innovators, eat sushi off a naked woman's body, preferably that of a virgin. Have you heard about the "no hands" restaurants in Thailand? Surely you saw Marlon Brando use butter to ease his taboo union with Maria Schneider in *Last Tango in Paris*? And do you know about the "wet and sloppy" crowd (punch up that phrase on Yahoo or Google to see what I'm talking about, but wait until the kids are asleep).

There's also a philosophical, or religious, side. What are the five pillars holding up the tradition of tantra, an action system—as opposed to the study systems offered by Hinduism and Buddhism—that promises nirvana in a single lifetime to those who nurtured pleasure and ecstasy? Fish, meat, wine, cereal, and sexual intercourse.

Erotic art with a food theme is ageless. Etruscan amphora and early Greek plates and goblets were decorated with the most vivid sexual union...a Mayan plate shows a monkey caressing a naked woman...for centuries in Japan sake was drunk from cups adorned with copulating couples, some of the cups phallic in shape, with holes in the glans through which the horny salarymen drank.

It's in the language, too. Can you translate the slang euphemisms "cherry," "salami," "bearded clam," and "to eat"?

And finally we come to aphrodisiacs. Perhaps in no other area of gastronomy has the mind been more inventive or deluded.

Alan Davidson wrote in *The Oxford Companion to Food* (1999), arguably the finest encyclopedia of gastronomy, that a study of the literature on the subject "shows that most foods have, in one culture or another, been perceived as aphrodisiacs. No doubt food which contain nutrients and therefore help to maintain human bodies in working order can be said to be aphrodisiacs in the very weak sense that they help to maintain the sexual function as well as the numerous others which our bodies are expected to perform. But this sense is so attenuated as to be without significance."

The 15th century work, *The Perfumed Garden* suggested a mixture of nutmeg, incense, and honey for premature ejaculation, while a paste of honey and ginger dabbed on the penis was recommended for increasing the size of the male organ, and a daily cocktail of honey, ginger, cinnamon, and cardamom was prescribed for impotence.

The *Kama Sutra*, the notorious Hindu guide to love, urged the erection-challenged to boil the testicles of a goat or ram in milk and sugar, or simmer sparrow's eggs in milk, honey, and butter. The Chinese preferred deer antler, rhino horn, ginseng, and tiger penises, served in a hearty drink or soup.

Ancient Greeks swore by carrots and onions. (Ovid wrote in his *Amaroriae*, "Some mingle pepper with the seed of the boiling nettle, and yellow chamomile ground up in old urine; but the goddess...will not thus be driven to her joys. Let white onions...be eaten.") In Rome in Pliny's day, garlic was ground up with coriander and white wine. Elizabethans put their trust in the humble potato. Indians say garlic is the answer. Yemenites chew nutmeg, which consumed in bulk can produce hallucinations. Residents of the South Pacific drank *kava kava*, a liquid made by women chewing the root of a plant and spitting the flavored saliva into a drinking bowl, which is then passed from guest to guest.

For centuries in much of the world, oysters have been consumed by the dozen as a sexual fortifier. Aphrodisiac recipes were very much in vogue throughout the 18th century, when, according to *Larousse Gastronomique*, the great epicurean encyclopedia, a typical repast may have included turtle soup with ambergris, sole *a la normande*, reindeer fillet in cream sauce, salmis of teal, roasted young pigeon, watercress salad, asparagus in hollandaise sauce, bone-marrow pudding, a nice Bordeaux wine, port, and coffee. The Elizabethan writer, Henry Buttes, prescribed in his *Dyets Dry Dinner* chestnuts which "much resembleth testes, the instrument of lust." In Paris, street-sellers shouted "Artichokes! Artichokes! Heats the body and the spirit. Heats the genitals!"

What is an aphrodisiac, exactly? Usually, it is considered to be any substance, animal, vegetable, or mineral—or in the age of Viagra, pharmaceutical—that is used to stimulate a man's or woman's libido, increase sexual energy, encourage and maintain the erection of the penis or increase feeling in the clitoris, intensify orgasm for all partners, and in any way possible, enhance the enjoyment of sex.

No secret, then, why such "foods" have been popular.

Absinthe, champagne, black tea, sarsparilla, sweetbreads, *ani-*

melles (French for testicles), amourettes, brains, kidneys, oysters, lobster and crayfish, caviar and roe, starfish, cuttlefish, smoked or salted mullet, anchovies, turtle, prawns, sea urchins, whelks, mussels, truffles and moral mushrooms, celery (what's the full stalk like?), red peppers, cola nuts, wild mint, pimiento, marjoram, parsley, roots of chervil and of fern, radish, lotus, pistachio nuts, cumin, thyme, sage, borage, walnuts, almonds, dates, quinces, mint, musk, caraway, sage, vanilla, cloves, saffron, shark's fin, the blood of many creatures, most notably snakes (again the shape), dove and pigeon (because of their exotic courtship behavior), shark's fin, the penis of any animal...the list of foods credited with powers that no one can prove goes on and on and on. If all these foods delivered what myth promised, would it be any wonder that so many of us walk around in a near constant state of lust?

Probably the most notorious food is Spanish Fly, or cantharides, a "spice" made from the powdered bodies of a bright green beetle of North Africa; this is considered quite dangerous and its sale is banned virtually everywhere. Another substance hailed for its improvement of blood circulation is johimbine, derived from a South American tree, but this is a drug, not a food.

Davidson concluded, saying that if anyone knew of a "seemingly innocuous food which, when ingested by the prospective partner would immediately produce a flood of sexual desire, how happy that human being would be and how often would this knowledge be utilized! In short, the concept of a truly aphrodisiac food is on par with that of finding a crock of gold at the end of a rainbow."

Alex Comfort, whose name graces books about the joy of sex, said that the best aphrodisiacs were, in order, "rest, boredom, sleep, red meat, and women, followed by wine and prosperity, fun, music and pleasant surroundings." Others insist that there are only two guaranteed aphrodisiacs when it is the man trying to get the woman into bed, and they have nothing to do with food: money and power.

Which, to me, sounds like no fun at all.

Excrement

A lot of people think it's a worthy subject. Scatology, scatography, and coprophilia have a lengthy and serious history, chronicled by Krafft-Ebbing and many scholars since. Scatology is the study of interest in excrement and scatalogic language is sometimes used as a stimulant during sexual encounters, especially those involving anal eroticism. Scatography is the practice of writing any kind of material, including graffiti, relating to eliminative functions, as a means of expressing or arousing sexual interest. Coprophiles generally are characterized—by the psychiatric establishment, anyway—as having a "pathological preoccupation" with excreta or filth, telling jokes about defecation, hoarding feces, creating fecal fantasies, experiencing sexual excitement during evacuation and, in some cases, smearing shit on walls or other objects. (In New York a few years ago, the mayor tried to shut down an art gallery when it displayed a painting of the Madonna that was decorated with buffalo crap.)

Now, none of this may be your cup of kaka, but for uncounted millions of years, it's been more than a hobby. Some people even eat it, a practice that's called coprophagia, sometimes scatophagy. Nowadays this is regarded as one of the most extreme behaviors, occasionally found in deteriorated schizophrenics, but also among a sizeable number of fetishists. But it wasn't, and isn't, always that way.

Some of the associations are obvious. Food becomes excrement, recall, after passing through the alimentary tract and in many parts of the world it is called "night soil" and is used matter-of-factly to fertilize crops. It can be argued similarly that excrement finds its way into our diet after it seeps or is flushed into our ground water supply.

The *Bible* predictably took a negative tack when Rabshakeh said, "Hath my master sent me to thy master, and to thee, to speak these words? Hath he not sent me to the men which sit on the wall, that they may eat their own dung, and drink their own piss with you?" (Isaiah: 36:7). The level of contempt was again clear when the prophet Malachi put the following scatophagous threat into the mouth of Jehovah: "If ye will not hear, and if ye will not lay it to heart, to give glory unto my name, saith the Lord of hosts, I will even send a curse upon you, and I will curse your blessings: yea, I have cursed them already, because ye do not lay it to heart. Behold I will corrupt your seed, and spread dung upon your faces, even the dung of your solemn feats; and one shall take you away with it" (Malachi 2:2–3). On the other hand—and the *Bible* is full of ambiguity and contradiction—in Ezekiel 4: 12–15, human excrement is mixed with cake flour.

Despite strong attack, excrement held a tenuous positive grip, mostly in the field of medicine, from the time of Hippocrates to its peak in the 16th century and through the 19th, when "filth-pharmacy," or Dreck Apotheke, its German name, was commonplace. Paul Spinrad notes in his *Guide to Bodily Fluids*: "Filth Pharmacy cures use virtually any kind of excrement you can name (badger dung, wild boar urine, crocodile dung, dung of milk-feeding lambs, the urine of an undefiled boy, hare urine, hawk dung, human feces, etc.), prescribe them in pretty much any manner you can imagine (to ingest, to apply as a lotion or poultice, to fumigate and inhale, to inject, to mix with food and drink and ingest, to reduce to ashes and plug into tooth cavities, to use as infusion for tea, as a suppository, as snuff, and so on), alone or in various combinations, in order to treat pretty much any ailment you can think of (dysentery, tuberculosis, deafness, dandruff, melancholia, delirium, baldness, snakebite, sore breasts, warts, cancer, insomnia, cataract, plague, etc.)." Some recipes were also used, unsurprisingly, simply to induce vomiting. Medical texts written and used by many of history's greatest doctors contained long lists of these eliminative remedies. Up until at least half a century ago, India's *sanyasi*, men dwelling in the highest state of exaltation a Brahmin could attain, drank regular draughts of *pancha gavia*, the blessed beverage composed of equal parts of the five gifts of the Sacred Cow: milk, curds, ghee (clarified butter), urine, and dung. Modern thinkers scoff at such reports, of course, insisting that, like urine, dung is waste, saying it has been excreted by the system and thus contains neither cure nor nourishment, medicinal or spiritual.

Nonetheless, the connection to food is so deep as to be in the language itself. *Pumpernickle* bread, for example, gets its name from the German words for farting (*pumpern*) and the devil (*nickel*). Germans also bake rosewater shortbread biscuits called *nonnenfürzchen* (nun's farts) and make little candies in the shape of a man squatting and defecating a large coin. Giving someone the "raspberry" by vibrating the tongue and lips to simulate the sound of flatulence comes from England's cockney rhyming slang: "raspberry tart, rhymes with fart." In the early 1990s, there was a popular restaurant in Berlin called The Klo (The Toilet), where the diners sat on porcelain thrones, meals were served in chamber pots, and toilet paper took the place of napkins; the latter is also widespread in Thailand and some other parts of Asia today, not because of any connection to excrement but because toilet paper is cheaper than napkins.

Other social associations are numerous. In India and elsewhere, food is eaten with the right hand only because the left is used when going to the paperless toilet. A less picky society existed earlier at dinner parties in Greece when handsome bronze pans were provided both for vomiting and urinating and at numerous locations around the room, chamber pots, a practice that continued for hundreds of years, with dinner guests evacuating their bowels, in one report, "as a matter of course, and occasions no interruption of the conversation." Eating and shitting, it was all one happy continuum.

Most interesting, of course, is the actual consumption of what most people believe is waste, such as was common in some of the oldest cultures in North America, where Indians made a broth from rabbit and caribou dung and near what is today Chicago, boiled rabbit feces with their wild rice. While in Southeast Asia, mouse shit is still believed by some to be an aphrodisiac in Thailand and in Vietnam and Indonesia, coffee beans are roasted after passing through the digestive track of weasels (or foxes or civet cats or monkeys; the story varies), the resulting drink said to be good for whatever ails you, save the dementia that tempted you to try it. There is reason to believe that such coffee really is no more than a reason to charge a high price for it, reportedly as much as US$300 a pound. Also in Thailand, the cloudy green liquid from the second bovine ruminant sac is called *khi phia*, the prefix being the word from excrement, using the bitter stuff to flavor spicy salads.

Similarly, Native Americans sorted through their own feces or that of animals for undigested grains or seeds of the pitahaya cactus, then roasted, ground and re-ingested them—a practice called "the second harvest." (In the same way that for reasons of survival, prisoners forced by the Japanese to build the "death railway" linking Thailand with Burma during the Second World War, removed undigested peanuts and kernels of corn from the chamber pots of their captors.) The Hindu god Utanka became immortal by eating bull dung. Persians ate melons with pigeon dung and Hindu Brahmins considered whole grains found in cow dung to be sacred. In Siberia, Central Africa, and North America, cooks prepared intestines without emptying them first.

Redmond O'Hanlon tells a wonderful story in his book about his travels in the *Amazon, In Trouble Again*, in which a Brazilian crocodile called a cayman is disemboweled with an axe and the guts become a cocktail. O'Hanlon described how his guide, Yavateiba, "grasped one end of the fishy tube in his right hand and slowly pulled the whole length through the tight sphincter made by his fingers, squeezing out the grey sludge of half-made cayman shit. The boy disappeared briefly into the forest and came back with a few large leaves. Yavateiba then wrapped up the bundle of guts, secured it with a piece of twine, arranged one leaf at the side into a spout, and pushed the whole gently into the ashes at the edge of the fire. We sat down to wait and in about five minutes Yavateiba decided it was ready; he pulled out the leaf vessel and held the spout in front of me; honoured, I opened my mouth and he tipped in a half a cupful of liquid. It was warm, thick, slimy, like a mixture of cod-liver oil and the recycled juice from old sardine tins."

More shocking, as was intended, was the scene in the John Waters film, *Pink Flamingo* (1974), where a 300-pound drag queen who held the title "The Filthiest Person in the World," watched a poodle shit outside her mobile home and fetched it in and ate it; this was an unedited scene, thus viewers of the cult film were assured of its realism.

Finally, we must consider the consumption of excrement as sexual aberration. The Marquis de Sade's early works remain classic, describing pleasure-seeking men who eat feces that have been aged a week, preferring it moldy; another man who prefers diarrhea, especially that of women suffering from indigestion or who have taken laxatives; a third who kept a woman in his home and restricted her diet (low fat, much poultry, no fish, salted meat, eggs, dairy products or bread) to enhance the flavor; and so on. No less outrageous is a character in Thomas Pynchon's 20th century novel *Gravity's Rainbow* who visits his mistress, has her whip him, then he drinks her urine, eats her feces, and masturbates. There is even a three-times-a-year magazine on the subject, costing US$20 per issue and published in the Netherlands.

Nicholas Bornoff tells a story in his excellent book about contemporary sex in Japan, *Pink Samarai* (1991): "a group of men were seated around a long, lacquer table bearing only a silver tray. A beautiful woman entered, stepped onto the table and stood astride the tray, raised her kimono, and evacuated her bowels. She then left the room and the event's hostess divided the leavings with a silver cake knife, serving a portion to each of the guests on a silver plate with a silver spoon.

afterword

ONLY WHEN WE'RE INFANTS are we willing to put just about anything into our mouths, usually as a means of identification. As we age, we become more selective and by the time we're adults most of us are set in our ways about what we eat and drink, and what we consumed when we were young generally is what we consume for the rest of our lives, with rarely much if any experimentation. This attitude, called neophobia, "the fear of the new," protects us from eating unknown, possibly harmful substances. It also denies us much joy.

There is a contrary point of view about what we consume called neophilia, "the love of the new." Margaret Visser, author of the superb book *The Rituals of Dinner: The Origins, Evolution, Eccentricities, and Meaning of Table Manners* (1991), believes that the neophiles are gaining on the neophobes, that diners are becoming more daring.

"Human beings are capable of seeking for variety, almost in itself," she wrote. "They will try new ways of cooking, new ingredients, new combinations of tastes. They hunt through books describing the food of cultures very different from their own, searching for new things to eat, new flavors and textures to try. Such people have usually had occasion to conquer and break out of their 'fear of the new' through contact with other cultures and the availability of a wide assortment of 'strange' foods. We admire and envy such people, and feel we should try to imitate them, thinking how sophisticated, knowledgeable, and broad-minded they are. Yet neophilia, in fact, is a typical human reaction to eating. Our own culture is experiencing at the moment a strong bias, or perhaps more specifically a pull exerted by the trend-setting 'upwardly mobile' classes, toward neophilia."

Ms. Visser wrote this before the SARS "epidemic" became, in late 2002 and through the early months of 2003, the latest Big Scare to shake the dinner table. When the outbreak of Severe Acute Respiratory Syndrome was tracked back to its apparent origin in the wild game market in Guangzhou, China, and quite possibly to the civet, a brown, furry creature with a cat-like body, long tail, and striped weasel-like face, and scientists found it carried a virus similar to that causing SARS, the exotic food market took a serious hit. Investigators discovered similar viruses in bats, snakes, and wild pigs in the same marketplace and further determined that approximately half of the exotic animal vendors in Guangdong Province tested positive for the virus, although evidently they were unaffected by it. Thousands of animals were destroyed and hundreds of vendors were put out of business, pushing what remained of the market underground and the prices for the animals up, while the world got another reason to curtail any urge it might have felt to taste something unusual or new.

I still count myself among the neophiles. I remain convinced that caution is wise—as it always has been—but also that it shouldn't be wrapped in fear. It's likely that the next time I'm in Guangzhou, I'll eat differently from the way I ate there the last time I visited. But I will not put handcuffs on my curiosity and my willingness to take some gastronomical risk. I believe that all of life is defined by risk and that those who do everything they can to avoid it, might just as well be dead. Just because there were outbreaks of Mad Cow Disease in England several years ago, an affliction that could reoccur somewhere else at any time (as it did in Canada in 2002), does that alone mean we should give up beef? Back in the Sixties, those who did drugs were advised to know their dealer and the source. So, too, it is wise, so far as it's possible, to consider the source of what we eat. I further believe that just because some scientist found a bad cobra in China, that doesn't mean I shouldn't eat rattlesnake in the United States.

Bottom line is that I hope Ms. Visser is right, that the neophiles are gaining on the neophobes, and there's growing evidence that she is. At the same time, there also still exists a yawning gastronomical gap between them, at least geographically and culturally. When it comes to eating "strange" food—that which is considered odd in most of the developed world, but elsewhere may merely be lunch—more people do it than don't. For example, I live in Thailand, where just about anything that moves, and a lot of what doesn't, is welcomed to the plate, and after a few years of a predominantly Asian cuisine, I was somewhat taken aback when I visited the United States, where I was born and raised. There, I asked many of the people I met what the strangest thing was they ever ate. Snails was about as weird as it got. North America, I learned, is where neophobes rule the kitchen and what comes out of it.

My former father-in-law was one of them. A rich real estate developer in California, a dedicated tennis player and an avid reader, he had learned more than half a dozen languages and played numerous musical instruments, yet when the dinner bell rang, he subscribed to the philosophy of Wittgenstein who hated being confronted with a change in his diet, regarding the effort involved in adapting to it a waste of his energy. I don't know if it was limited energy or imagination that governed my wife's father's appetite, or that of Wittgenstein's, for that matter. All I do know for sure is that my father-in-law told me that in all his numerous visits to the world's capitals he always stayed in a Sheraton hotel because he knew that every morning his plate of scrambled eggs would be exactly the same.

My mother, alas, was formed in the same uninteresting mold. As exciting as it ever got in my house was on Thursday nights when my father took his picky palate to his weekly Lions Club meeting and Mom added sliced onions to the hamburger goulash. She also once told me that she didn't see any wisdom in spending time on what would be consumed in fifteen minutes. While I eventually learned that if it was worth eating, a meal could go on for hours, delightfully.

The worst neophobe I ever met was, ironically, a woman who ran a cooking school and catering service in British Columbia. When I visited that city, my publisher hired her to follow some of the recipes in my book *Strange Foods* (1999) so I'd have some dishes for show-and-tell when I appeared on two Canadian television shows.

It wasn't the thinly sliced, deep-fried pigs' ears or the roasted bone marrow or the prickly pear veggie dish or the tomatoes stuffed with humus and fried crickets that caused her upset. It was the deep-dish bulls' ball pie, made from a recipe I found that dated back to 16th century Rome.

Following the instructions of Bartomolo Scappi, chef to Pope Pius V, she boiled four bulls' testicles with salt, then cut them into slices and sprinkled the result with more salt, pepper, nutmeg, and cinnamon. Next, in a pie crust she layered the sliced testicles with mince of lamb kidneys, ham, marjoram, cloves, and thyme. I must say it looked delicious and I enjoyed describing the contents and history on the show. But thinking the pie was going to be used again on the second program, I resisted eating any. When I arrived at the studio for that show, however, the woman told me that all the dishes were different and she didn't have the pie with her.

"How'd it taste?" I asked.

"You must be joking," she said. "I threw it away."

"You threw it away? Without tasting it? Weren't you even just a little bit curious?"

She said something genteel that really meant "Hell, no!" and then she explained her distress. "You can't just walk into a market and buy this sort of thing," she said. "I had to call my regular butcher and he had to order it from the abattoir. This is a man I use for all my meat orders, and when I told him what I wanted..."

She seemed at a loss for words, but finally said, "I can't tell you what this has done to my reputation in Vancouver."

It got worse. When she returned to her kitchen, she told me, she had to peel the primary objects in the recipe to remove their thick, veinous sack. Well! One of them slipped from her hands and it fell to the floor, bouncing several times on its way toward the back door as if trying to escape.

By now, I was having some trouble controlling myself. This sounded a great story, one I wanted her to tell on the show. However, I doubted she'd ever tell it again, it was clear that she was mortified, and somehow I kept my laughter in check.

"The worst part," she went on, "was when I started to slice them. They squirted at me! Squirted!"

I gave it up at that point and nearly fell off my chair.

Fast-food chains—now a gastronomical blight upon nearly every inhabited spot on the planet—and other mass producers of foodstuffs further encourage neophobia. They want us to settle for food that is prepared simply and quickly, without a care for quality or variety. In a time when busy schedules are crowded by the demands of hundreds of cable television stations and porn and game sites on the Internet, along with the press of daily life, too many of us head for the golden arches.

All that said, it's true that for some people an experimental attitude prevails. These are the people who were among the first to belly up to a North American sushi bar and go to the first Thai restaurant in town to try the spicy soup. Once upon a time, eating Chinese was considered exotic. Now more is required. So these dining adventurers check out the new Afghan or Colombian hole-in-the-wall that just opened in town, and if they live in a major metropolis they may actually attend a charity event held by the local zoo where insects and reptiles are on the menu. ("Just try a little bit, Herb. You don't have to eat the whole darned grasshopper!")

Neophilia also receives strong support from EuroAmerica's "health" craze, which has people swallowing such things as spirulina (made from green slime called algae), bee pollen, ginseng, and the foul-tasting noni fruit. Nowadays there are hundreds of odd foods and what retailers call "food supplements" to get around calling the products "drugs": cornucopia posing as pharmacy. The consumer movements that have grown up around vegetarianism and organic foods have contributed more choices, as has, most of all, the increased incidence of travel worldwide, accompanied by exposure to "extreme cuisine."

The point I wish to make is that if you're a neophobe, you don't know what you're missing. And to the neophiles and people who have any imagination at all I can only say: Follow me! This way! This is the direction of the future, after all, and to me it's always made sense, as the cliché goes, to ride the horse in the direction it's going.

A final story. During my visit back to the United States, on the plane from Portland to Seattle, I was handed a small bag of "Party Mix," described on the package as "a premium blend of zesty tastes including pretzels, ranch bagel chips, and cheddar corn sticks." The list of ingredients read as follows (take a very deep breath): "Enriched Wheat Flour (contains niacin, reduced iron, thiamine, mononitrate, riboflavin, folic acid), stone ground corn, bleached wheat flour (wheat flour, malted barley flour), sugar, cheddar cheese (pasteurized milk, cheese cultures, salt, enzymes, disodium phosphate and annatto), soybean oil, partially hydrogenated soybean oil, salt, malt, yeast, wheat gluten, oat bran, sour cream powder (sour cream solids, cultured nonfat milk, citric acid, TBHQ), whey solids, milk solids, guar gum, onion powder, tomato powder, tomato solids, garlic powder, cheddar cheese powder [cheddar cheese (whole milk, cheese cultures, salt enzymes), disodium phosphate, buttermilk, sodium bicarbonate, annatto vegetable color, citric acid, modified food starch, malic acid, artificial color (including yellow #6 and yellow #5), spices, natural and artificial flavor, paprika, yellow 6 lake, dried whey, dextrose monohydrate, lactic acid, silica gel-anticaking agent and turmeric."

And some people call what I eat "strange."

Defending the right to eat what we will

"Do you remember that food scare a few years ago when everybody was in a twist about the dangers of eating raw shellfish? I was having dinner around that time with an athletic friend, a captain of industry who showed up proudly wrapped in bandages and slings He had earned these by crashing into a large shrub on the slopes of Aspen. He needed help turning the pages of his menu. And then he refused to share my lavish platter of cold, plump, briny, crisp, and succulent oysters. 'Raw shellfish,' he gulped. 'Don't you read the papers?'

"In the days that followed, I tracked down the facts. The Food and Drug Administration had done a risk assessment study and discovered that one out of every 2,000 serving of raw mollusks is likely to make you sick. But you can expect to suffer a substantial injury in every 250 days of skiing, especially if you include gondola crashes and pain that blossom after the hapless skier returns home. So it turns out that a day of skiing is eight times more dangerous than a delicious plate of raw oysters. It was then that I decided to give up skiing so that I could eat oysters to my heart's delight."

—*Jeffrey Steingarten, writing in the New York Times, 2001*

Folk Wisdom

I'll eat anything with two legs except a ladder, anything with four legs except a table, anything that flies except an airplane, and anything that swims except a submarine.

—*Popular folk saying in a number of Asian countries*

selected bibliography

NO NEWSPAPER STORIES and only a few magazine articles are credited here, although they contributed much information; they numbered in the thousands. Nor are there specific citations from various editions of the *Collier's Encyclopedia*, *Encyclopedia Americana*, *Macmillan Family Encyclopedia*, *New Standard Encyclopedia*, and the *World Book Encyclopedia*. Many Internet connections and television documentaries also go unmentioned, with humble apologies to all.

Allen, Jana; and Gin, Margret. *Innards and Other Variety Meats*. 101 Productions, San Francisco, 1974.

Angier, Bradford, *Feasting Free on Wild Edibles*, Stackpole Books, Harrisburg, PA, 1966.

Barash, Cathy Wilkinson. *Edible Flowers: From Garden to Palate*, Fulcrum Publishing, Golden, CO, 1993.

Bates, H.W. *The Naturalist on the River Amazons*. John Murray, London, 1863.

Behnke, Frances L. *Natural History of Termites*, Charles Scribner's Sons, New York, 1977.

Blunt, Wilfrid. *The Ark in the Park: The Zoo in the Nineteenth Century*, Hamish Hamilton in association with The Tryon Gallery, London, 1976.

Boraiko, Allen A., "The Indomitable Cockroach," *National Geographic*, Jan. 1981.

Brennan, Jennifer. *Thai Cooking*. Warner Books, London, 1992.

Bridgeman, Richard Thomas Orlando, Earl of Bradford. *The Eccentric Cookbook*. Robson Books, London, 1985.

Bruman, Ray. "Ray's List of Weird and Disgusting Foods."
www.andreas.com/ray/food.html

Burkhill, I.H. *A Dictionary of the Economic Products of the Malay Peninsula, Vols. I & II*. Published for the Malay Government by Crown Agents, London, 1935.

Bushnell, G.H.S. *The First Americans*. Thames & Hudson, London, 1968.

Burton, Sir Richard. *The Hindu Art of Love*. Castle Books, New York, 1967.
—*The Perfumed Garden*. Castle Books, New York, 1965.

Cadwallader, Sharon. *Savoring Mexico: Classic Recipes of Traditional Cuisine from All Regions of Mexico*. Chronicle Books, San Francisco, 1987.

Canby, Thomas. "The Rat: Lapdog of the Devil." *National Geographic*, July 1997.

Cherry, Ron. "Use of Insects by Australian Aborigines." *American Entomologist* (32: 8-13).

Conniff, Richard. "From Jaws to Laws: Now the Big, Bad Shark Needs Protection from Us." *Smithsonian*, Jun. 1990.

Cornwall, I.W. *Prehistoric Animals and Their Hunters*. Faber & Faber, London, 1968.

Cost, Bruce. *Bruce Cost's Asian Ingredients: Buying and Cooking the Staple Foods of China, Japan and Southeast Asia*. William Morrow and Company, Inc., New York 1988.

Courtine, Robert J., introduction. *Larousse Gastronomique*. Paul Hamlyn, London, 1988.

Daniélou, Alain (trans.), *The Complete Kama Sutra*, Inner Traditions India, Rochester, VT, 1994.

David-Perez, Enriqueta, *Recipes of the Philippines*, National Book Store, Manila, 1973.

Davidson, Alan, *The Oxford Companion to Food*, Oxford University Pres, 1999.

DeFoliart, Gene R. "Edible Insects as Minilivestock." *Biodiversity and Conservation*, 4, 306-321 (1995).

—"Insects as a Source of Protein." Bulletin of the Entomological Society of America, Vo. 21, No. 2 (161-163), 1975.

—"Insects as Human Food." *Crop Protection*, Vol. 11, Oct. 1992.

Densmore, Frances. *How Indians Use Wild Plants for Food, Medicine & Crafts*. Dover Publications, New York, 1974.

Detrick, Mia. *Sushi*. Chronicle Books, San Francisco, 1981.

Doling, Annabel, *Vietnam on a Plate: A Culinary Journey*, Roundhouse Publications, Hong Kong, 1996.

Dorje, Rinjing. *Food in Tibetan Life*. Prospect Books, London, 1985.

Dowell, Philip; Bailey, Adrian; Ortiz, Elisabeth Lambert; Radecka, Helena. *The Book of Ingredients*. Mermaid Books, London, 1983.

Eighner, Lars, *Travels with Lizbeth*, St. Martin's Press, New York, 1993.

Ellis, Eleanor A., ed. *Northern Cookbook*. Ottawa: Ministry of Indian Affairs, 1998.

Eppele, David L. On the Desert: *Arizona Cactus*. Self-published on the Internet,

http://www.arizonacactus.com, 1998.

Etkin, Nina L., editor. *Eating on the Wild Side*. University of Arizona Press, Tucson and London, 1994.

Fisher, M.F.K. *The Art of Eating* (includes: *Serve It Forth, Consider the Oyster, How to Cook a Wolf, The Gastronomical Me*, and *An Alphabet of Gourmets*). Collier Books, New York, 1990.

Gattey, Charles Neilson. *Excess in Food, Drink and Sex*. Harrap Ltd., London, 1986.

Griffin, Gary M., *Aphrodisiacs for Men: Herbs, Drugs & Concentrated Virilizing Foods*, Added Dimensions, Los Angeles, 1991.

Groll, Jonathan. "Introduction to Cassava." Department of Biology, University of Witwatersrand, Johannesburg, 1998.

Headquarters, Department of the Army. *US Army Survival Manual: FM 21-76*. Dorset Press, New York, 1994.

Herbst, Sharon Tyler, *Food Lover's Companion*, Barron's Educational Series, Hauppauge, NY, 1995.

Holt, Vincent M. *Why Not Eat Insects?* E.W. Classey Ltd., Faringdon, Oxon, UK, 1978.

Humphries, Bronwen. "What Did Our Ancestors Eat?" Personal information file, http:/environlink.org/arrs/essays/man_eat.html

International Starch Institute. "ISI Technical Memorandum on Production of tapioca starch." Aarhus, Denmark: 1998.

Jackson-Doling, Annabel. *The Food of Vietnam*. Periplus Editions, Singapore, 1997.

Jamaican Information Service. "Jamaican Cuisine." jiz@jamaica-info.com, Kingston, 1998.

Jenkins, D.T. *Amanita of North America*. Mad River Press, Eureka, OR, 1986.

Konto, Fumihiro & Pei, Sheng-ji, editors. *Proceedings of the International Symposium on Flower-Eating Culture in Asia*. Kunming, 1989.

—& Guo, Huijin; Li , Yanhui; and Tsui, Jingyun. "Record of Ethnobotanical Investigation of Flower-eating Culture in Yunnan Province of China," 1990.

Kurlansky, Mark. "Better Red: Caviar lovers mourn the demise of communism." *Scanorama*, Dec. 1994-Jan.1994.

Kyle, Russel. *A Feast in the Wild*. Kudu Publishing, Oxford,1987.

Lever, Christopher. *They Dined on Eland: The Story of the Acclimatisation Societies.* Quiller Press, London, 1992.

Lincoff, G.H. National Audubon Society *Field Guide to North American Mushrooms.* Alfred A. Knopf, New York, 1981.

Livingston, A.D.; and Livingston, Helen. *Edible Plants and Animals: Unusual Foods from Aardvark to Zamia.* Facts on File, New York, 1993.

Luard, Elisabeth. *European Peasant Cooking.* Bantam, New York, 1988.

Lucan, Medlar; and Gray, Durian. *The Decadent Cookbook.* Sawtry, Cambs., Dedalus, UK, 1995.

Majupuria, Indra; and Lobsang, Diki. *Tibetan Cooking.* S. Devi, Lashkar, India, 1994

McPhee, John, "Travels in Georgia," *New Yorker*, Apr. 28, 1973.

McGee, Harold. *On Food and Cooking: The Science and Lore of the Kitchen.* Charles Scribner's Sons, New York, 1984.

McKie, Robin. "The People Eaters." *New Scientist*, Mar. 14, 1998.

Miller, Richard Alan. *The Magical and Ritual Use of Aphrodisiacs.* Destiny Books, Rochester, VT 1985 & 1993.

Morris, Sallie. *South-East Asian Cookery: The Authentic Taste of the Orient.* Grafton Books, London, 1989.

Nancarrow, Loren; and Taylor, Janet Hogan. *The Worm Book.* Ten Speed Press, Berkeley, CA, 1998.

Niethammer, Carolyn, *American Indian Food and Lore*, Collier Macmillan Publishers, London, 1974.

Nobel, Park S. *Remarkable Agaves and Cacti.* Oxford University Press, New York, 1994.

Noh, Chin-hwa. *Traditional Korean Cooking.* Hollym Corporation, Seoul, 1985.

Novick, Alvin, M.D. "Bats Aren't All Bad." *National Geographic*, May 1973.

O'Hanlon, Redmond. *In Trouble Again.* Hamish Hamilton, London, 1988.

Palmer, Joan. *All About Cats.* Ward, Lock & Uitgeverij Het Spectrum, London, 1986.

Pan, Lynn. *Sons of the Yellow Emperor: A History of the Chinese Diaspora.* Kodansha International, Tokyo, 1990.

Pearman, Rosemary. *Even More Wild Ways with Cooking.* KwaZulu-Natal Region of the Wildlife Society of South Africa, Linden, South Africa, 1998.

Peterson, B.R. (Buck), *The Original Road Kill Cookbook*, 10 Speed Press, Berkeley, CA, 1985.

—*Buck Peterson's International Roadkill Cookbook*, 10 Speed Press, Berkeley, 1994.

Peiris, Doreen. *A Ceylon Cookery Book.* published by the author, Colombo, Sri Lanka, 1995.

Ponting, Clive. *A Green History of the World: The Environment and the Collapse of Great Civilizations.* Penguin, New York, 1993.

Pope, Clifford H. *The Reptile World.* Alfred A. Knopf, New York, 1955.

Ross, Philip E. "Man Bites Shark." *Scientific American*, Jun. 1990.

Scott, David; and Inwood, Kristiaan. *A Taste of Thailand: A Practical and Atmospheric Guide to Thai Cuisine.* Rider, London, 1986.

Shreeve, James. "Infants, Cannibals, and the Pit of Bones." *Discover*, Jan. 1994.

Schwabe, Calvin W., *Unmentionable Cuisine*, University Press of Virginia, 1979.

Sing, Phia. *Traditional Recipes of Laos.* Prospect Books, London, 1981.

Smith, Leona Woodring. *The Forgotten Art of Flower Cookery.* Pelican Publishing Co., Gretna, LA, 1990.

Sonnenfeld, Albert, *Food: A Culinary History from Antiquity to the Present*, Penguin, New York, 2000.

Sterling, Richard, ed. *Travelers' Tales: Food—A Taste of the Road.* Travelers Tales, Inc., San Francisco, 1996.

—*World Food: Vietnam*, Lonely Planet, Hawthorne, Victoria, Australia, 2000.

Stewart, Matthew. *The Incredible Edible Wild: A Rare Collection of Wilderness Recipes.* Stewart Associates, Milan, IN, 1998

Stobart, Tom. *The Cook's Encyclopedia.* Harper and Row, New York, 1981.

Stolzenburg, William. "Hunting Dragons: On Safari for the Big Game of the Insect World." *Nature Conservancy*, May/June 1994.

Tannahil, Reay. *Food in History.* Penguin, London, 1973.

—*Sex in History*, Scarborough House, London, 1992.

Unger, Lana. "Bugfood III: Insects Snacks from Around the World." Cooperative Extension Service, University of Kentucky, 1998.

University of Hawaii Sea Grant College. "Ono Hawaiian Shark Recipes." Honolulu, May 1997.

US Department of the Interior. "American Alligator." US Fish and Wildlife Service, Washington DC, 1995.

Ventura, Emma. "Dinner with a Twist." *Heritage*, Mar.-Apr, 1998.

Vietmeyer, Noel D. "The Preposterous Puffer." *National Geographic*, Aug. 1984.
—"The Puffer—World's Deadliest Delicacy." *Reader's Digest*, Jun. 1985.

Visser, Margaret, *The Rituals of Dinner: The Origins, Evolution, Eccentricities, and Meaning of Table Manners*, Penguin Books, New York, 1991.

Warren, William. *The Food of Thailand*. Periplus Editions, Singapore, 1995.

Wedeck, Harry E., *Love Potions Through the Ages*, Philosophical Library, New York, 1963.

Whitaker, Zai. "Winning the Rat Race in India." *International Wildlife*, Nov.-Dec. 1992.

Wiseman, John. *The SAS Survival Handbook*. Harper Collins, New York, 1995.

Young, Mark C., ed. *The Guinesss Book of Records*. Bantam, by arrangement with Guinness Publishing, Ltd., New York, 1977.